EASTERN OJIBWA
GRAMMATICAL SKETCH, TEXTS AND WORD LIST

EASTERN OJIBWA

GRAMMATICAL SKETCH, TEXTS AND WORD LIST

BY

LEONARD BLOOMFIELD

ANN ARBOR
THE UNIVERSITY OF MICHIGAN PRESS

All rights reserved

Library of Congress Catalog Card No. 57-5140

Paperback ISBN : 978-0-472-75030-6

FOREWORD

Shortly after Leonard Bloomfield's death, in 1949, it was agreed between Bernard Bloch, his scholarly executor, and myself, that I should undertake the collation and editing of all of Bloomfield's unpublished Algonquian materials. The present monograph was at that time already in the hands of the editorial staff of The University of Michigan Press. But it was felt that, despite its advanced state of preparation, the work might well undergo further editorial scrutiny by an Algonquianist before being published; and the authorities of The University of Michigan Press agreed to the proposal.

Editorial revision of the monograph has been along the following lines:

(1) Correction of misprints, especially in Ojibwa forms. That these were rather numerous can be ascribed only to the author's poor health as he brought his work on the monograph to an end.

(2) Checking and, when necessary, correction of cross references.

(3) The addition of occasional phrases, sentences, or paragraphs to fill obvious lacunae. For example, the Word List originally contained no preliminary explanatory material; I have supplied fuller explanatory detail in 11.1.

(4) The supplying of examples at certain places in the Grammatical Sketch where the author had given none. In particular, in Chapters 5 and 20 Bloomfield often illustrated a point, not by citing a sentence, but by referring to those of the numbered sentences of Part II which were relevant. In most such cases I have cited at least one of the sentences, or the needed portion of it, at the relevant place in the Sketch (without, of course, removing the sentence from Part II).

(5) The establishment of uniform typographical conventions for citation of forms, glosses, cross references, and the like. In this connection I have departed from those practices most often used, and seemingly preferred, by Bloomfield. My only justification for the departure is that I have been able to achieve greater accuracy in my editorial work by adhering to the conventions with which I am most at ease.

It is perhaps unnecessary to say that the portrayal of Ojibwa contained in the monograph is entirely Bloomfield's. Although I am in some small measure an Algonquianist, there are very few aspects of Algonquian pattern on which I am so well informed that I would venture to disagree with Bloomfield's interpretations. On two such points, both admittedly rather trivial, I feel somewhat strongly. On both points, Bloomfield's portrayal has of course been left unaltered; but I mention them here:

(1) The units which Bloomfield transcribes as *pp tt kk cc ss šš* and calls "fortis consonants"—that is, single phonemes (1. 1, 11-3)—seem clearly to me to be clusters, entirely comparable to the clusters *šp št šk sk mp nt nc nk*.

(2) The term "passive" does not seem apt in the application which Bloomfield makes of it (5. 7). Algonquian "passives" are not like those of Latin or Greek; rather, they are special inflected forms for INDEFINITE ACTOR, showing the same inflectional indication of object shown by other inflected forms of the same kind of verb. Some such term as "indefinite actor form" would seem preferable.

Certain features of Bloomfield's monograph should be especially noted by the reader. The collection of texts (Part III) is outstanding in that it contains in several instances two or three versions of a single story or reminiscence. Such varia are of inestimable value for the study of certain linguistic and near-linguistic matters, such as style, and only very rarely have investigators of American Indian languages collected them. The chapter on syntax (20) should be highly prized, especially by Algonquianists: it is the only reasonably extended treatment of Algonquian syntax which we shall ever have from Bloomfield, for, in all the vast quantity of Bloomfield's Algonquian notes now in my care, no more syntactical discussion is to be found.

Miss Grace E. Potter, formerly of the University of Michigan Press, was most graciously helpful to me throughout my work, as she had been, earlier, to the author. I wish to express both my own sincere thanks for this, and also the conviction that the author, had he been able, would have expressed similar gratitude.

CHARLES F. HOCKETT

Cornell University
February, 1956

PREFACE

The words, phrases, and texts which are here described and presented were dictated for writing or recorded on phonograph disks during the summer of 1938 by Mr. Andrew Medler, of Walpole Island, Ontario. Mr. Medler was employed as informant by the University of Michigan in co-operation with the Linguistic Institute of the Linguistic Society of America. The dictations were written down for the most part by the author of the present volume; some were written down at the same time, and a few independently, by Professor Charles F. Voegelin of DePauw University (now of Indiana University), and by Professor Zellig S. Harris, of the University of Pennsylvania. An extremely valuable control for part of the material was contributed, in the shape of a narrow phonetic rendering, by Professor Bernard Bloch of Brown University (now of Yale University). It is an interesting fact that this narrow transcription by a very accurate phonetic observer who was entirely free from prepossessions about the language included all the phonemic features and would probably suffice to establish them. The recording by several observers has lessened the number of errors; the present writer is alone responsible for the many that doubtless remain.

Great thanks are due the staffs of the University of Michigan and of the Linguistic Institute: especially Professor Charles C. Fries, who indefatigably aided our work. Above all, this record was made possible through the unfailing kindness and helpfulness of Mr. Medler.

The Central Algonquian language whose dialects are known variously as Ojibwa or Chippewa, Ottawa, Algonquin, and Salteaux is spoken in the area of Lakes Superior, Huron, and Michigan, in the states of Minnesota, Wisconsin, and Michigan, and in the provinces of Ontario, Manitoba, and Saskatchewan. Older studies, such as those of the missionary fathers Baraga, Cuoq, and Lemoine, are listed in Pilling's "Bibliography of the Algonquian Languages," *Bulletin* 28 (1891) of the Bureau of American Ethnology, Smithsonian Institution, Washington, D.C. More recently there have appeared texts and a vocabulary from Minnesota by J. P. B. de Josselin de Jong, in Beiheft 5 (1913) of the *Baessler-Archiv*, and an extensive collection of texts from the north shore of Lake Superior by William Jones, edited by

Truman Michelson, as Volume 7, Parts 1 and 2 (1917) of the *Publications of the American Ethnological Society*. These works largely fail to solve the two great phonetic difficulties of the Ojibwa language: the distinction of lenis and fortis consonants and the distinction of long and short vowels; in these respects the present record will show some improvement, though it, too, doubtless contains many errors.

Mr. Medler's dialect represents the southern and eastern type of Ojibwa. He was born and brought up near Saginaw, Michigan, but has lived most of his adult life on Walpole Island. As a youth he spent three years at the Carlisle Indian School. He played in a band at the Chicago World's Fair in 1893.

Our record of the dialect is of course fragmentary. In the grammatical exposition and in the Word List, nouns are cited in unpossessed singular, intransitive verbs in the third person singular of the indicative mode of the independent order, and transitive verbs (in order to avoid the citation of forms that have a prefix) in the form for third person singular animate actor and obviative object of the simple tense of the indicative mode of the conjunct order. These citation-forms were constructed when they did not appear in the record.

We may note here a few words which Mr. Medler mentioned as foreign to his speech; some of these he characterized as "Ottawa": *uki·n* 'his mother', used by some speakers on Walpole Island; AI verb stem *akkanto·-:* Mr. Medler quotes, evidently from a narrative, *uki·-ena·n eniw uki·man ke·-ekkanto·necin* 'so he said to those chiefs who were to stand guard'; TA verb stem *atim-: nenka·wi·-kekwe·-etima·* 'I shall try to overtake him'; *nenta·nekkama·nak* 'my suspenders', Ottawa; *nemi·kkeno·t* 'my trousers', Ottawa; *ni·mena·weʔam* 'he goes out on the open water'; *sa·ko͞* 'monkey', Ottawa; *uci·k* 'fisher', pl. *uci·kok*.

LEONARD BLOOMFIELD

CONTENTS

Part I: Grammatical Sketch 1
  1. Sounds 3

  Forms:

    2. Morphology 11
    3. Internal Combination 15
    4. Morphologic Processes. 23

    Inflection:

      5. Categories of Inflection 31
      6. Inflection of the Noun and Pronoun 39
      7. Inflection of the Independent Verb 44
      8. Inflection of the Conjunct Verb 51
      9. Inflection of the Imperative Verb; Compounding
         Form 59
    10. Composition 61

    Word Formation:

      11. Noun Finals 63
      12. Animate Intransitive Finals. 76
      13. Inanimate Intransitive Finals 90
      14. Transitive Animate Finals 95
      15. Transitive Inanimate Finals 102
      16. Particle Finals 108
      17. Medial Suffixes 113
      18. Accretions of Suffixes 121
      19. Roots 127
  20. Syntax 130

Part II: Sentences 145
Part III: Texts 179

  1. Dialects 181
  2. Grandmother 181
  3. The White Man 181
  4. Falling in the Water (First Dictation) 182
  5. Falling in the Water (Second Dictation) 183

6. Falling in the Water (Phonograph Record) 183
 7. Fishing. 185
 8. Carlisle Indian School (Dictation) 185
 9. Carlisle Indian School (Phonograph Record) 187
10. Spring Thunderstorm 190
11. A Visit Home (Dictation) 192
12. A Visit Home (Phonograph Record) 192
13. End of the Summer's Work 193
14. The Fish Trap 194
15. Means of Livelihood 194
16. The Walpole Island Fair (First Dictation) 195
17. The Walpole Island Fair (Second Dictation) 197
18. The Walpole Island Fair (Phonograph Record) . . . 198
19. The Sweating Cure (First Dictation) 200
20. The Sweating Cure (Second Dictation) 201
21. The Sweating Cure (Phonograph Record) 201
22. Fasting (Dictation) 202
23. Fasting (Phonograph Record) 203
24. Burial Rites (Phonograph Record) 205
25. Indian Bread (Dictation) 206
26. Indian Bread (Phonograph Record) 207
27. Cats' Eyes 208
28. Love Medicine (Dictation) 208
29. Love Medicine (Phonograph Record) 209
30. The Doctor's Love Medicine 210
31. The Mirror Vision 213
32. Fighting (Phonograph Record) 216
33. Rabbit (Dictation) 218
34. Rabbit (Phonograph Record) 219
35. Nenabush and the Partridges (Dictation) 220
36. Nenabush and the Partridges (Phonograph Record) . . . 222
37. Nenabush and the Ducks (Dictation) 224
38. Nenabush and the Ducks (Phonograph Record) 226

Part IV: Word List 229
Index 269

ABBREVIATIONS

AI:	animate intransitive	M:	medial
AN:	animate (noun)	N:	noun final
an.:	animate	obv.:	obviative
exc., excl.:	exclusive	P:	particle final
II:	inanimate intransitive	pl.:	plural
inc., incl.:	inclusive	sg.:	singular
inan.:	inanimate	TA:	transitive animate
		TI:	transitive inanimate

CROSS REFERENCES

3	Grammatical Sketch, Chapter 3
3.7	Grammatical Sketch, Chapter 3, paragraph 7
3.7-9	Grammatical Sketch, Chapter 3, paragraphs 7, 8, 9
4.10.3	Grammatical Sketch, Chapter 4, paragraph 10, Position 3
17	(Grammatical Sketch, Chapter 17; reference made to alphabetically listed entry)
S9	Sentence 9 (Part II)
T4	Text 4 (Part III)

ALPHABETICAL ORDER

a a· c e e· ʾ i i· k m n (N) o o· p s (S) š t u w y

PART I
GRAMMATICAL SKETCH

CHAPTER 1

SOUNDS

1. 1. The phonemes of Eastern Ojibwa will here be represented as follows:

Vowels:
short: *a*   *i*   *o*
long: *a·*   *e·*   *i·*   *o·*
Consonants:
fortis: *pp*   *tt*   *kk*   *cc*   *ss*   *šš*
lenis: *p*   *t*   *k*   *c*   *s*   *š*
glottal stop: *ʔ*
nasals: *m*   *n*
final nasalization: ~

We shall use the following additional symbols for non-phonemic variants:

semivowels: *y*   *w*
reduced vowels: *e*   *u*

In grammatical formulae we shall also use the symbols *N, SS*.

Wherever forms are listed alphabetically the symbols for the fortis consonants are treated as two successive letters.

For phrase-final and sentence-final there seem to be two phonemic features of pitch and stress: a phrase-final (, ;) and a sentence-final (. ?).

In narration, Mr. Medler used occasional English words without adapting their pronunciation to fit his Ojibwa phonetic habits; for these we use ordinary English spelling: *Walpole Island* (S17 and texts passim), *Carlisle Indian School, Carlisle, school, rooms, carpenter shop, Girls' Quarters, Menomini girl, order* (T8).

'Walpole' was sometimes spoken with Ojibwa sounds as *wa·pow*. 'Automobile' was spoken largely with Ojibwa sounds as *etamo·pi·l* or *etomo·pi·l* (*etamo·pi·link* 'in a car, by car' T16-8); *l* occurs only here.

1. 2. The word is the phonetic unit: phonetic variants are governed largely by position in the word. However, each member of a compound word is treated phonetically like a separate word; we write hyphens between the members. The term WORD, accordingly, will in this chapter be used of simple (uncompounded) words and of simple (uncompounded) members of compound words.

SHORT VOWELS

1. 3. The short vowels *i* and *o* occur in three well-marked positional variants: unreduced syllabic, nonsyllabic, and reduced. The short vowel *a* occurs unreduced and reduced.

1. 4. Short *a* ranges between the vowel of German *hat, kann* and that of English *cut, come: essassan* 'nest'. In the final syllables *-yan*, *-yank* the *a* is often fronted and resembles the vowel of English *pen, yen: e·nta·yan* 'where thou dwellest', *e·nta·yank* 'where we dwell'.

Short *i* resembles the vowel of English *pit, pin: ekkikk* 'kettle'. In final position, however, it is very open, resembling the vowel of English *pet: enini* 'man'.

Short *o* resembles the vowel of English *book, put: eškote·* 'fire'. In final position it is very open, resembling the vowel of English *cut: ekkito* 'he says so'.

The short vowels are weakly nasalized after *m, n: emikk* 'beaver'. They are strongly nasalized before *n* plus *s, š;* often the closure of the *n* is then omitted, so that the *n* is represented only by the nasalization: *peššanše·ʔekan* 'whip'.

1. 5. The semivowels *y, w* are positional variants of *i, o*.

At the end of the word, in the sequence *oi*, the *o* is nonsyllabic, yielding *wi·epwi* 'paddle', *muwi* 'he weeps'. In all other combinations, final *i* and *o* after a vowel are nonsyllabic: *nentay* 'my dog', *pešiw* 'lynx'.

Before a syllabic vowel *i* and *o* are nonsyllabic; the determination is made from the end of the sequence toward the beginning: *eninuwak* 'men', *kwi·wesse·ns* 'boy'.

The successions are such that no sequences of syllabic vowels remain, and such that the semivowel *y* occurs after a consonant only in the sequence of long vowel plus *ny: ki·ko·nyak* 'fishes'.

From this point on, we shall use the term VOWEL for syllabic vowels only. For nonsyllabic vowels we shall use the term SEMIVOWEL. The term NONSYLLABIC will include consonants, semivowels, and clusters.

1. 6. In sound, the semivowels resemble those of English *yes, well*.

After *y* before a reduced vowel there is often a glide resembling a glottal stop: *no·ntuwiyeminkit* 'if he hears us'.

Between *p, t, m*, or *n* and *w* there is often a glide resembling a short back vowel: *epwi* 'paddle', *enwi* 'bullet'.

After a consonant the sequences *wa, wi* occur only in the second syllable of a word whose first syllable contains a short vowel, and in the last syllable: *ekwaci·nk* 'out of doors', *wa·ka·kkwat* 'axe'. Even in these positions several words seem to have, indifferently, *wa* and *o*: *ekwa, kwa* (emphatic postpositive), *ekkwa, kkwa* (iterative), *ke·kwa* (prohibitive), *nenkwaci* 'somewhere', *nenkwatink* 'at some time'.

1. 7. The reduced vowels *e, u* are positional variants of the unreduced short vowels *a, i, o*.

Within a word, in any succession of (one or more) short vowels, the vowels of the odd-numbered (first, third, etc.) syllables are reduced, with the exception that the last vowel of a word is never reduced.

Before *w* a short vowel is reduced to *u*:

> *enini*   'man',
> *eninuwak*   'men'.

Otherwise the vowels *a* and *i* are reduced to *e*, and the vowel *o* is reduced to *u*:

> *nentakuššin*   'I arrive',
> *tekoššin*   'he arrives',
> *tekoššeno·k*   'they arrive'.

Occasionally, after the reduced vowel of a prefix, a short vowel in the first syllable of a stem is reduced, quite as if the prefix were not present: *umettikwa·pi·n* 'his bow' like *mettikwa·p* 'bow'.

1. 8. The reduced vowels are rapidly spoken and often whispered or entirely omitted. They have less loudness than unreduced vowels.

In its more distinct forms, *e* resembles sometimes the *a* of the dialect, sometimes the *i*, and sometimes it has other colorings, resembling the vowel of English *pet* or the unstressed types of English *petted, lettuce, hammock*. The coloring varies even in utterances of one and the same form.

In its more distinct shape, *u* resembles the *o* of the dialect, but has weaker stress. It usually causes labialization of preceding *k* or *kk*: *pi·kuška·* 'it breaks'.

In these clearest variants the two reduced vowels seem to be distinctive: *eninc* 'a hand', *uninc* 'his hand'.

In the weaker variants, where the reduced vowels are whispered or, it would seem, entirely omitted, their presence is largely indicated by the consonant pattern. Thus, in *pemipetto·* 'he runs', even if the *e*'s are inaudible, their presence is manifest because there are otherwise no such sequences as *pm* or *ptt*. In *eššama·t* 'if he feeds him', when the *e* is inaudible, both the *šš*, which would not otherwise occur initially, and the unreduced *a*, guarantee an initial vowel.

However, there remain doubtful cases and our renderings surely contain errors in this respect. We set up reduced vowels in the following words which were recorded only without them: *ma·meppi·* 'here', *mencikekkan* 'fence' (second *e*), *mi·šeškoto·nsan* 'grass'.

Initial sequences of nasal, reduced vowel, nasal, lenis stop (*p, t, k, c*) are spoken sometimes in their full shape, sometimes without the second nasal, sometimes without the vowel and with the second nasal syllabic, and sometimes without the vowel and with a single syllabic nasal (*m* before *p*, otherwise *n*): *nempo·p* 'soup', *menta·min* 'maize', *nenkwiss* 'my son', *nenci·ma·n* 'my canoe'.

Within the word, in sequences of nasal, reduced vowel, lenis stop, a second nasal is occasionally heard before the stop: *pe·ma·tesine(n)cin* 'another person'; here we regard the shorter form as phonemic.

Between initial nasal and a fortis a reduced vowel is often omitted and the nasal whispered: *mettik* 'tree', *nessa·kkunan* 'open it'.

Between consonant and nasal a reduced vowel is usually dropped and the nasal made syllabic: *pemosse·* 'he walks'. The nasal may then be assimilated to the preceding consonant: *nuwa·penta·n* 'I see it' may be spoken with syllabic *m* instead of *n*.

After *y* a reduced vowel may be preceded by a glide resembling a glottal stop (1.6).

In the phrase (or in a compound word) a nondistinctive glottal stop is usually spoken between a final vowel and a reduced initial vowel; even when the latter is omitted, the glottal stop glide remains: *ma·pa ekkwe·* 'this woman', *pi·eša·* 'he comes'. Occasionally, this glide takes on rather the character of a *y* or *w*.

The on-glide which resembles a glottal stop is often made also after the pronouns *aw, iw: aw ekkwe·* 'that woman', *iw essin* 'that stone'.

After the compound member *ka* 'thou (future)', initial *e* is often dropped without a glottal glide: here the loss of *e* is apparently phonemic, and we omit it in transcription: *ka-ššamik* 'he will give thee food', beside *ka-eššamik*.

Within the phrase, similarly, the initial reduced vowel of ENCLITIC PARTICLES is often dropped without any glide or other trace, after both vowels and nonsyllabics. These particles are *ekwa, eko* (emphatic postpositive), *ekkwa, ekko* (iterative), *ena* (interrogative), *ema·, ena·* (emphatic), *essa* (emphatic of novelty), *ešša* (predicative emphatic); also the *e* of the preverb *eni·* 'going on'.

LONG VOWELS

1. 9. Long *a·* resembles the vowel of *calm, father: a·kim* 'snowshoe'. After *w* it tends towards the vowel of *walk: nuwa·pema·* 'I see him'.

Long *e·* resembles the vowel of French *tête;* lower variants range towards the vowel of English *bad: e·ka·c* 'slowly'.

Long *i·* resembles the vowel of French *rive*, German *tief: ni·pit* 'my tooth'.

Long *o·* resembles the vowel of French *chose*, German *so;* occasional higher variants tend toward the vowel of French *blouse*, German *gut: po·si* 'he embarks'.

The long vowels are weakly nasalized after *m, n: ni·š* 'two'. Occasionally this weak nasalization appears also in other positions, apparently as a rhetorical or emphatic feature; thus, for instance, quite often in the word *eka·wa·* 'just barely'.

The long vowels are strongly nasalized before the sequences of *n* plus *s, š, ʾ, y;* often before *s, š*, and always before *ʾ, y*, the closure of the *n* is then omitted and the *n*, accordingly, is represented only by the strong nasalization: *ekkikko·ns* 'small kettle', *neški·nšik* 'my eye', *epino·ci·nʾuwi* 'he is a child', *epino·ci·nyak* 'children'.

Long vowels are strongly nasalized when the closure of final *n* is omitted (1.14).

1. 10. Strong nasalization of a final long vowel occurs as a phonemic feature. We write a tilde after the vowel to indicate both length and the distinctive nasalization: *ki·ko˜* 'fish'.

CONSONANTS

1. 11. The fortes are voiceless, vigorously articulated, and often rather long. The stops, *pp, tt, kk, cc*, are often preceded by a slight aspiration: *eto·ppuwin* 'table'. The sibilants, *ss, šš*, are often weakened between the vigorous onset and the vigorous opening, with a clear division into two syllables: *ni·ssa·ntuwe·* 'he climbs down, descends'.

The fortes occur only after vowels. However, within the phrase the particles *ekkwa, essa, ešša* often lack the initial vowel (1.8). The final *ns* of noun stems before the vowel of an ending seems often to have fortis-like *s: kwi·wesse·nsak* 'boys'. In the word *ma·meppi·* 'here', the reduced vowel seems to be always omitted but the *pp* decidedly fortis (1.8). In *pa·ma·* 'later on', the *p* seems often to have fortis character.

The lenes are usually voiceless; between vowels and especially after a nasal they are often partly or wholly voiced: *ekate·ntam* 'he is ashamed'. The lenes are quite vigorously articulated, but less so than the fortes; they are decidedly short and are never aspirated.

The lenes occur initially, after vowels, and after nasals.

In the clusters *šp, št, šk, sk*, the sounds seem to be intermediate between lenes and fortes; we use the lenis symbols: *ešpimink* 'up aloft', *meskomin* 'raspberry'. These clusters occur only after a vowel.

The foreign ear has great difficulty in distinguishing the less extreme variants of fortes and lenes; our record doubtless contains errors in this regard. Moreover, sequences in which a reduced vowel is unarticulated between lenes, fortes, or lenis and fortis, may be confused by a foreign ear with fortes: *pepa·* 'going about', *kekkina* 'all'.

1. 12. The stops *pp, p* are bilabial.

The stops *tt, t* are postdental or gingival with flattened blade.

The stops *kk, k* are velars, fronted or retracted according to the following vowel, or, in final position, according to the preceding vowel. Before a front vowel they may have a *y*-like off-glide; this is especially marked before *e·: ke·ttin* 'really'. Before *o* and the reduced *u* they are labialized, and an off-glide like a *w* may be decidedly prominent: *ekkokkupina·kan* 'basket'. Final *k* after *n*, as in *wa·pank* 'tomorrow', is often left off and is then represented only by the velar character of the *n* (1.14).

The affricates *cc, c* resemble the type of *church;* the longer duration of the fortis lies in the stop-like component.

The hiss sibilants *ss*, *s* are formed with flattened blade; they resemble the French type of *cesse* rather than the English type of *sis*.

The hush sibilants *šš*, *š* have the quality of the English type in *shall*. Before a front vowel they seem sometimes to be palatalized; especially before *e·* a *y*-like off-glide is often prominent: *menišše̼* 'island'.

1. 13. The glottal stop ˀ is fairly well articulated: *pi·kuˀank* 'if he breaks it'; before a reduced vowel it seems often to be weakened: *pe·šeko·pi·ˀekan* 'ace'. In its weakest variants it resembles English *h* as in *ahead*. In *wa·ˀo·ne̼* 'whippoorwill' the sound seems to be persistently like English *h*.

The glottal stop occurs between vowels, between *n* and vowel, and finally after a vowel.

Nondistinctive glides resembling a glottal stop occur before reduced vowels initially (1.8), and after *y* (1.6).

1. 14. The nasals are voiced.

The *m* is bilabial.

The *n* is produced in the same position as *tt* and *t*, except before *k*, where it is velar, as in English *sink: penki·* 'a little'. In final position, as in *wa·pank* 'tomorrow', the stop is often omitted, but is represented then by the velar character of the *n*, resembling the final of English *sing*. After *pp*, *p* plus omitted reduced vowel, the *n* is often equivalent to *m* (1.8).

Often before *s*, *š*, and always before ˀ, *y*, the *n* is reduced to nasalization of a preceding vowel (1.4,9).

At the end of a word, *n* is sharply cut off from a preceding vowel: the tip or blade of the tongue makes closure as soon as nasalization begins, or, often, an instant sooner, so as to produce a glide resembling an English *d*: *kemiwan* 'it is raining', *peka·n* 'nut'.

After long vowels, however, Mr. Medler has an alternative pronunciation, in which no closure is made for the *n* and the vowel, instead, is strongly nasalized: in this variant, final *n* seems to coincide with ̼. (See Text 1.)

Certain forms are spoken both with and without final *n;* we regard these as genuine phonemic doublets. They are: *ni·n* 'I' (both forms with weak nasalization, 1.6), *ki·n* 'thou', *wi·n* 'he, it, however', and the verb endings *-min* 'we', *-pan* (preterit), *-pa·n* 'I (preterit)': *ketiša·min*, *ketiša·mi* 'we go there', *nenki·-enokki·na·pan*, *nenki·-enokki·na·pa* 'I then worked'.

THE WORD

1. 15. The word may begin with any vowel; it may begin with any one nonsyllabic except a fortis, $ˀ$, or *y;* initial *p t k* may be followed by *w: pwa·* 'fail to, not', *twa·šsin* 'he falls through the ice', *kwi·-wesse·ns* 'boy'. Forms with initial nasal plus short vowel plus nasal plus *p, t, k, c* vary freely with forms that lack the second nasal; we take the longer forms as basic (1.8).

Between the vowels of a word there is always a nonsyllabic. This may be:

(1) Any one nonsyllabic phoneme: *eya·* 'he is there', *mettik* 'tree';

(2) One of the clusters *šp, št, šk, sk: meškikki* 'herb', *meskomin* 'raspberry';

(3) Nasal plus lenis; before *p* the nasal is *m*, otherwise *n: umpinank* 'if he lifts it up', *pi·ncesse·* 'he steps or falls in';

(4) Any one of the preceding followed by *w*, provided the next vowel is not *o* or *o·; wa* and *wi* after consonant occur only in the positions named in 1. 6: *epwi* 'paddle', *meskwi* 'blood', *penkwi* 'ashes';

(5) *nˀ* and *ny* after a long vowel; here the *n* appears only as a strong nasalization (1. 9); *nˀ* occurs before front vowels (including *u* reduced from *i* before *w*), *ny* before back vowels.

The word ends with any vowel or with any nonsyllabic of the types 1, 2, 3; a final long vowel may have the distinctive nasalization (1. 10).

CHAPTER 2

MORPHOLOGY

2. 1. In inflection, suffixes and sometimes prefixes are added to a stem; in some forms (all without prefix) the first syllable of the stem is altered by INITIAL CHANGE.

Stem: *wa·pam-:* with suffix only, *wa·pema·* 'he is seen'; with prefix, *nuwa·pema·* 'I see him'; with initial change *eya·pemak* 'when I saw him; he whom I see'.

To the suffixes that appear in inflection we shall give the name ENDINGS. We shall say that every inflected word has at least one ending; where there is actually none, we shall speak of an ending reduced to the shape ZERO. For instance, we say that *wa·pam* 'see thou him' contains an ending *-yi* which after any but the shortest stems is reduced to zero; compare *ešši* 'place thou him', from the stem *aSS-*.

An inflected form may contain several endings; according to the order in which they appear, endings are divided into nine POSITIONS. Some of the endings of earlier positions form THEMES, to which endings of later positions are added quite as they are added to stems. Thus, the stem *ko·kko·šš-* with the ending *-im* of Position 1 (and with a prefix) forms the theme *ninko·kko·ššim-*, and, with endings of Position 9, we have then

ko·kko·šš 'pig'   *nenko·kko·ššim* 'my pig'
ko·kko·ššak 'pigs'   *nenko·kko·ššemak* 'my pigs'.

The stem may be a compound; prefixes and initial change affect the first member, endings the last member. Thus, from the compound stem *ki·-wa·pam-; nenki·-wa·pema·* 'I have seen him', *ka·-wa·pemak* 'when I had seen him; he whom I have seen'.

In a few irregular forms the stem, or the final member of a compound stem, is replaced by zero.

The forms of one part of speech, namely particles, are uninflected stems.

2. 2. In composition, stems are combined; phonetically the members are treated like words in a phrase: stem *kicci-makkw-*, as in *kecci-mekkwa* 'big bear'; stem *ki·-wa·pam-* (2. 1); particle *meno--menikk* 'quite enough'.

2. 3. In secondary derivation and in primary word formation, stems are formed by means of FINALS, suffixes which appear at the end of the stem and determine its part of speech. We shall say that every stem contains a final; where none is apparent, we shall say that the final has the shape ZERO. Thus, we shall say that the unanalyzable stem *ako·n-* (e.g., *eko·n* 'snow') consists of a root *ako·n-* and a final zero which characterizes the stem as a noun.

2. 4. In secondary derivation a final is added to a stem, forming a derived stem. Thus, from the stem *ko·kko·šš-* there is derived, with final *-e·ns*, the stem *ko·kko·šše·ns-*, e.g., *ko·kko·šše·nsak* 'little pigs'. The underlying stem may be a compound: *kecci-kwi·wesse·ns* 'big boy', with final *-iwi* forms *kecci-kwi·wesse·nsuwi* 'he is a big boy'.

In a few types, secondary derivation is made not from a stem, but from an inflectional theme: *šo·neya·* 'money', *ušo·neya·m* 'his money'; with final *-i*, *ušo·neya·mi* 'he has money'.

Irregularly, in some instances, secondary derivation is accompanied by initial change: stem *šo·škosse·-* 'to glide', *šwa·škusse·* 'sleigh'.

The underlying stem need not occur in inflected forms. Thus, *pe·šeko·pi·ʔekan* 'ace' is derived from a stem *pe·šiko·pi·ʔike·-* 'to write things as a unit'; this, in turn, from a stem *pe·šiko·pi·ʔ-* 'to write it as a unit', but it is not likely that either of these successive underlying stems will occur in inflected forms.

2. 5. In primary word formation, a final is added to a root or to a root combined with a MEDIAL suffix.

Root *ki·šk-* with final *-aʔ* gives the stem *ki·škaʔ-*, e.g., *ki·škeʔank* 'if he cuts it through'; to the same root with medial *-a·kkw* the same final is added, giving the stem *ki·ška·kkwaʔ-*, e.g., *ki·ška·kkuʔank* 'if he cuts it through as wood'.

Certain stems, which we call DEPENDENT, contain a medial suffix but no root. A medial cannot begin a word: dependent stems occur only with prefixes. Thus, the medial *-nincy* with final zero gives the dependent stem *-nincy*, e.g., *neninc* 'my hand'.

2. 6. Some finals contain a PREFINAL element. Thus, a prefinal -SS appears in the following finals:

-ssin: penkissin 'it falls',
-ššin: (-SS plus -yin) penkiššin 'he falls',
-ssito·: ešisseto·t 'if he lays it so',
-ššim: (-SS plus -yim) pi·kuššima·t 'if he breaks him'.

The prefinal may resemble a medial; that is, a complex consisting of a medial and a final may serve as a final. For instance, the noun *meskomin* 'raspberry' could be viewed as consisting of the root *miskw-* 'red', the medial *-imin* 'grain, berry', and a final of the shape zero, but *-imin* is added also, in secondary derivation, to stems, e.g., *menito·mene·ns* 'wampum bead', from *menito·* 'manitou'; hence it is convenient rather to describe *-imin* as a complex final consisting of a final zero with the medial *-imin* serving as a prefinal.

The prefinal may resemble a root; in such cases the final part is usually the same final as is used after this root, and the entire final accordingly resembles a stem and is a DEVERBAL final. Thus, in *ena·pentank* 'he sees it so', a deverbal final *-a·pant* is added to the root *iN-;* this final resembles the stem *wa·pant-* (*wa·pentank* 'he sees it') and analyzes therefore into a prefinal *-a·p* resembling the root *wa·p-* 'see', and the final *-ant*.

2. 7. Medials may contain a PREMEDIAL element or a POSTMEDIAL element or both. Beside the medial *-kam* 'liquid', as in *sesswe·kemiššin* 'he leaps splashing', there appears, with a premedial *-a·-*, the form *-a·kam-*, as in *menwa·kemippetank* 'he likes the taste of it as a liquid'. Beside the medial *-imin* (2. 6), there appears, with postmedial *-ak*, a form *-iminak*, as in *meskaweminekisi* 'hard-grained corn'.

Some medials are DEVERBAL: they resemble some root or stem, usually in a somewhat altered form. Thus, *-imin* 'grain, berry fruit' resembles the root or stem of the noun *mi·n* 'blueberry'.

2. 8. Roots may contain a POSTRADICAL element. Thus, beside the root *kip-*, as in *kepa·kkuʔank* 'he closes it with or as a solid', there is the extended root *kipo·-*, as in *kepo·pecikan* 'bag with a drawstring'. In some instances the unextended root does not occur: *nant-aw-* appears in *nentawa·pema·t* 'if he looks for him'; *nant-w-* appears in *nentoma·t* 'if he calls him'.

Roots are often REDUPLICATED. In the regular type of reduplication the syllable *a·y-* is prefixed to an initial vowel (*a·nikko·-* : *a·ya·-nikko·-*); to roots with an initial nonsyllabic there is prefixed this nonsyllabic followed by *a·* (*ki·n-* : *ka·ki·n-*). However, there are various irregular types of reduplication (e.g., *pim-* : *papim-*, *papa·m-*).

CHAPTER 3

INTERNAL COMBINATION

3. 1. Words meeting in a phrase or members meeting in a compound word are but slightly modified in shape; these modifications have been described in Chapter 1. In contrast with this, the constituent parts of a simple word or compound-member appear in greatly differing shapes, according to the other constituents with which they are combined. We shall set up each constituent in a theoretical BASE FORM and then describe the ways in which this constituent, in various combinations, deviates in shape from that base form. These modifications constitute the habits of INTERNAL COMBINATION (INTERNAL SANDHI) of the dialect.

Since the habits of combining the inflectional prefixes with stems differ from the other habits of internal combination, we shall leave the sandhi of prefixes for Chapter 4. In the present chapter we shall consider all other cases of internal sandhi.

3. 2. In our base forms y and w appear as independent units and not merely as positional variants of i and o (1. 5). Likewise, we write N and SS in certain base forms instead of n and ss. These MORPHOPHONEMES, when not dropped or replaced, appear in actual speech forms as $y, w, n, ss;$ thus, a theoretical combination $niSS\text{-}a\cdot\text{-}t$ appears actually as $nessa\cdot t$ 'he kills him'.

VOWELS

3. 3. When long vowels come together, y is inserted between them; root *pakone·-* with suffix *-a·kkas* gives *pekone·ya·kkesank* 'he burns a hole in it'.

3. 4. A short vowel drops after a vowel; thus, the suffixes *-anše·* and *-aʔ* appear in *peššanše·ʔank* 'he whips it'.

IRREGULAR VOWEL COMBINATIONS

3. 5. Before certain verb endings y is inserted between vowels regardless of length (8. 2, 21, 23).

3. 6. The medial *-iti·* with postmedial *-e·* yields *-itiye·* (17).

3. 7. Suffixes *-ke·* and *-aw* yield *-kaw* (14. 31).

3. 8. The *o·* of verb stems in *to·*, *--tto·* is dropped before suffixes of secondary derivation: *ešitto·t* 'he does it so': *ešičceke·* 'he does things so' (11. 27; 12. 16, 57; 13. 15; 14. 31, 36; 15. 26).

3. 9. The final short vowel of certain inflectional endings is dropped at the end of a word; in most (or all?) of these forms, however, the vowel is retained when the base form of the word consists of two short-vowel syllables. Thus, the ending *-a* of animate singular nouns is lost in *ši·šši·p* 'duck', but remains in *mekkwa* 'bear' (6. 1; 7. 2, 9, 14, 22, 24, 27; 9.2).

After a short vowel has thus been lost, final *y* and *w* after a consonant are dropped by 3. 27, 31: the stems *assapy-*, *akkikkw-* with ending *-a* yield *essap* 'net', *ekkikk* 'kettle'. Final *y* after a vowel remains: stem *-ay-* with ending *-a* yields *nentay* 'my dog'. Final *w* after a vowel drops by 3. 31: stem *ininiw-* with ending *-a* yields *enini* 'man'; however, in certain irregular cases the *w* is here kept: *pešiw* 'lynx' (3. 22).

Where the final vowel is present in a form, it is kept also when a prefix is added: *epwi* 'paddle', hence also *nentapwi* 'my paddle'; but *nentay* 'my dog', because the stem *-ay-* is used only with prefixes.

3. 10. Against 3. 9, the ending *-i* is retained in the singular of the noun *takkipy-* : *tekkipi* 'spring of water' (6. 4).

3. 11. Final *o* of the verb stem *nimpo-* drops before the ending *-w* (7. 2).

3. 12. Final *i* of the ending *-iNi* drops before certain other endings (7. 25; 8. 13).

3. 13. In some forms *i* is lengthened before *w* plus vowel: stem *maškikkiw-* (*meškikkuwan* 'herbs') with suffix *-yi·niniw* gives *meškikki·wenini* 'medicine man' (11. 58, 89, 104; 12. 65).

3. 14. A vowel immediately after the root *ay-* is lengthened: contrast *eya·nk* 'if he has it' with *mekkank* 'if he finds it' (8. 32; 14.31).

3. 15. Other irregular alternations of vowel quantity occur at 4. 9; 14. 41b; 17 s.v. *-a·kky*, *-mot*.

3. 16. Before certain suffixes final *e·* is replaced by *a·*. Thus, *a·sso·kke·* 'he tells a sacred story', with suffix *-n* yields *a·sso·kka·n* 'sacred story' (11. 25, 27; 12. 132, 133; 13. 14, 15; 14. 7, 16; 15. 23).

This includes cases where the *e·* is preceded, in the base form, by consonant plus *y*, and the alternation, accordingly, under 3. 26, 27, appears in the actual speech forms as one of *i·* and *a·*: *entaʾepi·* 'he draws water' : *entaʾepa·n* 'place from which one draws water' (11. 25, 27; 14. 16; 15.23).

3. 17. Before certain suffixes, final *e·* is replaced by *a: pi·nteke·* 'he enters' with suffix *-to·* gives *pi·ntekato·t* 'he brings it in' (11. 25; 14. 6, 16b; 15. 47a).

CONNECTIVE -*yi*-

3. 18. When an element ending in a nonsyllabic is followed by the initial consonant of a suffix, a CONNECTIVE -*yi*- appears between them: root *po·n-* with suffix *-m* gives *po·nema·t* 'he ceases talking to him'. Before initial *w* of a suffix, connective -*yi*- is used only after roots consisting of a single short-vowel syllable: root *iN-* with suffix *-we·p* gives *ešiwe·pesi* 'he acts so, fares so'; contrast, with root *si·k-*, *si·kwe·penank* 'he pours it out'.

Where the vowel *i* otherwise appears before *w*, we set up the suffix with initial *iw*, e.g. *-iwi* (12. 92). For this and similar reasons (3. 21, 35), we set up some suffixes in doublet form, with and without initial *i*.

IRREGULARITIES OF CONNECTIVE -*yi*-

3. 19. The root *iN-* with the suffix *-we·* takes no connective -*yi*-: *enwe·* 'he speaks so' (12. 38).

3. 20. In certain combinations connective -*yi*- is not used: *kemiwan* 'it is raining', with ending *-k: kemiwank* 'if it rains'. When this happens, the consonants combine as follows:

m-k: nk   8. 32; 12. 16.
m-kk: nk   9.8.
m-n (at end of word): *n*   9. 3.
m-ss: ns   7. 28.
m-t: nt   12. 63, 87, 138; 15. 30ff.
n-k: nk   8. 2, 9, 10, 11.
n-kk: nk   9. 6.
n-p: mp   8. 5, 8, 26, 27, 31, 34.
n-s: ns   12. 131; 14. 49; 15. 17.
n-ss: ns   7. 28.

n-š: nš   14. 49.
n-t: nt   4. 3; 13. 14; (but at end of word *t*, 19, 15).
N-k: kk   8. 30; 12. 146.
N-kk: kk   12. 96.
N-p: pp   12. 136, 149; 13, 52; 15. 50.
N-pp: pp   12. 11.
N-ss: ss   7. 25.
t-p: pp   8. 5, 17, 26; 12. 129.
t-k: kk   8.9.
t-ss: ss   7. 10.

MUTATION

3. 21. The consonants *t, tt, N, SS* before *y* are replaced by *c, cc, š, šš*. The *y* is then treated as in 3. 26, 27.

Root *pi·nt-* with connective *-yi-* appears in *pi·ncesse·* 'he steps or falls in'.

Stem *išitto·* -, after loss of *o·* (3. 8), with connective *-yi-* appears in *ešicceke·* 'he does so'.

Root *iN-* with connective *-yi-* appears in *ešitto·t* 'he does it so'.

Stem *aSS-* with ending *-yi* gives *ešši* 'place thou him'.

IRREGULARITIES OF MUTATION

3. 22. Mutation of *t* to *c* takes place also before the suffixes *-we·p* (14. 25; 15. 15) and *-aya^ʔi·* (16. 17), and at the end of certain particles (16. 1).

3. 23. Mutation of *N* to *š* is made in the suffix *-ca·N* when noun final zero is added: *uca·š* 'his nose' (11. 65); *SS* is mutated in *neššwa·-sswi* 'eight' (19. 14).

3. 24. In certain combinations *t* before *a·, i, i·* of a suffix is ASSIBILATED to *s:* root *a·nt-* with suffix *-ikkonaye·* gives *a·nsekkoneye·* 'he changes his clothes' (12. 64, 65; 13. 4, 33; 15. 10, 32).

POSTCONSONANTAL *y*

3. 25. The combination *ny* after a long vowel is replaced by *n^ʔ* before a front vowel and by ˜ at the end of a word: stem *apino·ci·ny-* (*epino·ci·nyak* 'children') with suffix *-iwi* gives *epino·ci·n^ʔuwi* 'he is a child' (*i* reduced to *u* by 1. 7); with ending -*a*, dropped by 3. 9, it gives *epino·ci⁻* 'child'.

When *y* comes after a nonsyllabic in combinations other than the above, it first causes mutation (3. 21) and then is treated as in the following paragraphs.

3. 26. The combinations *ya, yi, ye·* after a nonsyllabic are replaced by *i·:* stem *assiny-* with endings -*an, -ink* yields *essini·n* 'stones', *essini·nk* 'on the stone'; stem *apwy-* with ending -*an* yields *epwi·n* 'paddles', with suffix -*e·ns* it yields *epwi·ns* 'small paddle'.

3. 27. In all other positions *y* after a nonsyllabic is dropped: stem *assiny-* with ending -*i* (dropped by 3. 9) gives *essin* 'stone'; stem *mittikwa·py-* with suffix -*a·kkw* gives *mettikwa·pa·kk* 'hickory tree'.

IRREGULAR TREATMENT OF POSTCONSONANTAL *y*

3. 28. When the ending -*i* is kept, by 3. 9, 10, after a noun stem in nonsyllabic plus *y*, the combination *yi* is replaced by *i:* stem *apwy-* with ending -*i* yields *epwi* 'paddle'.

3. 29. In the combination of the noun stem *assapy-* with the suffix -*ikke·, yi* is replaced by *i: asapikke·-* (12. 20).

3. 30. Elements which we set up in base form with *yi* (and not with *yi·*) appear after nonsyllabics with *i:* so connective -*yi-* (3. 18) and the ending -*yi* 'me' of verbs (7. 13; 8. 13; 9.2); -*yiya·* (12. 13; 13. 10).

FINAL *w*

3. 31. At the end of a word *w* drops: root *a·pittaw-* with particle final zero gives *a·petta* 'half'. This loss takes place after the loss of final short vowels by 3. 9: stems *ininiw-, akkikkw-* with ending -*a* dropped give *enini* 'man', *ekkikk* 'kettle'.

IRREGULAR TREATMENT OF FINAL *w*

3. 32. In certain cases, especially (or always?) where the base form ends in *wyi* (3. 9, 27), final *w* after a vowel is kept: *pešiw* 'lynx', *po·ntaw* 'hear thou him' (6. 3; 7. 2, 22; 9. 2; 16. 47).

POSTCONSONANTAL *w*

3. 33. In the combination *wy* after a consonant, the *y* is treated according to 3. 26-30, but the *w* may then receive a special treatment (3. 35).

The combination *ww* after a consonant is treated like a single *w*: root *kettikw-* with suffix *-we·p* appears in *kuttikwe·penank* 'he tips it over'.

3. 34. After a consonant the combination *wi*, when not arising from *wyi* (3. 28, 30), is replaced by *o:* stem *akkikkw-* with ending *-ink* yields *ekkikkonk* 'in the kettle'.

3. 35. After a consonant the combination *wa*, and the combination *wi* which arises from *wyi* by 3. 28, 30, are kept in the second syllable of words whose first syllable contains a short vowel: *ekwaci·nk* 'out of doors', *mekkwa* 'bear', *ekwiwin* 'garment' (root *akw-* with suffix *-yi*), *epwi* 'paddle' (stem *apwy-* with ending *-i*).

These combinations are kept also in the last syllable of a word: *wa·ka·kkwat* 'axe', *nentapwi* 'my paddle'.

In all other positions, *wa* and *wi* after a consonant yield *o:* thus root *pi·miskw-* and suffix *-at* in *pi·meskotessi~* 'snail'; *ušikwan* 'his fishtail' in *we·šekonit* 'one who has a fishtail'; suffixes *-kw* and *-yiya·* in *ka·ki·nekoya·* 'it is pointed at both ends'.

3. 36. After a consonant, *w* drops before *o* and *o·:* root *ne·kw-* with suffix *-o·te·* gives *ne·ko·te·* 'he crawls under'; suffixes *-a·w* and *-o* in *ekoteʔo* 'he canoes upstream.'

3. 37. In the sequence *ʔw*, the *ʔ* is dropped whenever the *w* is not merged with a following vowel: stem *ki·-pakkitte·ʔw-* with ending *-ikw* gives *nenki·-pekkitte·ʔok* 'he beat me'; with ending *-a·t*, *pekkitte·wa·t* 'he beat him'; and with ending *-yi* dropped, *pekkitte·w* 'beat thou him'.

IRREGULAR TREATMENT OF POSTCONSONANTAL *w*

3. 38. Postconsonantal *w* with the ending *-yi* 'me' yields *o* in final syllables: stem *pakkitte·ʔw-* : *pekkitte·ʔot* 'if he beats me '(8. 23).

3. 39 Postconsonantal *w* with the plural endings *-ak*, *-an* and the obviative ending *-an* yields *-wak*, *-wan* only in the second syllable of a word whose first syllable contains a short vowel; in words longer than this, these conbinations yield -o·k, -o·n immediately after a short-vowel syllable, and -ok, -on immediately after a long-vowel syllable: *mekkwak* 'bears', *ekkikko·k* 'kettles', *šeka·kok* 'skunks' (6. 2; 7. 2, 19). See, however, 6. 2.

3. 40. Certain words fluctuate between *wa* and *o* in the second syllable (1. 6).

3. 41. In certain forms, *we·* after a consonant is replaced by *o·:* stem *akkikkw-* with suffix *-e·ns* gives *ekkikko·ns* 'small kettle' (11. 58, 104).

INTERVOCALIC w

3. 42. In the sequence *i·wo*, the *w* is optionally replaced by *y:* *ki·wusse·*, *ki·yusse·* 'he hunts'.

3. 43. In the sequence *e·wo*, the *w* is replaced by *y:* stem *owo·ssi-* with initial change of *o* to *we·* yields *we·yo·ssecik* 'they who have (someone as) a father'.

IRREGULAR TREATMENT OF INTERVOCALIC w

3. 44. In certain combinations the sequence *wi* drops after a vowel and this vowel, if short, is lengthened: stem *pašikkiw-* (*pešikku-wak* 'cows') with ending *-im* appears in *kepašekki·mak* 'thy cows'. This CONTRACTION takes place always when final *aw* of a verb stem is followed by *i* (not *yi*) of a suffix or ending: stem *no·ntaw-* with ending *-ikw* appears in *keno·nta·k* 'he hears thee'. So also as indicated at 6. 9, 14; 7. 13, 19; 8. 13, 21; 11. 58; 12. 17, 81, 82, 88.

3. 45. In certain cases *awi* is contracted to *o·* (instead of *a·*): *no·ntaw-* with ending *-iNi* yields *keno·nto·n* 'I hear thee' (7. 13, 24; 8. 13; 11. 44; 12. 25, 140; 15. 41, 42; 16. 41; 17 s.v. *-ci·*).

IRREGULAR LOSS OF w

3. 46. Initial *w* drops as indicated at 4. 2; compare also 4. 6, 7.

3. 47. Final *w* of an element drops in certain formations. Thus the noun stem *ikkwe·w-* (*ekkwe·wak* 'women') loses its final *w* in the deverbal suffix *-kkwe·:* *uškeni·kekkwe·k* 'young women'. See 6. 11; 11. 2, 10, 93; 16, 5.

NASALS

3. 48. When the sequence of initial nasal plus short vowel precedes *p, t, k, c*, a nasal (*m* before *p*, otherwise *n*) is inserted: prefix *ni-* with stem *pimosse·-* gives *nempimusse·* 'I walk', with stem *taNisi-* gives *nentanis* 'I dwell there'.

Where roots exhibit this form, the nasal seems to be treated as part of the root: *nempwa* 'he dies' : *ne·mpot* 'when he died'.

3. 49. Apart from the above, there is fluctuation in the sequence nasal, reduced vowel, lenis stop (1. 8; cf. 12. 87). In *mi·nkwan, mi·-kwan* 'feather', we seem to have a genuine doublet.

IRREGULAR LOSS OF NASAL

3. 50. Final *an* of a noun stem is replaced by *a·* before the suffixes *-ins* and *-iny: mi·kkan* 'road' : *mi·kka·ns* 'path' (11. 58, 104).

3. 51. Apparently *t* replaces *nt* at 12. 87.

SPECIAL IRREGULARITIES

3. 52. The final consonant of a root is dropped in the formation of certain particles; thus from the root *te·p-* there is formed the particle *te·* 'sufficiently' (16. 1).

3. 53. In a few instances where like consonants are separated by a vowel, the vowel together with one of the consonants is dropped; thus the suffixes *-e·nim* and *-t* would combine by 3. 20 to give *-e·nint*, but what actually occurs in *-e·nt: kekke·nema·t* 'he knows him', but *kekke·-ntank* 'he knows it' (4. 10. 4 *a·n*; 7. 26; 12. 87; 15. 35).

3. 54. The ending *-iN* 'thee' is doubled in certain forms (8. 31); the suffix *-we·we·* occurs beside *-we·* (17).

3. 55. Deverbal medial and final suffixes differ in various ways from the underlying roots or stems; most commonly an initial non-syllabic is dropped: root *wa·p-* (stems *wa·pam-, wa·pant-*) : prefinal *-a·p* (finals *-a·pam, -a·pant*). See 17; 18.

CHAPTER 4

MORPHOLOGIC PROCESSES

4. 1. Inflection is made by means of INITIAL CHANGE, PREFIXES, and ENDINGS.

INITIAL CHANGE

4. 2. Initial change consists of the following replacements in the first syllable of the stem.

Before *a·* or *e·* the syllable *ay* is added: *na·nkan* 'it is light of weight' : *neya·nkeninekin* 'those which are light of weight'; *te·-wi·ssenit* 'if he had eaten enough' : *teye·-wi·ssenit* 'when he had eaten enough'.

Before this *ay*, initial *w* drops: *wa·pete·* 'it is ripe' : *eya·pete·k* 'one which is ripe'.

i· is replaced by *a·*: *ki·-pi-eya·* 'he came here' : *ka·-pi-eya·t* 'when he came here'.

o· is replaced by *wa·*: *no·ntuwa·t* 'if he hears him' : *nwa·ntuwa·t* 'when he heard him'.

a and *i* are replaced by *e·*: *nenkamot* 'if he sings' : *ne·nkemot* 'when he sang'; *kemiwank* 'if it rains' : *ke·muwank* 'when it rained'.

o is replaced by *we·*: *uncicuwan* 'it flows from there' : *we·nceciwank* 'whence it flows'.

4. 3. The roots *taN-* 'there', *taSS-* 'so many', and the verb *ta·* 'he dwells there, exists' prefix *e·n-* without connective: *e·nteniseya·n* 'where I dwell'; *e·ntessotepaʔekane·k* 'how much o'clock it is'; *e·nta·ya·n* 'where I dwell, at my house'. Beside the particle *tasso* 'so many', there is also *entasso*, from which the changed form *e·ntasso* is regularly made.

4. 4. The preverb particle *ta* (future) is not used under initial change; instead, one uses *ka* (changed *ke·*): *ke·-nenkamot* 'he who will sing'. Occasionally, unchanged *ta* appears where one expects initial change.

4. 5. The preverb particles *ci* 'may', *pi* 'hither' remain unchanged; the changed form of stems beginning with the preverb particle *pwa·* 'fail to, not' seems to be avoided.

PREFIXES

4. 6. The prefixes are *ki-* 'thou', *ni-* 'I', *o-* 'he', *i-* (indefinite possessor). All four are used with certain dependent nouns, indicating the person of a possessor: *keninc* 'thy hand', *eninc* 'a hand', The first three are used with other nouns, and with transitive and pseudo-transitive verbs in the independent order, indicating the person of an actor or of an object: *nuwa·pema·* 'I see him'; *nuwa·pemik* 'he sees me'. The first two are used with intransitive verbs in the independent order, indicating the person of an actor: *nenametap* 'I sit' (but *nematepi* 'he sits').

Where more than one person is involved, *ki-* is preferred to *ni-* and *ni-* to *o-*: *ko·ssena·n* 'our father (thine and mine)'; *no·ssena·n* 'our father (mine and his but not thine)'; *keno·nto·n* 'I hear thee'; *keno·ntaw* 'thou hearest me'; *neno·ntuwa·* 'I hear him'; *uno·ntuwa·n* 'he hears the other one'.

Before the initial vowel of a stem the prefixes add *t: eša·* 'he goes there' : *ketiša·* 'thou goest there'. After this *t* an initial *o* is lengthened: *ukima·* 'chief' : *nento·kema·m* 'my chief'.

Occasionally, a stem with initial nonsyllabic is treated as if *o* preceded: *neme·* 'sturgeon' : *nento·neme·m* 'my sturgeon'; *pekakkettank* 'if he hears it distinctly' : *nento·pekakketta·n* 'I hear it distinctly'; *sesswe·pi·keʔantuwa·t* 'if he sprinkles him with water' : *uto·sesswe·pi·keʔantuwa·n* 'he sprinkles him with water'.

One instance was recorded in which apparently *wa* is treated as if it were *o: wene·nema·t* 'if he forgets him' : *nento·ne·nema·* 'I forget him'.

The noun *emikk* 'beaver' has *nento·mekkom* 'my beaver'.

In a few instances both the vowel of the prefix and a short vowel in the first syllable of the stem are reduced; see 1. 8.

The preverb particle *wi·* (future) with prefix *ni-* appears as *ni·* beside *nuwi·;* the noun *wi·teke·ma·kan* 'wife' gives *ni·teke·ma·kan* 'my wife'.

4. 7. Before the initial *i·* of certain dependent stems, the prefixes *ki-*, *ni-* lose their vowel and the prefix *o-* appears as *w-*: *ki·n* 'thou', *ni·n* 'I', *wi·n* 'he, it'; *ki·yaw*, *ni·yaw*, *wi·yaw* 'thy, my, his body'. Occasionally, the *o-* seems then to be added again: *uwi·cekkiwe·nyan* beside *wi·cekkiwe·nyan* 'his friend'.

Before the initial *o·* of a few dependent stems, the prefixes *ki-*, *ni-* lose their vowel and *o-* disappears: *ko·ss*, *no·ss*, *o·ssan* 'thy, my, his father'.

4. 8. The medial suffixes *-kakkwan* 'shin', *-ka·t* 'leg', *-ka·ttikw* 'forehead', *-kwan* 'liver', *-pikkwan* 'back', replace the initial lenis by fortis after the prefixes: *nekka·t* 'my leg'.

4. 9. The preverb *ta* (future) lengthens its vowel after prefixes: *nenta·*; alternatively it is replaced by *ka: nenka*. Before this *ka*, the prefix *ki-* usually disappears: *ka-pi·to·n* 'thou art to bring it', rather than *keka-pi·to·n*. After this combined *ka*, initial *a* sometimes disappears (1. 8). Compare the forms with initial change (4. 4.).

ENDINGS

4. 10. When inflectional endings are added to a stem, or follow each other, the habits of internal sandhi (3) come into effect.

The following are the inflectional endings, listed by positions. In citing an inflectional ending hereafter (except in this list itself), it will be preceded by a subscript numeral indicating its position.

POSITION 1

In position 1, immediately after the stem, appear theme-signs which mark the possessed noun and the main types of objects of transitive verbs.

-im (possessed noun theme); vowel plus *w* of the stem contract with the *i* (6. 13).

-a· (third person object): 7. 13, 26; 8. 13, 14, 16, 17, 19, 20; 9. 5, 7.

-ikw (inverse forms of the TA verb); before this ending the verb stem *iN-* is reduced to zero: 7. 13; 8. 13, 21.

-yi (first-person object; imperative object); not replaced by *i·* after a consonant; in word-final the *i* drops except after a stem consisting of a single short-vowel syllable: 7. 13; 8. 13; 9. 2, 4, 5, 7.

-iNi (second-person object); the *i* drops in word final: 7. 13. Alternate form *-iN* (occasionally *-iNiN*): 8. 13, 30, 31.

-am (object of TI verb): 7. 27; 8. 32, 33, 34, 35; 9. 3, 5, 8. Alternate form *-amo:* 8. 32, 35, 36; 9. 3.

POSITION 2

Here appear mode-signs of the negative and of the imperative and prohibitive with first person object; also supplementary TA theme-signs for inanimate actor and for the passive of the first and second person.

-ssi· (negative mode): 7. 4, 7, 10, 16, 18, 20, 23; 8. 7. Alternate form -ssi: 7. 25; 8. 4, 16, 25, 27.
-šš (first person object of imperative and prohibitive): 9. 2, 4, 5, 7.
-i (obviative actor): 8. 21.
-i (inanimate actor): 8. 21.
-o· (passive of first and second persons): 7. 19, 21; 8. 21.

POSITION 3

-kk (delayed imperative and prohibitive): 9. 4.
-n (inanimate object and pseudo-object): 7. 3, 4, 6, 9, 26.

Here also appear personal endings of the first and second persons of the conjunct verb. In the negative and dubitative modes these have w before their vowel; otherwise they are preceded by a connective y after a vowel:

-a·n 'I': 8. 2, 5, 21, 30, 31, 32, 34.   -wa·n: 8. 4, 6, 8.
-an 'thou': 8. 2, 21, 23, 26, 32, 34.   -wan: 8. 25, 27, 28.
-a·nk 'we (excl.)': 8. 2, 21, 23, 32, 34; in prohibitive, 9. 7.   -wa·nk: 8. 28.   -na·nk in imperative: 9. 2.
-ankw 'we (incl.)': 8. 2, 14, 21, 30, 31, 34.   -wankw: 8. 20.
-e·kw 'ye': 8. 2, 14, 21, 23, 34.   -we·kw: 8. 6, 28.
-ak 'I-him': 8. 14, 17.   -wak: 8. 16, 19, 20.
-at 'thou-him': 8. 14.   -wat: 8. 19, 20.
-ankit 'we (excl.) -him': 8. 14.
-akok 'I-you': 8. 30.
-amink 'he-us (excl.)': 8. 23.

POSITION 4

Many endings of several types belong here:

Plural and obviative signs:

-ina·n (first person plural in possessed noun and independent transitive verb): 6. 5, 13; 7. 3, 14, 15, 19.   -a·n (haplologic): 7. 26.
-iwa· (second and third persons plural in possessed noun, independent transitive verb, and conjunct verb): 6. 13; 7. 8, 14, 15, 19; 8. 2, 6, 14, 21, 23 ,26, 32, 35; compare -ₑwa·.   -a·wa·: 7. 3, 26, 28.   -owa·: 8. 2.
-ini (obviative): 7. 9; 8. 2, 6, 7, 8, 12, 14, 32, 35.   -iniw: 6. 11,13.
-iwi 'we' (pronominal): 6. 22.

Personal endings of the independent verb:
-*min* 'we': 7. 2, 4, 21, 22, 23, 24.
-*m* 'ye': 7. 2, 22, 24.
-*w* (third person): 7. 2, 4, 9, 14, 27, 29.
-*m* (passive): 7. 2.
-*iwa·n* (passive): 7. 2, 14.

POSITION 5

Here belong third-person endings of the conjunct verb, in part also of the independent dubitative.
-*t:* 8. 2, 5, 14, 17, 21, 23, 26, 32.
-*k:* 8. 2, 4, 11, 16, 30, 32, 34.
-*kw:* 7. 8, 12; 8. 6, 7, 8, 12, 19, 20, 28, 31, 35, 36.
-*okw:* 8. 12.
-*nk* (passive): 8. 2, 32.
-*int* (passive): 8. 14.

POSITION 6

Instead of the plural ending -$_4$*iwa·*, certain forms of the conjunct verb pluralize the third person by -*wa·* in position 6: 8. 4, 14, 23, 30.

POSITION 7

Here belong mode-signs of the preterit and independent dubitative.
-*pan* (preterit): 7. 5, 8, 12, 16; 8. 5, 8, 11, 17, 20, 26, 27, 29, 31, 34, 36. -*ipan* after -$_3$*at:* 8. 20. (See also end of 1. 14.)
-*pa·n* (first person conjunct preterit): 8. 5, 8, 31, 34. (See also end of 1. 14.)
-*na·pan* (independent preterit): 7. 5.
-*tik* (independent dubitative): 7. 6, 7, 11, 17, 18, 21. -*a·tik:* 7. 6, 21. -*itik:* [Bloomfield gives no cross reference and the editor cannot discover this variant.]

POSITION 8

Here belong mode-signs:
-*e·n* (dubitative): 7. 6, 7, 17, 18; 8. 6, 7, 8, 12, 19, 20, 28, 29, 35, 36.
-*a* (delayed imperative): 9. 4.
-*e·* (prohibitive): 9. 5.

POSITION 9

Number and obviation endings of the third person:

-a (animate singular); drops (3. 9) except after stems consisting of a single short-vowel syllable: 6. 1, 23; 7. 2, 14, 27.

-i (inanimate singular); drops like the preceding: 6. 1, 23; 7. 9.

-ak (animate plural); the *a* merges (3. 39) to *o·* or *o* with preceding postconsonantal *w*, except after stems consisting of a single short-vowel syllable: 6. 1; 7. 2, 4, 6, 7, 14, 15, 19, 20, 29; 8. 8. *-k* (in pronouns and participles): 6. 23, 24; 8. 1, 15, 24. *-ik* (after *-₄ina·n*): 6. 5; 7. 14, 19. *-i·k* (after *-₇pan*): 7. 16.

-an (obviative): 6. 1; 7. 2, 6, 14, 15, 17, 18, 19, 20; 8. 8. *-n* (in pronouns and participles): 6. 23, 24; 8. 1, 15, 22. *-in* (after *-₄ina·n*): 6. 5. *-i·n* (after *-₇pan*): 8. 18.

-an (inanimate plural): 6. 1; 7. 3, 9, 26, 28. *-n* (in pronouns and participles): 6. 23, 24; 8. 1, 10, 33. *-in* (after *-₄ina·n*): 6. 5.

Other noun and pronoun endings:

-ink (local form): 6. 8. *-a·nk:* 6. 10.

-i (compounding form): 6. 12.

-tik, -tok (plural address): 6. 7.

-i, -ti, -e·ti (demonstrative): 6. 23.

-šš (interrogative): 6. 25.

Imperative and prohibitive endings:

-n 'thou': 9. 1, 2, 3, 4, 6, 7, 8.

-k 'ye': 9. 1, 2, 3. *-kon:* 9. 2, 6, 7, 8.

-ta· 'we': 9. 1.

Tense and mode signs:

-n (iterative conjunct): 8. 1, 10, 15, 22.

-no·n (negative): 7. 10, 25.

WORD FORMATION

4. 11. The suffixes used in primary and secondary derivation are subject to the habits of internal sandhi (3).

4. 12. The final suffixes which appear at the end of a stem are of the following principal types:

(1) Zero final: *eko·n* 'snow', an unanalyzable noun stem; we say root *ako·n-* with noun-final zero.

(2) Simple final: *-ins*, in *pene·ns* 'young partridge', from *pene·* 'partridge'.

(3) Final containing a purely formal prefinal: -e·ns, consisting of final -ins with prefinal -e·, in ko·kko·šše·ns 'little pig', from ko·kko·šš 'pig'.

(4) Final containing a significant prefinal: -ssin, consisting of final -in with prefinal -SS 'lie, fall', in penkissin 'it falls'.

(5) Deverbal final, resembling a stem, hence (2. 6) analyzable into a significant prefinal and a final: -a·pant, deverbal from the stem wa·pant- (wa·pentank 'he sees it'), hence analyzable into a prefinal -a·p corresponding to the root wa·p-, and a final -ant, in ena·pentank 'he sees it so'.

(6) Complex of finals- -išš-e·ny in penki·šše ~ 'a little bit', composed of -išš and -e·ny. Similarly, -ant in par. (5) above consists of -am (wa·pam- 'see an animate object') and -t (action on inanimate object).

(7) Complex of medial plus final: -a·pikkw 'stone, metal', in pi·wa·pikk 'iron'; the medial is -a·pikk, the final -w; cf. keša·pekkite· 'it is heated as stone or metal'.

(8) Complex of deverbal medial plus final: -aškw 'grass, herb' (11. 99) medial -ašk, deverbal from the root mašk-, plus noun-final -w.

4. 13. Medials in their more independent use, when they are not closely tied up with some final, appear as variable elements between a root and a final, especially in verb stems: -a·khw 'wood, solid' in kinwa·kkusi 'he is a tall tree, a long timber', ki·ška·kku ᵖank 'he chops it through as wood'. Some appear also as finals in dependent nouns: -site· 'foot' (with postmedial -e·) in wi·nesite·ššin 'he gets his feet dirty', -sit in nesit 'my foot'.

Some medials are deverbal, resembling stems, as -a·konak 'snow' (with premedial -a· and postmedial -ak) in ešpa·kunaka· 'there is deep snow', from the noun eko·n 'snow'.

4. 14. On the border between medial and root there is the DEPENDENT ROOT -i·t-, as in ni·ci (prenoun particle) 'my fellow-' and ni·cekkiwe˜ 'my male friend', which is used only with prefixes, forming dependent stems, but behaves otherwise like a root. From it there is derived the ordinary root wi·t- 'accompany', as in wi·teke· 'he dwells with someone, is married'.

4. 15. Secondary derivation is sometimes accompanied by initial change: šwa·škusse· 'sleigh', from a stem šo·škosse·- 'glide' (11. 2, 82, 114; 16. 1, 15, 16, 21; compare initial change in composition, 10.2, 4).

4. 16. Secondary derivation is in certain cases made from a possessed noun theme in the form for third person singular possessor: *ušo·neya·mi* 'he has money', from *šo·neya·* 'money', *ušo·neya·m* 'his money' (12. 65; 14. 6). This theme seems always to be used for secondary derivation from dependent nouns: *uški·nšekokka·cekanan* 'eyeglasses', from *uški·nšik* 'his eye'.

When secondary derivation is made from dependent nouns with the irregular types of prefixation of 4.7, *o-* is prefixed to *wi·-* and *ow-* to *o·-: owi·cikkiwe·nʔim-* 'have someone as a friend', *owo·ssi-* 'have a father'.

4. 17. Reduplication is best viewed as a modification of roots, hence as a feature of primary word formation: *ka·ki·we·wak* 'they severally go home' is made from the reduplicated root *ka·ki·w-*, just as *ki·we·* 'he goes home' is made from the simple root *ki·w-* .

The meaning of reduplication seems to be plurality, diversity, repetition, and occasionally perhaps intensity of action.

CHAPTER 5

CATEGORIES OF INFLECTION

5. 1. The parts of speech are NOUN, PRONOUN, VERB, and PARTICLE. The categories of inflection are GENDER, NUMBER, and PERSON; in the verb, also ORDER, MODE, and TENSE. Nouns and intransitive verbs have also a compounding form; and nouns also a local form and a few forms for address.

5. 2. Every noun belongs to one of two genders, ANIMATE and INANIMATE. To the animate gender belong all nouns which denote persons, animals, spirits, or trees: *enini* 'man', *enim* 'dog', *menito·* 'manitou', *mettikumi·šš* 'oak'. The remaining nouns belong to the inanimate gender: *essin* 'stone', *peka·n* 'nut', *pekkwe·šekan* 'bread', *wa·wan* 'egg'.

However, certain nouns of meanings other than those specified belong to the animate gender. These will hereafter be marked AN. The following have come to notice; the first six are dependent nouns (2. 5) :. *-e·škan: ute·škanan* 'his horn(s)'. *-kitikw: nenkitik* 'my knee'. *-naškiti·: unašketi·n* 'his (bird's) tail'. *-na·n: nena·n* 'the calf of my leg'. *-ninkwi·ˀikan: uninkwi·ˀekanan* 'his wing(s)'. *-škanšy: neškanš* 'my claw, nail, hoof'.

a·kim 'snowshoe'. *a·semakuma·pesowinak* (pl.) 'suspenders'. *a·sso·- kka·n* 'sacred story'. *a·šo·nekkokenak* (pl.) 'suspenders'. *ekkikk* 'kettle, pot'. *eko·n* 'snow'. *enank* 'star'. *epakkwe·yašk* 'reed'. *epateniss* 'button'. *essap* 'seine, net'. *esse·ma·* 'tobacco'. *eškote·ta·- pa·n* 'railway train'. *ka·way* 'quill'. *ki·siss* 'sun, moon, month'. *mekkom* 'ice'. *mencinekka·wan* 'mitten'. *menta·min* 'maize'. *mesko- min* 'raspberry'. *meskoti·ssemin* 'bean'. *meškaweminekisi* 'hard-corn'. *meškote·ta·pa·n* 'railway train'. *mešsi·min* 'apple'. *mettik* 'tree'· *mettikwa·p* 'bow'. *mi·kwan, mi·nkwan,* 'feather'. *penakesikan* 'hard corn'. *pessaka·kk* 'board'. *po·kketo·nš* 'pear'. *šeka·kuwi·nš* 'onion'. *ši·kwan* 'grindstone'. *šwa·škusse·* 'sleigh'. *teko·* 'wave'. *tepaˀeki·sesswa·n* 'clock'. *te·we·ˀekan* 'drum'. *uppin* 'potato'. *uppwa·kan* 'pipe' (for smoking). *utatteka·kumin* 'blackberry'. *uta·pa·n* 'wagon'. *wa·kk* 'fish egg'. *wi·mpenakkesi* 'hollow tree'.

Diminutives of animates are animate, e.g., *ekkikko·ns* 'small kettle'.

Persons remain animate in transferred use; thus *ukima·* 'chief' is animate also in the sense of 'king-card'.

Inanimates are animate as personal designations; thus *wa·wa·pemowin* 'mirror' is animate in the part of T 31 where it means the Mirror Spirit.

The noun *mettik* shows class cleavage: when animate it means 'tree', when inanimate it means 'piece of wood'.

Reference to speaker or hearer is in the animate gender.

5. 3. The numbers are SINGULAR and PLURAL. The representative singular is frequent: *eniššena·pe·* 'the Indians'.

5. 4. The persons are FIRST (speaker), SECOND (person addressed), and THIRD. In the plural of the first person distinction is made between INCLUSIVE and EXCLUSIVE: *ko·ssena·n* 'our (incl.) father', when speaker is addressing, say, a brother, *no·ssena·n* 'our (excl.) father', when he is addressing someone who has not the same father.

5. 5. In any close context, one animate third person, singular or plural, is PROXIMATE, and any other animate third persons are OBVIATIVE; also any intransitive verb with inanimate actor then appears in a form for obviative actor.

Thus, *nuwa·pema· aw enini* 'I see that man', but *uwa·pema·n eniw eninuwan* 'he sees that man', with obviative object. Similarly, *nuwa·pemik aw enini* 'that man sees me', but *uwa·pemiko·n eniw eninuwan* 'that man sees him', with obviative actor. Inanimate verb: *ena·kuššik nenka-pi-tekoššin* 'when it is evening I shall arrive here', but *ena·kuššinik ta-pi-tekoššin* 'when it (obv.) is evening he will arrive here'.

In obviative forms singular and plural are not distinguished: *eninuwan* 'the (other) man or men.'

In any but the closest contexts, the proximate person often changes, so that obviatives are avoided; even in close contexts proximates occasionally appear instead of obviatives, especially in the case of the possessor of a noun and of the actor of an inanimate intransitive verb.

5. 6. The noun has forms for the two numbers and, if animate, also an obviative form: *enini* 'man', *eninuwak* 'men', *eninuwan* 'the other man or men'.

The noun is inflected also for personal-anaphoric mention of a POSSESSOR by person and number—also, presumably, by gender, but no forms with inanimate possessor were recorded. Thus *ukima·* 'chief', *nento·kema·m* 'my chief', *nento·kema·mena·n* 'our (excl.) chief'. An animate noun with a third person animate possessor is always obviative, the possessor being treated as proximate: *uto·kema·man* 'his chief or chiefs'. Obviation of the possessor of an inanimate noun is often neglected: *usi·sepa·kkutom* 'his sugar' where the syntax would lead one to expect *usi·sepa·kkutomeni* 'the other's sugar'.

The pronouns show gender and number; one set shows person and number.

5. 7. Verbs contain personal-anaphoric reference to an ACTOR, but have also PASSIVE forms in which this reference is omitted. Transitive verbs contain also personal-anaphoric reference to an OBJECT.

Each intransitive verb stem is specialized for animate or for inanimate actors; hence there are ANIMATE INTRANSITIVE (AI) verbs and INANIMATE INTRANSITIVE (II) verbs: *penkiššin* 'he falls', *penkissin* 'it falls'.

Each transitive verb stem is specialized for animate or for inanimate objects; hence there are TRANSITIVE ANIMATE (TA) verbs and TRANSITIVE INANIMATE (TI) verbs: *nuwa·pema·* 'I see him, *nuwa·penta·n* 'I see it'.

5. 8. In some instances intransitive stems tend to be specialized for number of the actor; so especially *eka·cci·nʔi* 'he is small' : *pi·weši-nʔuwak* 'they (an.) are small'; *eka·ccin, eka·cceno·nʔi* 'it is small' : *pi·wa·no·n* 'they (inan.) are small'.

Quite often stems containing reduplication are used for plural actor or for plural objects; so especially *mentito* 'he is big' : *mema·-ntetowak* 'they (an.) are big'; *mecca·* 'it is big' : *mema·cca·no·n* 'they (inan.) are big'.

5. 9. AI verbs have some PSEUDO-TRANSITIVE forms, which add anaphoric reference to a third person PSEUDO-OBJECT: *ki·škekkoceke·* 'he whittles through' : *uki·škekkoceke·n* 'he whittles it through'. Plural and obviative pseudo-objects have a special form.

Some AI verbs are used only with a pseudo-object, e.g., stem *minikkwe·-* : *neminekkwe·n* 'I drink it'. Most of these replace a lacking TI verb. Thus, the TA stem *amw-* (*nentamwa·* 'I eat him') has no TI pendant; instead, the pseudo-transitive (AI) stem *mi·ci-* is used: *nemi·cin* 'I eat it'. Especially, there is a large class of pseudo-TI verbs in *-to·*, *-tto·* which serve as pendants to some types of TA verbs: *nempi·-na·* 'I bring him' : *nempi·to·n* 'I bring it'.

Pseudo-transitive forms exist only in a few modes of the independent order; for the most part the pseudo-transitive forms are the same as ordinary AI forms.

5. 10. II verbs distinguish number of the actor only in the independent order and in the participle. Some II verbs occur only with singular actor and form no participles; these are IMPERSONAL verbs, e.g., *kemiwan* 'it is raining'. II verbs have no passive form.

5. 11. The TA verb is inflected for gender, number, and person of the actor and for number and person of the object; in addition, there are passive forms, which mention no actor, and at least one passive form which omits mention also of the object.

Where both actor and object are animate third persons, one of the two is obviative. There is at least one form where both actor and object are obviative: *wa·pema·nit* 'if the other sees still another'. On the other hand, where a first or second person is conjoined with an animate third person, no obviative forms are distinguished: *nuwa·pema·* 'I see him', but also *nuwa·pema· ukwissan* 'I see his son'.

Where the actor or object is first person plural, the number of a second person object or actor is not distinguished: *mi·šeššina·nk* 'give thou (ye) it to us'.

In some modes of the TA verb the number of a third person object is not distinguished; so notably in the modes of command: *mi·š* 'give thou it to him or them'.

Some TA verbs govern two objects as to syntax, but these DOUBLE-OBJECT verbs are inflected with reference to only one object: *nemi·na·* 'I give (it, him, them) to him', *nemi·na·k* 'I give (it, him, them) to them',

5. 12. The TI verb distinguishes the number of the object only in some of the independent forms and in the participle.

Some TI verbs have special PSEUDO-INTRANSITIVE forms which are used when the object is purely FORMAL: *nentina·penta·n* 'I see it thus; I thus look at it' : *nentina·pentam* 'I have such a vision'. The pseudo-intransitive forms are distinct from ordinary TI forms only in the independent modes. They occur especially in stems ending in *-a·pant* 'see', *-e·nt* 'think' (*ekate·ntam* 'he is ashamed'), and *-aʔ* 'by tool or medium' (*ekoteʔam* 'he paddles upstream').

5. 13. The verb is inflected also for order, mode, and tense.

The three orders are INDEPENDENT, CONJUNCT, and IMPERATIVE. The last appears in commands and prohibitions; the other two cover a parallel system of modes, the independent in principal clauses, the conjunct in subordinate clauses and participles.

The independent and conjunct orders have each an INDICATIVE, a PRETERIT, a DUBITATIVE, and a DUBITATIVE PRETERIT mode; each of these four modes, moreover, has by its side a corresponding NEGATIVE mode.

The modes of the independent order form principal clauses. The occurrence is negated by the particle *ka·* with the several negative modes. The modes of the conjunct order form subordinate clauses and participles. The occurrence is negated by the several negative modes or, more often, by composition with the particle *pwa·*.

5. 14. The independent indicative is the general form of statements and yes-or-no questions, the latter marked by the postpositive particle *ena: kemiwan* 'it is raining'; *nenta·-ki·-pi-eša·* 'I would have come here'; *ka-pi·to·n* 'thou art to bring it'; *ketaye·kkos ena?* 'art thou tired?' Negative: *ka· wi·n nentaye·kkusissi·* 'I am not tired'.

5. 15. The independent preterit is used of occurrences in a period of past time that does not extend into the present: *ki·-nempopan* 'he then died'.

The occurrence may be decidedly remote in time: (S469) *kecci-ša·ši kwa ki·-nempopan nemišše·miss* 'my grandfather died a very long time ago'.

The occurrence may be continuous with emphasis on its being cut off in the past: (S 484, first clause) *neni·puwina·pan essini·nk, (mi·tašš ki·-šo·škuššina·n)* 'I was standing on a stone, (but then I slipped and fell off)'.

Similarly, the preterit is used of repeated occurrence whose prevalence has been cut off: *nenki·-nessituttawa·peni·k* 'I formerly used to understand them (but have now forgotten their language)'.

The preterit is used also of intended actions that were not realized: (S 622) *ke·ko· ni·-ki·špenato·na·pan ota·we·wekamekonk* 'I was going to buy something at the store (but got there too late)'.

5. 16. The independent dubitative forms statements of doubtful occurrence: (S 453) *kenapac uwaya pi-eya·tik* 'someone seems to be coming here'.

5. 17. The independent dubitative preterit is used like the independent preterit (5. 15), but the occurrence is known by inference or tradition: (S 471) *a·ppeci kena·cuwikupan uškinuwe·* 'the young man must have been very handsome'; S 472.

5. 18. The conjunct indicative forms subordinate clauses and participles. It has four tenses: SIMPLE, CHANGED, ITERATIVE, and PARTICIPLE.

5. 19. The simple conjunct is the general form of subordinate clause verbs: (S 473) *ki·špin enokki·yan ka-tepaʾemo·n* 'if you work I will pay you'; S 474-551.

5. 20. The changed conjunct has initial change (4.2-5). It is the form of subordinate clause verbs naming an actual prior occurrence; also it is the form used with predicative particles and pronouns (except *mi·* 'it is that, it was then' and *a·ppi·*, *a·ppi·šš*, *a·ni·ppi·šš* 'where is it?', which are followed by the simple conjunct unless the verb contains a relative root): (S 607) *ki·-kecci-kemiwan eppane· me·no·kkemik* 'it rained hard all last spring'; S 613, 646, 560, 585; but simple conjunct in S 481: *mi· šikwa wi·-ni-ma·ca·ya·n* 'now I must leave right away'; and in S 618.

If the verb contains a RELATIVE ROOT, the changed conjunct may form a phrase which centers round this root; for instance, with the relative root *iN-* 'thither, thus', the simple conjunct *ešicceke·t* 'if he does so', the changed conjunct *e·šeccike·t* 'the way he does'; similarly *e·ši-keškitto·t* 'the way he manages it', *ka·-esi-keškitto·t* (the initial change affects the first syllable, here the preverb *ki·*) 'the way he has managed it'. (See S 553, 561, 566, 584.)

The relative roots are:

akkw- 'so long': *e·kko-keškiʾe·wesiyan* 'as long as thou art able';

appi·tt- 'so far': *e·ppi·tta·kunaka·k* 'as deep as the snow lies';

iN- 'thither, thus': *e·ša·t* 'whither he goes' (the verbs *to·tam* 'he does so', *to·tuwa·t* 'he does so to him', are treated as if they contained *iN-*; *it-* in *eta·kkusite·* 'he has feet of that length' may be a by-form of *iN-*);

ont- 'thence, therefore': *ka·-oncipa·t* 'whence he comes' (the verb *entaʾepa·* 'he draws water from there' is treated as if it contained *ont-*);

taN- 'there': *e·nteši-enokki·ya·n* 'where I work' (the verb *ta·* 'he exists there, dwells there' is treated as if it contained *taN-*: *e·nta·ya·n* 'where I dwell');

taSS- 'so many': *e·ntassotepa ʾekane·k* 'how many o'clock it is' (the root *tatt-* in *teccink* 'so many times' is a by-form).

When not so used, the relative roots normally require an antecedent (20. 5).

5. 21. The iterative tense of the conjunct indicative has initial change and adds the ending -$_9n$ to the simple conjunct endings; it forms clauses of repeated occurrence: *ke·muwankin* 'whenever it rains'; S 661-4.

5. 22. The participle has initial change. It forms clauses of substantive function: *wa·-pi-eša·t* 'he who will come'; *wa·cenokki·mak* 'the one with whom I work'; *me·cca·k* 'one which is big'; *me·cca·nik* 'one (obv.) which is big'.

If the participle denotes an animate obviative or an inanimate plural (proximate or obviative), it adds -$_9n$ to the simple conjunct endings: *wa·-pi-eša·necin* 'the other(s) who will come'; *me·ma·cca·kin* 'those which are big'; *me·ma·cca·nekin* 'those (obv.) which are big'.

If the participle denotes an animate plural, it adds -$_9k$ to the simple conjunct endings of the singular form (instead of -$_4iwa·$ or -$_6wa·$ of the other tenses): *wa·-pi-eša·cik* 'those who will come' (contrast the simple conjunct *wi·-pi-eša·wa·t* 'that they will come'); *wa·cenokki·mekik* 'those with whom I work'.

5. 23. The preterit conjunct, with ending -$_7pan$, -$_7pa·n$, forms clauses of unrealized occurrence: *ci-eša·ya·mpa·n* 'that I would go there'; and clauses of contrary-to-fact condition: (S 691) *ki·špin pwa·-untametta·ya·mpa· nenta·-ki·-eša·* 'if I were not busy I would go there', S 692-707. Otherwise, it parallels, in subordinate clauses, the use of the independent preterit: (S 708) *me·yo·ša ki·-no·ntema·mpa·* 'I heard it a long time ago'. It forms participles (8. 18).

5. 24. The dubitative conjunct has initial change and ending -$_8e·n$. It forms clauses of doubt or question: *e·ša·wa·ne·n* 'whether I go there'; S 668-89. It probably has a participle.

5. 25. The preterit dubitative conjunct combines the endings -$_7pan$, -$_7pa·n$ of the preterit and -$_8e·n$ of the dubitative conjunct. It parallels in clauses the use of the independent preterit dubitative: (S 709) *neme·tto· ssa wi· kwa ka·-pi-eša·kupane·n* 'he has left traces which show that he must have come here'. Also it forms clauses of doubtful or questionable hypothetical occurrence: *e·ša·wa·mpa·ne·n* 'whether I would go there'; S 712-4. It forms a participle: *ka·-mi·ka·-supane·nak* 'those who (by tradition) are said to have fought'.

5. 26. The negative modes corresponding to these conjunct modes are used without a negative particle: (S 666) *ki·špin no·ntuwa·ssuwak* 'if I do not hear him'; S 667-8. They are usually replaced by positive forms with the preverb *pwa·* 'fail to, not': (S 476) *ki·špin pwa·-pi--eya·t* ... 'if he does not come, ...'; S 691.

5. 27. The modes of the imperative order are a SIMPLE IMPERATIVE, a DELAYED IMPERATIVE, and a PROHIBITIVE.

The (simple) imperative forms ordinary positive commands: *pi·nteke·n* 'enter thou'.

The delayed imperative forms commands for action after an intervening event: *pi·nteke·kkan* 'do thou then afterward enter.'

The prohibitive is used with the negative particle *ke·kwa: ke·kwa pi·nteke·kke·n* 'do thou not enter'.

CHAPTER 6

INFLECTION OF THE NOUN AND PRONOUN

NOUN: NUMBER AND OBVIATION

6. 1. Number and obviation of the noun are indicated by the following endings:

Animate singular: $-_9a$, dropped after stems (or final members of compounds) longer than a single short-vowel syllable (3. 9).

Inanimate singular: $-_9i$, dropped like the preceding.

Animate plural: $-_9ak$.

Obviative, and inanimate plural: $-_9an$.

Thus, with stem *ko·kko·šš-: ko·kko·šš* 'pig', *ko·kko·ššak* 'pigs', *ko·kko·-ššan* 'pig(s) (obv.)'; stem *makkw-* 'bear': *mekkwa, mekkwak, mekkwan*; stem *ki·ko·ny-* 'fish': *ki·ko͞, ki·ko·nyak, ki·ko·nyan*; stem *assapy-* AN 'net': *essap, essapi·k, essapi·n*; stem *ikkwe·w-* 'woman': *ekkwe·, ekkwe·wak, ekkwe·wan*; stem *oškini·kikkwe·-* 'young woman': *uškini·-kekkwe·, uškini·kekkwe·k, uškini·kekkwe·n*; stem *makkisin-: mekkisin* 'moccasin', *mekkisenan* 'moccasins'; stem *si·pi·we·ny-* 'brook-: *si·pi·we͞, si·pi·we·nyan*; stem *assiny-* 'stone': *essin, essini·n*; stem *apwy-* 'paddle': *epwi, epwi·n*; stem *maškikkiw-* 'herb': *meškikki, meškikkuwan*. Likewise, with theme *ninko·kko·ššim-* 'my pig': *nenko·kko·ššim, nenko·kko·-ššemak, nenko·kko·ššeman*; theme *ko·ssiwa·-* 'your father': *ko·ssuwa·, ko·ssuwa·k, ko·ssuwa·n*; theme *omakkisin-* 'his moccasin': *umakkesin, umakkesinan.*

An animate noun with animate third person possessor is always obviative: *uko·kko·ššeman* 'his pig(s).

Themes consisting of a prefix and a stem of only a single short-vowel syllable (without the ending $-_1m$), form the singular like the unprefixed stem: *nentapwi* 'my paddle'.

6. 2. Stems in consonant plus *w* longer than a single short-vowel syllable, have coalescence of *wa* to *o* after a long-vowel syllable, and to *o·* after a short-vowel syllable (3. 39): stem *šika·kw-* 'skunk': *šeka·k, šeka·kok, šeka·kon*; stem *akkikkw-* AN 'kettle': *ekkikk, ekkikko·k, ekkikko·n*; stem *wa·ka·kkwatw-* 'axe': *wa·ka·kkwat, wa·ka·kkuto·n.*

If the plurals *nenkikok* 'otters' and *pepikok* 'fleas' are correctly recorded, the above statement does not cover all the cases.

6. 3. When the singular ending is dropped, the following retain final *w* (3. 32): *-e·naniw-* 'tongue' (*nente·neniw*), *-i·yaw-* 'body' (*ni·yaw*), *o·te·naw* 'town', *pekiw* 'pitch', *pešiw* 'lynx'; *ne·kaw* 'sand' is probably to be viewed as a stem in *-wy* (6. 8).

6. 4. Other irregularities of the singular are sporadic. The stem *takkipy-* 'spring of water' retains $-_ə i$: *tekkipi*. The stem *-kaššiw-* 'mother' has *nenkašše·* beside regular *nenkašši*. In story, *wa·peka·kwa*, *wa·peka·ko·* occur beside normal *wa·peka·k* 'white porcupine'; similarly *ne·nepo·šo·* beside *ne·nepoš* as the name of the Culture Hero.

6. 5. Possessed themes in $-_ɑ ina·n$ 'our' and stems in *-i·k* 'cloth' have *i* instead of *a* in the endings: *no·ssena·n* 'our (excl.) father' : *no·ssena·nik*, *no·ssena·nin;* *eppiššemoni·k* 'mat' : *eppiššcmoni·kin*.

6. 6. The stem *sa·kikki·-* 'plant' forms the plural with *-no·n*, like an II verb in the independent indicative (7. 9): *sa·kekki·*, *sa·kekki·no·n*.

NOUN: ADDRESS

6. 7. Two dependent nouns have a special form for singular address with possessor 'I': 6. 21.

A special form for plural address, with ending $-_ə tik$, $-_ə tok$, appears in *menta·kukkwe·tik* 'ladies!', *menta·kuninuwitok* 'gentlemen!'

NOUN: LOCAL FORM

6. 8. A local form, with the syntactic function of a particle, is made with the ending $-_ə ink$: *ci·ma·n* 'canoe': *ci·ma·nink* 'in the canoe'; *nenci·ma·n* 'my canoe': *nenci·ma·nink;* *essin* 'stone' (stem *assiny-*): *essini·nk* 'on the stone'; *epwi* 'paddle' (stem *apwy-*): *epwi·nk* 'on the paddle'; *ne·kaw* 'sand' (stem *ne·kawy-*): *ne·kuwi·nk* 'on the sand'; *wi·mpenakketo˜* 'hollow stump': *wi·mpenakketo·nᵊink;* *uwi·kuwa·muwa·* 'their house'; *uwi·kuwa·muwa·nk;* *ekkikk* AN 'kettle' (stem *akkikkw-*): *ekkikkonk*.

6. 9. Stems in vowel plus *w* drop the *w* and lengthen a preceding short vowel (3. 44): *si·pi* 'river' (stem *si·piw-*): *si·pi·nk;* *o·te·naw* 'town': *o·te·na·nk* 'in town, at Detroit'.

6. 10. A few stems take -₉a·nk: uma·nuwa·nk 'on his cheek'; unikka·nk 'on his arm'; uppikkuna·nk 'on his back'; mi·kkena·nk 'on the road'.

6. 11. Themes in -₄iniw 'obviative possessor' drop w (3. 47): ukka·tenink 'on the other one's leg'.

NOUN: COMPOUNDING FORM

6. 12. As prior members of compounds, noun stems take the ending -₉i: neme·pin 'sucker (fish)': neme·peni-ki·siss AN 'April'; mettik 'wood' (stem mittikw-): mettiko-tesso·na·kan 'wooden trap'; essin 'stone' (stem assiny-): essini·-wi·kuwa·m 'stone house'.

Occasionally, this -i seems to be lacking: meškote·ta·pa·n-mi·kkan 'railway track'.

NOUN: POSSESSED THEMES

6. 13. Possessed themes are formed by means of prefixes and the ending -₁im; to this -₄iniw is added for obviative possessor, -₄ina·n for plural possessor of the first person, -₄iwa· for other plural possessors. ko·kko·šš 'pig': nenko·kko·ššim 'my pig'; ukima· 'chief': nento·kema·m 'my chief'; essassã 'nest': utassessa·nᵊim 'his nest'; uppin AN 'potato' (stem oppiny-): nento·ppeni·mak 'my potatoes'; mettik 'wood' (stem mittikw-): kemittekom 'thy stick'.

Obviative possessor: si·sepa·kkwat 'sugar' (stem in -tw): usi·sepa·-kkutomeni 'the other's sugar'.

First person plural possessor: nento·kema·mena·n 'our (excl.) chief', keto·kema·mena·n 'our (incl.) chief'.

Second and third person plural possessor: keto·kema·muwa· 'your chief', uto·kema·muwa·n 'their chief(s) (obv.)'.

6. 14. Stems in vowel plus w drop w and lengthen the vowel if it is short (3. 44): pešikki 'cow' (stem pešikkiw-): kepašekki·mak 'thy cows'.

Stems in m or n do not take -₁im: nuwi·kuwa·m 'my house', nenci·-ma·n 'my canoe'.

IRREGULAR POSSESSED THEMES

6. 15. The stems akkan- (ekkan 'bone') and mi·kwan, mi·nkwan AN 'feather', contrary to 6. 14, take -₁im: nentakkenim 'my bone', nemi·-kunim 'my feather'.

6. 16. The following stems do not take -₁*im*: *ekkikk* AN 'kettle': *nentakkikk;* *enitt* 'fish spear'; *nentanitt;* *epwi* 'paddle': *nentapwi;* *esse·ma·* AN 'tobacco': *nentasse·ma·;* *kepo·ssenẽ* 'trousers': *nenkipo·-ssenẽ;* *meškimot* 'bag': *nemaškemot;* *mettikwa·p* AN 'bow': *umettikwa·pi·n;* *pekkwakk* 'arrow': *upakkwakk;* almost all dependent nouns (see 6. 19).

6. 17. The noun *neᵃ·nkišš* 'son-in-law' forms *nenaᵃ·nkešši·m*.

6. 18. The noun *enim* 'dog' and its diminutives *enimošš* 'dog' and *enimo·ns* 'little dog, puppy' do not make possessed themes: these are replaced by the dependent noun *nentay* 'my dog'.

DEPENDENT NOUNS

6. 19. Dependent nouns are used only with prefixes, in possessed themes. The ending -₁*im* is lacking in most; it appears optionally in *nempa·pa·m*, *nempa·pa* 'my father'; it is present, but is followed by a derivational suffix, in *nemiššo·miss* 'my grandfather', *nešši·mẽ* 'my younger brother or sister', *no·kkumiss* 'my grandmother'. It seems to be lacking even in those which are formed from ordinary nouns by composition with the dependent prenoun -*i·ci*: *ni·ci-enišsena·pe·* 'my fellow Indian' (10. 6).

Some dependent stems begin with a cluster: *neštikwa·n* 'my head'. Others, owing to the treatment of prefixes in 4. 8, have a fortis: *nekka·t* 'my leg'. A number with initial *i·* take the prefixes in the form *n-, k-, w-*: *ni·pit* 'my tooth', *ki·pit, wi·pit;* so those with -*i·ci* (10. 6). Occasionally *uw-* is used instead of *w-* (4. 7). Three with initial *o·* take the prefixes in the form *n-, k-,* zero: *no·ss* 'my father', *ko·ss, o·ssan*.

6. 20. The prefix *i-* (indefinite personal possessor) is used with those dependent nouns which do not denote relatives: *eninc* 'a hand'. No forms were obtained for the type with initial *i·*.

Those which denote relatives are replaced by verbal derivatives when the possessor is indefinite, e.g., *we·yo·ssecik* 'they who have someone as a father', i.e., 'a man's children'.

6. 21. Two dependent nouns have special forms for singular address with possessor 'I': *nemiššo·* 'O my grandfather', for *nemiššo··miss* 'my grandfather'; *no·kko·* 'O my grandmother', for *no·kkumiss* 'my grandmother'.

PRONOUNS

6. 22. The dependent stem -*i·n*- forms a set of pronouns denoting person and number. The singular has zero ending, the first persons plural have -₄*iwi*, the other plurals -₄*iwa·*: *ni·n* 'I', *ki·n* 'thou', *wi·n* 'he, it' (also *ni·*, *ki·*, *wi·*, I. 14); *ni·nuwi* 'we (excl.)', *ki·nuwi* 'we (incl.)'; *ki·nuwa·* 'ye', *wi·nuwa·* 'they'.

The form *wi·n* is used also as a contrastive postpositive particle, especially after *ka·* 'not'.

6. 23. There is a set of pronouns differentiated for gender, number, and obviation for nearer demonstrative use and one for farther; the latter are modified, for more remote reference, by endings -₉*i*, -*ti*, -*e·ti*. The forms show some use of *k* for animate plural and of *n* for obviative and for inanimate plural; there is also a partial contrast of animate *a* with inanimate *i*.

	'this'	'that'	'that over there'
an. sg.	*ma·pa*	*aw*	*uwiti, uwe·ti*
inan. sg.	*ma·nta*	*iw*	*uwiti, uwe·ti*
an. pl.	*ekonta*	*ekiw*	*ekiwi, ekiwe·ti*
obv., inan. pl.	*eninta*	*eniw*	*eniwi, eniwe·ti*

6. 24. There is a set for 'that sort': sg. *tenawa*, an. pl. *tenawak* (and, presumably, obv. and inan. pl. in -*n*).

6. 25. The interrogative pronouns are based on -*awe·*-, an., and *we·kw*-, inan. They in part contain -₉*šš*: *uwe·ne·*, *uwe·ne·šš* 'who is it?', *we·kune·šš* 'what is it?'

The dubitatives, based on the same stems, contain -₅*kw* and -₈*e·n*: *uwe·kwe·n* 'whoever it be', *we·kutakwe·n* 'whatever it be'.

6. 26. The indefinite pair is suppletive: *uwaya* 'someone', *ke·ko·* 'something'.

6. 27. The particles of place *ma·meppi·* 'here', *uwiti* 'there, yonder' resemble demonstrative pronouns; not so *ema·* 'there'.

CHAPTER 7

INFLECTION OF THE INDEPENDENT VERB

7. 1. In forms of the independent order, intransitive and pseudo-intransitive verbs take prefixes only for the first and second persons. Transitive and pseudo-transitive verbs take prefixes for all but the passive forms of the third person.

ANIMATE INTRANSITIVE

7. 2. The indicative mode has the following endings:

'I, thou': zero. *nempimusse·* 'I walk', *kepimusse·* 'thou walkest', *nenka-tekoššin* 'I shall arrive', *ka-tekoššin* 'thou wilt arrive'. A final short vowel of the stem is dropped (3. 9): *nempima·tis* 'I live', *kepima·tis* 'thou livest', stem *pima·tisi-;* then postvocalic *w* remains (3. 32): *kekwi·wesse·nsiw* 'thou art a boy', stem *kwi·wisse·nsiwi-*.

'we': $-_4min$. *nempimusse·min* 'we (excl.) walk', *kepimusse·min* 'we (incl.) walk'.

'ye': $-_4m$. *kepimusse·m* 'ye walk'.

passive: $-_4m$. *ni·meʔitim* 'there is dancing'. Probably also $-_4iwa·n$ implying plurality of actors: *wi·-wa·pentaʔuwe·wa·n* 'there will be an exhibition'.

The third person forms take $-_4w$, followed by sg. $-_9a$, pl. $-_9ak$, obv. $-_9an$. After any but a single short-vowel syllable, $-_9a$ drops (3. 9), and then the final *w;* between consonants, *wa* merges to *o·* (3. 39): *pemosse·* 'he walks', *pemosse·wak* 'they walk', *pemosse·wan* 'the other walks'; *pema·tesi* 'he lives'; *tekoššin* 'he arrives', *tekoššeno·k* 'they arrive', *tekoššeno·n* 'the other arrives'. The stem *nimpo-* drops *o: nempwa* 'he dies', *nempwak* 'they die', *nempwan* 'the other dies'.

7. 3. The pseudo-transitive forms have $-_3n$ for the pseudo-object, which is pluralized by $-_9an$:

'I, thou, he (-it)': $-_3n$. *nempi·to·n* 'I bring it', *kepi·to·n* 'thou bringest it', *upi·to·n* 'he brings it'.

'I, thou, he (-them)': $-_3n$, $-_9an$. *nempi·to·nan* 'I bring them', *kepi·to·nan* 'thou bringest them', *upi·to·nan* 'he brings them'.

'we (-it)': -₃n, -₄ina·n. nemi·cena·n 'we (excl.) eat it', kemi·cena·n 'we (incl.) eat it'.

'ye, they (-it)': -₃n, -₄a·wa·. kemi·cena·wa· 'ye eat it', umi·cena·wa· 'they eat it'.

'ye, they (-them)': -₃n, -₄a·wa·, -₉an. utata·we·na·wa·n 'they sell them'.

One form with animate pseudo-object was recorded: uki·-nettama·ke·nan 'he killed something for the other'.

7. 4. In the negative mode -₂ssi· is added to the stem, with further endings as in the indicative:

'I, thou': ka· wi·n nentaye·kkusissi· 'I am not tired'; ka· wi·n ketikketossi· 'thou dost not say so'.

'we': ka· wi·n ka-pi·nta·kkwe·ssi·min 'we (incl.) shall not smoke'.

'he': ka· wi·n ne·sse·ssi· 'he is not breathing'.

'they': ka· wi·n pekisussi·wak 'they do not go swimming'.

'I, thou, he (-it)': ka· wi·n nemi·cessi·n 'I do not eat it'; ka· wi·n ukašketto·ssi·n 'he cannot manage it'.

7. 5. In the preterit 'I' takes -₇na·pan, 'he' -₇pan: neni·puwina·pan 'I was standing', nenki·špenato·na·pan 'I used to buy it'; nempopan 'he died then'.

7. 6. Dubitative:

'he': -₇tik, after consonant -₇a·tik. eya·tik 'he may be there'; ki·-wenišsena·tik 'he must have got lost'.

'they': -₇tik, -₈e·n, -₉ak. ki·weškwe·pi·teke·nak 'they seem to be drunk'.

obviative: -₇tik, -₈e·n, -₉an. ki·weškwe·pi·teke·nan 'the other seems to be drunk'.

'he (-it)'; -₃n, -₇a·tik, ki·-kemo·tena·tik 'he must have stolen it'.

7. 7. Negative dubitative:

'he': -₂ssi·, -₇tik. ka· wi·n enokki·ssi·tik 'he seems not to be working'.

'they': -₂ssi·, -₇tik, -₈e·n, -₉ak. ka· wi·n enokki·ssi·teke·nak 'they seem not to be working'.

7. 8. Preterit dubitative:

'he': -₅kw, -₇pan. kena·cuwikupan 'he must have been handsome'.

'they': -₄iwa·, -₅kw, -₇pan. ki·-pepa·tti·nuwa·kupan 'they must have been many'.

INANIMATE INTRANSITIVE

7. 9. Indicative:

'it': -$_4$w, -$_9$i, dropping (by 3. 9). *enakente·* 'it is priced so'; *penkissin* 't falls'.

'they': -$_4$w, -$_9$an, with merging of *wa* to *o·* (3. 39); after a vowel -$_3$n precedes these endings. *penkisseno·n* 'they fall'; *enakente·no·n* 'they are priced so'.

obviative: -$_4$ini. *pi·nette·ni* 'it (obv.) lies clean'; *ma·ca·mekateni* 'it (obv.) goes away.'

7. 10. Negative:

'it': -$_2$ssi·, -$_9$no·n; -$_2$ssi· is added to a consonant without connective. *ka· wi·n we·wi·pe·nta·kussi·no·n* 'there is no hurry' (stem ending in *t*).

7. 11. Dubitative:

'it': -$_7$tik. *pena·tessinetik* 'it must be spoilt'.

7. 12. Preterit dubitative:

'it': -$_5$kw, -$_7$pan. *po·kkuška·kupan* 'it must have got broken'.

TRANSITIVE ANIMATE

7. 13. The independent forms of the TA verb are made from four themes.

Forms in which at most one of the first two persons appears as actor or object:

DIRECT forms: the prefix (chosen by 4. 6) agrees with the actor; theme sign -$_1$a·. Here belong also the passives of the third person; these passives have no prefix.

INVERSE forms: the prefix does not agree with the actor; theme sign -$_1$ikw, with *awi* replaced by *a·* (3. 44). Here belong also the forms with inanimate actor and the passives of the first two persons. Before -$_1$ikw the stem *iN-* is replaced by zero.

Forms in which both the first and second persons appear as actor or object:

THOU-ME forms: the prefix (*ki-*) agrees with the actor; theme sign -$_1$yi (3. 9, 30).

I-THEE forms: the prefix (*ki-*) agrees with the object; theme sign -$_1$iNi. Final *aw* of the stem coalesces with *i* to *o·* (3. 45).

GRAMMATICAL SKETCH

DIRECT FORMS

7. 14. Indicative:

'I, thou—him': zero. *neno·ntuwa·* 'I hear him', *keno·ntuwa·* 'thou hearest him'.

'I, thou—them': -$_9$*ak*. *neno·ntuwa·k* 'I hear them', *keno·ntuwa·k* 'thou hearest them'.

'we—him': -$_4$*ina·n*. *neno·ntuwa·na·n* 'we (excl.) hear him', *keno·ntuwa·na·n* 'we (incl.) hear him'.

'we—them': -$_4$*ina·n*, -$_9$*ik*. *neno·ntuwa·na·nik* 'we (excl.) hear them', *keno·ntuwa·na·nik* 'we (incl.) hear them'.

'ye—him': -$_4$*iwa·*. *keno·ntuwa·wa·* 'ye hear him'.

'ye—them': -$_4$*iwa·*, -$_9$*ak*. *keno·ntuwa·wa·k* 'ye hear them'.

'he—obv.': -$_9$*an*. *uno·ntuwa·n* 'he hears the other'.

'they—obv.': -$_4$*iwa·*, -$_9$*an*. *uno·ntuwa·wa·n* 'they hear the other'.

'he' passive: -$_4$*w*, -$_9$*a*, dropping (by 3. 9). *pekkinuwa·* 'he is defeated'.

'they' passive: -$_4$*w*, -$_9$*ak*. *kutacema·wak* 'they are tested in the cold'.

impersonal passive: -$_4$*iwa·n*. *ki·-no·ppenanuwa·n* 'there was pursuing of animate objects'.

7. 15. Negative: -$_2$*ssi·* is added to the theme.

'I, thou—him': *ka· wi·n nuwa·pema·ssi·* 'I do not see him', *ka· wi·n ka-mi·na·ssi·* 'thou shalt not give it to him'.

'I, thou—them': *ka· wi·n nenka-mi·na·ssi·k* 'I will not give it to them'

'we—him': *ka· wi·n ka-pa·pi·ʔa·ssi·na·n* 'we (incl.) shall not wait for him'.

'he—obv.': *ka· wi·n uki·-emwa·ssi·n* 'he has not eaten the other'.

'they—obv.': *ka· wi·n uki·-wa·pema·ssi·wa·n* 'they have not seen the other'.

7. 16. Preterit:

'I—him': -$_7$*pan*. *nenki·-no·ntuwa·pa* (final *n* lost by 1. 14) 'I used to hear him'.

'I—them': -$_7$*pan*, -$_9$*i·k*. *nenki·-nessituttawa·peni·k* 'I used to understand their speech'.

7. 17. Dubitative:

'he—obv.': -$_7$*tik*, -$_8$*e·n*, -$_9$*an*. *uki·-nessa·teke·nan* 'he must have killed the other'.

7. 18. Negative dubitative:

'he—obv.': -₂ssi·, -₇tik, -₈e·n, -₉an. *ka· wi·n uki·-nessa·ssi·teke·nan* 'he probably did not kill the other'.

INVERSE FORMS

7. 19. Indicative:

'he—me, thee': zero. *nuwa·pemik* 'he sees me'; *nenki·-ka·nteʔok* 'he gave me a push' (stem *ka·ntaʔw-*); *nenki·- no·nta·k* 'he has heard me' (stem *no·ntaw-*); *nenki·-ik* 'he said so to me' (stem *iN-*, replaced by zero); *keki·-wa·pemik* 'he has seen thee'.

'they—me, thee': -₉ak. *nenki·-wi·kkumiko·k* 'they have invited me'.

'he—us': -₄ina·n. *nenki·-no·ppenanekona·n* 'he pursued us (excl.)'; *ka-ššamekona·n* 'he will give us (incl.) food' (stem *aššam-*).

'they—us': -₄ina·n, -₉ik. *keno·nta·kuna·nik* 'they hear us (incl.)'.

'he—you': -₄iwa·. *keki·-keno·nekowa·* 'he spoke to you'.

'obv.—him': -₉an. *uki·-no·nta·ko·n* 'the other has heard him'; *uki·-eko·n* 'the other said so to him' (stem *iN-* replaced by zero).

'I' passive: -₂o·. *nenki·-ešiweniko·* 'I was led thither'.

7. 20. Negative: -₂ssi· is added to the theme-sign.

'he—me, thee': *ka· wi·n nenki·-pesinta·kussi·* 'he did not listen to me' (stem *pisintaw-*); *ka· wi·n keta·-tekkomekossi·* 'he will not bite thee'.

'they—me, thee': *ka· wi·n nente·pwe·tta·kussi·k* 'they do not believe me' (stem *te·pwe·ttaw-*); *ka· ke·ko· keta·-to·ta·kussi·k* 'they will not do anything to thee' (stem *to·taw-*).

'obv.—him': *ka· wi·n unissetawena·kussi·n* 'the other did not recognize him' (stem *nissitawinaw-*).

7. 21. Dubitative:

'he—me': -₇tik. *nenki·-petakkeʔokutik* 'he must have stung me' (stem *patakkaʔw-*).

'we' passive: -₂o·, -₄min, -₇a·tik. *kenantuwa·-pemiko·mena·tik* 'we (incl.) are probably being looked for'.

THOU—ME FORMS

7. 22. Indicative:

'thou—me': zero (with loss of the final vowel, by 3. 9, but retention of *w* after vowel, by 3. 32). *keki·-no·ntaw* 'thou hast heard me'; *kemi·š* 'thou givest it to me' (stem *mi·N-*).

'thou, ye—us': -₄*min*. *keki·-wa·pemimin* 'thou hast (ye have) seen us'.
'ye—me': -₄*m*. *keno·ntuwim* 'ye hear me'.

7. 23. Negative: -₂*ssi·* is added to the theme.
'thou, ye—us': *ka· wi·n keta·-wi·ci·wessi·min* 'thou art not (ye are not) to accompany us'.

I—THEE FORMS

7. 24. Indicative.
'I—thee': zero (with loss of final vowel by 3. 9). *kemi·nin* 'I give it to thee'; *keno·nto·n* 'I hear thee' (stem *no·ntaw-*).
'we—thee, you': -₄*min*. *keno·nto·nemin* 'we hear thee (you)'.
'I—you': -₄*m*. *keno·nto·nim* 'I hear you'.

7. 25. Negative: the theme sign loses its final vowel (by 3. 12); -₂*ssi* is added without connective.
'I—thee': -₉*no·n*. *ka· wi·n ka·pekkitte·ʔussino·n* 'I will not strike thee' (stem *pakkitte·ʔw-*).

TRANSITIVE INANIMATE

7. 26. Indicative: the theme signs are -₁*u·*, -₃*n*.
'I, thou, he—it': zero. *nenki·-kwa·peʔa·n* 'I ladled it up'; *keta·-ka·ta·n* 'thou wilt plant it'; *uki·-wa·penta·n* 'he has seen it'.
'I, thou, he—them': -₉*an*. *nənki·-no·nta·nun* 'I have heard them'; *keta·-ka·ta·nan* 'thou wilt plant them; *upi·ssekka·nan* 'he dons them'.
'we—it': -₄*a·n*. *nentišenikka·ta·na·n* 'we (excl.) name it thus'; *keta·-tešinta·na·n* 'we (incl.) will talk about it'.
'they—it, them': -₄*a·wa·*, -₉*an*. *uki·-si·kena·na·wa·n* 'they poured it out'.

7. 27. The pseudo-intransitive forms have the theme sign -₁*am*.
'I, thou—(it)': zero. *nentine·ntam* 'I think so'.
'he—(it)': -₄*w*, -₉*a* (dropped, by 3. 9). *ekate·ntam* 'he is ashamed'.

7. 28. Negative. The theme-sign is -₁*am*, to which -₂*ssi·* is added without connective, giving *-ansi·;* and -₃*n*.
'I, thou, he—it': zero. *ka· wi·n neminwa·kemippetansi·n* 'I do not like the taste of it as a liquid'.

'they—it': $-_4a\cdot wa\cdot$, $-_9an$. *ka· wi·n ute·pwe·ttansi·na·wa·n* 'they do not believe it'.

7. 29. The pseudo-intransitive forms in the negative lack $-_3n$.

'I, thou—(it)': zero. *ka· wi·n nenka-to·tensi·* 'I shall not do thus'.

'they—(it)': $-_4w$, $-_9ak$. *ka· wi·n nessituttansi·wak* 'they do not understand.'

CHAPTER 8

INFLECTION OF THE CONJUNCT VERB

8. 1. The verb forms of the conjunct order have no prefixes. The indicative forms have initial change in the changed and iterative tenses and in the participle. In the iterative tense there is an ending $-_9n$; in the obviative participle and the inanimate plural participle there is $-_9n$, in the animate (third person) plural participle there is $-_9k$ instead of $-_4iwa\cdot$ or $-_6wa\cdot$. The dubitative forms have initial change.

ANIMATE INTRANSITIVE

8. 2. Indicative: those endings which begin with a, $a\cdot$, $e\cdot$ prefix y after a vowel (3. 5).

'I': $-_3a\cdot n$. *ni·meya·n* 'if I dance', stem *ni·mi-;* *tekoššena·n* 'when I arrive'.

'thou': $-_3an$. *enokki·yan* 'as thou workest'; *pi·to·yan* 'if thou bringest it (pseudo-transitive; 5. 9)'; *ka·- a·šekiteko·cenan* 'when thou didst fall backwards'.

'we (excl.)': $-_3a\cdot nk$. *ni·meya·nk* 'if we (excl.) dance'; *tekoššena·nk* 'when we (excl.) arrive'.

'we (incl.)': $-_3ankw$. *ni·meyank* 'if we (incl.) dance'.

'ye': $-_3e\cdot kw$. *ni·meye·k* 'if ye dance'.

'he': $-_5t;$ after consonant, $-_5k$ without connective. *ni·mit* 'if he dances'; *tekoššink* 'when he arrives'. $-_5k$ appears also in *e·-penkiššemok* 'where he (the sun) sets; in the west'.

'they': $-_4iwa\cdot$, $-_5t;$ after consonant $-_4owa\cdot$, $-_5t$. *ni·muwa·t* 'if they dance'; *tekoššenowa·t* 'when they arrive'.

obviative: $-_4ini$, $-_5t$. *ki·-kecci·-muwinit* 'as the other wept bitterly'.

passive: $-_5nk$. *mi·ka·tink* 'if there is fighting'.

8. 3. Iterative tense: *me·no-ešiwe·pesicin* 'whenever he behaves well'.

Obviative participle: *pi-eya·necin* 'the other one who is coming', stem *aya·-;* *ka·-utapeʔaki·sesswa·nuwa·cin* 'the other whom they had as a clock', stem *otapaʔaki·sisswa·ni-* with pseudo-object.

Animate plural participle: *pe·ma·tesicik* 'those who live; people'; *e·-pwa-wi·ssencik* 'those who do not eat'.

8. 4. Negative: -₂*ssi* is added to the stem. The endings of the first two persons are in the form with initial *w* (4. 10. 3).

'I': -₃*wa·n*. *ušo·neya·messiwa·n* 'if I have no money'.

'they': -₅*k*, -₆*wa·*. *ta-ešicceke·ssekwa·* 'that they shall not do thus'.

8. 5. Preterit: -₇*pan*, *-pa·n* are added to *n* and *t* without connective.

'I': -₃*a·n*, -₇*pa·n*. *ci-eša·ya·mpa·n* 'that I would go there'; *pa·tti·-netto·ya·mpa·n* 'if I had much of it'.

'he': -₅*t*, -₇*pan*. *eya·ppan* 'if he were there'.

8. 6. Dubitative: the endings of the first two persons are in the form with initial *w* (4. 10. 3). The forms have initial change. All end in -₈*e·n*.

'I': -₃*wa·n*. *ne·mpa·wa·ne·n* 'whether I was asleep'.

'ye': -₃*we·kw*. *e·ya·we·kwe·n* 'whether ye were there'.

'he': -₅*kw*. *ke·pepa·-ki·wusse·kwe·n* 'whether he will go out hunting'.

'they': -₄*iwa·*, -₅*kw*. *e·ya·wa·kwe·n* 'whether they are there '.

obviative: -₃*ini*, -₅*kw*. *e·nukki·nekwe·n* 'whether the other does work'.

8. 7. Negative dubitative: -₂*ssi·* is added to the stem; the form ends in -₈*e·n*.

obviative: -₄*ini*, -₅*kw*. *e·nukki·ssi·nekwe·n* 'whether the other does not work'.

8. 8. Preterit dubitative:

'I': -₃*wa·n*, -₇*pa·n* (no connective), -₈*e·n*. *ke·-eša·wa·mpa·ne·n* 'whether I would go there'.

'he': -₅*kw*, -₇*pan*, -₉*e·n*. *ka·-nenkamukopene·n* 'whether he would have sung'.

'they': -₅*kw*, -₇*pan*, -₈*e·n*, -₉*ak*. *ka·-pi-eša·kupane·nak* 'whether they would have come'.

obviative: -₅*kw*, -₇*pan*, -₈*e·n*, -₉*an*. *ka·-pi-eša·kupane·nan* 'whether the other would have come'. An alternative form has -₄*ini* instead of -₉*an*: *ka·-pi-eša·nekopene·n*.

INANIMATE INTRANSITIVE

8. 9. Indicative:

'it': -₅*k*, added to consonant without connective. *ena·kuššik* 'when evening comes', *e·na·kuššik* 'when evening came'; *kemiwank* 'if it rains', *ke·muwank* 'when it rained'; *ki·šekakk* 'when it is day', stem *ki·šikat-*. Stems in *-tapaʔikane·t* drop *t: e·ntessotepaʔekane·k* 'what time it is'.

obviative: $-_4ini$, $-_5k$. *ena·kuššinik* 'when evening comes'; *ci·pwa·tepikketinik* 'before nightfall', stem *tipikkat-*.

8. 10. Iterative tense: *ke·muwankin* 'whenever it rains'.

Plural participle: *e·sa·wa·kin* 'those which are yellow'; *neya·nkeninekin* 'those (obv.) which are light of weight', stem *na·nkan-*.

8. 11. Preterit: 'it': $-_5k$ (without connective), $-_7pan$. *pwa·-kemiwankepan* 'if it were not raining'.

8. 12. Dubitative: the forms end in $-_8e·n$.

'it': $-_5kw$; after consonant $-_5okw$. *e·na·pi·kwe·n* 'whether it is strung thither'; *ke·muwanukwe·n* 'whether it is raining'.

obviative: $-_4ini$, $-_5kw$. *eya·pete·nekwe·n* 'whether the thing is ripe', stem *wa·pite·-*.

TRANSITIVE ANIMATE

8. 13. The conjunct forms of the TA verb are made from four themes, like the independent forms, but the distribution of the forms is not the same.

DIRECT forms: the theme sign $-_1a·$ is lacking in the indicative and preterit forms with other than third person actor.

INVERSE forms: theme sign $-_1ikw$ (with replacement of *awi* by *a·*, 3. 44); the forms with first and second person objects (and animate actor) are not in this group. The stem *iN-*, as in the independent order (7. 13), is replaced by zero.

ME forms: theme sign $-_1yi$ (3. 9, 30); forms with first person object and second or third person actor.

THEE forms: theme sign $-_1iN$ (not *-iNi*), with replacement of *awi* by *o·* (3. 45); forms with second person object and first or third person actor.

DIRECT FORMS

8. 14. Indicative:

'I—him': $-_3ak$. *pwa·-no·ntuwak* 'if I do not hear him'; *eya·pemak* 'when I saw him', stem *wa·pam-*.

'I—them': -₃ak, -₆wa·. mo·nuwakwa· 'if I dig them up', stem mo·naʔw-
'thou—him': -₃at. wa·pemat 'if thou seest him'.
'thou—them': -₃at, -₆wa·. ci-wi·ntemawetwa· 'that thou tell it to them'.
'we (excl.)—him': -₃ankit. no·ntuwankit 'if we (excl.) hear him'.
'we (excl.)—them': -₃ankit, -₆wa·. ci-mi·ka·nenkitwa· 'that we fight them'.
'we (incl.)—him': -₃ankw. pi·nank 'if we (incl.) bring him'.
'ye—him': -₃e·kw. no·ntuwe·k 'if ye hear him'.
'ye—them': -₃e·kw, -₆wa·. no·ntuwe·kwa· 'if ye hear them'.
'he—obv.': -₁a·, -₅t. wa·pema·t 'if he sees the other', ne·ntuwe·nema·t 'the one who wants the other'.
'they—obv.': -₁a·, -₄iwa·, -₅t. wa·pema·wa·t 'if they see the other'.
'obv.—obv.'; -₁a·, -₄ini, -₅t. wa·pema·nit 'if the other sees still another'.
'he' passive: -₅int. wi·-wi·kkwe·penint 'that he be put under a charm', wa·-wi·kkwe·penint 'he who is to be put under a charm'.

8. 15. Iterative tense: eya·pema·cin 'whenever he sees the other', stem wa·pam-.

Animate plural participle: wa·cenokki·mekik 'the ones with whom I work', stem wi·cinokki·m-; wa·-mi·ka·nenkicik 'the ones with whom we (excl.) are to fight'; ne·ntuwe·nema·cik 'the ones who want the other'.

Obviative participle: ne·ntuwe·nema·cin 'the other whom he wants', ne·ntuwe·nema·necin 'the other who desires still another'.

8. 16. Negative: the theme sign -₁a· is used throughout; it is followed by -₂ssi. The first and second person endings have initial w (4. 10. 3).
'I—him': -₃wak. no·ntuwa·ssuwak 'if I do not hear him'.
'he—obv.': -₅k. kekke·nema·ssik 'as he does not know about the other'.
'obv.—obv.': -₄ini, -₅k. ci-uta·ppena·ssenik 'that the other does not take up that other one'.

8. 17. Preterit: -₇pan, added to -₅t without connective. Presumably -₇ipan would be used after -₃at 'thou-him' (8. 20).
'I—him': -₃ak, -₇pan. eya·wekipan 'if I had him'.
'he—obv.': -₁a·, -₅t, -₇pan. nessa·ppan 'if he killed the other'.

8. 18. A participle form, with -$_9i\cdot n$ for obviative: *ka·-we·pena·ppeni·n* 'the other whom he had abandoned'.

8. 19. Dubitative: the theme sign -$_1a$· is used throughout; the first and second person endings have initial *w* (4. 10. 3); the forms end in -$_8e\cdot n$.

'I—him': -$_3wak$. *ci-wa·pema·weke·n* 'whether I might see him'.

'thou—him': -$_3wat$. *ta-etimene·wa·wete·n* 'whether thou wilt overtake him'.

'he—obv.': -$_5kw$. *ka·-wa·pema·kwe·n* 'whether he has seen the other'.

8. 20. Preterit dubitative: the forms are as in the dubitative, but with -$_7pan$ before -$_8e\cdot n$; after -$_3wat$, -$_7ipan$ is used.

'I—him': *ta-ki·-meŝwa·wekipene·n* 'whether I would have hit him'.

'thou—him': *ta-ki·-meŝwa·wetipene·n* 'whether thou wouldst have hit him'.

'we (incl.)—him': -$_3wankw$. *me·ŝwa·wenkopene·n* 'whether we (incl.) would hit him'.

"he—obv.': *ta-ki·-meŝwa·kupane·n* 'whether he would have hit the other'.

INVERSE FORMS

8. 21. Indicative: theme-sign -$_1ikw$. The forms with obviative or inanimate actor add -$_2i$, the passives -$_2o$·; upon these follow the endings of the AI verb (8. 2), with *y* before their vowel (3. 5).

'obv.—him'; -$_2i$, -$_5t$. *no·nta·kot* 'if the other hears him'; *e·kot* 'that which the other says to him', stem *iN*-, replaced by zero, and initial change.

'obv.—them': -$_4iwa$·, -$_5t$. *no·nta·kuwa·t* 'if the other hears them'.

'it—us (excl.)': -$_2i$, -$_3a\cdot nk$. *ta-wi·ci·wekoya·nk* 'that it accompany us (excl.)'.

'it—him': -$_2i$, -$_5t$. *ci-ŝuwe·nemikot* 'that it take pity on him'.

'I' passive: -$_2o$·, -$_3a\cdot n$. *no·nta·ko·ya·n* 'if I am heard'; *e·ŝena·ŝekka·ko·ya·n* 'whither I was sent', stem in *-ikkaw*.

'thou' passive: -$_2o$·, -$_3an$. *no·nta·ko·yan* 'if thou art heard'.

'we (excl.)' passive: -$_2o$·, -$_3a\cdot nk$. *ki·-mi·neko·ya·nk* 'as we (excl.) were given it'.

'we (incl.)' passive: -$_2o$·, -$_3ankw$. *no·nta·ko·yank* 'if we (incl.) are heard'.

'ye' passive: -$_2o$·, -$_3e\cdot kw$. *no·nta·ko·ye·k* 'if ye are heard'.

8. 22. Iterative tense: *e·ššemikucin* 'whenever the other gives him food'.

Obviative participle: *wa·-nessikucin* 'the other who intends to kill him', *wa·-nessikuwa·cin* 'the other who intends to kill them'.

ME FORMS

8. 23. Indicative: after the theme sign $-_1yi$, the endings of the first two persons have intervocalic *y* (3. 5).

'thou—me': $-_3an$. *pwa·nekkwe·ttuwiyan* 'that thou dost not answer me'.

'thou, ye—us': $-_3a·nk$. *pwa·-nekkwe·ttuwiwa·nk* 'that thou dost not (ye do not) answer us'.

'ye—me': $-_3e·kw$. *no·ntuwiye·k* 'if ye hear me'.

'he—me': $-_5t$. *ki·-wi·kkupišit* 'that he managed to pull me', stem *wi·kkopiN-*.

'they—me': $-_4iwa·$, $-_5t$. *na·temawuwa·t* 'if they help me.'

'he—us (excl.)': $-_3amink$, $-_5t$. *keno·šeyamenkit* 'if he addresses us (excl.)' stem *kano·N-*.

'they—us (excl.)': $-_3amink$, $-_5t$, $-_6wa·$. *no·ntuwiyeminketwa·* 'if they hear us (excl.)'.

8. 24. Plural participle: *e·-pwa·-na·temawecik* 'they who do not help me'.

8. 25. Negative: to the theme sign $-_1yi$ there is added $-_2ssi$. The endings of the first two persons have initial *w* (4. 10. 3).

'thou—me': $-_3wan$. *na·temawessiwan* 'if thou dost not help me.'

8. 26. Preterit: $-_7pan$ is added, to *n* and *t* without connective.

'thou—me': *na·temaweyampan* 'if thou wouldst help me'.
'he—me': *wa·pemippan* 'if he saw me'.
'they—me': *wa·pemiwa·ppan* 'if they saw me'.

8. 27. Negative preterit: $-_2ssi$ is added to the theme sign; the endings of the first two persons have initial *w* (4. 10. 3); $-_7pan$ is added, to *n* and *t* without connective.

'thou—me': *na·temawessiwempan* 'if thou didst not help me'.

8. 28. Dubitative: the endings of the first two persons have initial *w*. The forms end in $-_8e·n$.

'thou—me': *ke·-na·temawuwane·n* 'whether thou wilt help me'.

'thou, ye—us': *ke·-na·temawuwa·nke·n* 'whether thou wilt (ye will) help us'.

'ye—me': *ke·-na·temawuwe·kwe·n* 'whether ye will help me'.

'he—me': *na·temawekwe·n* 'whether he helps me'.

8. 29. Preterit dubitative: -$_8e·n$ is preceded by -$_7pan$.

'he—me': -$_5kw$. *ke·-na·temawekopene·n* 'whether he would have helped me'.

THEE FORMS

8. 30. Indicative: the theme sign -$_1iN$ is followed by -$_5k$ without connective.

'I—thee': -$_3a·n$. *ta-wi·ci·wena·n* 'that I accompany thee'.

'I—you': -$_3akok$. *no·nto·nekok* 'if I hear you', stem *no·ntaw-*.

'he—thee': -$_5k$. *no·nto·kk* 'if he hears thee'.

'they—thee': -$_5k$, -$_6wa·$. *no·nto·kkwa·* 'if they hear thee'.

'he—us (incl.)': -$_3ankw$. *no·nto·nank* 'if he hears us (incl.)'.

'they—us (incl.)': -$_3ankw$, -$_6wa·$. *no·nto·nenkwa·* 'if they hear us (incl.)'.

8. 31. Preterit: -$_7pan$, -*pa·n* are added, to *n* without connective.

'I—thee': *wa·pemina·mpa·n* 'if I saw thee'.

'he—thee': -$_5kw$, -$_7pan$. *wa·pemikkupan* 'if he saw thee'.

'they—thee': -$_5kw$, -$_6wa·$, -$_7pan$. *wa·pemikkwa·pan* 'if they saw thee'.

'he—us (incl.)': -$_3ankw$, -$_7pan$. In both of the examples that were obtained, the theme-sign -$_1iN$ is added twice: *wa·peminenankupan* 'if he saw us (incl.)'; *na·temo·nenankupan* 'if he helped us (incl.)', stem *na·tamaw-*.

TRANSITIVE INANIMATE

8. 32. Indicative: the theme sign is -$_1am$, in some forms -$_1amo$. To this -$_5k$ is added without connective. Number of the object is not distinguished.

After the stem *ay-* a vowel is lengthened (3. 14).

'I—it'; -$_1am$, -$_3a·n$. *ki·-wa·pentama·n* 'that I have seen it'; *ci-eya·ma·n* 'that I have it', stem *ay-*.

'thou—it'; -$_1am$, -$_3an$. *ki·-mekkaman* 'that thou hast found it'.

'we (excl.)—it': -$_1am$, -$_3a·nk$. *ki·-a·nsekkama·nk* 'that we (excl.) have changed them'; *e·nte^{ʔ}ama·k* 'where we (excl.) draw water', stem *inta^ʔ-*.

'he—it': $-_1am$, $-_5k$, without connective: *ki·-pi·ssekkank* 'that he has donned it'; *eya·nk* 'if he has it'.

they—it': $-_1amo$, $-_4iwa\cdot$, $-_5t$. *mekkamuwa·t* 'if they find it'.

'obv.—it': $-_1am$, $-_4ini$, $-_5t$. *ka·-ena·pentamenit* 'when the other has had a vision'.

'it' passive: $-_1am$, $-_5nk$. *wi·-te·penamink* 'that it will be reached'.

8. 33. Inanimate plural participle: *te·pe·ntema·nin* 'those which I own'; *wa·-pepa·-eya·ma·nin* 'those which I intend to carry about', stem *ay-*.

8. 34. Preterit: to endings in *n*, $-_7pan$, $-pa\cdot n$ are added without connective.

'I—it': *ki·-no·ntema·mpa·n* 'if I had heard it'; *eya·ma·mpa·n* 'if I had it'.

'thou—it': *ke·-ene·ntemampa* 'that thou wouldst think so' (1. 14); *eya·pempan* 'if thou hadst it'.

'we (excl.)—it'; *eya·ma·nkepan* 'if we (excl.) had it'.

'we (incl.)—it': $-_1am$, $-_3ankw$, $-_7pan$. *eya·menkopan* 'if we (incl.) had it'.

'ye—it': $-_1am$, $-_3e\cdot kw$, $-_7pan$. *eya·me·kupan* 'if ye had it'.

'he—it': *ka·-ena·pentankepan* 'that which he had seen in a vision'.

8. 35. Dubitative: the forms end in $-_8e\cdot n$.

'he—it': $-_1amo$, $-_5kw$. *ne·ntuwe·ntemokwe·n* 'whether he wants it'.

'they—it': $-_1amo$, $-_4iwa\cdot$, $-_5kw$. *ka·-mekkamuwa·kwe·n* 'whether they have found it'.

'obv.—it': $-_1am$, $-_4ini$, $-_5kw$. *ka·-ena·pentamenikwe·n* 'whether the other has seen a vision'.

8. 36. Preterit dubitative: $-_7pan$ precedes $-_8e\cdot n$.

'he—it': $-_1amo$, $-_5kw$. *e·ne·ntemokupane·n* 'whether he would think so'.

CHAPTER 9

INFLECTION OF THE IMPERATIVE VERB; COMPOUNDING FORM

IMPERATIVE MODE

9. 1. The imperative of the AI verb has the following endings:
'thou': $-_9n$. *pi·nteke·n* 'enter thou'; *pi·to·n* 'bring thou it'; *šenkiššenin* 'lie thou down', stem *šinkiššin-*.
'ye': $-_9k$. *pi·nteke·k* 'enter ye'.
'we': $-_9ta·$. *pi·nteke·ta·* 'let us enter'.

9. 2. The TA forms ('we—him' was not obtained) all contain $-_1yi$, which (by 3. 4) loses *i* in final position, except after a stem consisting of a single short-vowel syllable (where *i* appears, by 3. 30). The forms with first person object add $-_2šš$. Number of a third person object is not distinguished.
'thou—him': $-_1yi$. *nešši* 'kill thou him', stem *niSS-*; *mi·š* 'give thou it to him', stem *mi·N-*; *tekkopiš* 'tie thou him fast', stem *takkopiN-*; *pekitin* 'set thou him down', stem *pakitin-*; *pi·taw* 'bring thou it to him', stem *pi·taw-* (3. 32); *ki·škaw* 'cut thou him though', stem *ki·ška ʔw-* (3. 37); *necci·wiʔ* 'scold thou him', stem *nicci·wiʔ-*.
'ye—him': $-_1yi$, $-_9kon$. *mi·šekon* 'give ye it to him'.
'thou—me': $-_1yi$, $-_2šš$, $-_9n$. *mi·šeššin* 'give thou it to me'.
'thou, ye—us': $-_1yi$, $-_2šš$, $-_3na·nk$. *mi·šeššina·nk* 'give thou (ye) it to us'.
'ye—me': $-_1yi$, $-_2šš$, $-_9k$. *mi·šeššik* 'give ye it to me'.

9. 3. The TI verb has for singular actor the theme sign $-_1am$, to which $-_9n$ is added without connective, yielding *-an*. The form for plural actor has $-_1amo$. Number of the object is not distinguished.
'thou—it': *ekintan* 'count thou them'.
'ye—it': $-_1amo$, $-_9k$. *wa·pentamok* 'look ye at it'.

DELAYED IMPERATIVE MODE

9. 4. After the AI stem, or after $-_1yi$, $-_2šš$ added to TA stems, come the mode signs $-_3kk$ and $-_8a$. The following forms were obtained:

'thou': -₉n. *pi-eša·kkan* 'come thou then hither'; *pi·to·kkan* 'bring thou it then'.

'thou—me': -₉n. *wi·ntemawešsikkan* 'tell thou it then to me'.

PROHIBITIVE MODE

9. 5. To the AI stem, to the TA theme with -₁*a·* for third person object or with -₁*yi*, -₂*šš* for first person object, and to the TI stem with theme sign -₁*am*, the mode sign -₃*kk* is added; this is followed by -₈*e·*.

9. 6. To an AI stem in *n*, -₃*kk* is added without connective, giving *-nk*. After vowels, -₃*kk* seems to be occasionally spoken as lenis *k*.

'thou': -₉n. *ke·kwa ni·mekke·n* 'do thou not dance'; *ke·kwa mi·cekke·n, ke·kwa mi·ceke·n* 'do thou not eat it'; *ke·kwa weniššenke·n* 'do thou not get lost'.

'ye': -₉*kon*. *ke·kwa ni·mekke·kon* 'do ye not dance'.

9. 7. TA forms: theme signs -₁*a·* 'him', -₁*yi*, -₂*šš* 'me'. Number of third person object is not distinguished.

'thou—him': -₉n. *ke·kwa mi·na·kke·n* 'do thou not give it to him'; *ke·kwa wi·-kussa·kke·n* 'do thou not fear him'.

'ye—him': -₉*kon*. *ke·kwa mi·na·kke·kon* 'do ye not give it to him'.
'thou—me': -₉n. *ke·kwa mi·šeššikke·n* 'do thou not give it to me'.
'thou, ye—us': -₃*a·nk*, -₉n. *ke·kwa mi·šeššikka·nke·n* 'do thou (ye) not give it to us'.

'ye—me': -₉*kon*. *ke·kwa mi·šeššikke·kon* 'do ye not give it to me'.

9. 8. TI forms: the theme sign -₁*am* and the mode sign -₃*kk* are joined without connective. Number of the object is not distinguished.

'thou—it': -₉n. *ke·kwa pi·kuʔanke·n* 'do thou not smash it'.

'ye—it': -₉*kon*. *ke·kwa nessa·kkunanke·kon* 'do ye not open it'.

COMPOUNDING FORM

9. 9. Intransitive verb stems ending in a vowel have a compounding form equal to the stem; examples in 10. 3. Stems ending in a consonant presumably take *-o*.

CHAPTER 10

COMPOSITION

10. 1. The members of a compound word are treated phonetically like words in a phrase.

10. 2. Nouns in compounding form (6. 12) appear as prior members with nouns: *essini·-wi·kuwa·m* 'stone house'. In some instances the singular form seems to be used: *meškote·ta·pa·n-mi·kkan* 'railway track'. Occasionally, such compounds appear beside unit words: *mettiko-una·kan* 'wooden bowl', beside the unit word *mettikuna·kan* with suffix *-na·kan* (11. 29).

The prior member has initial change in *še·ma·keni-uwe·ssi* 'wasp' (*šema·kan* 'soldier').

10. 3. Intransitive verbs in compounding form (9. 9) occur as prior members with nouns and verbs: *mento·to·-essini·n* 'stones for the steam bath', *si·sepa·kkutokke·-ki·siss* 'the sugar-making month, March'; *ena·kušši-wi·sseniwak* 'they eat the evening meal'.

10. 4. Some particles, PRENOUNS, are used as prior members with nouns: *kecci-mekkwa* 'big bear'; *kecci-mo·kkuma·n* 'Big-Knife: white American'; *esa·wi-ci·ss* 'yellow turnip: carrot'; *pekwaci-meno·min* 'wild rice'.

Initial change appears in *me·yeki-pa·kkeʔa·kkwa·n* 'strange fowl: pheasant'; compare *meyaki-enišsena·pe·k* 'strange Indians'.

10. 5. Dependent nouns after a prenoun appear in the form for indefinite possessor: *kecci-eninci·n* 'big hands', *kecci-eštikwa·n* 'a big head'.

10. 6. The dependent particle *-i·ci* 'fellow' forms dependent compound nouns: *ni·ci-eniššena·pe·* 'my fellow Indian'.

10. 7. Some prenouns join nouns in singular form to make EXOCENTRIC particle compounds. Some of these are local in meaning: *ekici-eto·ppuwin* 'on top of the table'; *na·mi-mekkom* 'under the ice'; *na·mi-nempa·kan* 'under the bed'. Occasionally the noun is in local form: *me·kwe·-eškote·nk* 'in the fire'. Other such compounds, with numeral prenouns, denote groups of things, but function syntactically as particles: *nesso-pepo·n* 'for three years'; *ni·šo-tepaʔeka·ns* 'for two hours'; *ni·šo-mekkakkussak* 'to the amount of two barrels'. The numeral particles higher than ten do not occur as prior members; they appear as antecedents (20. 10) of compounds with *tesso* 'so many': *neššwa·ssumitena tesso-pepo·n* 'eighty years'.

10. 8. Many particles, PREVERBS, are used as prior members with verbs: *we·pi-kemiwan* 'it is starting to rain'. For irregularities of prefixation and initial change see 4. 3-5, 9.

10. 9. The preverb *a* (with initial change, *e·*) is used with conjunct verbs only; it denotes place or person. (S 534) *unci·yē nenki·-nematap a-nematepit* 'I sat next to him where he sat'; S 535, 634, 655.

10. 10. The preverbs *a, ci, ki·, ta, wi·* precede other preverbs: *ki·-eškwa·-na·wekkwe·k* 'after it is noon'. The combination *ta-ki·* denotes unrealized action (S 691).

10. 11. The preverbs *ekko, entasso, eši, taši, unci*, formed from relative roots, give the compound a relative function (5. 20, 20. 5).

10. 12. Occasionally a word or a short phrase is INCLUDED after a preverb: *ci-pwa·-kekkina-kencipeʔiwe·wa·t* 'before they all get away' (included *kekkina* 'all').

10. 13. Compound particles differ from phrases in that the prior member, a PREPARTICLE, does not occur alone: *meno-menikk* 'quite enough' (*meno* also as a preverb); *e·ntesso-kekiše·p* 'every morning'; (*menta·sswi*) *ešši-pe·šik* 'eleven'; *ni·štena ešši-ni·š* 'twenty-two'; *enameʔe·-ki·šik* 'on Sunday'.

Some particles have by-forms with ending *-yi* (16. 16) serving as preparticles: beside *nemanc* 'however it be', there is *nemanci-i·tik* 'however it may turn out to be'. Similarly, beside *eno·c* 'variously', with a pronoun as second member there is *eno·ci-ke·ko·* 'all manner of things'.

10. 14. A prior compound member may serve as antecedent of a relative root (20.5) in a subsequent member: *meno-ešiwe·pesi* 'well he-behaves-so', i.e., 'he behaves well'.

CHAPTER 11

NOUN FINALS

11. 1. The order of presentation in this chapter and in chapters 12-16 is alphabetical by the last sounds of the suffix. In general we list all available examples of a formation. When only a representative sample is given, the incompleteness is indicated by "etc." at the end of the examples, or by "for example" or "e.g." before them, or, in some cases, by such a wording as "freely added" in the description of the formation.

Throughout chapters 11-16 intransitive verbs are cited, as far as possible, in the independent indicative form for third person singular actor. Transitive and pseudo-transitive verbs, however, are cited in the corresponding conjunct indicative form, in which the structure of the stem appears more clearly. The translation is in all cases that appropriate for the independent indicative.

In this chapter dependent nouns of relationship are analyzed only for obvious final suffixes, not for medials.

Dependent noun stems consisting of a medial plus a noun final of shape zero are treated in the following paragraphs: 11. 11, 18, 20, 23, 32, 34, 35, 36, 37, 38, 39, 45, 46, 54, 57, 61, 65, 69, 70, 71, 72, 75, 76, 80, 91, 92, 94, 103, 118.

11. 2. A noun final of the form ZERO can be set up for unanalyzable nouns, e.g., *eko·n* AN 'snow'. It may be worth noticing, however that many such stems end in *w*: *ekkwe·* 'women' (stem *ikkwe·w-*), *enim* 'dog' (stem *animw-*), *pešiw* 'lynx'. In general, the root in such nouns does not occur in other primary formations. An exception is *meskwi* 'blood', root *miskw-* 'red'.

Final *w* of the root is lost in *mekkate·* 'gunpowder', root *makkate·w-* 'black'.

In secondary derivation, zero as a noun final makes nouns of agent from intransitive verbs that end in a long vowel; cf. 11. 73. Thus, *šekaška·ntuwe·* 'flying squirrel' consists of an AI stem in *-a·ntawe·* 'climb, especially on wood', plus noun final zero. Similarly, *sa·kekki·* 'plant' is formed with noun final zero from the II verb *sa·kekki·* 'it grows forth'. Nouns from II stems in *-kka·* are used especially in local form: *ne·kuwi·kka·nk* 'on the sand'. An additional noun final may then be added; thus doubtless *wa·wa·ssekkoneⁿ* 'flower' with diminutive noun final *-iny* implies a noun stem *wa·wa·ssakkone·-*, made with noun final zero from an II stem which occurs in the compound *wa·wa·ssekkone·-ki·siss* 'May' (10. 3).

Some of the nouns so formed have initial change: *me·kkete·wekkoneye·* 'priest', from an AI stem *makkate·wikkonaye·-* 'he has a black robe' (formed by 12. 64); *se·kete·pwe·* AN 'burr' doubtless represents some AI formation on the root *sak-* 'take hold'; *šwa·škusse·* AN 'sleigh' from an AI stem *šo·škosse·-* (root *šo·škw-* 'smooth', with AI final *-sse·*, 12. 28); *e·ssepikkeⁿ* 'spider' has the noun final *-iny* added to a noun stem *e·ssapikke·-*, formed in turn with initial change from an AI *assapikke·-* 'make nets' (12. 20).

11. 3. *-ana·* 'baked thing': *nempakena·* AN 'corn-bread'; *a·nekkonaⁿ* 'biscuit, cracker', with added diminutive noun final *-iny*.

11. 4. *-a·nke·*: *wi·na·nke·* 'turkey buzzard'.

11. 5. *-na·pe·* 'man', perhaps deverbal from a noun of the same form: *eniššena·pe·* 'human being, Indian'.

11. 6. *-sse·* 'bird', medial with noun final zero: *pa·ppa·sse·* 'red-headed woodpecker'; *mesisse·* 'turkey'.

11. 7. *-še·*. (a) *kekkiše·* 'charcoal'. (b) 'body', consisting of medial *-še·* plus noun final zero: *keno·še·* 'pike' (fish).

11. 8. *-ite·*, probably an II final (13. 17) plus noun final zero, but independent of any II verbs: *eškote·* 'fire'; *meškote·* 'prairie'.

11. 9. *-nawe·* 'body', medial *-naw* with noun final *-e·* (or with AI final *-e·* and noun final zero): *uškinuwe·* 'young man'.

11. 10. *-kkwe·* 'woman', deverbal from the noun *ekkwe·* 'woman'; the noun final, however, lacks the final *w* of the noun (*ekkwe·wak* 'women', *uškini·kekkwe·k* 'young women').

Added to nouns: *me·kkete·wekkoneye·kkwe·* 'nun'; *ukima·kkwe·* 'queen'.

Added to an AI verb stem: *uškini·kekkwe·* 'young woman'.

Primary: *mencikekkwe·* 'bad woman'; *menta·kukkwe·* 'well-behaved woman, lady'.

-anikkwe·, with prefinal *-an*, is added to the noun stem *naʔa·nk-* (in *neʔa·nkišš* 'son-in-law', with diminutive *-išš*): *neʔa·nkenikkwe·* 'daughter-in-law'.

11. 11. *-te·ʔ* 'heart', medial plus noun final zero: *nente·ʔ* 'my heart'; perhaps also *nempi·ʔepi·sete·ʔ* 'my lungs'.

11. 12. *-ci·* 'small round body', medial plus noun final zero. Except for a single perhaps erroneous recording of *epino·ci·* 'child', all the stems contain an additional diminutive noun final: *epino·ci·ns* 'child'; *ekkokkuci·šš* 'woodchuck'; *ekko·ci·šš* 'louse'; *epino·cĩ* 'child'; *wa·wa·pekono·cĩ* 'mouse'. With initial change: *me·na·kucĩ* 'bedbug'.

11. 13. *-akki·* 'land', deverbal medial from the noun stem *akky-* (*ekki* 'land'), with a postmedial *-e·*: *wa·peškokki·* 'marsh'.
-a·kki·, added to a noun stem: *mettikwa·kki·ns* 'plot of wooded land', with added diminutive noun final *-ns*.

11. 14. *-makkakki·* 'frog': *pepi·kumakkekki·* 'toad'.

11. 15. *-kaši·* 'hoof', medial with noun final *-e·*: *pe·šeko·keši·* 'horse' (could be described also as noun final zero added to an AI stem).

11. 16. *-piši·* 'lynx', deverbal from the noun *pešiw* 'lynx': *mešših̃peši·* 'Great Lynx'.

11. 17. *-iti·* 'rump, tail', medial plus noun final zero: *unašketi·n* AN 'his (bird's) tail'; *meskoti·ssemin* AN 'bean', with following diminutive *-iss* and *-imin* 'berry, grain, fruit'.

11. 18. *-tto·wak* 'ear', medial plus zero: *netto·wak* 'my ear'.

11. 19. *-yi·k* 'cloth', medial plus zero; added to a noun: *eppišše-moni·k* 'mat' (noun stem *appiššimon-* 'thing to step on', formed with noun final *-n*).

11. 20. *-nikk* 'arm', medial plus zero: *nenikk* 'my arm.'

11. 21. *-wa·m*: *wi·kuwa·m* 'house'.

11. 22. *-kiwa·m* 'house', deverbal from *wi·kuwa·m* 'house'; added to a noun stem: *mi·šeškokuwa·m* 'barn' (noun stem *mi·šaškw-*).

11. 23. *-pwa·m* 'back of thigh', medial plus zero: *nempwa·m* 'my thigh'.

11. 24. -a·nte·m, medial -a·nte· 'wood' with a noun final -m: eškwa·nte·m 'door'.

11. 25. -n, freely used in forming abstract nouns (action, product, place, instrument) from AI stems ending in e· (cf. 11. 52), which is replaced by a· (3. 16): a·sso·kka·n AN 'sacred story'; kettika·n 'farm, field'; pemikkuwa·n 'footprint'; etc.

Similarly from AI stems in i· (3. 16) representing postconsonantal ye·: enta ᵓepa·n 'place from which one draws water'.

Before this noun final, stems in AI -ke· (12. 16) replace e· by short a (3. 17): mentwe·cceke· 'he plays music' : mentwe·ccekan 'flute'. However, the resulting combination -kan is treated as a unit: it is used in combinations where there is no corresponding AI verb in -ke·. This and other extensions of the noun final -n will appear in the following paragraphs.

In the noun which underlies eppiššemoni·k (11. 19), the -n is added to an AI stem in -o: appiššimo- 'lie, step on something'. In the noun which underlies ekawa·nekamik (11. 89), the -n is added to an AI stem in a·: ekawa· 'he fishes through the ice'.

In primary use, -n, with preceding e· unchanged, appears in mo·šwe·n 'shawl'.

11. 26. -an appears in various primary nouns: epikkan 'pack strap, tumpline, harness'; pepikwan 'musical instrument'; etc. Several of the medials which are used with noun final zero end in -an; see the next few paragraphs.

11. 27. -kan is a complex of AI -ke· (12. 16) and -n (11. 25). Accordingly, like AI -ke·, it is added to TI stems, and to pseudo-TI stems in -to·, -tto·, which lose the o·: ci·ketaᵓank 'he sweeps it' : ci·keta-ᵓekan 'broom'; ki·škepo·to·t 'he saws it through' : ki·škepo·cekan 'crosscut saw'; etc. In some cases the occurrence in separate inflected forms of the underlying TI stem is very unlikely: uninkwi·ᵓekanan AN 'his wing, his wings', with TI final -aᵓ; so also the card names pe·šeko·pi·-ᵓekan 'ace', ni·šo·pi·ᵓekan 'deuce'; etc. The final -kan is not added to TI stems whose TA pendant has -aw (14. 31c).

In a few instances -kan is added to AI stems: nempa·kan 'bed'. Preceding e· is replaced by a· (3. 16): ekkwa·ntuwa·kan 'ladder, stairway'; so also i· for ye·: ni·mepa·kan 'water pail'.

-kan also occurs as a primary noun final: uninci·kanan 'his fins'; a·šo·nekkokenak AN pl. 'suspenders'; wa·pekan 'clay'; etc.

11. 28. *-a·kan*, consisting of *-kan* with prefinal *a·*, is added to TA stems: *eko·na·t* 'he hangs him up' : *eko·na·kan* 'tree house'; etc.

It is added to a few TI stems: *kuntank* 'he swallows it' : *kunta·kan* 'throat'; etc.

Primary: *pema·kan* 'cream'; *pi·nta·kan* 'pocket'; *una·kan* 'bowl'.

-ama·kan, with further prefinal *-am*, appears in *pi·wekkotema·kenan* pl. 'shavings', from a stem in TI *-ikkot* 'carve, whittle'.

11. 29. *-na·kan* 'dish', deverbal from *una·kan* (11. 28), is added to noun stems: *mettikuna·kan* 'wooden bowl'; *pi·wa·pekkona·kan* 'iron dish'.

11. 30. *-wa·kan*, prefinal *-w* with final *-a·kan*, is added to an AI stem ending in a long vowel: *mi·si·wa·kan* 'privy'.

11. 31. *-o·cikan*, a complex of a TI final *-o·t* with noun final *-kan*, is added to the TA verb *eššama·t* 'he feeds him': *eššamo·cekan* 'bait'.

11. 32. *-e·škan* 'horn', medial with noun final zero: *ute·škenan* AN 'his horn, his horns'.

11. 33. *-wan: mencinekka·wan* AN 'mitten'.

11. 34. *-kwan* 'liver', medial with noun final zero: *nekkwan* 'my liver' (4. 8).

11. 35. *-šikwan* 'fish tail', medial with noun final zero: *ušikwan* 'his (fish's) tail'.

11. 36. *-kakkwan* 'shin', medial with noun final zero: *nekkakkwan* 'my shin' (4. 8).

11. 37. *-pikkwan* 'back', medial with noun final zero: *uppikkuna·nk* 'on his back' (4. 8).

11. 38. *-ci·nkwan* 'thigh', medial with noun final zero: *nenci·nkwan* 'my thigh'.

11. 39. *-to·skwan* 'elbow', medial with noun final zero: *nento·skwan* 'my elbow'.

11. 40. *-a·n* appears at the end of some primary nouns, such as *peka·n* 'nut', *uta·pa·n* AN 'wagon'.

11. 41. *-wika·n* 'house', a complex of the AI final *-wike·* with noun final *-n: mente·weka·n* 'lodge for the Mystic Rite'.

11. 42. *-ikka·n*, a complex of AI final *-ikke·* with noun final *-n*, is added to a noun: *ni·nemokka·n* 'my sister-in-law' (man speaking), 'my brother-in-law' (woman speaking), alongside *ni·nim* with the same meaning.

11. 43. *-ma·n*, primary: *ekkwassema·n* 'pumpkin'.

11. 44. *-ikkoma·n* 'knife', prefinal *-ikkw* 'cut' and noun final *-ma·n*: *pi·ntekkoma·n* 'knife sheath'; with contraction of *awi* to *o·* (3. 45), *mo·kkuma·n* 'knife'.

11. 45. *-na·n* 'calf of leg', medial with noun final zero: *nena·n* AN 'my calf'.

11. 46. *-štikwa·n* 'head', medial with noun final zero: *neštikwa·n* 'my head'.

11. 47. *-kkwa·n*, primary: *e·mekkwa·n* 'ladle'; *na·pekkwa·n* 'ship'.

11. 48. *-ta·pa·n* 'wagon', deverbal from the noun stem *ota·pa·n-* (11. 40); added to noun stems: *eškote·ta·pa·n* AN and *meškote·ta·pa·n* AN 'railway train'.

11. 49. *-aya·n* 'garment', added to a noun stem: *mekkwaya·neˉ* 'caterpillar'.
-iwiya·n, primary in *pepakuwiya·n* 'shirt'.
-o·wiya·n, primary in *wa·po·weya·n* 'blanket'.

11. 50. *-imin* 'berry, grain, fruit', deverbal from *mi·n* 'blueberry'.
Added to nouns: *ute·ᵖemin* 'strawberry'; *menito·mene·ns* 'wampum bead'. From noun stems not otherwise recorded: *meskoti·ssemin* AN 'bean'; *meški·kemin* 'cranberry' (probably "marsh-berry"); *utatteka·kumin* AN 'blackberry' (presumably "backbone-berry").
Primary: *essasswe·min* 'cherry'; *meskomin* AN 'raspberry'; etc.
-yi·min: *mešši·min* AN 'apple'.

11. 51. *-pin*, added to a noun stem: *neme·pin* 'carp, sucker'.

11. 52. *-win*, noun final *-n* with prefinal *-w*, is freely added to AI stems not ending in *e·* (cf. 11. 25), forming nouns of action, product, place, instrument: *a·kkusiwin* 'sickness'; *tenakki·win* 'place of residence'; *ekkituwin* 'way of speaking'; etc.
In two instances it is added to AI stems in *e·*: *enwe·win* 'way of speaking'; *menwa·peme·weᵖiwe·win* 'blessing'.

11. 53. *-amowin*, a prefinal *-amo* (cf. inflectional ending *-₁amo*) with noun final *-win*, is added to a TI stem: *ena·pentamuwin* 'vision'.

11. 54. *-to·n* 'mouth', medial with noun final zero: *nento·n* 'my mouth'.

11. 55. *-a·po·* 'liquid', a medial with noun final zero, is added to nouns: *eni·pi·šša·po·* 'tea'; *meškikkuwa·po·* 'herb, infusion'; etc.
-wa·po·, after a noun ending in a long vowel: *eškote·wa·po* 'whiskey'.
-iwa·po·, after a noun in consonant plus *y*: *mekkomi·wa·po* 'ice water'.

11. 56. *-o·so·*: *wa·po·so·* 'rabbit'.

11. 57. *-i·nintip* 'brain', medial with noun final zero: *wi·nentip* 'his brain' (4. 7).

11. 58. *-ins*, along with *-iny* (11. 104), is a freely used diminutive noun final.
It is added to noun stems ending in a long vowel: *eniššena·pe·ns* 'young Indian'; *eškote·ns* 'match'; etc.
It is added to noun stems ending in vowel plus *w*; the *w* is dropped and a preceding short vowel is lengthened (3. 44): *pešikki·ns* 'calf'.
It is added to noun stems in *-an*; the *n* is dropped and the *a* lengthened (3. 50): *mi·kka·ns* 'path, trail'.
-e·ns is added to nouns of other than the above-named shapes: *e·mekkwa·ne·ns* 'spoon'; *ko·kko·šše·ns* 'little pig'; etc.
After nonsyllabic plus *y*, there is the regular replacement of *ye·* by *i·*: *epwi·ns* 'small paddle'; *essapa·pi·ns* 'thread'.
When *-e·ns* is added to stems in consonant plus *w*, the combination *we·* is replaced by *o·* (3. 41): *mekko·ns* 'bear cub'; *enimo·ns* 'little dog'.
As an irregularity, the stem *si·piw-* (*si·pi* 'river') takes *-e·ns*, lengthening the *i* (3. 13): *si·pi·we·ns* 'brook'.
Primary: *ka·šeke·ns* 'cat'.

11. 59. *-isse·ns*, a complex of the noun finals *-iss* and *-e·ns*, is added, with loss of *w*, to the noun stem *ikkwe·w-* (*ekkwe·* 'woman'): *ekkwe·sse·ns* 'girl'.
Primary: *kwi·wesse·ns* 'boy'.

11. 60. *-išši·ns* consists of the noun final *-išš*, treated as if it were *-iššy*, plus the noun final *-e·ns*. It is added to a noun in *pene·šši·ns* 'little bird'.

11. 61. *-ta·ss* 'legging', medial with noun final zero: *nenta·ss* 'my legging'.

-mita·ss: ekokkumita·ss 'sock'.

11. 62. *-iss* has diminutive flavor, but is largely primary. It appears in dependent nouns of relationship, for example *nenkwiss* 'my son', *nešiniss* 'my father-in-law'; in *nemiššo·miss* 'my grandfather', *no·nkumiss* 'my grandmother', it is preceded by inflectional *-₁im*. In other primary nouns: *menko·ss* 'awl'; *šenkwass* 'weasel'; etc.

In secondary use it appears in *nenta·niss* 'my daughter', beside *nenta·n* with the same meaning; with contraction of *awi* to *a·* (3. 44), *wi·ya·ss* 'meat, flesh' (*wi·yaw* 'his body'); *ni·kka·niss* 'my brother, my male friend' (man speaking) (*ni·kka·ne͂* 'my brother', man speaking). Beside *neni·ca·niss* 'my child', there is a noun stem *-ni·ca·n-* underlying the AI verb *uni·ca·ni* 'she has a child'. In *nempiss* 'lake', from the stem *nimpy-* (*nempi* 'water'), postconsonantal *yi* is not replaced by *i·*.

The final *-iss* forms part of the longer finals *-isse·ns, -isse·ny, -issi·ny*.

11. 63. *-ississ*, primary, as though *-iss* were twice added: *nesikussiss* 'my mother-in-law'; *ni·nessiss* 'my (single) hair (on head)'.

11. 64. *-wiss*, noun final *-iss* with prefinal *-w*, is added to a few nouns ending in a long vowel: *ni·tta·wiss* 'my cousin'; *mencikekkwe·wiss* 'eldest sister'.

11. 65. *-ca·š* 'nose', medial *-ca·N* with noun final zero and mutation: *nenca·š* 'my nose'.

11. 66. *-nš: po·kketo·nš* AN 'pear'.

11. 67. *-išš*, diminutive with pejorative flavor, added to noun stems: *nentayišš* 'my dog'; *enimošš* 'dog'; *nempi·šš* 'water in portable quantity'; etc.

Primary: *eni·pi·šš* 'leaf'; *ko·kko·šš* 'pig'.

This forms part of the noun final *-išše·ny* and, with combination as though it were *-iššy*, of the noun finals *-išši·ns, -išši·ny* (cf. also 11. 89; 12. 125).

-wišš is added to a noun ending in a long vowel: *mencikekkwe·wišš* 'bad girl'. Primary: *šekina·wišš* 'angleworm'.

11. 68. *-at* 'stomach', medial with noun final zero: *missat-*, apparently always in possessed form: *nemissat* 'my stomach'.

11. 69. *-ka·t* 'leg', medial with noun final zero: *nekka·t* 'my leg' (4. 8).

11. 70. *-i·pit* 'tooth', medial with noun final zero: *ni·pit* 'my tooth' (4. 7).

11. 71. *-sit* 'foot', medial with noun final zero: *nesit* 'my foot'.

11. 72. *-mot* 'bag', medial with noun final zero: *meškimot* 'bag'. *-mo·t: nemo·te·ns* 'my pocket'.

11. 73. *-w* is freely added to intransitive verb stems that do not end in a long vowel (11. 2), forming nouns of agent: *wi·mpenakkesi* AN 'hollow tree' (AI final *-isi*); *ki·šekat* 'day'; etc. (Cf. 13. 28).

As a primary noun final it appears in *ša·wenonk* 'in the south', *tepikkonk* 'at night'.

11. 74. *-naw: o·te·naw* 'town'.

11. 75. *-ma·naw* 'cheek', medial with noun final zero: *uma·nuwa·nk* 'on his cheek'.

11. 76. *-i·yaw* 'body', medial with noun final zero: *ni·yaw* 'my body, myself' (4. 7).

11. 77. *-iw: enini* 'man'.

11. 78. *-kkiw: meškikki* 'herb'.

11. 79. *-yi·kkiw: menci·kkuwiss* 'eldest brother'.

11. 80. *-e·naniw* 'tongue', medial with noun final zero: *nente·neniw* 'my tongue'.

11. 81. *-niniw* 'man', deverbal from the noun stem *ininiw-* (11. 77). Added to a noun stem with *iw* lengthened to *i·w: meskikki·-wenini* 'medicine man'. Primary: *menta·kunini* 'well-behaved man, gentleman'; *mente·wenini* 'participant in the Mystic Rite'.

-wininiw is added to AI stems ending in a long vowel: *ešike·wenini* 'carpenter'; *eta·we·wenini* 'trader, storekeeper'.

11. 82. *-ssiw* appears in designations of animals; in all our examples it follows upon a long vowel. It is added to a noun stem in *pene·ssi* 'bird' (of any larger species). It is added, with initial change, to an AI stem in *kwe·šku·ʔiwe·ssi* 'Little Startler', from an AI stem *koškwiʔiwe·-* (12. 47).

Primary: *wa·wa·te·ssi* 'firefly'; etc.

11. 83. *-e·šši̯w*, primary, in designations of animals: *ša·nkwe·šši* 'mink'; *wa·wa·ške·šši* 'deer'.

11. 84. *-a·nakw*, primary: *uso·wa·nak* 'his (quadruped's) tail'; *pi·wa·nak* 'arrowhead'.

11. 85. *-ssakw* 'board', medial with noun final *-w;* added to a noun stem: *mekkakkussak* 'barrel'. Primary: *ešpimessakonk* 'upstairs'.

11. 86. *-a·kw*, primary: *e·sseka·k* 'wood-tick'; *utatteka·kumin* AN 'blackberry' containing, apparently, a dependent stem *-tattaka·kw-* 'backbone'.

11. 87. *-ka·kw* 'porcupine', deverbal from the noun *ka·k: wa·peka·k* 'white porcupine'.

11. 88. *-ame·kw* 'fish', deverbal from the noun *neme·* 'sturgeon', with a noun final *-kw: esikume·k* 'dogfish'; *etikkume·k* 'whitefish'. This latter may be secondary from a noun stem *atikkw-* 'caribou', not recorded.

11. 89. *-kamikw* 'house', medial with noun final zero, added to noun stems: *enake·kkukamik* 'bark house'; *mettikukamik* 'log house'; etc.

-wikamikw is added to a noun stem ending in a long vowel: *pe·šeko·keši·wekamik* 'stable'; and to AI stems ending in a long vowel: *eta·we·wekamik* 'store', *mento·to·wekamik* 'tent for the steam bath'.

Final *i* of an AI stem is lengthened in *kekkino·ʔema·ti·wekamik* 'school', from a stem in AI *-iti* (12. 88).

-yi·wikamikw is added to a noun stem in *-išš* (11. 67): *enimošši·wekamik* 'kennel'.

11. 90. *-akkamikw* 'place', medial with noun final *-w: na·mekkamekokka·te·* 'it is made with a cellar' (12. 20; 13. 14), implying a noun stem *na·makkamikw-*.

11. 91. *-ški·nšikw* 'eye', medial with noun final zero: *neški·nšik* 'my eye'.

11. 92. -*kitikw* 'knee', medial with noun final zero: *nenkitik* AN 'my knee'.

11. 93. -*a·ttikw* 'stick', prefinal with noun final zero, added to noun stems: *peššanše·ʔekana·ttik* 'whipstock'; *po·tta·kena·ttik* 'pestle-stick'.

The underlying stem loses final *w* (3. 47) in *wa·ka·kkuta·ttik* 'axe-handle'.

Primary: *enina·ttik* AN 'hard maple'.

-*e·ya·ttikw*, added to a noun stem: *peššanše·ʔekane·ya·ttik* 'whipstock' (cf. above).

11. 94. -*ka·ttikw* 'forehead', medial with noun final zero (4. 8): *ukka·ttekonk* 'on his forehead'.

11. 95. -*anakkw* 'tree', medial with noun final -*w*: *šo·šo·penakkonk* 'in the treetop'.

11. 96. -*a·kkw* 'wood, solid', medial with noun final zero; added to noun stems: *ekwa·wa·na·kk* 'kettle hanger'; *peka·na·kk* AN 'walnut tree'. Primary: *essikena·kk* 'blackbird'; *pessaka·kk* AN 'board'; etc.

11. 97. -*kkina·kkw* 'turtle': *te·te·pekkina·kk* 'soft-shell turtle'.

11. 98. -*pikkw* 'stone, metal', medial with noun final -*w*. This shorter form appears in *a·šepikk* 'cliff, mountain'.

-*a·pikkw* is added to a noun stem in *wa·sse·ccekana·pikk* 'pane, glass'; it is primary in *esa·wa·pikk* 'brass', *pi·wa·pikk* 'iron', *ušo·ma·nekkiwa·pikk* 'copper'.

11. 99. -*aškw* 'grass, herb', medial with noun final zero, deverbal from the root *maškw*-. Added to a noun stem: *epakkwe·yašk* AN 'cattail reed;' perhaps primary in *mi·šeško·ns* 'blade of grass'.

11. 100. -*mo·w* 'dung', medial with noun final zero: *umo·wan* pl. 'his dung'.

11. 101. -*a·nakkwatw* 'cloud', deverbal from the noun *a·nekkwat* 'cloud': *wa·pa·nekkwat* 'white cloud'.

11. 102. -*ay: ka·way* AN 'quill of porcupine'; *epakkwe·yašk* (11. 99) implying a stem *apakkwe·y*- 'thatch'.

-*e·nkway* 'face', medial with noun final zero: *nente·nkway* 'my face'.

11. 103. *-nincy* 'hand', medial with noun final zero: *neninc* 'my hand'; *aškwe·nincy-* always possessed: *nentaškwe·ninc* 'my little finger'.

11. 104. *-iny* diminutive, much like *-ins* (11. 58), but tending more to primary use. It is added to noun stems ending in a long vowel (e.g. *pene͂* 'young partridge'), in vowel plus *w* (*uwe·ssi͂* 'creature'), and in *an*, with loss of *n* and lengthening of *a* (3. 50) (*essassa͂* 'nest').

Where no underlying noun is found, we should perhaps set up such a stem. Thus *wa·wa·ssekkone͂* 'flower' seems to have by its side *wa·wa·-ssekkone·-*, though the latter is attested only as a compound member (11. 2). Similarly, but with initial change: *e·ssepikke͂* 'spider', from a stem with the AI final *-ikke·* (12. 20; 11. 2).

There are many primary nouns: *me·mi·kwa͂* 'butterfly'; *menciko·te͂* 'skirt'; *e·ssi͂* 'clam'; *ki·ko͂* 'fish'; etc. (Cf. 12. 68, 93.)

-e·ny is added to nouns ending in a nonsyllabic, except those in *an:* *nenkwisse͂* 'my little son'; *neme·pene͂* beside *neme·pin* 'carp, sucker'. Nouns in consonant plus *w* replace *we·* by *o·* (3. 41): *uššaško͂* beside *uššašk* 'muskrat'; *pi·wa·neko͂* 'flint' from *pi·wa·nak* 'arrowhead'. (Cf. 13. 28.)

The stem *si·piw-* has the same irregularity as 11. 58: *si·pi·we͂* 'creek'.

11. 105. *-isse·ny*, a combination of diminutive noun finals *-iss* and *-e·ny;* primary in *nemisse͂* 'my elder sister', *ko·kusse͂* 'frog'.

11. 106. *-išše·ny*, a combination of diminutive noun finals *-išš* and *-e·ny;* primary in *nešišše͂* 'my uncle', *wa·kušše͂* 'fox'. (Cf. 16. 48).

11. 107. *-we·ny*, added to a noun in a long vowel: *meškote·we·nˀink* 'at Flint' (Michigan).

11. 108. *-kkiwe·ny* 'man', deverbal as though from a noun stem *akkiwe·ny-* formed by 11, 104 (actually there seems to be only the formation of 11. 110): *ni·cekkiwe͂* 'my male friend'.

11. 109. *-piniwe·ny* 'owl': *neninkepinuwe͂* and *wa·kepinuwe͂* 'screech owl'.

11. 110. *-e·nsi·ny: ekkiwe·nsi͂* 'old man' (cf. 11. 108).

11. 111. *-kkiwe·nsi·ny* 'man', deverbal from the preceding: *ni·cekkiwe·nsi͂* 'my male friend' (man speaking).

11. 112. *-issi·ny: meskwa·te·ssi*̃ 'small turtle'; *pi·meskotessi*̃ 'snail'.

11. 113. *-išši·ny*, consisting of *-išš*, treated as if it were *-iššy*, plus *-e·ny*. Added to a noun: *pene·šši*̃ 'bird' (of any smaller species). In a verb final: see 12. 67. Primary: *ešša·ke·šši*̃ 'crawfish'; *untama·- kkume·šši*̃ 'monkey'.

11. 114. *-amo·ny: ecitemo*̃ 'squirrel'; with initial change, hence secondary in flavor: *e·škettamo*̃ 'watermelon'.

11. 115. *-a·py* 'string, cord', medial with noun final zero; added to nouns: *essapa·p* 'cord'; *mettikwa·p* AN 'bow'.
-e·ya·py: menkiskene·ya·p 'fishing line'.

11. 116. *-ipy* 'liquid', medial with noun final zero, deverbal from *nimpy-* (*nempi* 'water'; 3. 48): *nempo·p* 'soup, broth'; *tekkipi* 'spring of water' (3. 10).

11. 117. *-kopy* 'bark', deverbal as though from a noun stem *wi·kopy-* (cf. 11. 120): *uša·ššekop* 'slippery-elm bark'.

11. 118. *-škanšy* 'claw, nail, hoof', medial with noun final zero: *neškanš* AN 'my claw, nail, hoof'.

11. 119. *-awi·nšy* 'plant'. From a noun *šeka·kuwi·nš* AN 'onion'. Primary: *eninuwi·nš* 'milkweed'; *ši·keme·wi·nš* AN 'soft maple'.

11. 120. *-mi·ššy* 'tree'. From nouns: *mettikumi·šš* AN 'oak tree'; *wi·kupi·mi·šš* AN 'linden' (cf. 11. 117). Perhaps primary: *pa·kkwa·- nemi·šš* AN 'sumac'.

CHAPTER 12

ANIMATE INTRANSITIVE FINALS

12. 1. Some combinations of medials with AI finals, especially with AI *-e·*, seem to be treated as units and are listed here.

Corresponding to some AI finals there are II finals; in such cases cross reference will be made here and in Chapter 13. Where there is no paired II final, an II verb is derived from the AI by addition of *-makat* (13. 45).

Pseudo-intransitives ending in *o·* are given in Chapter 15.

For order of presentation see 11. 1.

12. 2. Several primary stems end in *-a·: ekawa·* 'he spears fish through the ice'; *eya·* 'he is there' (II same); *nempa·* 'he sleeps'; *ta·* 'he exists, he dwells there'.

12. 3. *-oʔa·: tekkamuʔa·* 'he goes across'.

12. 4. *-ka·:* (a) 'leak' (II same): *uncika·* 'he (a kettle) leaks'. (b) 'dance', in *wi·ceka·ma·t* 'he dances with him' (14. 6).

12. 5. *-a·taka·* 'swim': *pema·teka·* 'he swims on, along, past'; *tekkama·teka·* 'he swims across'.

12. 6. *-ikka·* 'move, go' (II same), prefinal *-ikk* with AI final *-a·: kepikka·na·t* 'he passes him' (14. 16); *keši·kka·* 'he goes fast'; *nempwa·-kka·* 'he is wise'.

12. 7. *-nikka·* 'arm', medial *-nikk* with AI final *-a·: e·ši-keccinekka·-yan* 'at thy right'; *e·ši-nemancenikka·yan* 'at thy left'.

12. 8. *-iška·* 'move, go' (II same), prefinal *-išk* with AI final *-a·: pemiška·* 'he travels by canoe'; *uniška·* 'he gets up from lying'; *we·wi·-peška·* 'he goes hurrying'; etc.

12. 9. *-pa·* 'come': *uncipa·* 'he comes from there'.

12. 10. *-tta·* 'work, act': *po·netta·* 'he quits working'; *untametta·* 'he is busy'; *we·wi·petta·* 'he hastens his work'; etc.

-yi·tta·: ki·ši·tta· 'he finishes his work'; *uši·tta·* 'he gets ready for his work or action'.

12. 11. *-ppwa·* 'smoke', prefinal *-ppw* with AI final *-a·: mene·ppwa·* 'he is in want of a smoke'; added without connective to the root *oN-* in *uppwa·kan* AN 'pipe for smoking' (11. 28).

12. 12. *-ya·: eša·* 'he goes thither'; *ma·ca·* 'he starts on his way'.

12. 13. *-yiya·* (II same): *ešiya·* 'he is there' (3. 30).

12. 14. *-e·: eššakuwe·* 'he vomits'; *ka·we·* 'he is jealous'; *ki·we·* 'he goes back, home'; *ne·sse·* 'he breathes'. Secondary, from a noun: *pekkwa·kkutwe·* 'he plays ball'.

12. 15. *-a·tti ʔe·: šo·škwa·tte ʔe·* 'he skates'.

12. 16. *-ke·* freely forms verbs for action on indefinite object from TI stems whose TA pendant does not end in *aw;* and from pseudo-TI stems in *-to·, -tto·*, which lose their *o·* (cf. 11. 27; 13. 15). Thus *sekakkenank* 'he stores it away' : *sekakkenike·* 'he stores things away'; *kucitto·t* 'he tries it' : *kucicceke·* 'he tries'. (Contrast 12. 55.)

As an irregularity, *-ke·* without connective (instead of *-yiwe·*, 12. 47) is added for action on indefinite persons to the TA stem *tekkoma·t* 'he bites him' : *tekkonke·* 'he bites people.'

See also 12. 18.

12. 17. *-ike·* freely forms verbs of action on indefinite persons from TA stems in *-aw* (cf. *-yiwe·*, 12. 47): *na·temawa·t* 'he helps him' : *na·tema·ke·* 'he helps someone, he helps people' (3. 44); etc.

12. 18. *-ike·* 'house', medial with AI final *-e·: keša·teke·* 'he stays alone in the house'; *kettike·* 'he farms'; *pi·nteke·* 'he enters'; *wi·teke·* 'he lives with someone, he (she) is married'.

-ke· appears after the root *aN-: ešike·wenini* 'carpenter' (11. 81).

-wike· underlies the noun final complex *-wika·n* (11. 41).

12. 19. *-a·ssike·* 'flash', complex of a TI final *-a·ss* with AI final *-ke·: peta·sseke·* 'Petoskey' ("Flasher" ?)—noun by 11. 2).

12. 20. *-ikke·* 'make, gather', freely added to noun stems: *si·sepa·-kkutokke·* 'he makes sugar'; *uški·nšekkoka·cekanan* 'eyeglasses' (11. 27; 15. 23).

Postconsonantal *yi* does not yield *i·* (3. 29) in *e·ssepikkẽ* 'spider' (*assapy-* 'net', 11. 2, 104).

Primary: *a·sso·kke·* 'he tells a sacred story'; *kessikke·* 'he flies up'; *ci·ssekka·n* 'conjuror's tent' and *wa·nekka·n* 'pit' with AI verbs implied by 11. 25.

12. 21. -*tto·ke·* 'ear', medial with AI final -*e·*: *keši·petto·ke·* 'his ear itches'; *ni·šo·tto·ke·* 'he has two ears'.

12. 22. -*kki·kime·* 'nose', medial with AI final -*e·*: *si·nekki·keme·* 'he blows his nose'.

12. 23. -*a·kkokane·* 'bone', medial with AI final -*e·*: *te·wa·kkukane·* 'his bones ache'.

12. 24. -*ca·Ne·* 'nose', medial with AI final -*e·*: *keši·peca·ne·* 'his nose itches'; *wa·keca·ne·* 'he has a curved nose'; etc.

12. 25. -*iškine·* 'fill' (II presumably same), prefinal -*iškin* with AI final -*e·*: added to the root *maw*- with contraction of *awi* to *o·* (3. 45) in *mo·škene·* 'he (kettle) is full'.

12. 26. -*a·ppine·* 'die': *kunta·ppene·* 'he drowns'.

12. 27. -*intipe·* 'head', medial with AI final -*e·*: *keši·pentipe·* 'his head itches'; *wa·peškintepe·* 'he is white at the head'; etc.

12. 28. -*sse·* 'fly, fall, speed' (II same), prefinal -*SS* with AI final -*e·*: *ecitekki·sse·* 'he falls forward, face down'; *mo·kkesse·* 'he (sun) moves into view, rises'; *no·kesse·* 'he stops in his course'; *pi·ncesse·* 'he steps or falls in '; etc. Added to an AI stem: *pecipeʔike·sse·* 'he falls striking something' (-*ke·* 12. 16).

12. 29. -*ne·sse·* 'breathe', deverbal from *ne·sse·* 'he breathes' (12. 14): in *pi·cene·sseto·t* (15. 47).

12. 30. -*osse·* 'walk': *enimusse·* 'he walks along, away'; *pemosse·* 'he walks on, along, past'; etc.

12. 31. -*še·* 'body', medial with AI final zero: *kesi·pi·keše·* 'he takes a bath'.

12. 32. -*šše·*, medial with AI final zero: (a) 'skin': *keši·pešše·* 'he itches', *pa·kešše·* 'he has a swelling'. (b) 'ear': *mema·nkešše·* 'he has big ears', *nentošše·* 'he listens'.

12. 33. -*ate·* 'stomach', medial with AI final -*e·*: *a·kkuškate·* 'he has a stomach-ache'; *pekkate·* 'he is hungry'.

12. 34. -*ka·te·* 'leg', medial with AI final -*e·*: *keka·nuka·te·* 'he is long-legged'; *keši·peka·te·* 'his leg itches'; *teta·kkuka·te·* 'he is short-legged'.

12. 35. -a·pite· 'tooth', medial with AI final -e·: šo·šwa·pete· 'his teeth are on edge'.

12. 36. -site· 'foot', medial with AI final -e·: ekko·sete· 'he is so long at the foot'; ki·kemanesite· 'his foot is asleep'; mema·nkesite· 'he has big feet'; etc.

12. 37. -o·te· 'crawl': keto·te· 'he crawls forth'; ne·ko·te· 'he crawls under'; sa·keto·te· 'he crawls out'. From an AI stem: pi·nteke·yo·te· 'he crawls in'.

12. 38. -we· 'vocal sound', medial with AI final zero: enwa·we· 'he hiccoughs'; te·pwe· 'he speaks true'; etc. Added to the root iN- without connective (3. 19): enwe· 'he speaks so'.

12. 39. -awe·: epassekkawe· 'she plays shinney'; po·tuwe· 'he makes a fire'.

12. 40. -kkawe· 'make tracks', prefinal -kk with AI final -awe·: mema·nkekkawe· 'he makes big tracks'; pemikkuwe· 'he leaves tracks'; pepi·wekkawe· 'he makes small tracks'.

12. 41. -acinawe·: šo·škucinuwe· 'he toboggans'.

12. 42. -a·ntawe· 'go on wood, climb', medial with AI final -awe·: ekkwa·ntuwe· 'he climbs up on something'; ni·ssa·ntuwe· 'he climbs down'; etc.

12. 43. -yawe·, added to an AI stem: na·nepayuwe· 'he yawns' (cf. nempa· 'he sleeps').

12. 44. -kwiyawe· 'neck', medial with AI final -e·: keši·pekoyuwe· 'his neck itches'.

12. 45. -a·we·: eta·we· 'he gives credit, sells'; ekwa·wa·na·kk 'hook on kettle-hanger' (11. 25, 96); pa·nešša·wa·n 'strip of jerked meat' (11. 25).

12. 46. -a·pa·we· 'wet' (II same), medial with AI final -e·: nekka·- pa·we· 'he (snow) melts'; nenka·pa·weto·t 'he wets it' (with TI -to·, 15. 47); nessa·pa·weto·t 'he wets it'.

12. 47. -yiwe· is freely added to TA stems (except those in -aw, 12. 17; takkom-, 12. 16; makkam-, 12. 63; ano·N-, 12. 96), forming AI verbs of action on indefinite persons: wa·penta^ʔuwe· 'he exhibits to people' from TA wa·panta^ʔ- 'show something to' (14. 3).

From stems in TA -*paʔ* 'run from', these derivatives are used in the meaning 'run', of plural actors (cf. -*patto·*, 12. 149): *kencipeʔiwe·wak* 'they run away'; *ma·ci·peʔiwe·wak* 'they run off'.

12. 48. -*akkošiwe·* 'paddle, swim': *ekotekkošuwe·* 'he paddles or swims upstream'; *enakkušiwe·* 'he paddles or swims thither, thus'; *kesi·kkušiwe·* 'he paddles or swims fast'; etc.

12. 49. -*yi·we·* 'flesh, muscle, strength', medial with AI final -*e·*: *a·nci·we·nʔuwi* 'he renews his effort' (with -*nʔiwi*, 12. 93); *wa·peški·we·* 'he has white flesh'.

12. 50. -*na·pa·kwe·* 'thirst': *ka·skena·pa·kwe·* 'he is thirsty'; *te·pena·pa·kwe·* 'he quenches his thirst'.

12. 51. -*ški·nšikwe·* 'eye', medial with AI final -*e·*: *keši·peški·nšekwe·* 'his eye itches'; *mekkate·weški·nšekwa·n* 'pupil of the eye' (11. 25).

12. 52. -*kkwe·*: (a) 'head', medial with AI final zero: *te·wekkwe·* 'he has a headache'; *wi·wekkwa·n* 'hat' (11. 25).

(b) In *menikkwe·t* 'he drinks it' (pseudo-transitive).

12. 53. -*akkwe·* 'thatch', medial -*akkw* with AI final -*e·*: *epakkwa·n* 'thatch' (11. 25); *epakkwe·yašk* 'cattail reed' (11. 99, 102).

12. 54. -*a·kkwe·* 'wood, solid', medial -*a·kkw* with AI final -*e·*: *ci·pa·kkwe·* 'he cooks'; *pa·keʔa·kkwa·n* 'hen, cock' (11. 25); *pi·nta·kkwe·* 'he smokes'; *po·ta·kkwe·na·t* 'he puts him in the kettle' (14. 16).

12. 55. -*e·kkwe·*, added to a TI stem in -*is* (15. 17) for action on indefinite object: *menose·kkwe·* 'he cooks' (cf. 12. 16).

12. 56. -*anake·kkwe·* 'bark of tree', deverbal medial with AI final -*e·*: *peššakenake·kkwe·* 'he peels bark'.

12. 57. -*akkikkwe·* 'kettle', medial -*akkikkw* (deverbal from the noun *akkikkw-*) with AI final -*e·*; added to a pseudo-TI stem in -*to·* with loss of *o·*: *eko·to·t* 'he hangs it up' : *eko·tekkikkwa·n* 'hook or limb on the kettle hanger' (11. 25).

12. 58. -*a·nikkwe·* 'hair of head', medial with AI final -*e·*: *keka·nwa·nekkwe·* 'he has long hair'; *mekkate·wa·nekkwe·* 'he has black hair'.

12. 59. -*yi·nkwe·* 'eye, face', medial with AI final -*e·*: *kesi·pi·ki·nkwe·* 'he washes his face'; *ki·ci·nkwe·* 'he has a sore eye'; *ki·ši·nkwe·* 'he (maize) is ripe'.

-*a·kami·nkwe·* 'pupil of eye', a complex medial -*a·kam-yi·nkw* with AI final -*e·*: *mekkate·wa·kemi·nkwe·* 'he has black eyes'; *wa·pa·kemi·nkwe·* 'he has gray eyes'.

From an II stem: *na·wekkwe·* 'it is noon': *na·wekkwe·ya·kemi·nkwe·* 'his pupils are in the noon state'.

From a noun: *wa·kk* AN 'fish egg' : *wa·kkwa·kemi·nkwe·* 'he has gray eyes'.

12. 60. -*mo·we·* 'dung', medial with AI final -*e·*: *wa·weye·mo·we·* 'he has round droppings'.

12. 61. -*te·pwe·*: *se·kete·pwe·* AN 'burr' (11.2).

12. 62. -*aki·sisswe·* 'sun', medial -*aki·sissw* (deverbal from the noun *ki·siss* 'sun') with AI final -*e·*: *tepaʔeki·sesswa·n* AN 'clock' (11. 25).

12. 63. -*twe·*, added without connective to a TA stem, for action on indefinite persons (cf. 12. 47): *mekkama·t* 'he robs him' : *mekkantwe·* 'he robs people'.

12. 64. -*kkonaye·* 'garment', medial with AI final -*e·*: *ki·ssekkoneye·* 'he undresses'; *pi·ssekkoneye·* 'he dresses'; cf. *me·kkete·wekkoneye·* 'priest' (11. 2).

With replacement of *t* by *s* (3. 24): *a·nsekkoneye·* 'he changes his clothes'.

12. 65. -*i*. (a) Primary: *epi* 'he is there, at home' (II *ette·*); *kena·cuwi* 'he is handsome' (II -*an*); *kusi* 'he moves camp'; *kwa·škuni* 'he disembarks'; etc. Here also belong the pseudo-TI verbs *kemo·tit* 'he steals it' and *na·tit* 'he fetches it'.

(b) From a noun in -*iw*, with the *i* lengthened (3. 13): *meškikki·wenini·wi* 'he is a physician' (cf. 12. 90, 92).

(c) Freely added to possessed noun themes for third person singular possessor, forming AI verbs of possession: *ušo·neya·m* 'his money' : *ušo·neya·mi* 'he has money'; *uni·ca·ni* 'she has a child'; *uwo·ssi* 'he has a father'.

12. 66. -*aci* 'cold' (II -*atin*), prefinal -*at* with AI final -*yi*: *tekkaci* 'he catches cold'.

12. 67. *-išši·n ᵊi*, diminutive, a complex of noun final *-išši·ny* (11. 113) and AI final *-i: pi·wešši·n ᵊuwak* 'they are small'.

12. 68. *-yi·n ᵊi*, diminutive, prefinal *-yi·* with noun final *-iny* (11. 104) and AI final *-i: eka·cci·n ᵊi* 'he is small'.

12. 69. *-ki* 'grow' (II *-kin*), prefinal *-k* with AI final *-i: ma·ci·ki* 'he starts to grow'; *netta·wekitto·t* 'he makes it grow' (15. 54).
  -ni·ki 'be born', deverbal from an AI stem *ni·ki-* (12. 65): *uškini·ki* 'he is a young man'.

12. 70. *-kki: ekacekki* 'he is bashful'.

12.71. *-ški*, pejorative: *kettimeški* 'he is lazy'; *ki·nuwiški* 'he tells a lie'. Secondary, with the meaning of habitual action, from an AI verb: *keša·we·nceke·ški* 'he is of envious disposition' (from a stem in *-ke·*, 12. 16).

12. 72. *-ni: no·ni* 'he sucks at the breast'.
After medials, 'move a part of the body': *ka·ci·nkwe·ni* 'he makes an ugly face'; *šo·mi·nkwe·ni* 'he smiles'; *sa·keninci·ni* 'he sticks out his hand'.

12. 73. *-ipani: nentopeni* 'he goes on the war path'.

12. 74. *-api* 'be in place, sit' (II *-atte·*), deverbal from *api-* (12. 65): *a·ntepi* 'he changes his seat'; *enwe·pi* 'he rests'; *nematepi* 'he sits down, he sits'; etc.

12. 75. *-a·pi* 'look', deverbal from an AI type *wa·pi* 'look' (12. 65): *a·pena·pi* 'he looks back'; *ekkawa·pi* 'he watches'; *ena·pi* 'he looks thither'; etc.

12. 76. *-a·ppi* 'laugh', deverbal from *pa·ppi* 'he laughs' (12. 65): *nempašša·ppe ᵊa·t* 'he makes fun of him' (14. 2).

12. 77. *-isi* 'state, shape'. This is the most widespread AI final. It is widely used after roots (e.g., *a·kkusi* 'he is ill', *se·kesi* 'he is frightened'); often with postradical *-a·t* (*pema·tesi* 'he lives'); also with root plus medial (*kenwa·kkusi* 'he—a tree—is long as wood'), especially with postmedial *-ak* (*kenwa·pi·kesi* 'he—a snake—is a long string'). Where a corresponding II verb exists it has II final *-at* or *-ya·*. The next few finals are extensions of *-isi*. (Cf. also *-isi·*, 12. 105.)
  -e·wisi, with prefinal *-e·w*, is added to a TA stem in *menwa·peme·wesi* 'he has good luck'.

12. 78. *-we·pisi*, with prefinal *-we·p* deverbal from the root *we·p-:* *ešiwe·pesi* 'he behaves so, fares so'.

12. 79. *-a·kosi* 'subject to action' (II *-a·kwat*), prefinal *-a·* and AI final *-ikosi*, added to a TI stem: *kekke·nta·kusi* 'he is known'.

12. 80. *-ma·kosi* 'be smelled' (II *-ma·kwat*), prefinal *-ma·* and AI final *-ikosi: pi·cema·kosi* 'the smell of him comes hither'.

12. 81. *-na·kosi* 'be seen' (II *-na·kwat*), a complex of TA final *-naw* (14. 37) and AI final *-ikosi: wi·nena·kusi* 'he looks dirty'.

12. 82. *-ikosi* 'subject to act' (II *-ikwat*), prefinal *-ikw* (cf. inflectional ending *-₁ikw*) with final *-isi;* added to TA stems in *-aw* (cf. 12. 81): *kekkino·ʔema·kusi* 'he is taught, gets schooling'; *no·nta·kusi* 'he is audible, he calls out'; *te·petta·kusi* 'he is within hearing'.

12. 83. *-a·mikosi* 'subject to act' (II *-a·mikwat*), prefinal *-a·m* with final *-ikosi;* added to a TI stem *kott-* (15. 43): *kutta·mekosi* 'he is terrible, formidable'.

12. 84. *-ippokosi* 'subject to taste' (II *-ippokwat*), prefinal *-ippw* with final *-ikosi: menoppukosi* 'he tastes good'.

12. 85. *-šši* 'spend time': *pepo·nešši* 'he winters'.

12. 86. *-nkwašši* 'sleep', prefinal *-nkw* with AI final *-ašši: ki·ki·-penkošši* 'he is sleepy'; *wena·cenkošši* 'he has a nightmare'.

12. 87. *-ti*, reciprocal; added, without connective, to TA stems ending in *m* (cf. *-iti* below): *wa·pema·t* 'he sees him' : *wa·pentiwak* 'they see each other'; *uwi·cekkiwe·nʔetiwak* 'they (men) are friends together' (14. 6), apparently with *t* for *nt*.

Stems in TA *-e·nim* lose *ni* haplologically (3. 53): *pekite·nema·t* 'he holds funeral rites over him' : *pekite·ntuwak* 'they hold funeral rites one for another' (cf. 15. 35).

12. 88. *-iti*, reciprocal; freely added to TA stems (except those in *m*, 12. 87, and *mi·ka·N-*, for which see below): *nessa·t* 'he kills him' : *nessituwak* 'they kill each other'; *wi·ntemawa·t* 'he tells it to him' : *wi·ntema·tuwak* 'they tell it one to another'.

Instead of this secondary formation from TA *mi·ka·N-*, the reciprocal *-iti* is added to the root *mi·ka·-: mi·ka·tuwak* 'they fight each other'.

12. 89. *-e·nti* 'stay away': *ene·nti* 'he stays away so long'.

12. 90. *-wi* 'be, become' (II same), freely added to noun stems ending in a long vowel (cf. *-i*, 12. 65b, and *-iwi*, 12. 92): *ukima·* 'chief' : *ukima·wi* 'he is chief'.

12. 91. *-ka·pawi* 'stand': *no·keka·puwi* 'he comes to a standing halt'; *uncika·puwi* 'he stands on that side, at that distance'.

12. 92. *-iwi* 'be, become', freely added to noun stems (except those in vowel plus *w*, 12. 65b, and those in a long vowel, 12. 90): *epino·ci⁻* 'child' : *epino·ci·nʔuwi* 'he is a child'; *kwi·wesse·ns* 'boy' : *kwi·wesse·nsuwi* 'he is a boy'.

Perhaps primary in *nempa·ssuwi* 'he instructs'.

12. 93. *-nʔiwi*, a complex of noun final *-iny* (11. 104) and AI *-iwi;* added to an AI stem: *a·nci·we·nʔuwi* 'he renews his effort' (12. 49).

12. 94. *-yi:* *sekkwi* 'he spits'; also in pseudo-TI *mi·cit* 'he eats it', *ekwit* 'he wears it' (cf. 12. 66).

12. 95. *-i·:* *ekoški·* 'he is anxious'; *keši·pi·* 'he itches, scratches'; *pesikwi·* 'he gets up from a sitting position'; etc.

12. 96. *-kki·.* (a) Added without connective to the TA stem *ano·N-* (*eno·na·t* 'he orders, commissions him'), for action on indefinite persons: *eno·kki·* 'he commissions people' (cf. 12. 47).

(b) 'face', medial with AI final zero: *ekacekki·* 'he is bashful'.

12. 97. *-akki·* 'land', medial *-akky* with AI final *-e·:* *tenakki·* 'he dwells there'.

12. 98. *-ikki·:* *enokki·* 'he works'; *tekkokki·* 'he stamps his foot'.

12. 99. *-ninci·* 'hand', medial *-nincy* with AI final *-e·:* *kesi·pi·-keninci·* 'he washes his hands'; *keši·peninci·* 'his hand itches'; etc.

12. 100. *-nokki·* 'work', deverbal from *anokki·-* (12. 98): *wi·ceno·kki·ma·t* 'he works with him' (14. 6).

-anokki·: enanukki· 'he works thus'.

12. 101. *-kkomi·* 'ice', medial *-kkomy* (deverbal from the noun *mikkomy-*) with AI final *-e·:* *tekkamekkomi·* 'he crosses on the ice'.

12. 102. *-a·pi·* 'string' (II same), medial *-a·py* with AI final *-e·:* *ena·pi·* 'he is strung thither or thus'.

12. 103. -*ipi·* 'liquid' (II same), medial -*ipy* with AI final -*e·*: *ki·weškwe·pi·* 'he is drunk'; *šo·pi·* 'he is slightly drunk'. Added to TI stems: *enta ʾepi·* 'he draws water'; *twa·ʾepa·n* 'water hole in the ice' (11. 25).

12. 104. -*a·sipi·: pi·ta·sepi·* 'he belches'.

12. 105. -*isi·* appears, instead of -*isi* (12. 77), in *meškawesi·* 'he is strong'.

12. 106. -*akkoni·si·: ekotekkoni·si·* 'he climbs up a slope'.

12. 107. -*a·kkwi* 'shoot'; *unta·kkwi·* 'he shoots from there'.

12. 108. -*yi·wi·* 'muscle', medial -*yi·w* with AI final -*i·*: *pe·ci·wi·* 'he is weak'.

12. 109. -*inkwa·m* 'sleep', prefinal -*inkw* with AI final -*a·m*: *mi·tenkwa·m* 'he befouls himself in his sleep'; *šekinkwa·m* 'he wets his bed'; *usa·menkwa·m* 'he oversleeps'.

12. 110. -*pikkwan* 'back', medial with AI final zero: *keši·pepikkwan* 'his back itches'.

12. 111. -*cin* 'be fast' (II -*te·*), prefinal -*t* with AI final -*n: eko·cin* 'he hangs'.

12. 112. -*ako·cin* 'hang, fall' (II -*ako·te·*), deverbal from *ako·cin-* (12. 111): *a·šekiteko·cin* 'he falls backwards'; *untako·cin* 'he falls down from somewhere'.

12. 113. -*ššin* 'fall, land, step, lie' (II -*ssin*), prefinal -*SS* with AI final -*n;* one of the commonest AI finals. Added to roots: *eciceššin* 'he lies upside down', *penkiššin* 'he falls'; or to root plus medial: *ecitekki·ššin* 'he lies face down', *a·swa·kkuššin* 'he lies across a solid'.

-*iššin* has to be set up for *tekoššin* 'he arrives'.

12. 114. -*a·nakito·n* 'talk', complex medial with AI final zero: *tena·nekito·n* 'he talks there, he is engaged in talking'.

12. 115. -*o.* (a) *nempwa* 'he dies'; *pa·tti·no* 'he is numerous' (II -*at*); *pepa·tti·no* 'he is very numerous'; *wi·neno* 'he is fat'.

(b) Reflexive, from TA stems. The combinations of TA finals and reflexive AI -*o* are treated as unit AI finals and present many irregularities; it is simplest to regard them as AI formations parallel with the transitives. Hence the combinations are listed in the following paragraphs.

12. 116. -ʔo, reflexive corresponding to TA -ʔ: nena·ntuwiʔuwin 'doctoring' (11. 52); uwe·šeʔo 'he paints himself'.

12. 117. -aʔo, reflexive corresponding to TA -aʔw 'by tool', but partly specialized in the meaning 'go on water': ekoteʔo 'he canoes upstream'; nessikkwe·ʔo 'he combs his hair'; pe·nkuše·ʔo 'he dries himself'; sekkaʔuwin 'cane' (11. 52).

12. 118. -iko 'be transported', formed of the inflectional endings -$_1$ikw, -$_3$o which appear in the TA verb, but specialized as an AI final, and differing in the third person forms from the TA inflection. Added to TA stems: pemita·pa·neko 'he rides in a wagon' (TA -ta·pa·N 'draw'), pepa·meta·pa·neko 'he rides about in a wagon'; pemo·meko 'he rides horseback' (TA -o·m 'carry on back'); uta·ppeškate·peniko 'he has cramps' (TA -piN 'pull').

12. 119. -aʔoko, complex of TA -aʔw and AI -iko: umpaʔuko 'he swells up'.

12. 120. -mo, corresponding to TA -m, but entirely specialized: ca·ca·mo 'he sneezes'; nenkamo 'he sings'; no·cemoʔa·t 'he cures him' (with TA -ʔ, 14. 2).

From nouns, 'speak such-and-such a language': eniššena·pe·muttawa·t 'he speaks in an Indian language to him (14. 41); kecci-mo·kkuma·nemo 'he speaks English' ("American"); ucipwe·mo 'he speaks Ojibwa' (cf. 12. 125).

12. 121. -amo, corresponding to TA -am, but entirely specialized: mo·škemo 'he emerges'; wa·ssemo 'he flashes'; wa·wa·pemowin 'mirror' (11. 52).

12. 122. -imo, corresponding to TA -im, but specialized: ekomo 'he floats'.

12. 123. -a·cimo 'narrate', prefinal -a·t with AI final -mo, corresponding to TA -a·cim: tepa·cemo 'he reports, narrates'.

12. 124. -ššimo 'lie, step, dance', prefinal -SS with AI final -mo, corresponding to TA -ššim: epiššemoni·k 'mat' (11. 19, 25); kesi·sete·ššemowin 'door mat' (11. 52); kuwiššemo 'he lies down'; penkiššemo 'he (the sun) sets'.

From an AI stem: pessankwa·peššimo 'he dances with his eyes shut'.

12. 125. -*yi·mo* 'speak such-and-such a language', like -*mo* (12. 120); merely that a noun stem in -*išš* is treated as if it were -*iššy* (11. 67): *ša·kena·šši·mo* 'he speaks English'.

12. 126. -*o·mo* 'carry', prefinal -*o·* with AI final -*mo*, corresponding to TA -*o·m: pi·nto·mot* 'he carries it in the fold of his garment'.

12. 127. -*ino*, corresponding to TA -*in: untameno* 'he plays'.

12. 128. -*a·pono: tekkama·puno* 'he crosses'.

12. 129. -*po* 'eat', prefinal -*pw* with AI final -*o*; added without connective to the root *ato·t-: eto·ppuwin* 'table' (11. 52).

12. 130. -*o·ppo* 'eat', prefinal -*o·ppw* with AI final -*o: wi·to·ppuma·t* 'he eats with him' (14. 6).

12. 131. -*so* (II -*te·*). (a) 'by heat', corresponding to TA -*sw*; added without connective to root *on-: unso* 'he (kettle) comes to a boil'.

(b) Corresponding to TA stems in -*N* (14. 16 ff): *eko·so* 'he clings, hangs'; *enika·suwin* 'implement', *eno·suwin* 'name' (11. 52); *kešk̆iso* 'he forces himself, holds out, manages'; *mi·ka·so* 'he fights'; *na·nenkoso* 'he lies buried continuously'; *pekiso* 'he goes into the water'; *tesso·so* 'he gets trapped'.

12. 132. -*ka·so* 'undergo action' (II -*ka·te·*), a complex of -*ke·* (12. 16) with -*so*; added to TI stems: *nenkwaʔeka·so* 'he is buried'.

12. 133. -*ikka·so* 'feign', a complex of AI -*ikke·* (12. 20) and AI -*so*, with replacement of *e·* by *a·* (3. 16), corresponding to TA -(*i*)*kka·N*; added to an AI stem with lengthening of the final vowel: *nimpo-* (*nempwa* 'he dies') : *nempo·kka·so* 'he feigns dead'.

12. 134. -*nikka·so* 'be named' (II -*nikka·te·*), prefinal -*nikka·* and AI final -*so*, corresponding to TA -*nikka·N: ešinekka·so* 'he is named so'.

12. 135. -*iso* 'by heat' (II -*ite·*), corresponding to TA -*isw: epwe·so* 'he feels hot, he sweats'; *kešiso* 'he is hot'; *teniso* 'he is cooked there'; *wa·peso* 'he is ripe'.

12. 136. -*piso* 'speed, fly, fall; tie' (II -*pite·*), prefinal -*p* and AI final -*so*; corresponding to TA -*piN*, but largely specialized. Forms many verbs, e.g., *keši·peso* 'he goes fast'; *pemipeso* 'he speeds on, along, past'; *tepinenci·pesowin* 'ring for the finger' (11. 52).

It is added without connective to the root *iN-: eppiso* 'he speeds, flies thither or thus'.

12. 137. *-appiso, -ippiso* 'tie', corresponding to TA *-appiN, -ippiN: a·sentipe·ppeso* 'he carries his load with the pack strap round his head'; *etippesowin* 'apron' (11. 52).

12. 138. *-tiso*, explicit reflexive, a complex of AI *-ti* (12. 87) and AI *-so*. Freely added, without connective, to TA stems ending in *m*, as an explicit reflexive, in contrast with the vaguer forms in *-o: wa·pema·t* 'he sees him' : *wa·pentiso* 'he sees himself'.

12. 139. *-itiso*, explicit reflexive, a complex of AI *-iti* (12. 88) and AI *-so*. Freely added to TA stems (other than those ending in *m*): *tekkopena·t* 'he ties him fast' : *tekkopeniteso* 'he ties himself fast'; *pekkitte·wa·t* 'he strikes him' (TA final *-aʔw*) : *pekkitte·ʔutiso* 'he strikes himself'; *we·ppetawa·t* 'he strikes him' : *we·ppeta·teso* 'he strikes himself'.

12. 140. *-iško·so* 'by foot or body-movement' (II *-iško·te·*), a complex of TA *-iškaw* and AI *-iso* (with the contraction of 3. 45), reflexive corresponding to TA *-iškaw: tekkonekke·ško·so* 'he is caught by the arm'.

12. 141. *-ano·so* 'smoke': *te·penakkeno·so* 'he has had enough smoking'.

12. 142. *-a·wasso* 'child', added to a TA stem: *no·na·t* 'she suckles him' : *no·na·wesso* 'she suckles her child'.

12. 143. *-a·sso.* (a) 'sunshine' (II *-a·tte·*), corresponding to a TA final *-a·ssw: sa·ka·sso* 'he is exposed to the sun'.

(b) 'useful action', added to a TI stem: *mo·kkuta·sso* 'he carves, whittles'.

12. 144. *-kwa·sso* 'sew', prefinal *-kwa·* with AI final *-sso: keškikwa·-sso* 'he sews'.

Added to a TI stem: *ka·nteʔikwa·ssuwin* 'thimble' (11. 52), from TI *ka·ntaʔ-* (formed by 15. 3).

12. 145. *-ito: mentito* 'he is big'; *mema·tetowak* 'they are big'.

12. 146. *-kito* 'speak': *ka·ki·keto* 'he converses'; *ki·keto* 'he speaks'. Added without connective to the root *iN-: ekkito* 'he says so'.

12. 147. *-to·: mento·to·* 'he takes a steam bath'.

12. 148. *-tto·*. Apart from pseudo-transitives, the following AI verbs have this final: *neme·tto·* 'he leaves traces of his presence'; *o·te·tto·* 'he goes to town'; *senaketto·* 'he has difficulty'.

12. 149. *-patto·* 'run', inflected as AI, although in formation it is like a pseudo-transitive pendant to TA *-pa⸱* 'run from' (cf. 12. 47): *kencipettwa·tank* 'he runs away with it' (15. 26); *ma·ci·petto·* 'he starts to run'; *pemipetto·* 'he runs on, along, past'; *pe·cepatto·* 'he runs slowly'.

Added without connective to the root *iN-*; *eppatto·* 'he runs thither or thus'.

Added to AI stems: *keši·kka·petto·* 'he runs fast'; *ki·we·petto·* 'he runs back or home'; *pepa·ma·ntuwe·petto·* 'he runs climbing about'; *sa·keto·te·petto·* 'he runs crawling out'.

CHAPTER 13

INANIMATE INTRANSITIVE FINALS

13. 1. II finals are less varied than AI finals; where an AI final has no corresponding II, an II verb is derived from the AI by *-makat*. This final is also frequently added to II finals, with no apparent difference of meaning; we shall give these stems without comment under the II final that precedes *-makat*.

For order of presentation see 11. 1.

13. 2. *-ka·* 'leak' (AI same): *uncika·* 'it is leaky'.

13. 3. *-kka·* 'move', prefinal *-kk* with II final *-a·*, for usual *-ikka·*: *uncikka·mekat* 'it comes from there'.

13. 4. *-ikka·*. (a) 'move' (AI same), prefinal *-ikk* with II final *-a·*; preceding *t* is replaced by *s* (3. 24): *mema·sekka·* 'it moves'.

(b) 'quantity', freely added to nouns. These verbs appear especially in the simple conjunct indicative as expressions of place: *enimekki·* 'thunderer' : *enimekki·kka·* 'there is a thunderstorm'; *mettiko·ns* AN 'small tree' : *mettiko·nsekka·* 'it is a place of small trees'; *me·mi·kwa͞* 'butterfly' : *me·mi·kwa·nʔekka·* 'there are many butterflies'. From a particle: *me·kuya·k* 'in the woods' : *me·kuya·kekka·* 'it is woodland'.

-yi·kka· seems to underlie the noun form *ne·kuwi·kka·nk* 'on the sand' (11. 2).

13. 5. *-a·ška·* 'waves', prefinal *-a·* with II final *-iška·*: *mema·nka·-ška·* 'it runs in big waves'.

13. 6. *-iška·* 'move' (AI same), prefinal *-išk* with II final *-a·*: *kuttikuška·* 'it tips over'; *pi·kuška·* 'it breaks to pieces'; *po·kkuška·* 'it breaks in two'.

13. 7. *-kama·* 'water', medial *-kam* with II final *-a·*: *wi·kkwe·kema·* 'there is a bay'.

13. 8. *-ya·* is freely added to roots or combinations of root and medial; the AI correspondent in many cases has *-isi*. *esa·wa·* 'it is yellow'; *eya·* 'it is here' (AI same); *mecca·* 'it is big'; *pa·šketta·wenka·*

'there is loose soil, the road is dusty'. The medial may have postmedial -*ak: ešpa·kunaka·* 'there is deep snow'.

13. 9. -*e·ya·: tekke·ya·* 'it is cool weather'.

13. 10. -*yiya·: ešiya·* 'it is there' (AI same); *ka·ki·nekoya·* 'it is pointed at both ends' (3. 30).

13. 11. -*ane·* 'burn': *peskane·* 'it takes fire, kindles'.

13. 12. -*ine·: wa·wa·ssekkone͂* 'flower' (11. 2).

13. 13. -*sse·* 'fly, fall, speed' (AI same), prefinal -*SS* with II final -*e·: kuttikusse·* 'it tips over'; *kuwisse·mekat* 'it falls over'; *pemisse·* 'it goes by'; *pi·tte·wa·kemisse·* 'it is foamy liquid'; *tepiško·sse·* 'it reaches, it comes to the time'.

13. 14. -*te·*, reflexive (AI -*so*). (a) 'by heat', corresponding to TA -*sw*, TI -*s;* added without connective: *unte·* 'it comes to a boil.'

(b) Corresponding to TA -*N*, TI -*t;* preceding *e·* replaced by *a·* (3. 16). Added to an AI stem: *na·mekkamekokka·te·* 'it is built with a cellar', as though from AI *na·makkamikokke·-* 'make a cellar' (12. 20; 11. 90).

(c) Medial -*t* (for usual -*at*) with II final -*e·: mema·ccete·mekat* 'it grows big'.

13. 15. -*ka·te·*, reflexive or 'subject to act' (AI -*ka·so*), properly AI -*ke·* plus reflexive II -*te·* with replacement of *e·* by *a·* (3. 16). Corresponds to TA -*ka·N*, TI -*ka·t;* freely added to TI stems and to pseudo-transitives, the latter dropping final *o·: kepa·kkuʔank* 'he closes it' : *kepa·kkuʔika·te·* 'it is closed'; *ešitto·t* 'he makes it so, he makes it' : *ešicceka·te·* 'it is made so, it is made'.

13. 16. -*nikka·te·* reflexive, 'be named' (AI -*nikka·so*), corresponding to TA -*nikka·N*, TI -*nikka·t*, prefinal -*nikka·* with II final -*te·: ešinekka·te·* 'it is named so'.

13. 17. -*ite·*, reflexive or 'by heat', corresponding to TA -*isw*, TI -*is: keša·pekkite·* 'it is heated as stone or metal'; *kešite·* 'it is hot'; *menote·* 'it is cooked'; *meskwa·pekkite·* 'it is red hot'; *pekone·te·* 'it has a hole burned in it'; *wa·pete·* 'it is ripe' (cf. 11. 8).

13. 18. -*pite·*, reflexive, 'be pulled, speed, fly' (AI -*piso*), corresponding to TA -*piN*, pseudo-TI -*pito·;* prefinal -*p* with II final -*te·: pekamepite·* 'it arrives speeding'; *uncipete·* 'it speeds from there'.

13. 19. -*a·nte·* 'wood', medial with II final -*e·: eša·weškwa·nte·* 'it is a green house'.

-*wa·nte·*, added to a noun: *mi·šeško·nswa·nte·* 'it is a wooden thing'.

13. 20. -*akinte·*, reflexive, 'be counted' (AI -*akinso?*), corresponding to TA -*akim*, TI -*akint;* deverbal from a stem *akinte·*- which is formed with a reflexive II -*nte·* corresponding to TA -*m*, TI -*nt: enakinte·* 'it is priced so, costs so much'.

13. 21. -*po·te·*, reflexive, 'be ground, filed' (AI -*po·so?*), corresponding to TA -*po·N*, pseudo-TI -*po·to·;* prefinal -*po·* with II final -*te·: ki·nepo·te·* 'it is sharpened'.

13. 22. -*tte·*, reflexive. (a) *a·tte·* 'it is extinguished'.

(b) 'by heat' (AI -*sso?*), corresponding to TA -*ssw*, TI -*ss: pa·tte·* 'it is dry'.

(c) Corresponding to TA -*SS*, pseudo-TI -*tto·: ette·* 'it is placed, it is there'. The corresponding AI reflexive is replaced by *api-* (12. 65).

13. 23. -*atte·*, reflexive, 'be in place, be there', deverbal from *atte·*- (13. 22). Corresponds probably to a TA -*aSS*, pseudo-TI -*atto·;* the corresponding reflexive AI final is replaced by -*api. necci·wette·* 'it lies in disorder'; *pi·nette·* 'it lies clean'.

13. 24. -*a·patte·* 'smoke' (AI presumably -*a·passo*), prefinal -*a·p* with II final -*atte·: umpa·pette·* 'there is smoke or vapor rising'; *unta·pette·* 'there is smoke rising from there'.

13. 25. -*a·tte·*, reflexive or 'sunlight' (AI -*a·sso*), corresponding to TA -*a·ssw*, TI -*a·ss: keša·tte·* 'it is hot weather'; *sa·ka·tte·* 'it is in the sunlight'.

13. 26. -*akkwe·* 'sky', medial with II final -*e·: na·wekkwe·* 'it is noon'.

13. 27. -*i: tekwa·ki* 'it is autumn'.

13. 28. -*o·nʔi*, diminutive, a complex of noun finals -*w* (11. 73), -*e·ny* (11. 104), and II final -*i;* added to an II stem: *eka·cceno·nʔi* 'it is tiny'.

13. 29. -*kami* 'liquid', medial -*kam* with II final -*i: pekkwe·pi·kemi* 'it is muddy water'.

-*a·kami: menwa·kemi* 'it is good liquid'; *nempi·ška·kemi* 'it is watery liquid'; *pi·na·kemi* 'it is clean water'; etc.

13. 30. *-o·kkami: meno·kkemi* 'it is spring'.

13. 31. *-šši: ena·kušši* 'it is evening'.

13. 32. *-kki·* 'grow': *sa·kekki·* 'it grows forth'.

13. 33. *-a·pi·* (AI same), medial with II final *-e·*. (a) 'liquid'; preceding *t* replaced by *s* (3. 24): *kunsa·pi·* 'it founders'.

(b) 'string': *ena·pi·* 'it is strung thither or thus'.

13. 34. *-n: eka·ccin* 'it is small'; *pepo·n* 'it is winter'; *sa·te·wa·nk* 'on Saturday'; *uniššeššin* 'it is beautiful'.

13. 35. *-an: kemiwan* 'it rains'; *kena·cuwan* 'it is handsome' (AI *-i*); *kusikwan* 'it is heavy'; *na·nkan* 'it is light of weight'; *wa·pank* 'tomorrow'.

13. 36. *-aʔan* 'flood': *mo·škeʔan* 'there is a flood'.

13. 37. *-wan*, added to a particle: *a·pettaweyaʔi·wank* 'on Thursday'.

13. 38. *-ciwan* 'flow': *pekkiceciwan* 'it flows as rapids'; *pemicuwan* 'it flows on, along, past'; *uncicuwan* 'it flows from there'.

13. 39. *-in: pe·šekon* 'it is one'.

13. 40. *-kin* 'grow' (AI *-ki*), prefinal *-k* with II final *-in: netta·wekin* 'it grows up'.

13. 41. *-ssin* 'fall, land, lie' (A1 *-ššin*), prefinal *-SS* with II final *-in: a·swa·kkussin* 'it lies across a solid'; *penkissin* 'it falls'; *ucipwe·ssin* 'it is written in Ojibwa'; etc.

13. 42. *-atin* 'cold' (AI *-aci*), prefinal *-at* with II final *-in: kepatin* 'it is frozen over'.

13. 43. *-amo* 'path, streak': *enamo* 'it (road) goes thither or thus'; *pe·šša·pi·kemo* 'it makes a streak', *pe·ppe·šša·pi·kemo* 'it makes repeated streaks'; *šeya·we·mo* 'it is a straight road'.

13. 44. *-at* 'state, shape' (AI *-isi*), widely used after roots: *senakat* 'it is difficult', *we·neppanat* 'it is easy'; after root plus medial: *mešakkwat* 'the sky is clear', *šo·škwa·pekkat* 'it is smooth stone or metal'; especially after root plus medial when the latter has postmedial *-ak: ekkwa·pi·kat* 'it is so long a string', *ni·šukonekat* 'it is two days'.

13. 45. *-makat* is freely added to AI stems, to form corresponding II stems: *eša·mekat* 'it goes thither'; *ki·ši·tta·mekat* 'it finishes'; *ma·ca·mekat* 'it goes away'.

Added to II stems, it seems to produce no new meaning: *ette·mekat* 'it is in place, it is there'; *mecca·mekat* 'it is big'.

-o·makat is the form of the suffix after AI stems ending in a consonant: *tekoššeno·mekat* 'it arrives'.

13. 46. *-anat* 'decay', prefinal *-an* with II final *-at:* *pekaškenat* 'it rots so as to break'.

13. 47. *-a·kwat* 'subject to act' (AI *-a·kosi*), prefinal *-a·* with II final *-ikwat;* added to TI stems in *-e·nt: nentawe·nta·kwat* 'it is wanted'; *we·wi·pe·nta·kwat* 'it is urgent'.

13. 48. *-ma·kwat* 'be smelled' (AI *-ma·kosi*), prefinal *-ma·* with II final *-ikwat: pi·cema·kwat* 'its smell comes hither'.

13. 49. *-na·kwat* 'be seen' (AI *-na·kosi*), a complex of TA final *-naw* and II *-ikwat: ešina·kwat* 'it looks so'.

13. 50. *-ikwat* (AI *-ikosi*) is contained in the finals of 13. 47-9, 51-3.

13. 51. *-a·mikwat* 'subject to act' (AI *-a·mikosi*), prefinal *-a·m* and II final *-ikwat;* added to a TI stem: *kutta·mekwat* 'it is terrifying'.

13. 52. *-pokwat* 'be tasted' (AI doubtless *-pokosi*), prefinal *-pw* and II final *-ikwat;* added to the root *iN-* without connective: *eppokwat* 'it tastes so'.

13. 53. *-ippokwat* 'be tasted' (AI *-ippokosi*), prefinal *-ppw* with II final *-ikwat: menoppukwat* 'it tastes good'.

13. 54. *-a·nakkwat* 'cloud', deverbal from a stem *a·nakkwat-* (13. 44); cf. the noun *a·nekkwat* 'cloud' formed from this stem by 11. 73: *meskwa·nekkwat* 'it is a red cloud'; *nenkwa·nekkwat* 'the sky clouds over'; *wa·pa·nekkwat* 'white cloud' (11. 73).

CHAPTER 14

TRANSITIVE ANIMATE FINALS

14. 1. By the side of each TA final there is either a TI final or a pseudo-transitive AI verb which is used with inanimate objects.

Some TA finals are derived with final *-aw* or *-w* from TI finals.

For order of presentation see 11. 1.

14. 2. *-ʔ* (pseudo-TI *-tto·*) is the most abstract of the TA finals. It is freely added to AI stems in the meanings 'cause to' or 'act so upon': *mento·to·* 'he takes a steam bath' : *mento·to·ʔa·t* 'he gives him a steam bath'; *ekwit* (pseudo-transitive) 'he dons it' : *ekwiʔa·t* 'he clothes him'; *pa·pi·* 'he waits' : *pa·piʔa·t* 'he waits for him'.

It appears also in many primary formations: *keškiʔa·t* 'he controls him'; *sa·keʔa·t* 'he loves him'; *se·keʔa·t* 'he frightens him'.

14. 3. *-aʔ* 'cause': *menaʔa·t* 'he gives him drink'.

Added to a TI stem *wa·pentank* 'he sees it': *wa·pantaʔ-* 'he shows it to him', in *wa·pentaʔetiwak* 'they show it to each other' (12. 88), and in *wa·pentaʔuwe·* 'he exhibits' (12.47).

14. 4. *-paʔ* 'run from'; the AI final *-patto·* makes ordinary intransitive verbs (12. 149; cf. also 12. 47): *kencipeʔa·t* 'he runs away from him'.

14. 5. *-e·wiʔ*, added to TA stems in *-a·pam*: *menwa·peme·weʔiwe·win* 'blessing' (11. 52; 12. 47).

14. 6. *-m* has several uses. (a) It is added to AI stems formed with the root *wi·t-* 'along' (and presumably to AI stems compounded with the particle *wi·ci* 'along'); the AI stem need not occur in inflectional forms: *wi·teke·* 'he lives with someone; he (she) is married' : *wi·teke·ma·t* 'he lives with him; he (she) is married to her (him)'. Similarly, with the underlying AI stem not quotable in inflected forms: *wi·ceka·ma·t* 'he dances with him'; *wi·cenokki·ma·t* 'he works with him'; *wi·cesse·ma·t* 'he goes with him'; *wi·to·ppuma·t* 'he eats with him'.

(b) Added to possessed noun themes in the sense 'have as, treat as': *ni·cekkiwe˜* 'my male friend' : *owi·cikkiwe·nʔim-* in *uwi·cekkiwe·nʔetiwak* 'they (men) are friends together' (12. 87).

(c) Added to an AI stem with replacement of *e·* by *a* (3. 17): *eta·we·* 'he gives credit, he sells' : *eta·wema·t* 'he borrows something from him'.

(d) Primary, 'by speech, by mouth' (TI *-nt*, AI reflexive *-mo*), widely used: *kekwe·cema·t* 'he asks him'; *kuma·t* 'he swallows him'; *se·kema·t* 'he frightens him by speech'; etc.

14. 7. *-am* 'by mouth' and in abstract meanings (TI *-ant*): *enama·t* 'he bites him thus'; *eššama·t* 'he gives him food'; *wa·pema·t* 'he sees him'.

With replacement of *e·* by *a·* (3. 16): *pa·šketiya·ma·t* 'he bursts him at the rump'.

14. 8. *-a·pam* 'see', deverbal from *wa·pam-* (14. 7; TI *-a·pant*): *ekkawa·pema·t* 'he watches over him'; *minwa·pam-* (12. 77); *nentawa·pema·t* 'he looks for him'.

14. 9. *-ma·m* 'smell' (TI *-ma·nt*), prefinal *-ma·* with TA final *-m*: *pi·cema·ma·t* 'he gets the smell of him'.

14. 10. *-im* 'by speech' (TI *-it*), 'by mouth' (TI *-int*): *nentoma·t* 'he calls him'; *tekkoma·t* 'he bites him'.

14. 11. *-acim* 'by cold' (pseudo-TI *-acito·?*), prefinal *-at* with TA final *-m*: *kuta·cema·t* 'he tests him in the cold'.

14. 12. *-a·cim* 'narrate' (TI *-a·cit*, reflexive AI *-a·cimo*), prefinal *-a·t* with TA final *-m*: *tepa·cema·t* 'he tells of him'.

14. 13. *-e·nim* 'think' (TI *-e·nt*), prefinal *-e·n* with TA final *-m*; widely used: *kekke·nema·t* 'he knows him'; *nentawe·nema·t* 'he desires him'; *wene·nema·t* 'he forgets him'; etc.

14. 14. *-ššim* 'lay, throw' (pseudo-TI *-ssito·*, reflexive AI *-ššimo*), prefinal *-SS* with TA final *-m*: *ekwa·ššema·t* 'he takes him out of the water or other medium'; *pi·kuššima·t* 'he brings him down so as to break him'; *umpi·kwe·we·ššema·t* 'he flops him (wing) up with noise'.

14. 15. *-o·m* 'carry on back' (TI *-o·nt*, reflexive AI *-o·mo*), prefinal *-o·* with TA final *-m*: *pemo·meko* 'he rides horseback' (12. 118).

14. 16. *-N* has various uses. (a) Applies the action to an object (TI *-t*, reflexive AI *-so*, II *-te·*); added to AI stems: *tekkamuˀa·* 'he crosses' : *tekkamuˀa·na·t* 'he crosses over on him (a log)'. Preceding e· is replaced by a·: ešicceke· 'he makes things so' : ešicceka·na·t 'he works thus on him' (cf. the reflexives -ka·so, -ikka·so, 12. 132-3). Similarly, i· based on ye· is replaced by a·: tekkokki· 'he stamps his foot' : tekkokka·na·t 'he stamps on him'. Preceding e· is kept in po·ta·kkwe·na·t 'he puts him in the kettle'.

(b) Matched by pseudo-TI -to·; added to an AI stem with replacement of e· by a: pi·nteke· 'he enters' : pi·ntekana·t 'he brings him inside'.

(c) In many primary formations; the TI verb is formed with -t or represented by a pseudo-transitive in -to·; reflexives are as under (a) above: eka·wa·na·t 'he longs for him' (TI -t); eko·na·t 'he hangs him up' (pseudo-TI -to·); ena·t 'he says so to him' (TI probably -t); ma·ci·na·t 'he takes him away with him' (pseudo-TI -to·); mi·cena·t 'he defecates on him' (TI probably -t); pi·na·t 'he brings him' (pseudo-TI -to·); puwa·na·t 'he dreams of him' (TI -t).

The stem na·na·t 'he fetches him' is matched by the pseudo-TI verb na·tit 'he fetches it'.

The stem mi·na·t 'he gives it to him' (double object) has no corresponding TI.

14. 17. -aN: a·wena·t 'he carries him off' (probably pseudo-TI -to·); memašuwe· 'he copulates' (12. 47; probably TI -t); nenkana·t 'he abandons him' (probably TI -t).

14. 18. -aʔaN 'track' (pseudo-TI -aʔatto·): na·keʔana·t 'he tracks him'.

14. 19. -kkaN 'go from' (TI probably -t), prefinal -kk with TA final -aN: kekwe·cekkanetiwak 'they race with each other' (12. 88).

14. 20. -naN 'pursue, kill' (TI probably -nat), prefinal -na with TA final -N: no·ppenana·t 'he pursues, follows him'; uncinenituwak 'they kill each other therefor' (12. 88).

-inaN: eškonena·t 'he spares him from killing'.

14. 21. -nikka·N 'name' (TI -nikka·t, reflexives AI -nikka·so, II -nikka·te·), prefinal -nikka· with TA final -N: ešinekka·netiso 'he names himself so' (12. 139).

14. 22. -ta·pa·N 'drag', probably deverbal from a stem ota·pa·N- (TI -ta·pa·t): pekkopi·ta·pa·na·t 'he pulls him into the water' (cf. 12. 118).

14. 23. *-in* 'by hand' (TI *-in*), forms many stems: *a·kukwe·na·t* 'he hugs him'; *nuwatena·t* 'he takes hold of him'; *uta·ppena·t* 'he picks him up'; *we·pena·t* 'he throws him away, casts him off'.

14. 24. *-piN* 'pull' (pseudo-TI *-pito·*, reflexives AI *-piso*, II *-pite·*), prefinal *-p* with TA final *-N;* forms many stems: *keškipena·t* 'he manages to pull him'; *ki·ssekkoneye·pena·t* 'he pulls the clothes from him'; *wi·kkupina·t* 'he pulls him in'; etc.

-ipiN has to be set up for the stems *peškopena·t* 'he plucks him', *tekkopena·t* 'he ties him fast'.

14. 25. *-we·pin* 'throw by hand, push' (TI *-we·pin*), deverbal from the stem *we·pin-* (14. 23): *ekwa·we·pena·t* 'he flings him out of the water or other medium'; *menka·we·pena·t* 'he hinders, stops him'.

Preceding *t* is replaced by *c*: *ka·ncwe·pena·t* 'he shoves him'; *ema·cwe·pena·t* 'he wakes him' has rather *-we·piN*.

14. 26. *-appiN* 'tie' (pseudo-TI *-appito·*), prefinal *-app* with TA final *-N:* *na·pekwe·ppena·t* 'he ropes him round the neck'; *sekika·te·ppena·t* 'he ties him by the leg'.

14. 27. *-wiN* 'convey, lead' (pseudo-TI *-wito·*), prefinal *-w* with TA final *-N:* *ekwa·wena·t* 'he takes him out of the water'; *ešiwena·t* 'he leads him thither'; *ki·we·wena·t* 'he takes him home'.

14. 28. *-ikkoN* 'carve, whittle' (TI *-ikkot*), prefinal *-ikkw* with TA final *-iN:* *penakekkona·t* 'he peels him (potato)'.

14. 29. *-amo·N* 'cause' (TI *-amo·t*), added to TI stems: *kekke·ntank* 'he knows it' : *kekke·ntemo·na·t* 'he informs him'; *kuntank* 'he swallows it' : *kuntamo·na·t* 'he catches him with hook and line'.

14. 30. *-SS* forms a few stems: *essa·t* 'he places him' (pseudo-TI *etto·t*); *kussa·t* 'he fears him' (probably TI *kott-*); *nessa·t* 'he kills him' (probably pseudo-TI *nitto·-*).

14. 31. *-aw.* (a) Forms double object verbs from pseudo-TI stems in *-to·*, *-tto·*; the *o·* is dropped: *etto·t* 'he places it' : *ettawa·t* 'he contends, bets, gambles with him'; *ma·ci·to·t* 'he takes it away' : *ma·ci·tuwa·t* 'he takes it away for or from him'; *pi·to·t* 'he brings it' : *pi·tuwa·t* 'he brings it to him'. The formation with TA *-amaw* (14. 36) is commoner.

(b) Added to a stem in AI -ke·, with loss of e·: nena·ntuwiᵖekawa·t 'he does doctoring for him', from an AI stem nana·ntawiᵖike·- (12. 16).

(c) Added to certain TI finals, forming the corresponding TA finals, as listed in the following paragraphs. Corresponding to the TI stem ay-, with final zero, there is the TA eya·wa·t 'he has him', with the vowel lengthened after ay- (3. 14).

14. 32. -ikkaw 'by foot or body-movement' (TI -ikk) underlies the nouns na·pekkawa·kan 'article of neckwear' and pi·ssekkawa·kan 'jacket, coat' (11. 28).

14. 33. -na·šikkaw 'chase, send' (TI presumably -na·šikk), prefinal -na·N with a TA final -kkaw: ešina·šekkawa·t 'he sends him thither'; sa·kecina·šekkawa·t 'he chases him out'.

14. 34. -o·kkaw 'go' (TI -o·kk?), prefinal -o· with TA final -ikkaw: wi·to·kkuwa·t 'he goes with him, helps him'.

14. 35. -iškaw 'by foot or body-movement'(TI -išk, reflexives AI -iško·so, II -iško·te·): nekkwe·škuwa·t 'he goes to meet him'; tenkiš-kuwa·t 'he kicks him'; tetankeškawa·t 'he repeatedly kicks him'. Added to an II stem: sa·ka·tte·škuwa·t 'he (sun) shines on him'.

14. 36. -amaw freely forms double object verbs: (a) from TI stems, e.g., mekkank 'he finds it' : mekkamuwa·t 'he finds it for him'; wa·pentank 'he sees it' : wa·pentamuwa·t 'he sees it on or for him'.

(b) From pseudo-TI verbs in -to·, -tto·, with loss of the o·; more used than -aw (14. 30): e.g. etto·t 'he places it' : ettamuwa·t 'he places it for him'; ki·špenato·t 'he buys it' : ki·špenatemawa·t 'he buys it from him'; ma·ci·to·t 'he takes it away with him' : ma·ci·temawa·t 'he takes it away for or from him'.

(c) Beside the pseudo-TI stem na·tit 'he fetches it', there is the TA na·temawa·t 'he helps him'.

14. 37. -naw (TI -n), as a general transitivizer in pekkinuwa·t 'he wins from him'; in the meaning 'see' in nessituwinuwa·t 'he recognizes him' (cf. AI -na·kosi, 12. 81; II -na·kwat, 13. 49).

-inaw 'shoot': peškonuwa·t 'he misses him with a shot'.

14. 38. -taw (TI -t): to·tuwa·t 'he does so to him, treats him so'; we·ppetawa·t 'he strikes him'.

14. 39. *-ntaw* 'hear' (TI *-nt*): *no·ntuwa·t* 'he hears him'; *pesintuwa·t* 'he listens to him, obeys him'.

14. 40. *-antaw* added to a TI stem: *sesswe·pi·keʾantuwa·t* 'he sprinkles him with water', from a TI stem in *-aʾ*.

14. 41. *-ittaw* (TI *-itt*). (a) Freely added to AI stems, 'act in relation to': *enokki·* 'he works' : *enokki·ttuwa·t* 'he works for him'; *ucipwe·mo* 'he speaks Ojibwa' : *ucipwe·muttawa·t* 'he speaks Ojibwa to him'. The preceding vowel is lengthened in *neška·tesi·ttuwa·t* 'he is angry at him' from *neška·tesi* 'he is angry'.

(b) Primary, 'hear': *nekkwe·ttuwa·t* 'he answers him'; *nessituttawa·t* 'he understands him'; *te·pwe·ttuwa·t* 'he believes him'.

14. 42. *-yi·w: wi·ci·wa·t* 'he accompanies him'.

14. 43. *-aʾw* 'by instrument or medium' (TA *-aʾ*, reflexives AI *-aʾo*, II *-aʾoko*). Like most of the following finals, this consists of a TI final plus *-w*. TA *-aʾw* is very widely employed, e.g., *a·puwa·t* 'he unties him', *ka·ntuwa·t* 'he shoves him', *na·pekwe·wa·t* 'he catches him by the neck', *pekkitte·wa·t* 'he hits him with something'.

14. 44. *-kaʾw* 'by axe' (TI *-kaʾ*), prefinal *-k* with TA final *-aʾw*: *ta·škekawa·t* 'he splits him'.

14. 45. *-we·paʾw* 'fling by tool' (TI *-we·paʾ*), prefinal *-we·p* (deverbal from root *we·p-*) with TA final *-aʾw*: *ešiwe·puwa·t* 'he knocks him thither or thus'.

14. 46. *-ne·ʾw* 'approach': *etimene·wa·t* 'he overtakes him'; *muwi·ne·wa·t* 'he attacks him.

14. 47. *-na·šiʾw* 'chase, send', prefinal *-na·N* with a TA final *-ʾw*: *ešina·šuwa·t* 'he sends him thither'.
-ina·šiʾw: ekkona·šuwa·t 'he sends him away'.

14. 48. *-mw: emwa·t* 'he eats him', to which corresponds the pseudo-TI verb *mi·cit* 'he eats it'; *pemwa·t* 'he shoots him' (TI presumably a stem *pimot-*).

14. 49. *-sw* 'by heat' (TI *-s*, reflexives AI *-so*, II *-te·*), added without connective to root *on-*: *unswa·t* 'he brings him (kettle) to a boil'.

-isw: *menoswa·t* 'he cooks him'; *pa·škeswa·t* 'he shoots him with a gun'; *tekoswa·t* 'he cooks him along'.

14. 50. *-šw.* (a) In *mešwa·t* 'he hits him with a shot or missile' (TI stem *mišot-?*).

(b) 'cut' (TI *-š*), added without connective to the root *mo·n-:* *mo·nšwa·t* 'he cuts his hair'.

-išw 'by knife' (TI *-iš*): *ki·škešwa·t* 'he slices him through'; *pekaškešwa·t* 'he cuts him up'.

CHAPTER 15

TRANSITIVE INANIMATE FINALS

15. 1. We give first (15. 2-44) the TI finals and then (15. 45-57) the pseudo-TI finals.

For order of presentation in each part see 11. 1.

TI FINALS

15. 2. Zero appears in *eya·nk* 'he has it, gets it'; TA *-aw*.

15. 3. *-aʔ* 'by instrument or medium' (TA *-aʔw*); very widely used, sometimes with a formal object only: *a·tteʔank* 'he extinguishes it'; *ekoteʔam* 'he canoes upstream'; *ki·škeʔank* 'he chops it through'; *puwaʔank* 'he knocks it off'.

15. 4. *-kaʔ* 'by axe' (TA *-kaʔw*), prefinal *-k* with TI final *-aʔ*: *ca·kekaʔank* 'he chops it all'; *wa·weye·keʔank* 'he hews it round'.
-ikaʔ: *pekokeʔike·* 'he chops a hole' (12. 16).

15. 5. *-we·paʔ* 'throw by tool' (TA *-we·paʔw*), prefinal *-we·p* with TI final *-aʔ*: *ekwa·we·peʔank* 'he flings it out of the water by tool'.

15. 6. *-ataʔ* 'by stick' (TA presumably *-ataʔw*), prefinal *-at* with TI final *-aʔ*: *ci·ketaʔank* 'he sweeps it with a broom'.

15. 7. *-antaʔ* 'by tool' (TA *-antaʔw* ?): *pekakkekanteʔike·* 'he threshes' (12. 16).

15. 8. *-no·ʔ* 'point out': *ešino·ʔemawa·t* 'he points it out thus to him' and *kekkino·ʔemawa·t* 'he teaches it to him' (14. 36).

15. 9. *-kk* (TA probably *-kkaw*) : *mekkank* 'he finds it'.

15. 10. *-ikk* 'by foot or body-movement' (TA *-ikkaw*), prefinal *-ikk* with TI final zero: *ki·ssekkank* 'he doffs it'; *na·pekkank* 'he wears it round his neck'; *pi·ssekkank* 'he dons it'.

Preceding *t* is replaced by *s* (3. 24) in *a·nsekkank* 'he changes it (a garment)'.

15. 11. -*yi·kk* 'resort to, frequent' (TA presumably -*yi·kkaw*), prefinal -*yi·* with TI final -*ikk: untami·kkank* 'he amuses himself with it'.

15. 12. -*išk* 'by foot or body-movement' (TA -*iškaw*), prefinal -*išk* with TI final zero: *a·tte·škank* 'he extinguishes it with his foot'; *senikuci·škank* 'he rubs his foot on it'; *si·neškank* 'he has a tight fit of it'.

15. 13. -*we·pišk* 'fling by foot' (TA presumably -*we·piškaw*), prefinal -*we·p* with TI final -*išk: si·kwe·peškank* 'he spills it by kicking it or bumping into it.'

15. 14. -*in* 'by hand' (TA -*in*), very widely used: *a·pi·nenank* 'he unwraps it'; *kesi·pi·kenank* 'he washes it'; *pekitenank* 'he sets it down'; *uta·ppenank* 'he picks it up'; etc.

15. 15. -*we·pin* 'throw by hand' (TA same), deverbal from a stem *we·pin-* formed by 15. 14: *ekwa·we·penank* 'he flings it out of the water or other medium'; *kuttikwe·penank* 'he flips it upside down'; *si·kwe·penank* 'he spills it'.

Preceding *t* is replaced by *c: ka·ncwe·penank* 'he shoves it'; *pekicwe·penank* 'he flings it down'.

15. 16. -*appin* 'tie' (TA presumably the same): *nena·ʔetta·ppenank* 'he ties it in shape'.

15. 17. -*s* 'by heat' (TA -*sw*): added without connective to the root *on-*: *unsank* 'he brings it to a boil'.

-*is* (TA -*isw*): *ca·kesank* 'he gets a burn on it'; *menosank* 'he cooks it'; *pa·škesank* 'he shoots it with a gun'.

Added to an AI stem: *eššakuwe·* 'he vomits' : *eššakuwe·sekan* 'water weed' (11. 27).

15. 18. -*a·kkas* 'burn' (TA presumably -*a·kkasw*), prefinal -*a·kka* with TI final -*is: ena·kkesank* 'he burns it so'; *ki·ška·kkesank* 'he burns it through'; *pekone·ya·kkesank* 'he burns a hole in it'.

15. 19. -*a·ss* 'flash'; see 12. 19 and cf. 12. 143.

15. 20. -*iss* (TA presumably -*issw*): *etissank* 'he colors it'.

15. 21. -*tiss*, -*atiss* (TA presumably -*tissw*, -*atissw*), deverbal from the stem *atiss-* (15. 20): *wa·peškitessank* 'he paints it white'; *meskwatessank* 'he paints it red'.

15. 22. -*iš* 'by knife' (TA -*išw*): *ki·škešank* 'he slices it through'; *pekkwe·šekan* 'bread' (11. 27).

15. 23. -*t* (AI -*N*). (a) Added to AI stems: *kepikka·tank* 'he passes it', from an underlying AI in -*ikka·* (12. 6). Preceding *e·* is replaced by *a·*: *ešicceke·* 'he does things so' : *ešicceka·tank* 'he works on it thus'; *kettike·* 'he farms' : *kettika·tank* 'he plants it, raises it'; *uški·nšeko·kka·cekanan* pl. 'eyeglasses' (11. 27), from an AI in -*ikke·* (12. 20).

(b) Primary: *ka·tank* 'he plants it'; *pekitank* 'he throws it'; *puwa·tank* 'he dreams of it'. Preceding *i·* (representing *ye·*) is replaced by *a·* in *ka·škepa·cekan* 'razor' (11. 27).

(c) Preceding *e·* is kept in *eškwe·ta·kan* 'last-born child' (11. 28).

(d) TI -*t* is matched by TA -*taw* in *to·tam* 'he does so', and *we·ppecika·ns* 'hammer' (11. 27, 58).

15. 24. -*nika·t* 'carry on shoulder' (TA presumably -*nika·N*), prefinal -*nika·* with TI final -*t*: *pemineka·tank* 'he carries it along on his shoulder'.

15. 25. -*nikka·t* 'name' (TA -*nikka·N*): *ešinekka·tank* 'he names it so'.

15. 26. -*wa·t* (TA presumably -*wa·N*), added to AI stems in -*patto·* with loss of *o·*: *kencipettwa·tank* 'he runs away with it'.

15. 27. -*it* 'by speech' (TA -*im*): *nentotank* 'he asks for it'; *ussassetam* (formal object only) 'he coughs'.

15. 28. -*a·cit* 'narrate' (TA -*a·cim*), prefinal -*a·t* with TI final -*t*: *tepa·cetank* 'he tells of it'.

15. 29. -*akit* 'throw' (TA presumably -*akiN*), deverbal from the stem *pakit*- (15. 23): *eppaketank* 'he throws it, pitches it'.

15. 30. -*nt*. (a) 'by mouth, by speech' (TA -*m* with TI -*t* added without connective): *ekitank* 'he counts, prices, reads it'; *kuntank* 'he swallows it'; *tešintank* 'he speaks of it'.

(b) 'hear' (TA -*ntaw*): *no·ntank* 'he hears it'.

(c) TI -*nt* is presumably matched by TA -*n* or -*N* in *wi·ntemawa·t* 'he tells it to him' and *wa·wi·ntemawa·t* 'he promises it to him' (14. 36).

15. 31. *-ant* 'by mouth', also general transitive (TA *-am* with TI *-t* added without connective): *ki·škentank* 'he bites it through'; *kuta·- kumantank* 'he tries to eat it'; *to·kkuntamuwa·t* 'he (fish) nibbles at the bait for him' (14. 36); *wa·pentank* 'he sees it'.

15. 32. *-a·pant* 'see' (TA *-a·pam* with TI *-t* added without connective), deverbal from *wa·pant-* (15. 31): *ena·pentam* 'he has such a vision'; *menwa·pentam* 'he sees a good vision'; *nentawa·pentank* 'he looks for it'.

Preceding *t* is replaced by *s* (3. 24): *kusa·pentam* 'he uses the conjuror's tent', root *kot-* 'try'.

15. 33. *-ma·nt* 'smell' (TA *-ma·m* with TI final *-t* added without connective): *pi·cema·ntank* 'he gets the smell of it'.

15. 34. *-ana·nt* 'fasting': *usa·mena·ntam* 'he overfasts'.

15. 35. *-e·nt* 'think' (TA *-e·nim* with TI *-t* without connective, and haplology, 3. 53), very widely used, often with formal object: *ekate·ntam* 'he is ashamed'; *ene·ntam* 'he thinks so'; *kekke·ntank* 'he knows it'; *tepe·ntank* 'he owns it'.

15. 36. 'smoke, mist, light', prefinal *-ne·* with TI final *-nt: pekkwe·- ne·ncekan* 'smudge bucket' and *wa·ssa·kkune·ncekan* 'lamp' (11. 27).

15. 37. *-ane·nt* 'in mouth' (TA presumably *-ane·m*), prefinal *-ane·* with TI final *-nt: te·pene·ntank* 'he has enough of it in his mouth'.

15. 38. *-o·nt* 'carry on back' (TA *-o·m* with TI final *-t* without connective): *pemo·ntank* 'he carries it along on his back'.

15. 39. *-ikkot* 'carve, whittle' (TA *-ikkoN*), prefinal *-ikkw* with TI final *-it: ki·škekkotank* 'he whittles it through'; *pi·wekkotema·kenan* pl. 'shavings' (11. 28).

15. 40. *-o·t*, added to a TA stem; see 11. 31.

15. 41. *-iško·t* 'cause to move' (TA presumably *-iško·N*), complex of TA *-iškaw* and TI *-it* with the contraction of 3. 45: *kessa·pi·ško·cekan* 'sinker on fishing line' (11. 27).

15. 42. *-amo·t* (TA *-amo·N*), complex of TA *-amaw* and TI *-it*, with the contraction of 3. 45; added to a TI stem: *kuntamo·ceke·* 'he fishes with hook and line' (12. 16).

15. 43. *-tt* (TA *-SS*): *kott-* 'fear' (12. 83).

15. 44. *-itt* 'hear' (TA *-ittaw*): *nessituttank* 'he understands it'; *pekakkettank* 'he hears it distinctly'; *te·pettank* 'he gets the sound of it'; *te·pwe·ttank* 'he believes it'.

PSEUDO-TRANSITIVES

15. 45. *-i·: na·tit* 'he fetches it' (TA *na·N-*); *kemo·tit* 'he steals it' (12. 65).

15. 46. *-yi·: mi·cit* 'he eats it' (TA *amw-*); *ekwit* 'he wears it' (12.94).

15. 47. *-to·* (TA *-N*). (a) From AI stems, preceding *e·* replaced by *a* (3. 17): *nekka·pa·weto·t* 'he melts it'; *nenka·pa·weto·t* 'he wets it'; *nessa·pa·weto·t* 'he wets it'; *pi·ntekato·t* 'he brings it inside'; *pi·cene·sseto·t* 'he breathes it in'.

(b) Primary: *eko·to·t* 'he hangs it up'; *kekkito·t* 'he hides it'; *ma·ci·to·t* 'he takes it away with him'; *pi·to·t* 'he brings it'.

15. 48. *-ato·* (TA presumably *-aN*): *kišpenato·t* 'he buys it'.

15. 49. *-ccito·* 'snag' (TA presumably *-ccim*), prefinal *-tt* with pseudo-TI final *-tto·: ki·ška·kkuccito·t* 'he tears it on a snag'.

15. 50. *-pito·* 'pull' (TA *-piN*), prefinal *-p* with pseudo-TI final *-to·;* widely used, e.g., *keši·pepito·t* 'he scratches it'; *pa·ssepito·t* 'he smashes it in handling'.

Added to the root *iN-* without connective: *eppito·t* 'he pulls, handles it that way', beside *ešipeto·t* 'he pulls it in that direction'.

-ipito·: tekkopeto·t 'he ties it fast'.

15. 51. *-ssito·* 'lay, throw' (TA *-ššim*), prefinal *-SS* with pseudo-TI final *-to·;* widely used, e.g., *ešisseto·t* 'he places it so'; *kwe·kkussito·t* 'he turns it as it lies'; *pi·kussito·t* 'he brings it down so as to break it'.

15. 52. *-wito·* 'convey' (TA *-wiN*), prefinal *-w* with pseudo-TI final *-to·: ešiweto·t* 'he takes it thither'; *ki·we·weto·t* 'he takes it home'.

15. 53. *-po·to·* 'grind, file, handle violently' (TA presumably *-po·N*), prefinal *-po·* with pseudo-TI final *-to·: esipo·to·t* 'he sharpens it'; *ki·nepo·to·t* 'he sharpens it'; *ki·škepo·to·t* 'he saws it through'; *nessaškupo·ceke·* 'he pulls up weeds' (12. 16).

15. 54. *-tto·*. (a) 'cause', added to AI stems (TA -ʔ); *ma·ci·ketto·t* 'he makes it grow'; *pa·pi·tto·t* 'he waits for it'; etc.

Added to an II stem: *mecca·tto·t* 'he makes it big'.

Primary, in many forms: *a·pecitto·t* 'he uses it'; *ešitto·t* 'he makes it so'; *keškitto·t* 'he controls it, he can do it'; *ušitto·t* 'he arranges it, makes it'; etc.

(b) Matched by TA *-SS: etto·t* 'he places it'; *nettama·ke·* 'he kills things for people' (12 17; 14. 36).

15. 55. *-aʔatto·* 'track' (TA *-aʔaN*): *ma·teʔatto·t* 'he sets out to follow the trail of it'; *na·keʔatto·t* 'he follows the trail of it'.

15. 56. *-e·tto·: wa·sse·ccekan* 'window' (11. 27).

15. 57. *-a·pacitto·* 'use' (TA presumably *-a·paciʔ*), deverbal medial *-a·pat* (cf. the stem *a·pacitto·-*, 15. 54) plus pseudo-TI final *-tto·: ena·pecitto·t* 'he uses it thus'; *menwa·pecitto·t* 'he has good use of it'.

CHAPTER 16

PARTICLE FINALS

16. 1. For the order of presentation in this chapter, see 11. 1.

Many particles consist simply of a root; we set up a particle final of the form zero: e.g., in *a·petta* 'half, halfway, at the middle', from the root *a·pittaw-*: likewise in *usa·m* 'too much', *pe·šik* 'one', *we·wi·p* 'quickly'.

If the root ends in *t*, mutation takes place: *eno·c* 'variously'; *keki·pa·c* 'foolishly'.

Initial change appears in *e·nekokk* 'with all one's might'; initial change twice over appears in *ne·yi·š* 'both' beside *ni·š* 'two'.

The final consonant of the root is dropped in some particles that serve as preverbs: *eni* 'on the way, in the course', root *anim-*; *kekwe·* 'try to', root *kakwe·t-*; *ki·* 'completed', root *ki·š-*; *pepa·* 'about, around', root *papa·m-*; *te·* 'reaching, enough', root *te·p-*.

16. 2. *-a:* *no·nkwa* 'now, today'; with initial change, *e·ntakwa* 'it seems so'.

16. 3. *-na* 'body', medial *-naw* and particle final zero: *a·pettawena* 'round the middle'; *kekkina* 'all'; *nenkwana* 'so thus it is'; *ni·pena* 'much, many'; *ni·šena* 'two loaves'.

16. 4. *-akkana* 'road', medial with particle final *-a: eye·yi·tuwakkena* 'at both sides of the road'.

16. 5. *-tana* 'decade'; added without connective in *ni·štena* 'twenty'.

-mitana: nessimetana 'thirty'; *na·nemitena* 'fifty'; *nenkotwa·ssemitena* 'sixty'; *ni·šwa·ssemitena* 'seventy'; *neššwa·ssemitena* 'eighty'; *ša·nkessimetana* 'ninety'.

With loss of final *w: ni·metana* 'forty'.

16. 6. *-tta: uwaššetta* 'beyond'; *a·kuwi·tta* 'additional'.

16. 7. *-a·* appears in many particles, e.g. *eka·wa·* 'barely, with effort succeeding'; *eškwa·* (preverb) 'having finished, after'; *me·kwa·* 'while, during'; *nentawa·* 'necessarily, needs, had better'.

16. 8. *-ac: kenapac* 'perhaps'; *na·kac* 'later'. Added to other particles: *eškwa·c* 'last, at the end'; *me·kwa·c* 'now'.

16. 9. *-a·c: e·ka·c* 'slowly'; *una·c* 'pleasantly, with pleasure'. Compare postradical *-a·t* (19. 16).

Added to a particle: *eškwa·ya·c* 'last, at the end, late'.

16. 10. *-cc*, added to a particle: *kuma·ppi·cc* 'afterwards, finally'. *-špi·cc* 'time', added to a particle: *a·ni·špi·cc* 'when?'

16. 11. *-nc: na·winc* 'out on the open water'.

16. 12. *-e·* appears in many particles: *eppane·* 'always'; *ka·keke·* 'forever'; *me·kwe·* (exocentric prenoun) 'in the midst of, in'; *no·nte·* (preverb) 'too soon, before reaching the goal'.

16. 13. *-me·: uwašseme·* 'more'.

16. 14. *-ne·*, interrogative in pronouns: *uwe·ne·* 'who?'; *we·kune·šš* 'what?'

16. 15. *-i* is used after roots in consonant plus *w* to form particles that are used as prior members of compounds: *ekko* (preverb) 'so far, so long'; *entasso* (preverb) 'so many times'; *meno* (preverb, prenoun, preparticle) 'good, well'; *nento* (preverb) 'seek to'; *tesso* (exocentric prenoun) 'so many'. With initial change: *e·ntesso* 'every time, every one'.

The numeral roots (in the form that ends in consonant plus *w*) take this final to form exocentric prenoun particles (otherwise these roots take *-yi*): *nenko* 'one'; *ni·šo* 'two'; *nesso* 'three'; *ni·wo* 'four'; *na·no* 'five'.

16. 16. *-yi* forms prior member particles from roots that do not end in consonant plus *w*. There are many such formations, e.g. *a·nci* (preverb) 'changing place'; *ekici* (exocentric prenoun) 'on top of'; *esa·wi* (prenoun) 'yellow, brown'; *eša·wi* (prenoun) 'yellow'; *eši* (preverb) 'thither, thus'; *teši* (preverb) 'there'; *unci* (preverb) 'thence, therefore'; *nemanci, eno·ci* (10. 13).

Here belongs the dependent prenoun *-i·ci* 'fellow'.

Some of the numeral roots, in the form with final consonant plus *w*, take this final, in contrast with *-i*, to form independent particles: *nesswi* 'three'; *nenkotwa·sswi* 'six'; *ni·šwa·sswi* 'seven'; *neššwa·sswi* 'eight'; *ša·nkesswi* 'nine'; *menta·sswi* 'ten'.

Other particles that are prior members: *a·ppeci* 'much, completely'; *a·ši* 'already'; *ma·muwi* 'among them all' (also as preverb); *nenkwaci, nenkoci* 'somewhere'; *tepi* 'right there, wherever'; *we·we·ni* 'properly; thanks'.

With initial change: *me·yeki* (prenoun) 'strange, foreign', beside *meyaki*.

16. 17. *-aya ᵖi·* 'place' forms many particles; often inflectional *-ₒink* is added: *a·pettaweya ᵖi·* 'at the middle'; *kepe·ye ᵖi·* 'for a long while'; *na·meya ᵖi·* 'underneath'.

Preceding *t* is replaced by *c* in *ekiceya ᵖi·* 'on top'.

-yi·ya ᵖi·: pi·nci·ye ᵖi· 'inside'. Added, presumably, to a noun stem: *ma·netta·nešši·ye ᵖi·* 'woolen'.

16. 18. *-appi·: a·ni·ppi·šš* 'where?'; *ke·keppi·* 'after a while'; *kuma·ppi·* 'afterwards, finally'; *ma·meppi·* 'here'.

16. 19. *-yi·: nenkwaci·, nenkoci·* 'somewhere or other, off somewhere'; *penki·* 'little, a little, few.'

16. 20. *-ya·k: me·kuya·k* 'in the woods'.

16. 21. *-ik* 'house', medial with particle final zero: *pi·ntik* 'inside, indoors'.

-ikamik appears, with initial change, in *ka·wetta·kemik* 'all round the house'.

16. 22. *-akkamik* 'place', medial with particle final zero: *enikke·kkemik* 'in this part of the land'; *na·mekkamik* 'underground'.

16. 23. *-tik*, dubitative (cf. inflectional *-ₐtik*): *i·tik* 'I wonder, perhaps'.

16. 24. *-a·ttik* 'stick', prefinal with particle final zero: *ekkita·ttik* 'on a stick, tree, branch'.

16. 25. *-a·pi·k* 'string, row', medial with particle final zero: *pe·šekwa·pi·k* 'one string or row'; *ni·šwa·pi·k* 'two strings or rows'.

16. 26. *-ipi·k* 'water', medial with particle final zero: *ci·kepi·k* 'close to the water's edge'.

16. 27. *-a·kk* 'hundred', medial *-a·kkw* with particle final zero: *nenkotwa·kk* 'one hundred'; *ni·šwa·kk* 'two hundred'; etc.

16. 28. *-nikk* 'arm', medial with particle final zero: *eye·yi·tuwinikk* 'at both arms'.

16. 29. *-a·pikk* 'dollar', medial with particle final zero, with numeral roots: *pe·šekwa·pikk* 'one dollar'; *ni·šwa·pikk* 'two dollars'; *nesswa·pikk* 'three dollars'; *ni·šwa·sswa·pikk* 'seven dollars'; *neššwa·sswa·pikk* 'eight dollars'; *ša·nkesswa·pikk* 'nine dollars'.

16. 30. *-itipikk* 'night', deverbal from *tepikk* 'night'; with contraction of *awi* to *a·*: *a·petta·tepikk* 'at midnight'.

16. 31. *-nk: teccink* 'so many times'.

16. 32. *-e·ya·nk: eškwe·ya·nk* 'at the very end'.

16. 33. *-ink* (inflectional *-₀ink*). (a) Added to *-aya ʔi·*, *-yi·ya· ʔi·*: *ekiceya· ʔi·nk* 'on top of the thing'.

(b) Otherwise, in *ekwaci·nk* 'out of doors'; *ešpimink* 'up aloft'; *nenkwatink, nenkotink* 'once, at one time'; *ni·šink* 'twice'; *nessink* 'three times'.

16. 34. *-inonk: na·nenkotenonk* 'now and then, sometimes'.

16. 35. *-am: e·škam* 'gradually, in the course of time, increasingly'; *enittam, nettam* 'first, at first'.

16. 36. *-im: no·nkom* 'now'.

16. 37. *-an: na·nun* 'five'.

16. 38. *-e·wa·n* 'set, pair', medial with particle final zero: *nenkotwe·wa·n* 'one pair'; *ni·šwe·wa·n* 'two sets, two pairs'.

16. 39. *-e·n: na·nepe·n* 'only then, too late'.

-₈e·n, dubitative, with accompanying initial change: *e·ntekwe·n* 'I wonder whether it be'.

-takwe·n: we·kutakwe·n 'whatever it be'.

16. 40. *-in: ke·ttin* 'truly, really'; *ki·špin* 'if'; *ni·win* 'four'.

16. 41. *-iškin* 'full', prefinal with particle final zero; with contraction of *awi* to *o·*: *a·petto·škin* 'half a filling'.

16. 42. *-ikon* 'day', medial with particle final zero: *ni·wukon* 'four days'; *tessokon* 'so many days'.

16. 43. -*še·p* 'morning', medial with particle final zero: *kekiše·p* 'in the morning'.

16. 44. -*šš* added to predicative particles, especially for question: *a·ni·ppi·šš* 'where?'; *a·ni·šš* 'how?'; *a·ppi·šš* 'where?'; *mi·šš* 'then it is, that it is'; *uwe·ne·šš* 'who?'; *we·kune·šš* 'what?'

16. 45. -*aka·t* 'leg', medial with particle final zero: *eye·yi·tuwaka·t* 'on both legs'.

16. 46. -*e·tt: ke·ke·tt* 'truly, surely'.

16. 47. -*e·w*, with final *w* kept (3. 32): *tepe·w* 'along the bank'.

16. 48. -*išše·ny*, diminutive (cf. the noun final, 11. 106); added to a particle: *penki·šše˜* 'a little bit'.

16. 49. -*yi·ye·ny* (cf. noun final -*e·ny*, 11. 104); added to a particle: *unci·ye˜* 'near by, next in order'.

CHAPTER 17

MEDIAL SUFFIXES

The medial suffixes are here listed alphabetically, except that initial *i* is ignored. A colon following an entry, followed by another suffix, is a cross reference to the latter. Where a medial suffix serves as a prefinal, reference is made to 11-16.

We do not include the medials which appear only in dependent nouns of relationship, e.g., -*kw* in *nenkwiss* 'my son'.

-*aka·t*: -*ka·t*.

-*aki·sissw* 'sun', deverbal from the noun *ki·sissw*-; with AI final -*e·* 12. 62.

-*akkamik* 'place': *tenakkemikesi* 'he is busy there, plays there'; *wi·nekkamekisi* 'he makes a mess'; *nempi·wekkameka·* 'it is wet ground'; *pi·nekkameka·mekat* 'it is a clean place'; *we·pekkamekat* 'the doings begin'. Added to a noun stem: *ne·kuwakkemika·* 'it is a sandy place'. With noun final -*w* 11. 90; with particle final zero 16. 22.

-*akkan* 'road', deverbal from the noun *mi·kkan*; with AI final -*a* 16. 4.

-*akkikkw* 'kettle', deverbal from the noun *akkikkw*-; with AI final -*e·* 12. 57.

-*akki·*: -*a·kky*.

-*akkw* 'sky': *a·nekkwat* 'cloud'; *mešakkwat* 'it is clear sky'. With II final -*e·* 13. 26; 'thatch', with AI final -*e·* 12. 53.

-*akky*: -*a·kky*.

-*anake·kkw* 'bark', deverbal from the noun *enake·kk*: *peššakenake·kkuwa·t* 'he peels bark from him'. With AI final -*e·* 12. 56.

-*anakk* 'tree': *kepanekka'eke·* 'he stops up a hole in a tree'; *ki··škenakketo͞* 'stump of a tree'; *pekwanekka'eke·* 'he chops a hole in a tree'; *pi·ntenakkesse·* 'he falls into a hollow tree'; *wi·mpenakkesi* AN 'hollow tree'; *wi·mpenakketo͞* 'hollow stump'. With noun final -*w* 11. 95.

-*anikkwe·*: -*kkwe·*.

-*anše·*(?): *peššanše·'ank*, *pepaššenše·'ank* 'he whips it'.

8

-aškw 'grass', deverbal from the root *maškw-*: *nessaškupo·ceke·* 'he pulls up weeds'; *wa·peškokki·* 'marsh'. With noun final zero 11. 99. As postradical in the root *asa·waškw-*. — *-aškwe·: ki·weškwe·pi·* 'he is drunk'.

-at 'belly': *enatenank* 'he shapes it so'; *unatenank* 'he kneads it'. With noun final zero 11. 68. — *-ate·: menkate·ya·* 'it is wide'; *pi·meskote·ssĩ* 'snail'; *uta·ppeškate·peniko* 'he has cramps'. AI final 12. 33. — *-te·: eka·ccete·ya·* 'it is narrow'. II final 13. 14.

-ata·kke·: -a·kky.

-a·kam: -kam.

-a·kami·nkw: -yi·nkw.

-a·kkokan: -kan.

-a·kkome· 'louse'(?): *untama·kkume·ššĩ* 'monkey'.

-a·kkw 'wood, solid': *a·swa·kkussin* 'it lies across a solid'; *a·swa·kkuššin* 'he lies across a solid'; *a·swa·kkussito·t* 'he leans it on a solid'; *kinwa·kkusi* 'he (tree) is a tall stick'; *nessa·kkunank* 'he opens it (door) as a solid thing'; etc. Noun final 11. 96; particle final 16. 27; with AI final *-e·* 12. 54. As premedial: see *-kan* below.

-a·kky 'land', deverbal from the noun *akky-*: *ekkita·kki* 'on the hill'; added to a noun stem in *mettikwa·kki·ns* 'plot of wooded ground'. — *-ata·kke·: a·pettaweta·kke·ya·mekat* 'it is halfway up the slope'. — *-akky* with AI final *-e·* 12. 97. — *-a·kki·, -akki·* as noun final 11. 13.

-a·kom(?): *kuta·kumantank* 'he tries eating it'.

-a·konak 'snow', deverbal from the noun *eko·n* AN: *eppi·tta·kunaka·* 'the snow is so deep'; *ešpa·kunaka·* 'there is deep snow'; *no·kka·kunaka·* 'there is soft snow'.

-a·nakito·n: -to·n.

-a·nikkw: -kkw.

-a·nim 'wind': *pekanta·nemat* 'the wind strikes'; *unta·nemat* 'the wind blows from that direction'.

-a·nt 'wood'; with AI final *-awe·* 12. 42; with II final *-e·* 13. 19. — *-a·nte·:* with noun final *-m* 11. 24. — *-wa·nt:* with II final *-e·* 13. 19.

-a·pat 'use', deverbal from the root *a·pat-*: *ena·pete·ntam* 'he thus derives benefit'. With pseudo-TI final *-tto·* 15. 57.

-a·pa·w: -ipy.

-a·pikk 'stone, metal': a·pa·pekkaʔekan 'key'; keša·pekkisank 'he heats it as stone or metal'; keša·pekkite· 'it is heated stone or metal'; etc. With noun final -w 11. 98; with particle final zero 16. 29. — -pikk: with noun final -w 11. 98.

-a·pit 'tooth'; with AI final -e· 12. 35. — -i·pit: with noun final zero 11. 70.

-a·po·: -ipy.

-a·py 'string, elongated thing'; with noun final zero 11. 115; with AI final -e· 12. 102; with II final -e· 13. 33. — -e·ya·py: with noun final zero 11. 115. — -a·pi·: kessa·pi·ško·cekan 'sinker on fishing line'; peswa·pi·sseto·t 'he places it winding'. — -a·pi·k: ekkwa·pi·kat 'it is so long a string'; kenwa·pi·kesi 'he (snake) is a long string'; etc. With particle final zero 16. 25.

-a·py 'liquid': -ipy.

-a·sse·(?): meskwa·sse·ccekan 'red sash'.

-a·te·(?): meskwa·te·ssĩ 'small turtle'.

-a·ttatakw(?): pi·ma·ttetakunank 'he rolls it up in his hand'.

-a·wank 'ashes, dust': ena·wenkaʔank 'he moves, shapes it so, as or in dust or ashes'; pa·šketta·wenka· 'there is loose dust, it is dusty'.

-a·wikan 'backbone': with premedial -tattak in utatteka·wekan 'his backbone'.

-ca·N 'nose'; with noun final zero and mutation 11. 65; with AI final -e· 12. 24.

-ci· 'round small thing, belly': kucici·nank 'he feels it with his hand'; pa·škeci·ssin 'it falls and bursts'; etc. With noun final zero 11. 12. — -ici·: with contraction of awi to o· (3. 45) in a·petto·ci·na·t 'he holds him round the middle'.

-ci·nkwan 'thigh': with noun final zero 11. 38.

-e·k: -yi·k.

-e·naniw 'tongue': with noun final zero 11. 80.

-e·nkway 'face': with noun final zero 11. 102.

-e·škan 'horn': with noun final zero 11. 32.

-e·wa·n 'set, pair': with particle final zero 16. 38. — -e·wa·nak: nišwe·wa·nekisuwak 'they are in two families'.

-e·ya·py: -a·py.

-i·n 'hair of head': with noun final *-ississ* 11. 63.

-i·nintip: -intip.

-i·ntim 'body of water': *kenwi·ntema·mekat* 'it is deep water'; *tekkwi·ntema·mekat* 'it is shallow water'.

i·pit: -a·pit.

-i·yaw 'body': with noun final zero 11. 76.

-ik 'house': with particle final zero 16. 21; with AI final *-e·* 12. 18. — *-k:* with AI final *-e·* 12. 18. — *-wik:* with AI final *-e·* 12. 18. — *-ikamik:* with noun final *-w* 11. 89; with particle final zero 16. 21. — *-wikamik, -yi·wikamik:* with noun final *-w* 11. 89.

-kakkwan 'shin': with noun final zero 11. 36.

-kam 'liquid, water'; *sesswe·kemiššin* 'he leaps splashing'. With II final *-a·* 13. 7; with II final *-i* 13. 29. — *-a·kam: menwa·kemippetank* 'he likes the taste of it as liquid'; *pi·tte·wa·kemisse·* 'it is foaming liquid'. With II final *-i* 13. 29.

-ikamik: -ik.

-kan 'bone': with medial *-a·kkw* as premedial (thus *-a·kkokan*) and AI final *-e·* 12. 23.

-kašy 'claw, hoof, nail': with noun (or AI) final *-e·* 11. 15. — *-škanšy:* with noun final zero 11. 118.

-ka·t 'leg': with noun final zero 11. 69; with AI final *-e·* 12. 34. — *-aka·t:* with particle final zero 16. 45. — *-ka·te·: po·kkuka·te·peniteso* 'he breaks his leg'; *sekika·te·ppena·t* 'he ties him fast by the leg'; *se·ka·te·ššin* 'he lies with leg uplifted'.

-ka·ttikw 'forehead': with noun final zero 11. 94.

-kitikw 'knee': with noun final zero 11. 92.

-ikki· 'face': *ecitekki·sse·* 'he falls on his face'; *ecitekki·ššin* 'he lies face down'. With AI final zero 12. 96.

-kki·kim 'nose': with AI final *-e·* 12. 22.

-kkomy 'ice', deverbal from the noun *mikkomy-:* with AI final *-e·* 12. 101.

-ikkonay 'garment': with AI final *-e·* 12. 64. — *-ikkonaye·: ki·ssekkoneye·pena·t* 'he pulls off his clothes'.

-kkw 'head': with AI final *-e·* 12. 52. — *-kkwe·: ca·nka·kkwe·ššin* 'he lies with head uplifted'; *eššawe·kkwe·ššin* 'he lies with head to one side'; *nessikkwe·ʔo* 'he combs his hair'; *nuwakekkwe·ššin* 'he lies with lowered head.' — *-a·nikkw* 'hair of head': with AI final *-e·* 12. 58.

-kkwe· 'woman', deverbal from the noun *ikkwew-·* with noun final zero 11. 10. — *-anikkwe·:* with noun final zero 11. 10.

-ikon 'day': with particle final zero 16. 42. — *-ikonak: nessokunakat* 'it is three days'; *ni·šukonekat* 'it is two days'.

-kw 'beak, point': *ka·ki·nekoya·* 'it is pointed at both ends'; *ki·neko-keʔank* 'he chops it to a point'.

-kwan 'liver': with noun final zero 11. 34.

-kwe· 'neck': *a·kukwe·na·t* 'he hugs him'; *na·pekwa·ppena·t* 'he ropes him round the neck'; *na·pekwe·wa·t* 'he gets something round his neck'. — *-kwiyaw:* with AI final *-e·* (12. 44).

-makoma· 'shoulder'(?): *a·semakuma·pesowenak* AN pl. 'suspenders'.

-ma·naw 'cheek': with noun final zero 11. 75.

-imin 'berry, grain, bead', deverbal from the noun *mi·n* 'blueberry': with noun final zero 11. 50. — *-yi·min:* with noun final zero 11. 50. — *-iminak: eša·weškomenakat* 'green head of a plant'; *meškaweminekisi* AN 'hard corn'.

-mot, -mo·t 'bag': with noun final zero 11. 72.

-mo·w 'dung': with noun final zero 11. 100; with AI final *-e·* 12. 60.

-naw 'body': with noun (or AI) final *-e·* 11. 9; with particle final zero 16. 3.

-na·n 'calf of leg': with noun final zero 11. 45.

-na·pe· 'man': with noun final zero 11. 5.

-ne· 'mist, smoke, light': *pekkwe·ne·ya·* 'there is a fog'; *pi·cene·sseto·t* 'he places it to be wafted hither'; *pi·cene·ssin* 'it is wafted hither'. With TI final *-nt* 15. 36.

-nikk 'arm': with noun final zero 11. 20; with particle final zero 16. 28; with AI final *-a·* 12. 7. — *-nikka·: mencinekka·wan* AN 'mitten'. — *-nikke·: keškinekke·pesowin* 'arm garter'. — *-inikke·: tekkonekke·ško·-so* 'he is caught by his arm'.

-nincy 'hand, finger': with noun final zero 11. 103; with AI final *-e·* 12. 99. — *-ninci·:* *sa·keninci·ni* 'he sticks out his hand'; *tepinenci·pesowin* 'ring for the finger'; *wi·neninci·ššin* 'he gets his hands dirty'.

-ninkwi· 'wing': *mentwe·nenkwi·ššin* 'he moves with noise of wings'; *me·mettikuninkwi·ššē* 'swallow'; *uninkwi·ʾekanan* AN 'his wing, his wings'.

-intip 'head': with AI final *-e·* 12. 27. — *-intipe·:* *a·sentipe·ppeso* 'he carries his load by a strap around his head'; *pa·kentipe·ʾekan* 'war club'; *pa·kentipe·wa·t* 'he knocks him on the head'. — *-ntipe·: pi·centipe·wa·t* 'he smashes his head'. — *-i·nintip* 'brain': with noun final zero 11. 57.

-pak 'leaf': *nesso·pekat* 'it has three leaves'.

-pikk: -a·pikk.

-pikkwan 'back': with noun final zero 11. 37; with AI final zero 12. 110.

-ipi·: -ipy.

-pi· 'pen, brush'(?): *ušipi·ʾank* 'he pictures, draws, writes it'; *pe·šeko·pi·ʾekan* 'ace'; etc.

-pwa·m 'back of thigh': with noun final zero 11. 23.

-ipy 'liquid': with noun final zero 11. 116; with AI final *-e·* 12. 103. — *-ipi·:* *ka·škepa·cekan* 'razor'; *pekkopi·sse·* 'he falls into the water'; *pekkopi·ta·pa·na·t* 'he pulls him into the water'; *pekkwe·pi·kemi* 'it is troubled water'. — *-ipi·k:* *ekwa·pi·kena·t* 'he takes him out of the water'; *kesi·pi·kenank* 'he washes it'; *sesswe·pi·keʾantuwa·t* 'he sprinkles him with water'. As postradical in the root *kisi·pi·k-*. With particle final zero 16. 26. — *-a·py:* with II final *-e·* 13. 33. — *-a·pa·w:* with AI final *-e·* 12. 46. — *-a·po·, -wa·po·, -iwa·po·:* with noun final zero 11. 55.

-sit 'foot': with noun final zero 11. 71; with AI final *-e·* 12. 36. — *-site·:* *kesi·sete·ššemowin* 'door-mat'; *sa·kesite·ššin* 'he lies with a foot protruding'; *wi·nesite·ššin* 'he gets his feet dirty'.

-so·w 'quadruped's tail': with noun final *-a·nakw* 11. 84.

-ssak 'piece of wood, board', deverbal from *messan* 'firewood' with postmedial *-ak:* *kesi·pi·kessakenike·* 'he washes woodwork'. With noun final *-w* 11. 85.

-sse· 'bird': with noun final zero 11. 6.

-še· 'body': ci·cci·kkeše·ʔank 'he pokes it (the fire)'; pe·nkuše·wa·t 'he dries him'; pe·nkuše·ʔo 'he dries himself'. With noun final zero 11. 7.

-še·p 'morning'; with particle final zero 16. 43. — -še·pa·wak: kekiše·pa·wekat 'it is morning'.

-šikwan 'fish tail': with noun final zero 11. 35.

-škanšy: -kašy.

-ški·nšikw 'eye': with noun final zero 11. 91; with AI final -e· 12. 51.

-šše· 'skin': with AI final zero 12. 32.

-išše· 'ear': na·pešše·pesowin 'ear ring'. With AI final zero 12. 32.

-štikwa·n 'head': with noun final zero 11. 46.

-t: -at.

-tapaʔikane· 'hour, clock', deverbal from a noun tapaʔikan- (tepaʔ-eka·ns 'hour'): menta·ssutapeʔikene·t 'it is ten o'clock'; tessotepaʔekane·t 'it is so-many o'clock'.

-tattak 'backbone'(?): utatteka·kumin AN 'blackberry' 11. 86. As premedial: see -a·wikan.

-ta·ss 'legging, stocking': with noun final zero 11. 61. — -mita·ss: with noun final zero 11. 61. — -ta·sse·: keškita·sse·pesowin 'garter'.

-te·: -at.

-te·ʔ 'heart': po·kkete·ʔemin 'lemon'. With noun final zero 11. 11.

-iti· 'rump, tail': with noun final zero 11. 17. — -itiye·: eye·kkutiye·pi 'his buttocks are tired from sitting'; pa·šketiya·ma·t 'he bursts him at the rump'.

-to·n 'mouth': with noun final zero 11. 54. — -a·nakito·n: with AI final zero 12. 114. — -to·ne·: pekkiketo·ne·wa·t 'he hits him on the mouth'.

-to·skwan 'elbow': with noun final zero 11. 39.

-ttak(?): pi·mettakenike· 'he rolls a cigarette'.

-ttikwe· 'river': ešittekwe·ya· 'it flows in that direction'; nekkwe·tte-kwe·ya·no·n 'they come together as streams'.

-tto·k 'ear': with AI final -e· 12. 21. — -tto·wak: with noun final zero 11. 18.

-wa·nte·: -a·nt.

-wa·po·: ipy.

-we· 'noise': kesi·pwe·ška· 'he moves with scraping noise'. Cf. the root mantwe·-. With AI final zero 12. 38. — -we·we·: kesi·pwe·we·ška· 'he moves with repeated scraping noise'; umpi·kwe·we·ššema·t 'he lifts him (wing) with noise'.

-wik, -wikamik: -ik.

-yi·k 'cloth': a·pi·kenank 'he unwraps it'; eka·cci·kat 'it is a small piece of cloth'; ke·sepi·kenank 'he folds it up'; peššaki·kepina·t 'he skins him'. With noun final zero 11. 19. — -e·k: nempi·we·kat 'it is wet cloth'.

-yi·min: -imin.

-yi·nkw 'face, eye': with AI final -e· 12. 59. — -yi·nkwe·: ka·ci·nkwe·ni 'he makes an ugly face'; po·ci·nkwe·ʔekan 'Indian bread'; šo·mi·nkwe·ni 'he smiles'. — -a·kami·nkw 'pupil of the eye' (medial -a·kam as premedial): with AI final -e· 12. 59.

-yi·w 'flesh, muscle, strength': with AI final -e· 12. 49; with AI final -i· 12. 108.

-yi·wikamik: -ik.

CHAPTER 18

ACCRETIONS OF SUFFIXES

18. 1. In this chapter we list the elements which can be analyzed out of the finals of Chapters 11-16 and out of the medials of Chapter 17, as postmedials, premedials, and prefinals.

POSTMEDIAL ELEMENTS

18. 2. The following elements, appearing at the end of medials listed in Chapter 17, may, in one way or another, be analyzed out as postmedials. After each postmedial we list the medials in which it occurs:

-ak: -a·konak, -a·pi·k, -e·wa·nak, -ikonak, -iminak, -ipi·k, -še·pa·wak.
-amik: -ikamik, -wikamik, -yi·wikamik; cf. *-akkamik.*
-a·: -nikka·.
-a·w: -a·pa·w, -še·pa·wak.
-e·: -aškwe·, -ata·kke·, -ate·, -a·nte·, -a·pi·, -a·pi·k, -ka·te·, -ikkonaye·, -kwe·, -nikke·, -ninci·, -ntipe·, -ipi·, -ipi·k, -site·, -tapaʔikane·, -ta·sse·, -to·ne·, -yi·nkwe·; with preceding *i·* replaced by *iy: -itiye·.*
-o·: -a·po·.
-iyaw: -kwiyaw.

SIGNIFICANT PREFINALS

18. 3. Even though a final may have a fairly definite meaning, we analyze it into prefinal plus smaller final only in case its structure is quite clear. Thus such finals as AI *-tta·* 'move, act', or TA *-aʔw*, TI *-aʔ* 'by tool', are here viewed as unanalyzable.

We list alphabetically below the prefinal elements which seem to analyze out fairly well and to bear fairly definite meanings. After each are given the finals in which it occurs. The abbreviations "N" and "P" stand respectively for noun final and particle final. When the smaller final is zero, so that the larger one is homonymous with the prefinal, we do not repeat the shape. Cross references are made in the style of Chapter 17: a colon after an entry, followed simply by the entry to which reference is made.

-*a* 'place, put', deverbal from the root *a-:* II -*atte·* 13. 23.

-*acinaw*(?): AI -*acinawe·* 12. 41.

-*aʔ* 'flood': II -*aʔan* 13. 36.

-*aʔa* 'track': TA -*aʔaN* 14. 18, pseudo-TI -*aʔatto·* 15. 55.

-*ak* 'count', deverbal from the root *ak-:* II -*akinte·* 13. 20; 'throw', deverbal from the root *pak-:* TI -*akit* 15. 29.

-*akkoni·* 'climb': AI -*akkoni·si·* 12. 106.

-*akkošiw* 'paddle': AI -*akkošiwe·* 12. 48.

-*akkwi·* 'shoot': AI 12. 107.

-*ako·* 'hang', deverbal from the root *ako·-:* AI -*ako·cin* 12. 112.

-*ame·* 'fish', deverbal from the noun *name·-:* N -*ame·kw* 11. 88.

-*amo* 'path, streak': II 13. 43.

-*an* 'decay': II -*anat* 13. 46.

-*ana·* 'fast': TI -*ana·nt* 15. 34; 'baked thing': N 11. 3.

-*ane·* 'in mouth': TI -*ane·nt* 15. 37; 'burn': II 13. 11.

-*anokki·*: -*nokki·*.

-*ano·* 'smoke': AI -*ano·so* 12. 141.

-*ant*(?): TA -*antaw* 14. 40, TI -*antaʔ* 15. 7

-*ap* 'sit, be in place', deverbal from the root *ap-:* AI -*api* 12. 74.

-*app* 'tie': TA -*appiN* 14. 26, TI -*appin* 15. 16. — *ipp:* AI -*ippiso* 12. 137.

-*at, -t* 'color', deverbal from the root *at-:* TI -*atiss, -tiss* 15. 21.

-*at* 'cold': AI -*aci* 12. 66, II -*atin* 13. 42, TA -*acim* 14. 11; 'stick': TI -*ataʔ* 15. 6.

-*awi·nšy* 'plant': N 11. 119.

-*ayaʔi·, -yi·yaʔi·* 'thing, place': P 16. 17.

-*aya·n, -iwiya·n, -o·wiyan* 'garment': N 11. 49.

-*a·* 'shine': AI -*a·sso* 12. 143, II -*a·tte·* 13. 25, TI -*a·ss* 15. 19.

-*a·kka* 'burn': TI -*a·kkas* 15. 18.

-*a·nakkwat* 'cloud', deverbal from II *a·nakkwat-:* N -*a·nakkwatw* 11. 101, II 13. 54.

-*a·nke·*(?): N 11. 4.

-a·p 'see', deverbal from the root wa·p-: AI -a·pi 12. 75, TA -a·pam 14. 8, TA -a·pant 15. 32.

-a·pa 'smoke': II -a·patte· 13. 24.

-a·pon 'move': AI -a·pono 12. 128.

-a·pp 'laugh', deverbal from the root pa·pp-: AI -a·ppi 12. 76.

-a·ppin 'die': AI -a·ppine· 12. 26.

-a·sipi·(?): AI 12. 104.

-a·šk: -išk.

-a·t 'narrate': AI -a·cimo 12. 123, TA -a·cim 14. 12, TI -a·cit 15. 28.

-a·tak 'swim': AI -a·taka· 12. 5.

-a·tti?(?): AI -a·tti?e· 12. 15.

-a·ttikw 'stick': N 11. 93, P -a·ttik 16. 24. — -e·ya·ttikw: N 11. 93.

-a·wass 'child': AI -a·wasso 12. 142.

-ciw 'flow': II -ciwan 13. 38.

-e·n 'think': TA -e·nim 14. 13, TI -e·nt 15. 35.

-e·ya·ttikw: -a·ttikw.

-k 'grow': AI -ki 12. 69, II -kin 13. 40; 'axe': TA -ka?w 14. 44, TI -ka? 15. 4.

-ka· 'dance': AI 12. 4; 'leak': AI 12. 4, II 15. 4.

-ka·kw 'porcupine', deverbal from the noun ka·kw-: N 11. 87.

-ka·paw 'stand': AI -ka·pawi 12. 91.

-kit 'speak': AI -kito 12. 146.

-kiwa·m 'house', deverbal from the noun wi·kuwa·m: N 11. 22.

-ikk 'move': AI -ikka· 12. 6, II -ikka· 13. 4, TA -ikkaw 14. 32, TI 15. 10. — -kk: AI -kkawe· 12. 40, II -kka· 13. 3, TA -kkaN 14. 19, -kkaw 14. 33. — -o·kk: TA -o·kkaw 14. 34. — -yi·kk: II -yi·kka· 13. 4, TI 15. 11.

-kkina·kkw 'turtle': N 11. 97.

-kkiw 'man', deverbal from the root akkiw-: N -kkiwe·ny 11. 108, -kkiwe·nsi·ny 11. 111.

-kki· 'grow': II 13. 32.

-ikkw 'carve': N -ikkoma·n 11. 44, TA -ikkoN 14. 28, TI -ikkot 15. 39.

-*kkwe·* 'woman', deverbal from the noun *ikkwe·w-:* N 11. 10.

-*kopy* 'bark', deverbal from a noun *wi·kopy-:* N 11. 117.

-*kwa·* 'sew': AI -*kwa·sso* 12. 144.

-*makkakki·* 'frog': N 11. 14.

-*ma·* 'smell': AI -*ma·kosi* 12. 80, II -*ma·kwat* 13. 48, TA -*ma·m* 14. 9, TI -*ma·nt* 15. 33.

-*mi·šŠy* 'tree': N 11. 120.

-*na, -ina* 'kill': TA -*naN, -inaN* 14. 20.

-*na·kan* 'dish', deverbal from the noun *una·kan:* N 11. 29.

-*na·N* 'chase': TA -*na·šikkaw* 14. 33, *na·ši ʔw* 14. 47.

-*na·pa·kw* 'thirst': AI -*na·pa·kwe·* 12. 50.

-*na·pe·* 'man': N 11. 5.

-*nc* 'water'(?): P 16. 11.

-*ine·*(?): II 13. 12.

-*ne·* 'pursue': TA -*ne· ʔw* 14. 46.

-*ne·ss* 'breathe', deverbal from the root *ne·ss-:* AI -*ne·sse·* 12. 29.

-*nika·* 'carry on shoulder': TI -*nika·t* 15. 24.

-*nikka·* 'name': AI -*nikka·so* 12. 134, II -*nikka·te·* 13. 16, TA -*nikka·N* 14. 21, TI -*nikka·t* 15. 25.

-*niniw, -wininiw* 'man', deverbal from the noun *ininiw-:* N 11. 81.

-*ni·k* 'be born', deverbal from the root *ni·k-:* AI -*ni·ki* 12. 69.

-*inkw* 'sleep': AI -*inkwa·m* 12. 109. — -*nkw:* AI -*nkwašši* 12. 86.

-*nokki·, -anokki·* 'work', deverbal from AI *anokki·-:* AI 12. 100.

-*no·* 'point out': TI -*no· ʔ* 15. 8.

-*oss* 'walk': AI -*osse·* 12. 30.

-*o·* 'carry on back': AI -*o·mo* 12. 126, TA -*o·m* 14. 15, TI -*o·nt* 15. 38.

-*o·kk: -ikk.*

-*o·kkam*(?): II -*o·kkami* 13. 30.

-*o·ppw: -pw.*

-*o·t* 'crawl': AI -*o·te·* 12. 37.

-*o·wiya·n: -aya·n.*

-p, -ip 'pull, speed': AI -piso 12. 136, II -pite· 13. 18, TA -piN, -ipiN 14. 24, pseudo-TI -pito·, -ipito· 15. 50.

-pa 'run': AI -patto· 12. 149, TA -paʾ 14. 4.

-piniw 'owl': N -piniwe·ny 11. 109.

-piši· 'lynx', deverbal from the noun pišiw-: N 11. 16.

-po· 'grind': II -po·te· 13. 21, pseudo-TI -po·to· 15. 53.

-ipp: -app.

-ppw: -pw.

-pw 'by mouth': AI -po 12. 129, II -pokwat 13. 52. — -ppw: AI -ppwa· 12. 11. — -ippw: AI -ippokosi 12. 84, II -ippokwat 13. 53. — -o·ppw: AI -o·ppo 12. 130.

-SS 'fall, lie, speed': AI -sse· 12. 28, -ššin 12. 113, -ššimo 12. 124, II -sse· 13. 13, -ssin 13. 41, TA -ššim 14. 14, pseudo-TI -ssito· 15. 51. — -iSS: AI -iššin 12. 113.

-sse· 'bird': N 11. 6.

-išk 'move': AI -iška· 12. 8, II -iška· 13. 6, TA -iškaw 14. 35, TI 15. 12. — -a·šk: II -a·ška· 13. 5.

-iškin 'full': AI -iškine· 12. 25, P 16. 41.

-t 'hang, snag': AI -cin 12. 111. — -tt: pseudo-TI -ccito· 15. 49.

-t 'color': -at.

-tana, -mitana 'decade': P 16. 5.

-ta·pa· 'pull', deverbal from the root ota·pa·-: TA -ta·pa·N 14. 22, N -ta·pa·n 11. 48.

-te·pw(?): AI -te·pwe· 12. 61.

-itipikk 'night', deverbal from the root tipikk-: P 16. 30.

-tt 'hang, snag': -t.

-w 'lead, take': TA -wiN 14. 27, pseudo-TI -wito· 15. 52.

-we·p 'throw', deverbal from the root we·p-: AI -we·pisi 12. 78, TA -we·paʾw 14. 45, -we·pin, -we·piN 14. 25, TI -we·paʾ 15. 5, -we·pišk 15. 13, -we·pin 15. 15.

-wininiw: -niniw.

-iwiya·n: -aya·n.

-yi·yaʾi·: -ayaʾi·.

PREMEDIAL AND FORMAL PREFINAL ELEMENTS

18. 4. Both medials and finals are in some cases enlarged by sounds added at the beginning. We list these accretions; after each item there follows a list of the medials and finals in which it appears. The abbrevations are those of 18. 3, plus "M" for medial.

-a: M -aka·t, -aki·sissw.

-am: N -ama·kan 11. 28.

-amo: N -amowin 11. 53.

-an: N -anikkwe· 11. 10.

-at: M -ata·kke·.

-a·: N -a·kan 11. 28; AI -a·kosi 12. 79; II -a·ška· 13. 5, -a·kwat 13. 47; M -a·kam, -a·kky, -a·konak, -a·pikk, -a·pit, -a·py, -a·pa·w, -a·po·.

-a·kam (medial as premedial): M -a·kami·nkw.

-a·kkw (medial as premedial): M -a·kkokan.

-a·m: AI -a·mikosi 12. 83; II -a·mikwat 13. 51.

-a·n: M -a·nikkw.

-a·nak: M -a·nakito·n.

-e·: N -e·ns 11. 58, -e·ny 11. 104, -e·ya·ttikw 11. 93; II -e·ya· 13. 9; M -e·ya·py.

-e·w: AI -e·wisi 12. 77; TA -e·wi^ꝫ 14. 5.

-i·: M -i·pit.

-i·n: M -i·nintip.

-ikw (cf. inflectional -$_1$ikw): AI -ikosi 12. 82; II -ikwat 13. 50.

-mak: II -makat 13. 45.

-mi: N -mita·ss 11. 61; P -mitana 16. 5.

-o·: N -o·wiya·n 11. 49; AI -o·ppo 12. 130; II -o·makat 13. 45; TA -o·kkaw 14. 34.

-tattak (probably medial as premedial): M̠-tattaka·wikan.

-w (especially after long vowels): N -wa·kan 11. 30, -win 11. 52, -wiss 11. 64, -wišš 11. 67, -wininiw 11. 81, -wikamikw, -yi·wikamikw 11. 89, -we·ny 11. 107; AI -wike· 12. 18; M -wa·nt, -wik.

-yi·: N -yi·min 11. 50, -yi·wikamikw 11. 89; AI -yi·tta· 12. 10, -yi·n^{ꝫ}i 12. 68, -yi·mo 12. 125; II -yi·kka· 13. 4; TI -yi·kk 15. 11; P -yi·ya^{ꝫ}i· 16. 17, -yi·ye·ny 16. 49.

CHAPTER 19

ROOTS

19. 1. Apart from inflectional prefixes, roots are the only elements capable of beginning a word or a compound-member. Dependent stems contain no root and are used only with prefixes. The root is lacking also in the forms where the TA verb stem *iN-* is replaced by zero before the ending -$_1$*ikw* (7. 13; 8. 13).

19. 2. The root -*i·t*, which begins dependent nouns and the dependent prenoun particle -*i·ci* (10. 6), joins with the third person prefix to form the root *wi·t-* 'accompany': *wi·teke·* 'he lives with someone'; *wi·ceka·ma·t* 'he dances with him' (cf. 14. 6).

19. 3. The relative roots are listed at 5. 20.

19. 4. Roots are subject to REDUPLICATION. In the regular form of reduplication *a·y-* is prefixed to an initial vowel: *a·ya·nekko·peso* 'he is tied in successive lengths' (contrast *nenta·nekko·pecikan* 'my great-grandchild'). In roots with initial nonsyllabic, the reduplication consists of this nonsyllabic plus the vowel *a·*: *wa·wa·pema·t* 'he looks at him' beside *wa·pema·t* 'he sees him'. So *ka·ki·k-, ka·ki·n-, ma·mi·cit* 'he keeps eating it', etc.

19. 5. The commonest type of irregular reduplication has *a* instead of *a·*: *eyina·pi* 'he looks around' beside *ena·pi* 'he looks thither'; *pepimusse·* 'he walks on and on' beside *pemosse·* 'he walks'. So plainly *ayiN-, mama·t-, papakkik-, papank-, papašš-, papa·tti·n-, papim-, papi·w-, tatakkw-, tatank-, wawa·p-*.

19. 6. Reduplication with *e·* appears in *pe·pekka·n* 'variously', *me·mettikuninkwi·šše⁓* 'swallow', and *me·ma·twe·* 'he sings'.

19. 7. A widespread type of irregular reduplication has *a* in the reduplicative syllable and *a·* replacing the vowel of the first syllable of the root: *pemosse·* 'he walks' : *pepa·musse·* 'he walks about'. So from the roots *kinw-, mank-, mint-, mitt-, naʔ-, namat-, nantaw-, pim-, takkw-*.

19. 8. The following have other irregular vowels in the reduplication and in the first syllable of the root: *kip-* : *kaki·p-*, *ki·ki·p-*; *kot-* : *kakwe·t-;* *oN-* : *owe·N-*.

19. 9. In some reduplicated roots an initial lenis is replaced by fortis after the reduplication: *ki·šk-* : *ki·kki·šk-;* *pe·šš-* : *pe·ppe·šš-;* *šik-* : *ši·ššik-;* *sa·k-* : *sassa·k-*.

19. 10. Various other roots seem to contain reduplication, but corresponding unreduplicated forms were not recorded; for example *mamaN-*, *ci·cci·kk-*, *aye·yi·taw-*, *titti·tip-*, *ko·kko·kku*ʔ*o·*, *me·mi·kwa̰*, *neninkepinuwḛ*.

19. 11. Apparently with no difference of meaning there are double forms *aN-* and *oN-*, *ašk-* and *ošk-*. Beside *ninkot-* there is *ni·nkot-*, beside *kokkw-* there is *kwe·kkw-*. Compare also *asa·w-* and *aša·w-*. For 'big' we have *makk-*, *miSS-*, *mitt-* (*mama·tt-*), *mank-* (*mama·nk-*), *mint-* (*mama·nt-*).

19. 12. Many roots are amplified by POSTRADICAL elements. Some of these resemble verb final suffixes, quite as though a stem were used as a root: *ki·we·* 'he goes home' : *ki·we·petto·* 'he runs home'; *a·tte·* 'it is extinguished' : *a·tte·*ʔ*ank* 'he extinguishes it'; *eko·to·t* 'he hangs it up' : *eko·tekkikkwa·n* 'hook on the kettle hanger'. So *pakit-* beside *pak-*, *pi·t-* beside *pi·-*.

19. 13. Other postradical elements resemble medials, but are joined with the root in a unit which is treated in turn like a root: *aša·waškw-* (cf. medial *-aškw* 'herb, grass'), *kisi·pi·k-* (*-ipi·k* 'water'), *pakkopi·-* (*-ipi·* 'water'), *wi·we·k-* (*-e·k* 'cloth'?). So perhaps also *wi·-wakkwe·-* (*-akkwe·* beside *-kkwe·* 'head'?) and *wa·ssakkw-* (*-akkw* 'sky'?).

19. 14. The numeral roots *ninkotwa·ss-* 'six', *ni·šwa·ss-* 'seven' are formed from *ninkotw-* 'one' and *ni·šw-* 'two' with a postradical element *-a·ss;* *niššwa·ss-* 'eight' from *niSSw-* similarly but with mutation; *minta·ss-* 'ten' has no shorter form by its side, nor does *ša·nkass-* 'nine', with *-ass*.

19. 15. The numeral roots *ni·š-* 'two', *niSS-* 'three', *ni·w-* 'four', *na·n-* 'five', as well as those in 19. 14, appear in this form and also in forms with postradical *-w* or *-o·:* e.g. *ni·wa·kk* 'four hundred', *ni·win* 'four', *ni·metana·* 'forty' : *ni·wo·pi·*ʔ*ekan* 'four-spot' : *ni·wukon*, *ni·yukon* 'four days'.

The numeral roots for 'one' are *pe·šikw-*, *pe·šiko·-*, and *ninkw-*, *ninkot-* (*ninkwat-*), *ninkotw-*.

19. 16. The following postradical elements, in addition to those mentioned in the preceding paragraphs, appear with some clearness:

-a·: kiša·-.
-ine·: pakone·-.
-we·: mantwe·-.
-yi·: ma·ci·-, pašši·-.
-k: mancik-.
-ak: paššak-.
-nakk: te·pinakk-.
-šk: a·kkošk-, nimi·šk-, ota·ppišk-, wa·pišk-.
-ašk: ni·mašk-.
-m: išpim-.
-an: ki·wan-.
-o·: kipo·-; added to roots in consonant plus *w: akko·-, ako·-, a·nikko·-, kino·-, takko·-*.
-p: kisi·p-.
-t: pakant- (beside *pakam-*), *sa·kit-;* cf., above, 19. 12.
-a·t: minkoška·t-, niška·t-, pana·t-, papa·ma·t-, pima·t-, wana·t-.
-e·tt: wa·sse·tt-.
-w: nantw-, nimpi·w-, ša·pw-.
-aw: nantaw-.
-tta·w: ki·witta·w-.
-kkw: animikkw-, mikkw- (beside *mi-* in *mekkank* 'he finds it').
-ikokkw: iNikokkw-.
-skw: pi·miskw-.

CHAPTER 20

SYNTAX

20. 1. The syntactic signs are cross reference, concord, obviation, relative reference, verbal order and mode, and word order.

20. 2. In cross reference, a personal-anaphoric element of inflection (5. 6, 7, 9) is supplemented by an independent expression (word or phrase): *ca·n umo·kkuma·n* 'John his-knife', i.e., 'John's knife'.

20. 3. Concord as to gender, number, and person links expressions: *ma·pa ekkwe·* 'this woman'; *ma·nta wi·kuwa·m* 'this house'.

20. 4. Obviation (5. 5) distinguishes between several animate third person in a context; lack of it, accordingly, should identify third-person expressions; we could construct, for example, the contrast between *uki·-nuwatena·n uwi·wekkwa·n* 'he took his (own) hat' and *uki·-nuwatena·n uwi·wekkwa·neni* 'he took his (another person's) hat'. However, obviation is often neglected.

20. 5. Relative reference links a form containing a relative root (5. 20) to an ANTECEDENT: *ke·ko· ešiwe·pesi* 'something he-fares-so', i.e. 'something is the matter with him'; *neššwa·ssemitena tesso-pepo·n* 'eighty so-many-winters', i.e., 'eighty years'. A word containing a relative root is always, apparently, used with an antecedent, except in the following cases: (1) the word is in changed conjunct form, centering around the relative root (5. 20); (2) a prior compound member of the same word serves as antecedent (10. 14); (3) some words with relative roots occur in special meanings requiring no antecedent: *tešima·t* 'he talks about him', with root *taN-*, requiring no antecedent.

20. 6. Verbs in the conjunct order are subordinate verbs or participles. As subordinate verbs, they are joined with predicative pronouns and particles, or with independent verbs: *we·kune·šš we·šetto·ya·n?* 'what-is-it that-thou-art-doing?'; *mi· ki·-ni-ma·ca·t* 'then-it-was that-he-went away'; *ena·kuššik nenka-tekoššin* 'when-it-is-evening I-shall-arrive'. Participles have much the function of nouns: *aw ne·nkemot* 'that-one who-sings'.

Verbs in the negative modes of the independent order are preceded by the negative particle *ka·;* verbs in the prohibitive mode of the imperative order are preceded by the prohibitive particle *ke·kwa*. Verbs in the negative modes of the conjunct order are not joined to any negative particle (5. 26): (S 667) *ki·špin na·temo·ssuwan*. 'If you do not help me.'; S 665-6.

20. 7. Word order is decidedly flexible. Often words that belong together in meaning are spoken in succession; on the other hand, syntactically coherent words are often separated by other expressions (20. 16-18). Some modifiers always or almost always precede their head: *aw ekkwe·* 'that woman'. Predicative pronouns and particles, including interrogatives, begin their phrase. The enclitic particles come after the first word of the expression which they modify, but there is some freedom as to what they modify; generally one or more enclitics come second in a sentence; others may appear later, as modifiers of some part of the sentence.

ENCLITICS

20. 8. The enclitic particle *ma·* and those listed at the end of 1. 8 come after the first word of any expression which they modify, with the exception that they do not interrupt phrases of *ke·* plus personal pronoun (20. 11) or of *ka·*, *ke·kwa* plus modifying particle (20. 10): (S 2) *ke· ni· kwa ni·-ni-ma·ca·*. 'I too want to go.'; S 437, 844.

Most commonly they come after the first word of a verb expression and apply to the expression as a whole; so especially *etašš* 'and': (S 40) *ci·ma·nink nenki·-pemiška·mi, nenki·-kwa·škunimi tašš*. 'We (exc.) traveled in a canoe, and then we disembarked.' Or, in this same position, they may apply more to the opening word or to the verb: (S 17) *ma·meppi· enikke·kkemik nentaši-unta·tis, pa·ma· tašš mi·nuwa· nenki·--wa-tenakki· uwiti Walpole Island*. 'I was born here on this side of the border, but afterwards I went to live there on Walpole Island.'; (S 24) *keki·-meno·-nempa· na?* 'Did you sleep well?'; (S 32) *me·kwa· na ketanukki·?* 'Are you working now?'; (S 42) *kekkina kkwa nempa·ppemi*. 'We (exc.) all laugh every time.'; S 45, 599, 800.

The enclitic particles are often linked with shorter expressions and then come after the first word of these. Thus in *aw na· ko na· ma·no· mi·š*. (S 786) 'Oh, do give it to him anyway!', the first *na·* goes with the demonstrative *aw* (20. 9), and the following couple *ko na·*

goes with the verb expression as a whole. Fixed expressions are *a·ši kwa* 'already', *wi· kwa* 'he, that one (emphatic)'; (S 236) *ki·na·mekat tašš a·ši kwa.* 'It [a knife] is already sharp.'; (S 486) *mi· ko a·ši kwa we·pi-kemiwank.* 'Then it started to rain.'; (S 372) *ni·n ssa wi· kwa keta·-wi·ci·win.* 'I am the one who will go with you.'; (S 709) *neme·tto· ssa wi· kwa ka·-pi-eša·kupane·n.* 'He has left traces which show that he must have come here.'

Quite commonly the enclitics apply to a phrase of modifying demonstrative with noun (20. 16); they come after the demonstrative: S 786 (cited above); *ma·nta ssa pekwaci-meno·min* 'this wild rice'; *aw ma· menta·kunini* 'that same fine gentleman'.

20. 9. Where several enclitics come together, the order of precedence seems to be *etašš, essa, ena, ekwa, ena·*: (S 3) *nenta·-ni-ma·ca·na kwa?* 'May I go?'; (S 36) *ke·ke·tt ssa na· kemino-kwi·wesse·nsiw.* 'Really, now, you are a good boy.'; (S 52) *kuma·ppi·cc eko na· ki·-uniška·.* 'Only later did he get up.'; (S 651) *ki·nuwa· ko šša ekiwi ka·-ni·mecik.* 'You are the ones who danced.'; S 175.

PARTICLE EXPRESSIONS

20. 10. A PARTICLE EXPRESSION is a non-enclitic particle or a series of such. Where there is a sequence of two or more particles, we may sometimes view one as a head and another, whose position seems to be fixed, as a modifier. Thus *usa·m* 'too much', *nuwanc* 'more', *enikwa* 'until', preceding other particles may be viewed as modifiers: (S 7) *usa·m kepe·ye ᵖi·nk nenki·-nempa·.* 'I slept too long.'; (S 133) *nuwanc penki· eta·kkusite·wak.* 'They have smaller feet.'; (S 138) *ta·ni·-muwak keye· kwa enikwa a·petta·tepikk.* 'They will dance, and until midnight too.'; S 90, 208, 362.

Similarly perhaps *uwiti* 'over there', *ema·* 'there', *no·nkwa* 'now, today'; *mi·nuwa·* with numeral particle: (S 526) *kecci-enokki· aw mentimo·yẽ pi·necciket ema· ka·wetta·kemik.* 'That old woman works hard cleaning up all over the house.'; (S 707) *wa·wa·ške·šši nenki·-wa·pema· uwiti me·kuya·k.* 'I saw a deer over in the woods.'; (S 513) *wi·-kessina·mekat no·nkwa tepikkakk, ni·š etašš nentawe·nta·kuto·n wa·po·weya·nan.* 'It is going to get cold tonight; one will need two blankets.'; *mi·nuwa· pe·šik* 'another'. After other particles, *e·tta* 'only' may be viewed as a modifier: (S 14) *ecina e·tta nenki·-enokki·.* 'I worked only a short time.'; S 269, 408. A particle containing a relative root is modified by an antecedent particle: *no·nkwa unci* 'from this time'; *ni·pena teccink* 'many times'; S 21, 102.

The negative particles *ka·*, *ke·kwa* are modified by following *wi·n* and by *wi·kka·* 'ever'; *ka·* also by *kenake·*: (S 359) *uki·-wa·pema·n kene·peko·n, wi·cekkiwe·nyan taš̌ ka· wi·n*. 'He saw the snake, but his friend did not.'; (S 836) *ke·ko wi· ema· nematepikke·kon, kesa·ka·ssom*. 'Do (ye) not sit here; you are right in the sun.'; (S 431) *ka·wi·kka· ta-pi-eya·ssi·*. 'She will never come.'; (S 837) *ke·kwa· wi·kka· pekisukke-kon*. 'Do (ye) not ever go swimming.'; (S 623) *ka· kenake· pi-peska·pi-ssi·*. 'He is not coming back at all.'

The predicative particle *mi·* is followed and modified by inanimate demonstrative pronouns (*ma·nta, iw*) and by local particles (*ma·meppi·, ema·*): (S 568) *mi· ma·nta ka·- ešisseto·t*. 'This is the way he placed it.'; (S 560) *mi· ko na· iw eppane· e·ši-eya·t*. 'That is the way he always is.'; (S 587) *mi· nenkwana ema· e·nta·yan* 'And so this is where you live!'; S 567, 591.

The predicative particle *a·ni·šš* is modified in *a·ni·šš menikk* 'how many', and *a·ni·* is modified in *a·ni· eppi·* 'when': (S 619) *a·ni·šš menikk e·ya·nk ci·ma·nan?* 'How many canoes has he?'; (S 610) *a·ni· taš̌ eppi· ke·-peska·pi·yan?* 'And when are you coming back?'

Other sequences of particle expressions are *pa·ma· na·kac* 'later on' (S 47); *no·nko unci ni·ka·n* 'from now on' (S 21).

In general, however, our record is not extensive enough to establish closer linking between successive particles, or to decide whether a given order is fixed: *pa·ma· mi·nuwa·* 'later again' (S 17); *nentawa· pa·ma·* 'necessarily later' (S 46).

SUBSTANTIVE EXPRESSIONS

20. 11. A PERSONAL PRONOUN EXPRESSION is a personal pronoun with or without modifier. When *wi·n* serves as an emphasizer of contrast, it is treated as a particle, not as a pronoun.

The personal pronouns are preceded and modified by *ke·* (sometimes apparently *keye·*) 'as for'; nothing intervenes, not even an enclitic: (S 35) *ke· ki·n na kuwi·-wi·ssin?* 'Do you too want to eat?'; S 76, 131, 174.

Those of the first and second persons are followed and modified by the contrastive *wi·n;* an enclitic emphasizer intervenes: (S 372) *ni·n ssa wi· kwa keta·-wi·ci·win*. 'I am the one who will go with you.'

20. 12. A DEMONSTRATIVE PRONOUN EXPRESSION is a demonstrative pronoun with or without modifiers.

The demonstrative pronouns are followed and modified by *pe·šik* 'one', *a·nint* 'several', *tenawa* 'sort', *e·tta* 'only': (S 65) *kuyakk ma·pa enimošš, uwe·ti tašš pe·šik tekkonke·.* 'This dog is well behaved, but that one bites.'; *ma·pa pe·šik* 'this one'; *aw pe·šik* 'that one'; (S 784) *ma·pa tenawa pi·nta·kkwa·š.* 'Smoke this sort of tobacco.'; *iw tenawa* 'that sort'; S 650, 654.

ma·nta is preceded and modified by *menci* with intervening *ekwa:* *menci ko ma·nta* 'to this degree'; the phrase is a subordinator (20. 41).

20. 13. An INDEFINITE PRONOUN EXPRESSION is an indefinite pronoun with or without modifiers.

The indefinite pronouns are preceded and negatived by *ka·* or *ka· wi·n:* (S 843) *ka· wi· ke·ko· keta·-to·ta·kussi·k* 'They [dogs] won't do anything to you.'; *ka· uwaya* 'nobody'. Also with the modifier *a·pecci* 'completely': *ka· wi· a·pecci ke·ko·* 'nothing at all'.

The indefinite pronouns are preceded and modified by such particles as *kekkina* 'all', *ni·pena* 'much, many': (S 406) *nempwa·kka·, ni·pena ke·ko· ukikke·nta·n.* 'He is wise; he knows many things.'; *kekkina ke·ko·* 'everything'.

20. 14. An INTERROGATIVE PRONOUN EXPRESSION is an interrogative pronoun with or without modifiers.

The interrogative pronouns are followed and modified by *tenawa* 'sort': *uwe·ne·šš tenawa* 'what sort is he?'; *we·kune·šš tenawa* 'what sort is it?'

20. 15. A DUBITATIVE PRONOUN EXPRESSION is a dubitative pronoun with or without modifiers.

The dubitative pronouns are modified and followed by *i·tik:* *we·kutakwe·n i·tik* 'whatever it might be'.

20. 16. A NOUN EXPRESSION is a noun (not in local form) with or without modifiers.

Nouns are preceded and modified by pronoun expressions. The personal pronoun expressions *ke· wi·n, ke· wi·nuwa·* agree in number: (S 349) *ke· wi· kwa uki·-mo·nšwa·n epino·ci·nyan.* 'And he cut the child's hair too.'; S 457. However, also *ke· wi· eninuwak* 'the men' in T 17 (par. 1).

Nouns are preceded and modified by demonstrative pronoun

expressions agreeing in number, gender, and obviation: (S 77) *te·pwe· aw enini.* 'That man is speaking the truth.'; (S 142) *mekkate·wa·pekkisuwak ekonta ekkikko·k.* 'These kettles are black.'; (S 297) *uki·-necci·we ˀa·n eniw kwi·wesse·nsan.* 'He scolded that boy.'; S 65, 220, 874-81. The noun may be possessed: (S 684) *ma·pa nemišso·miss* 'this grandfather of mine'; (S 693) *aw no·ss* 'that father of mine'; (S 800) *iw uwi·wekkwa·n* 'that hat of his'. Other examples: *aw pe·šik ekkiwe·nsi͂* 'that (certain) old man'; *iw tenawa enokki·win* 'that sort of work'; *ekiw essa eniššena·pe·k* 'those Indians, you see'; *aw ma·menta·kunini* 'that same fine gentleman'; *ekiw a·nint epino·ci·nyak* 'those several children'.

Between the demonstrative pronoun and the noun there may intervene verbs and even larger parts of the sentence: (S 174) *ma·nta tašš ke· ni· nenka-mi·cin wa·wan.* '[You may eat that egg,] and I shall eat this egg.'; S 570, 647.

If a personal pronoun and a demonstrative pronoun both occur with a noun, the personal pronoun precedes: *ke· wi· aw ci·nti·ssi͂* 'that bluejay too'.

Nouns are preceded and modified by indefinite pronoun expressions agreeing in gender: (S 596) *ka· wi· uwaya ekko·ci·ššan.* 'There are no lice.' Other expressions may intervene: *kekkina ke·ko· wi·-eya·mekato·n eniw "games"* 'there will be all sorts of games'; S 357. The indefinite modifier precedes the demonstrative.

Nouns are preceded and modified by interrogative pronoun expressions agreeing in gender; the resultant phrase is interrogative (and therefore predicative): (S 857) *uwe·ne·šš tenawa pene·šši͂?* 'What sort of bird is it?'

20. 17. The link between a numeral particle and a following noun is lexical rather than syntactic; however, *pe·šik* 'one' goes with singular nouns and the other numerals go with plural: (S 882) *pe·šik mi·kwan.* 'One feather.'; (S 883) *ni·š ekkikko·k.* 'Two kettles.' These loose combinations contrast with exocentric numeral compounds: *na·no-una·ka·ns* 'five cupfuls'. However, *šenin* 'shilling' seems to keep the singular form not only after prenoun numerals (S 886: *nenkotwa·sso šenin.* 'Six shillings.'), but also after independent numeral particles: (S 884) *ni·š šenin.* 'Two shillings.'; S 885. The numeral particle may have modifiers of its own: *mi·nuwa· pe·šik ekkwe·* 'one woman besides'; (S 379) *pe·šik e·tta nenki·-mekka·n wa·wan.* 'I found only one egg.'

20. 18. Many particles which precede the noun, often at an interval, apply more or less closely to it in the way of lexical meaning; the closeness may apparently be shown by close collocation. However, there seems to be no real syntactic bond: the particles go with the sentence rather than with the noun. Such particles are *a·nint* 'some', *kekkina* 'all', *ni·pena* 'much, many', *ni·puwa* 'many', *penki·* 'little, few', *peššiššik* 'nothing but', *kuyakk* 'proper': (S 144) *nenkamuwak kekkina pene·šši·nyak.* 'All the birds are singing.'; (S 179) *ni·pena nenki·-pi·to·nan nenkamuwinan.* 'I have brought many songs.'; (S 290) *nenki·-menwa·peme·wis, ni·puwa nenki·-nessa·k ki·ko·nyak.* 'I have had good luck; I have caught lots of fish.'; (S 336) *peššiššik ko ki·ko" nuwi·-emwa·ne·n.* 'We (exc.) shall eat nothing but fish.'; (S 862) *kekkina kuyakk eninuwak.* 'They are all good men.'; S 134, 214, 232, 357, 414, 464, 489. The particle may apply lexically to only part of the noun: *a·ppeci ko kecci-ki·ko"* 'a very big fish'.

Occasionally the linking of a particle with the noun is produced by unusual position: *aw a·ppeci kwa menta·kunini* 'that extremely fine gentleman'. On the other hand, some particles, through closer linking with another element, may come after the noun: *aw ko·n kekkina ki-nekka·pa·we·* 'that snow melted entirely'.

If S 460 is correctly recorded, *ke·* may precede a noun.

20. 19. Nouns are modified by participles, with agreement in gender, number, and obviation. The participle may be accompanied by the adjuncts (actor, object, etc.) which it has as a verb form.

The participle may precede. With intervening verb: (S 631) *eya·pesot nentaya·wa· mešši·min.* 'I have a ripe apple.' In this case it may come before a demonstrative modifier: *ke·kke·ntema·n ma·nta wi·kkwe·pecikan* 'this love-charm which I know'. In closer linking it comes after a demonstrative modifier: *iw ke·kke·ntank wi·kkwe·pecikan* 'that love-charm which he knows'. The demonstrative may be repeated: *eniw eya·nik eniw essini·n* 'those stones which are there'.

More commonly the participle follows, especially when it has verbal adjuncts: (S 634) *aw epino·ci" e·-pwa·-wi·ssenit a·ppeci ta-pekka-te·.* 'The child that does not eat will be very hungry.'; S 542, 659; with intervening verb: (S 783) *menta·min na·š ka·ši·nkwe·t.* 'Fetch ripe corn.'

20. 20. The possessed noun is modified, in cross-reference with the personal-anaphoric possessor, by substantive expressions (20. 22); these usually precede: (S 156) *ma·pa enini uwi·teke·ma·kenan menci-*

-ešiwe·pesiwan. 'This man's wife behaves badly.'; S 416-7, 847, 853, 866. In the inflection of the noun, obviation of the possessor is often neglected: (S 321) uki·-ma·ci·tuwa·n uwi·teke·ma·kenan umasenaʔekan. 'He took his wife's book away with him.'

20. 21. Participles, part from the adjuncts which they take as verbs, are modified in the same manner as nouns: modification by a demonstrative pronoun: (S 632) aw ne·nkemot. 'The one who is singing.'; S 633, 635-6, 641, 645, 650-1, 654-5; modification by a particle: (S 640) nettam ke·-pi-eya·t nenka-mi·na· esse·ma·n. 'I shall give some tobacco to the one who comes here first.'; S 638-9, 660.

20. 22. Pronoun expressions (20. 11-15), noun expressions (20. 16-18), and participle expressions (20. 19) together make up the class of SUBSTANTIVE EXPRESSIONS.

LOCAL-NOUN EXPRESSIONS

20. 23. A LOCAL-NOUN EXPRESSION is a noun in local form with or without modifiers.

Nouns in local form are preceded and modified by certain particles, especially ma·meppi 'here', uwiti 'over there', ema· 'there', pi·ntik 'inside', and those formed with -ayaʔi·: (S 57) eppane· eya· pi·ntik wi·kuwa·mink. 'He is always inside the house.'; (S 214) usa·m ni·pena nempi·šš uki·-etto·n ema· nempo·pi·nk 'she has put too much water into the soup'; (S 335) nenki·-wi·kkupina·na·n pi·nci·yeʔi· uta·pa·nink 'and we pulled it [a calf] into the wagon'; (S 682) e·ntekwe·n ke·muwanukwe·n uwiti menišše·nʔink. 'I wonder if it is raining over on the island.'; S 303, 707; tepe·w si·pi·nk 'along the bank of the river'.

VERB EXPRESSIONS

20. 24. A VERB EXPRESSION is a verb with or without adjuncts and modifiers.

20. 25. The adjuncts of a verb are substantive expressions in cross reference with the personal-anaphoric actor, object, or pseudo-object that appears in the inflection of the verb. These adjuncts precede or, more often, follow the verb: (S 2) ke· ni· kwa ni·-ni-ma·ca·. 'I too want to go.'; (S 56) ki·ke·tta· neʔa·nkišš. 'Son-in-law is giving out food.'; (S 159) nempi·šš neminekkwe·n. 'I drank some water.'; S 12, 35, 58, 60, 62, 76, 162-3, 176, 178, 189-91, 282-3, 478, 630, 654.

20. 26. A verb with first person plural exclusive actor may be joined with a noun as actor, in the meaning 'so-and-so and I': (S 41) *ni·teke·ma·kan nenana·metapemi pi·ntik wi·kuwa·mi·nk.* 'My wife and I sat inside the house.'

20. 27. A double-object verb may be joined with an object noun that is not represented in the inflection: (S 272) *nempi·tuwa· esse·ma·n.* 'I am bringing him tobacco'.; S 321, 346, 350. Secondary derivative verbs from a double-object verb share this feature: (S 332) *etta·tuwak mesineʔika·nsan, pe·šik etašš ki·-pekkinuwa·.* 'They played cards, and one of them lost'.

20. 28. Other adjunct nouns not represented in the inflection occur largely as instruments: (S 6) *nenki·-meno-eya· neninci·n.* 'My hands are well again.'; S 180, 288, 339. They serve also as goals of movement, in rivalry with local nouns: *ki·-tekoššena·nk o·te·naw* 'that we arrived in the town'.

20. 29. If an adjunct consists of more than one word, the verb often comes between the parts of the adjunct: (S 130) *ni·štena ki·-pi--eša·wak eninuwak ci·na·kwa.* 'Twenty men came yesterday.' ("twenty they-came men yesterday"); S 134, 174, 179, 248, 269, 349, 411. Not so, for instance, in (S 410) *ni·š wi·wekkwa·nan nentaya·nan.* 'I have two hats.'

20. 30. A negative indefinite pronoun (20. 13) as adjunct precedes the verb and an independent verb is then is negative mode: *ka· wi· uwaya ki·-pi-eša·ssi·* 'nobody has come'; *ka· ke·ko· nuwa·pentansi·n* 'I don't see anything'.

20. 31. The indefinite pronoun *ke·ko·* may serve as antecedent of a verb that contains a relative root; if negated, the pronoun precedes: (S 843) *ka· wi· ke·ko· keta·-to·ta·kussi·k* 'they [dogs] won't do anything to you'.

20. 32. The verb is modified by local noun expressions, which may precede or follow: (S 4) *ni·-tekkama·teka· nempissink* 'I shall swim across the lake.'; S 17.

A closer linking appears when the local-noun expression is the antecedent of a relative root in the verb: (S 9) *nesso-pepo·n nenki·-eša kekkino·ʔema·ti·wekamekonk.* 'I went to school three years.'

20. 33. The independent verb is negated by *ka·* with or without modifiers; the verb is then in a negative mode: (S 426) *ka· wi· nenkoci ni·-eša·ssi·*. 'I shall not go off anywhere.' The prohibitive verb is preceded by *ke·kwa (wi·n)* 'do not': (S 831) *ke·ko wi· ki· pi-eša·kke·n ma·meppi·*. 'Don't you come here!'

The negative expressions precede the verb. If the negative particle is closely linked with some adjunct or modifier, this latter comes immediately after the negation: (S 429) *ka· wi· we·we·ni ketikketossi·*. 'You do not say it right.'; S 438, 445.

20. 34. Only a few particles may precede the negation: *nentawa·* 'needs', *kunima·* 'perhaps': (S 439) *nentawa· ka· wi· ka-pi·nta·kkwe·ssi·mi* 'We (inc.) shall have to refrain from smoking.'; (S 466) *kunima· ka· wi· enokki·ssi·tik*. 'It appears that he is not working.' But in S 464 *nentawa·* follows the negation: *ka· wi·n nentawa· ka-mi·na·ssi· uta·pa·-nan*. 'You had better not give him the wagon.'

Rarely an adjunct precedes: (S 451) *nemišSo·messina·nik ka· wi· uki·-eya·nsi·na·wa·n pa·škesikenan*. 'Our (exc.) grandfathers did not have guns.'

20. 35. If the verb contains a relative root, a particle may serve as antecedent. The particle usually precedes the verb, but not always: (S 8) *pe·ššo nenki·-eša·*. 'I went close by.'; (S 21) *no·nko unci ni·ka·n kuyakk nenka-ešiwe·pis*. 'From now on I will be good.'; S 9, 10, 17, 23, 39, 561.

20. 36. The verb is loosely modified by particle expressions. Some of these always appear at the beginning of the verb expression: *a·mpe·* 'please', *a·ssena·* 'look out', *eka·wa·* 'barely managing', *teka* 'do': (S 18) *a·mpe· ni·-wi·ssin*. 'Please, I should like to eat.'; (S 37) *a·ssena· ka-untako·cin*. 'Look out, you will fall down from there.'; (S 265) *eka·wa· kwa nenki·-keški ʔa·*. 'I barely managed to get him [a calf].'; (S 798) *teka kuwaw aw mettik*. 'Come, fell that tree.'; S 496, 734. Most particle expressions usually come first, but occasionally follow: *kepe·ye ʔi·* 'a long time' first in S 13, *kepe·ye ʔi· nenki·-enokki·*. 'I worked a long time.', but following in S 16, *nenki·-pa·pi· etašš kepe·ye·ʔi*. 'And I waited a long time.'; similarly S 1, 7, 21, 236, 459. Others more often follow, especially those of place and time, such as *ma·meppi·* 'here', *uwiti* 'there', *no·nkwa* 'now, today', *ci·na·kwa* 'yesterday', *tepikkonk* 'last night'; (S 12) *ni·n neššikke· nuwi·-eya· ma·meppi·*. 'I want to be here alone.'; S 11, 53, 61, 224. Still others, such as *i·tik* 'I wonder, I daresay', *e·tta* 'only' seem to come always after the verb: (S 226) *ki·-kemiwan i·tik ma·meppi·*. 'It must have been raining here.'; S 435.

20. 37. Where the verb has several adjuncts or modifiers, their order seems to be fairly free; those which are nearer to the verb are closely joined to it syntactically or in lexical meaning, for example *kuyakk* as antecedent in S 21 (cited 20. 35).

SUBORDINATE CLAUSES

20. 38. A verb expression whose verb is a participle has the same function as a noun, serving especially as adjunct of another verb (20. 25).

20. 39. A verb expression which is subordinate has its verb in the conjunct order; the meanings of the modes and tenses are outlined in 5. 18-26.

20. 40. A conjunct verb expression serves as modifier of a verb expression: (S 367) *pa·ma· na·kac ka-mi·š ci-pi·nta·kkwe·ya·n*. 'Later on you may give me a smoke.'; (S 483) *ci-pwa·-nempa·ya·n kwa nenak-kuwe·-pi·nta·kkwe·*. 'Before I go to bed I shall first have a smoke.'; S 497, 499, 546, 552, 561. So especially *wa·pank* 'tomorrow', *ena·kuššik* 'this (coming) evening', and the like. The clause occasionally interrupts the main verb phrase; especially it may come after some part to which it is closely linked: (S 510) *pa·ma· ki·-eškwa·-una·kušši-wi·sseniya·nk nenka-ni-ma·ca·mi*. 'After we (exc.) have eaten the evening meal we shall leave.'; S 828.

A conjunct verb expression is often preceded and modified by the demonstrative *iw*, which gives it a substantive flavor: (S 519) *uwi·-kka·ne·nyan uki·-pa·tta·meko·n iw ki·-kemo·tit wa·ka·kkuto·ns*. 'His brother accused him of having stolen the hatchet.'

20. 41. Subordinate clauses are introduced by various particles: *eppi·* 'when', *ki·špin* 'if, whether', *me·kwa·* 'while', *nena·š* 'until': (S 490) *eppi· ki·-pi-tekoššink nenka-kekwe·cema·*. 'When he arrives here I shall ask him.'; (S 473) *ki·špin enokki·yan ka-tepaʾemo·n*. 'If you work I will pay you.'; (S 608) *nemiššo·miss kkwa nenki·-na·tema·k me·kwa· pe·ma·tesit*. 'My grandfather used to help me when he was living.' (*me·kwa·* here accompanies the changed conjunct; the simple conjunct is commoner); S 612, 661-2, 669, 691. *menci ko ma·nta* 'to such a degree' (20. 12) also introduces a conjunct verb expression.

20. 42. A subordinate clause follows the predicative particle *mi·*, *mi·šš* 'c'est alors que', with or without modifiers: (S 481) *mi· šikwa wi·- -ni-ma·ca·ya·n.* 'Now I must leave right away.'; S 483. These clauses have the verb in the simple indicative conjunct; only if the verb contains a relative root is it in the changed conjunct: (S 560) *mi· ko na· iw eppane· e·ši-eya·t.* 'That is the way he always is.'; S 574.

Other particles are always or often predicative and then are supplemented by clauses: *e·ntekwe·n* 'I wonder if it is true that' (S 493, 626, 673, 712), *empe·kišš* 'would that '(S 496), *meyo·ša* 'it is long ago that' (S 708); *ke·ka·* 'it almost happened that' (changed conjunct); *we·we·ni* 'it is good (of you) that' (S 627), *uwiti* 'it is there that '(S 629); *wa·ssa* 'it is far', *pe·ššo* 'it is near '(S 580-1; contrast 582-3).

20. 43. Interrogative particles are predicative; they precede a clause. The clause has the verb in the changed indicative conjunct after *a·ni·*, *a·ni·šš* 'how is it', *a·ni·špi·cc* 'when is (was) it': (S 554) *a·ni·šš e·ši-eya·yan?* 'What is ailing you?'; (S 615) *a·ni·špi·cc ka·- -pi-peska·pi·yan?* 'When did you come back?'; S 619. After *a·ppi·*, *a·ppi·šš*, *a·ni·ppi·šš* 'where is it', the verb is in the changed conjunct when it contains a relative root, otherwise in the simple conjunct: (S 491, with simple conjunct) *a·ppi·šš ki·-mekkaman ušipi·ʔeka·ns?* 'Where did you find the pencil?'; S 617-8; (S 585, with changed conjunct) *a·ppi·šš e·nta·yan?* 'Where do you live?'; S 586.

20. 44. The interrogative pronouns are predicative and are modified by clauses with the verb in changed conjunct form: (S 573) *we·kune·šš we·šetto·yan?* 'What are you doing?'; S 645-6.

20. 45. The dubitative pronouns precede conjunct verbs as adjuncts; the clause so formed is an adjunct or modifier of the main verb. The mode is usually dubitative: (S 672) *uta·nessan ta-ešicceke·wan we·kutakwe·n e·na·kwe·n.* 'His daughter will do whatever he tells her.' Occasionally it is in participle form: (S 657) *ma·pa kwi·wesse·ns uko·ssan uwe·kwe·n pi-eya·necin.* 'This boy is afraid of everyone who comes here'.

CO-ORDINATION

20. 46. Co-ordinate expressions are connected by *keye·* 'and': (S 887) *pe·šik keye· ni·š.* 'One and two.'; (S 888) *ki·n keye· ni·n.* 'You and I.' This particle is treated as the first word of the second expression, being followed by enclitics, especially *ekwa:* (S 138) *ta-ni·muwak keye·*

kwa enikwa a·petta·tepikk. 'They will dance, and until midnight too.'; (S 484) *neni·puwina·pan essini·nk, mi· tašš ki·-šo·škuššina·n, keye· kwa mi· ki·-pekkopi·sse·ya·n.* 'I was standing on a stone, and then I slipped and fell into the water.'

20. 47. Expressions are very freely co-ordinated by parataxis, differing from successions of sentences only by the non-final sentence pitches on all but the last. Usually, *etašš* appears in the subsequent members: (S 239) *kunsa·pi·mekat ci·ma·n, a·petik ka-pema·teka·n.* 'The canoe is foundering; you will have to swim.'; S 17, 40, 241, 245, 362, 449.

Often the subsequent member is of a shape that could serve as adjunct or modifier in the prior member: (S 238) *kešite·mekat pi·ntik, usa·m.* 'It is hot indoors, too [hot].'

ANAPHORA

20. 48. Anaphora is made by inflectional elements of the verb and possessed noun: (S 51) *peci·nak ki·-ni-ma·ca·.* 'He went off a little ways.'; (S 98) *ki·-menci-ešiwe·pesi kkwa ma·pa kwi·wesse·ns, no·nko tašš meno-ešiwe·pesi.* 'This boy used to be naughty, but now he is good.'; (S 151) *eya·wan ukwissan.* 'He had a (his) son.'

20. 49. Various expressions are anaphorically represented by zero, especially substantives in the subsequent members of a co-ordination: (S 65) *kuyakk ma·pa· enimošš, uwe·ti tašš pe·šik tekkonke·.* 'This dog is well-behaved, but that one bites.'; S 208, 359, 453.

Less often the prior occurrence is omitted, so as to yield a periodic construction: (S 174) *uwe·ti ke· ki· ka-mi·cin, ma·nta tašš ke· ni·nenka-mi·cin wa·wan.* 'You may eat that [egg], and I shall eat this egg.'

SENTENCE TYPES

20. 50. The favorite sentence types are NARRATIVE, with independent verb, IMPERATIVE, with verb in imperative order, PREDICATIVE, with interrogative pronoun or predicative particle as center (20. 42-44), EQUATIONAL, with particle and substantive expression or two substantive expressions equated.

Narrative: (S 1) *a·petik nenka·-ni-ma·ca·.* 'I have to go now.'; (S 3) *nenta·-ni-ma·ca· na kwa?* 'May I go?'

Imperative: (S 715) *ma·ca·n ma·meppi·*. 'Come here!'; (S 831) *ke·ko wi· ki· pi-eša·kke·n ma·meppi·*. 'Don't you come here!'

Predicative: (S 853) *a·ppi· tašš ki·n kuwi·wekkwa·n?* 'And you, where is your hat?'; (S 858) *we·kune·šš iw?* 'What is that?'

Equational: (S 580) *wa·ssa e·nta·ya·n* 'It is far to where I live.'; (S 860) *ni·n ssa aw*. 'It's me.'; S 65, 581, 861-2. One member may be *ka·* with indefinite pronoun: (S 357) *kekkina nenki·-pekkina·k iw nešo·neya·m, ka· tašš ke·ko· no·nkwa šo·neya·*. 'He won all my money from me, and now I have no money left.'

20. 51. Minor sentences are of many shapes, e.g. *e·* 'yes', *ka· (wi·n)* 'no'; (S 849) *po·šo· no·kko·*. 'Good day, grandmother.'; (S 138, all but first word) (*ta-ni·muwak*) *keye· kwa enikwa a·petta·tepikk*. '(They will dance,) and till midnight, too,'; (S 452) *ka· wi·n kenapac* 'I guess not'. It is worth noting that words like *a·w* 'well', *a·mpe·, teka* 'please' are treated as part of a sentence: (S 825) *a·w, tašš wi· ekintan.* 'Come now, count them.'

PART II
SENTENCES

SENTENCES

1. *a·petik nenka-ni-ma·ca·.* I have to go now.
2. *ke· ni· kwa ni·-ni-ma·ca·.* I too want to go.
3. *nenta·-ni-ma·ca· na kwa?* May I go?
4. *ni·-tekkama·teka· nempissink.* I shall swim across the lake.
5. *nenki·-pi-tekkama·teka· nempissink.* I have swum here across the lake.
6. *nenki·-meno-eya· neninci·n.* My hands are well again.
7. *usa·m kepe·ye ʔi·nk nenki·-nempa·.* I slept too long.
8. *pe·ššo nenki·-eša·.* I went close by.
9. *nesso-pepo·n nenki·-eša kekkino·ʔema·ti·wekamekonk.* I went to school three years.
10. *na·winc nenki·-eša·.* I went out on the open water.
11. *nenko-pepo·n nenki·-eya· uwiti.* I was there one year.
12. *ni·n neššikke· nuwi·-eya· ma·meppi·.* I want to be here alone.
13. *kepe·ye ʔi· nenki·-enokki·.* I worked a long time.
14. *ecina e·tta nenki·-enokki·.* I worked only a short time.
15. *ni·-enokki· nenkitteka·ne·nsink.* I am going to work in my garden.
16. *nenki·-pa·pi· etašš kepe·ye ʔi·.* And I waited a long time.
17. *ma·meppi· enikke·kkemik nentaši-unta·tis, pa·ma· tašš mi·nuwa· nenki·-wa-tenakki· uwiti Walpole Island.* I was born here on this side of the border, but afterwards I went to live there on Walpole Island.
18. *a·mpe· ni·-wi·ssin.* Please, I should like to eat.
19. *a·ši meno-menikk nenki·-wi·ssin.* I have had enough to eat.
20. *a·ppeci nento·ntemis.* I am very busy.
21. *no·nko unci ni·ka·n kuyakk nenka-ešiwe·pis.* From now on I will be good.
22. *nesso-pepo·n nenki·-kekkino·ʔema·kos.* I have had three years' schooling.
23. *nenko-tepaʔeka·ns nuwi·-pepa·-ene·nt.* I shall be gone one hour.
24. *keki·-meno-nempa· na?* Did you sleep well?
25. *kuwi·-eša· na?* Do you want to go there?
26. *kemane·ppwa· na?* Are you in need of a smoke?
27. *kuma·ppi· keta-pi-eya·.* You are to come here later on.
28. *kepi-pemosse· na?* Did you walk here?

29. *keki·-po·ni-a·kkuškate· na?* Has your stomach-ache stopped?
30. *kuwi·-pi·nta·kkwe· na?* Do you want to smoke?
31. *ketanukki· na?* Are you working?
32. *me·kwa· na ketanukki·?* Are you working now?
33. *usa·m kekicci-enokki·.* You work too hard.
34. *usa·m kepe·cepatto·.* You run too slowly.
35. *ke· ki·n na kuwi·-wi·ssin?* Do you too want to eat?
36. *ke·ke·tt ssa na· kemino-kwi·wesse·nsiw.* Really, now, you are a good boy.
37. *a·ssena· ka-untako·cin.* Look out, you will fall down from there.
38. *a·ssena· ka-penkiššin.* Look out, you will fall.
39. *menišše·nᵖink nenki·-ta·mi.* We (exc.) camped on an island.
40. *ci·ma·nink nenki·-pemiška·mi, nenki·-kwa·škunimi tašš.* We (exc.) traveled in a canoe, and then we disembarked.
41. *ni·teke·ma·kan nenana·metapemi pi·ntik wi·kuwa·mink.* My wife and I sat inside the house.
42. *kekkina kkwa nempa·ppemi.* We (exc.) all laugh every time.
43. *uta·pa·nink nenki·-po·semi.* We (exc.) got on a wagon.
44. *uta·pa·nink nenki·-pemita·pa·nekomi.* We (exc.) rode on a wagon.
45. *pa·ma· kwa ka-eša·mi.* Afterwards we (inc.) shall go there.
46. *nentawa· pa·ma· ka-pi·nta·kkwe·mi.* We (inc.) shall have to smoke later on.
47. *pa·ma· na·kac ka-wi·ssenimi.* After a while we (inc.) shall eat.
48. *pa·ma· na·kac ka-enwe·pemi.* After a while we (inc.) shall rest.
49. *keki·-meno-nempa·m na?* Did you (pl.) sleep well?
50. *keki·-pi-pemosse·m na?* Did you (pl.) walk here?
51. *peci·nak ki·-ni·ma·ca·.* He went off a little ways.
52. *kuma·ppi·cc eko na· ki·-uniška·.* Only later did he get up.
53. *ki·-pi-eša· ci·na·kwa.* He came yesterday.
54. *ki·-eša ešpimessakonk.* He has gone upstairs.
55. *ekkita·kki ki·-eša·.* He went up on the hill.
56. *ki·ke·tta neᵖa·nkišš.* Son-in-law is giving out food.
57. *eppane· eya· pi·ntik wi·kuwa·mink.* He is always inside the house.
58. *uwaya na eya· ešpimessakonk?* Is anyone upstairs?
59. *kuyakk eši-eya·.* He is a proper person. (Cf. S 97).
60. *pene·šši⁓ ešpimink eya·.* There is a bird up above.
61. *eya· ma·meppi· no·nkwa.* He is here today.
62. *uwaya ki·-eya·.* There was someone there.
63. *pesa·n eya·.* He keeps quiet.

64. *nessink ki·-mentwe·seke·.* He shot three times.
65. *kuyakk ma·pa enimošš, uwe·ti tašš pe·šik tekkonke·.* This dog is well-behaved, but that one bites.
66. *mo·škene· ekkikk.* The kettle is full.
67. *ki·-pi·ncesse tekkipi·nk.* He stepped into a spring of water.
68. *pi-mo·kkesse· ki·siss.* The sun is rising.
69. *ki·-pemosse· ne·kuwi·nk.* He walked on the sand.
70. *eškwe·ya·nk pemosse·.* He walks in the rear.
71. *ni·ka·n pemosse·.* He walks in the lead.
72. *uškinuwe· pepa·-ki·yusse·.* The young man is off hunting.
73. *ni·šink ki·-pepa·-ki·yusse·.* He went hunting twice.
74. *pemikkuwe· wa·wa·ške·šši,.* A deer has left tracks.
75. *ki·-ekkwa·ntuwe· mettikonk.* He climbed a tree.
76. *ke· wi· pi·nta·kkwe·.* He too is smoking.
77. *te·pwe· aw enini.* That man is speaking the truth.
78. *ma·pa kwi·wesse·ns ki·-te·pwe·.* This boy has told the truth.
79. *a·ši kwa ki·-pi·ssekkoneye·.* He has already put on his clothes.
80. *o·te·na·nk tenakki·.* He lives in Detroit.
81. *netta·-enokki· aw ekkwe·.* That woman is a good worker.
82. *ekkita·kki ki·-eppatto·.* He ran to the top of the hill.
83. *eka·cci·nʾi ki·koˉ.* The fish is small.
84. *ma·ci·ki menta·min.* The corn is growing.
85. *nuwanc uškini·ki.* He is younger.
86. *ma·muwi uškini·ki.* He is the youngest of all.
87. *kettimeški aw ekkwe·.* That woman is lazy.
88. *ma·pa kwi·wesse·ns ki·-ki·nuwiški.* This boy has told a lie.
89. *kepe·-tepikk ki·-ni·mi.* He danced all night.
90. *usa·m ni·pena ki·-wi·sseni, pa·škeci·ška· tašš.* He ate too much, and so he burst open.
91. *uwaya pi-sa·keninci·ni.* Someone stuck his hand in here.
92. *ki·-se·kesi ekkwe·.* The woman was frightened.
93. *kenwa·pi·kesi kene·pik.* The snake is long.
94. *šo·škwa·pi·kesi kene·pik.* The snake is smooth.
95. *mekkate·wa·pekkisi ma·pa ekkikk.* This kettle is black.
96. *wi·n ma·muwi sesi·kkesi.* He is the oldest of them all.
97. *kuyakk ešiwe·pesi.* He behaves well. (Cf. S 59).
98. *ki·-menci-ešiwe·pesi kkwa ma·pa kwi·wesse·ns, no·nko tašš meno--ešiwe·pesi.* This boy used to be naughty, but now he is good.
99. *neššwa·ssemitena tesso-pepo·n ki·-pema·tesi.* He lived eighty years.

100. *ki·wena·tesi ma·pa ekkwe·*. This woman is insane.
101. *šeka·k pi·cema·kusi*. One can smell a skunk here.
102. *ni·pena teccink ki·-no·nta·kusi*. He called out many times.
103. *menoppukosi ma·pa ki·koʼ*. This fish tastes good.
104. *ni·kka·niss a·kkusi*. My brother is ill.
105. *kekkina ki·-nempi·wa·kkusi*. He was entirely drenched.
106. *usa·m keno·si nenta·sso·kka·n*. My sacred story is too long.
107. *kepe·yeʼi· ki·-pepa·-ene·nti*. He was out a long time.
108. *muwi epino·ciʼ*. The child is crying.
109. *uwaššeme· wi·n ekkiwe·nsi·n ʼuwi*. He is a still older man.
110. *ma·pa pene·ššiʼ nenkamo*. This bird sings.
111. *eni·penkiššemo ki·siss*. The sun is setting.
112. *pa·tti·no esse·ma·*. There is lots of tobacco.
113. *ki·-tekkama·puno mettikonk*. He crossed over on a log.
114. *netta·-pekiso epino·ciʼ*. The child can siwm.
115. *netta·-pekiso aw kwi·wesse·ns*. That boy can swim.
116. *wa·peso mešši·min*. The apple is ripe.
117. *pepa·mepiso pene·ššiʼ*. A bird is flying about.
118. *keši·peso eškote·ta·pa·n*. The train is going fast.
119. *pe·cepiso eškote·ta·pa·n*. The train is going slowly.
120. *espimink mettikonk eko·so*. He is up in the tree.
121. *nentawe·ma· netta·-keškikwa·sso*. My sister (man speaking) sews well.
122. *netta·-keškikwa·sso nenaʼa·nkenikkwe·m*. My daughter-in-law sews well.
123. *mentito na aw uppin?* Is that potato big?
124. *ki·koʼ ki·-sesswe·kemiššin*. A fish leaped up with a splash.
125. *wi· nettam ki·-tekoššin*. He arrived first.
126. *šeyi·kwa pi-tekoššin*. He will arrive in a moment.
127. *ni·teke·ma·kan ki·-nempwa*. My wife has died.
128. *ki·-pi-nenkotwa·sso·ška·wak ci·ma·nink*. They came here six in a canoe.
129. *ši·šši·pak ta-ma·ca·wak ša·wenonk*. The ducks will leave for the south.
130. *ni·štena ki·-pi-eša·wak eninuwak ci·na·kwa*. Twenty men came yesterday.
131. *ke· wi·nuwa· ki·-ekawa·wak*. They too speared fish.
132. *uškinuwe·k pepa·-ki·yusse·wak*. The young men are off hunting.
133. *nuwanc penki· eta·kkusite·wak*. They have smaller feet.

134. *kekkina ki·-ma·ci·petto·wak pe·šeko·keši·k.* All the horses started to run.
135. *nentayak menkiwak.* My dogs are barking.
136. *enimo·k menkiwak.* The dogs are barking.
137. *pi·weši·nᵊuwak ki·ko·nyak.* The fish are small.
138. *ta-ni·muwak keye· kwa enikwa a·petta·tepikk.* They will dance, and till midnight, too.
139. *ke· wi·nuwa· ni·muwak.* They too are dancing.
140. *kekkina ma·muwi ki·-nematepiwak.* They all sat together.
141. *ce·ci·pa·n ki·-nematepiwak.* They sat in separate places.
142. *mekkate·wa·pekkisuwak ekonta ekkikko·k.* These kettles are black.
143. *nenkamuwak pene·šši·nyak.* The birds are singing.
144. *nenkamuwak kekkina pene·šši·nyak.* All the birds are singing.
145. *wa·ssemowak enimekki·k.* There is lightning. ("The Thunderers flash.").
146. *mema·ntetowak ena uppini·k?* Are the potatoes big?
147. *eppane· kwa eškwa·ya·c tekoššeno·k.* They always arrive late.
148. *nentakkikk uncika·.* My kettle is leaking.
149. *ke· wi· kwa utakkekko·n uncika·wan.* Her kettle is leaking too.
150. *pesa·n eya·wan.* The other one is quiet.
151. *eya·wan ukwissan.* He has a son.
152. *wi·kka·nessan unci·ye͂ pemosse·wan.* His brother walks next in order.
153. *uwi·teke·ma·kenan kettimeškiwan.* His wife is lazy.
154. *ukwissan pa·ppuwan.* His son is laughing.
155. *uta·nessan tenakkemikesiwan ne·kuwi·kka·nk.* His daughters are playing in the sand.
156. *ma·pa enini uwi·teke·ma·kenan menci-ešiwe·pesiwan.* This man's wife behaves badly.
157. *ki·-tekoššeno·n o·ssuwa·n.* Their father has arrived.
158. *ki·-nempwan uko·kko·šševan.* His pig has died.
159. *nempi·šš neminekkwe·n.* I drank some water.
160. *a·ši kwa nenki·-menikkwe·n nempi·šš.* I have already had a drink of water.
161. *nempi·šš nenki·wa-menikkwe·n.* I went and took a drink of water.
162. *na·no-una·ka·ns nenki·-menikkwe·n.* I drank five glasses.
163. *nenki·ška·kkuccito·n nenta·ss.* I have snagged and torn my legging.

164. *nenki·-kekkito·n šo·neya· na·mekkamik.* I have hidden the money underground.
165. *wa·wan nenki·-pa·ssepito·n, a·ppeci tašš nuwi·neninci·.* I have smashed an egg, and my hands are all dirty.
166. *nenki·-tekkopeto·n nemakkesin.* I have tied my shoe.
167. *nenka-pi·to·n kwa mekkakkussak.* I shall bring the barrel.
168. *nempa·tti·netto·n wi·sseniwin.* I have lots of food.
169. *menko·ss nentašetto·n.* I am making an awl.
170. *menko·ss etašš nuwi·-ešitto·n.* Also I am going to make an awl.
171. *nentašitto·n a·šukan.* I am building a bridge.
172. *nento·šetto·n wi·kuwa·m.* I am building a house.
173. *kemi·cin na e·ššo͞?* Are you eating the cabbage?
174. *uwe·ti ke· ki· ka-mi·cin, ma·nta tašš ke· ni· nenka-mi·cin wa·wan.* You may eat that egg, and I shall eat this one.
175. *pa·ma· ko na· ka·-pi·to·n.* Later on is when you are to bring it.
176. *nenki·-tekkamuʔa·nan mettik.* I crossed over on a log.
177. *mettiko·n nenki·-pi·ntekato·nan, ni·teke·ma·kan etašš ki·-po·tuwe·.* I brought the wood inside, and my wife made a fire.
178. *nenki·-pi·kussito·nan nento·ški·nšekokka·cekanan.* I have broken my spectacles.
179. *ni·pena nenki·-pi·to·nan nenkamuwinan.* I have brought many songs.
180. *mo·kkuma·ne·ns uki·-ki·škekkoceke·n mettiko·ns.* With his pocket-knife he whittled through the stick.
181. *wi·ya·ss umi·cin.* He eats meat.
182. *e·ššo͞ umi·cin.* He is eating cabbage.
183. *uki·-mi·cin pekkwe·šekan.* He ate some bread.
184. *uki·-po·kkupito·n utapwi.* He broke his paddle.
185. *uki·-ki·we·weto·n uwi·wekkwa·n.* He took home his hat.
186. *uki·-ma·ci·to·n nemasenaʔekan.* He took my book away with him.
187. *nempi·šš uki·-etto·n ekkikkonk.* She put some water in the kettle.
188. *mencikekkan uto·šetto·n.* He is making a fence.
189. *uki·-nettama·ke·nan enimo·n.* He killed somebody's dog.
190. *uki·-po·ta·kkwe·nan ši·šši·pe·nyan.* She put the duck in the kettle.
191. *e·ššo·nyan utata·we·nan.* He sells cabbages.
192. *upi·to·nan mettiko·n.* He is bringing wood.
193. *ekiceyaʔi·nk keki·-etto·na·n.* We (inc.) put it on top of the thing.
194. *eškote· nento·šetto·na·n.* We (exc.) are making a fire.

195. *ni·š ci·ma·nan upapa·-a·pecitto·na·wa·n.* They use two canoes as they go about.
196. *e·škam pepaka· nuwa·po·weya·n.* My blanket is wearing thinner and thinner.
197. *mencikekkan pi·kuška.* The fence is broken.
198. *pe·šik ci·ma·n ki·-pi·kuška·.* One canoe was damaged.
199. *eye·yi·tuwayeˀi· ki·na·.* It is pointed at both ends.
200. *pekkwe·ne·ya· kwa.* There is indeed a fog.
201. *eka·ccete·ya· eškwa·nte·m.* The door is narrow.
202. *menkate·ya· eškwa·nte·m.* The door is wide.
203. *nenci·ma·n ki·-kuttikusse·.* My canoe tipped over.
204. *kepa·kkuˀika·te· eškwa·nte·m.* The door is shut.
205. *na·mekkamekokka·te· wi·kuwa·m.* The house has a cellar.
206. *ki·-pekone·te· nuwa·po·weya·n.* My blanket has got a hole burned in it.
207. *meskwa·pekkite· essin.* The stone is red-hot.
208. *ma·netta·nešši·yeˀi· nuwanc ni·pena enakente·.* Woolen things cost more.
209. *una·ka·ns unte·.* The vessel has come to a boil.
210. *wa·ka·kkwat wi·-ki·nepo·te·.* The axe needs sharpening.
211. *ki·-a·tte· eškote·ns.* The match went out.
212. *a·ppeci ki·-keša·tte· ci·na·kwa.* The weather was very hot yesterday.
213. *eka·cceno·nˀi essin.* The stone is very small.
214. *usa·m ni·pena nempi·šš uki·-otto·n emu· nempo·pi·nk, usa·m tašš wi·n iw nempo·p nempi·ška·kemi.* She has put too much water into the soup, and so now the soup is too watery.
215. *menwa·kemi nempo·p.* The soup is good.
216. *šeya·we·mo meškote·ta·pa·n-mi·kkan.* The railway track runs straight.
217. *ki·-so·kkeppo ci·na·kwa.* It snowed yesterday.
218. *mema·cca·no·n na esa·wi·ci·ssan?* Are the carrots big?
219. *usa·m pi·wa·no·n nemakkesinan.* My shoes are too small.
220. *wa·pete·no·n eniw peka·nan.* Those walnuts are ripe.
221. *ni·šeno·n eto·ppuwinan.* There are two tables.
222. *uto·na·kan uncika·ni.* Her bowl is leaking.
223. *kenapac ta-kemiwan.* I guess it is going to rain.
224. *ki·-kemiwan tepikkonk.* It rained last night.
225. *ci·na·kwa ki·-kemiwan.* It rained yesterday.

226. *ki·-kemiwan i·tik ma·meppi·.* It must have been raining here.
227. *kusikwan ma·nta.* This thing is heavy.
228. *nuwanc ma·nta kecci-eto·ppuwin, ma·nta nuwanc eka·ccin.* This table is bigger, and this one is smaller.
229. *pi·cene·ssin eškote·.* The smell of the fire is borne hither.
230. *keto·šepi·ʔeka·ns ki·-penkissin.* Your pencil has fallen down.
231. *nessa·kkussin eškwa·nte·m.* The door is standing open.
232. *kekkina si·pi ki·-kepatin.* The river is all frozen over.
233. *mecca·mekat ena esa·wi-ci·ss?* Is the carrot big?
234. *še·kwa·mekat enitt.* The spear is dull.
235. *ki·na·mekat enitt.* The spear is sharp.
236. *še·kwa·mekat nemo·kkuma·n, a·petik nenki·nepo·to·n. ši·kunink nenka-teši-esipo·to·n. ki·na·mekat tašš a·ši kwa. ki·na·mekat tašš no·nkwa.* My knife is dull; I must sharpen it. I shall whet it on the grindstone. It is already sharp. It is sharp now.
237. *ma·nta wi·kuwa·m wi·-kuwisse·mekat, kekkina pekaškenat.* This house will fall over; it is all rotted to pieces.
238. *kešite·mekat pi·ntik, usa·m.* It is hot indoors, too hot.
239. *kunsa·pi·mekat ci·ma·n, a·petik ka-pema·teka·n.* The canoe is foundering; you will have to swim.
240. *šo·škwa·pekkat essin.* The rock is smooth.
241. *ni·sa·nat ma·meppi·, ni·sa·ni-eya·, nese·kis.* It is dangerous here; things are dangerous; I am afraid.
242. *pa·tti·nat wi·ya·ss.* There is plenty of meat.
243. *wi·ya·ss pi·cema·kwat.* There is a smell of meat.
244. *menoppukwat wi·ya·ss.* The meat smells good.
245. *nenkwa·nekkwat, kenapac ta-kemiwan.* It is clouding over; maybe it is going to rain.
246. *pi·weno·n essini·n.* The stones are small.
247. *eni·pi·ššan penkisseno·n.* The leaves are falling.
248. *nesswi ki·-pi-eša·mekato·n ci·ma·nan menišše·nʔink.* Three canoes came to the island.
249. *pa·tti·neto·n essini·n.* There are many stones.
250. *pa·tti·neto·n messan.* There is lots of firewood.
251. *pa·tti·neto·n ekwassema·nan.* There are lots of pumpkins.
252. *nuwi·-nempwa·cceʔa· nešiššẽ·.* I am going to visit my uncle.
253. *nenki·-wa-nempwa·cceʔa· kkwa.* I used to go and visit him.
254. *nesa·keʔa· aw ekkwe·.* I love that woman.
255. *nenki·-wa·pema· kkwa.* I used to see him.

256. *nenkiˑ-waˑpema waˑwaˑškeˑšši.* I saw a deer.
257. *nuwaˑpemaˑ enimošš.* I see a dog.
258. *nuwaˑpemaˑ upeˑšekoˑkešiˑmuwaˑn.* I see the horse which they own. (Cf. S 261).
259. *nuwaˑpemaˑ utayuwaˑn.* I see their dog.
260. *nuwaˑpemaˑ ukwiˑwesseˑnsemiwaˑn.* I see their boy.
261. *nuwaˑpemaˑ utayeʔaˑmuwaˑn.* I see their horse. (Cf. S 258).
262. *nenantuwaˑpemaˑ nentoˑppwaˑkan.* I am looking for my pipe.
263. *nenkiˑ-kumaˑ mekkom.* I have swallowed the ice.
264. *nenkiˑ-peššakiˑkepinaˑ waˑpoˑsõ.* I have skinned the rabbit.
265. *nenkiˑ-naˑpekweˑppenaˑ pešikkiˑns, ekaˑwaˑ kwa nenkiˑ-keškiʔaˑ.* I roped the calf; I barely managed to get him.
266. *nenka-piˑnaˑ uppwaˑkan.* I shall bring a pipe.
267. *nenkiˑ-piˑnaˑ esseˑmaˑ.* I have brought tobacco.
268. *aˑši ko nenkiˑ-kuntamoˑnaˑ.* I have him on my hook now.
269. *peˑšik eˑtta nenkiˑ-nessaˑ essaˑweˑ.* I caught only one perch.
270. *nenkiˑ-nessaˑ kecci-mekkwa.* I killed a big bear.
271. *nenkiˑ-noˑcemottemawaˑ uniˑcaˑnessan.* I cured his child for him.
272. *nempiˑtuwaˑ esseˑmaˑn.* I am bringing him tobacco.
273. *nentasseˑmaˑ nenka-ni-eyaˑwaˑ.* I shall take my tobacco with me.
274. *nenkiˑ-miˑkkuwaˑ oˑciˑns.* I hit the fly as I struck at it.
275. *nenkiˑ-kuwawaˑ mettik.* I have felled the tree.
276. *nenkiˑ-pekoneˑwaˑ aw mekkom.* I made a hole through the ice.
277. *nenkiˑ-naˑpekweˑwaˑ pešikkiˑns.* I roped the calf.
278. *šekaˑkonk nenkiˑ-ešinaˑšuwaˑ.* I sent him to Chicago.
279. *nentoˑnswaˑ ekkikk.* I bring the kettle to a boil.
280. *nentaˑ-kiˑ-mešwaˑ kwa aw waˑwaˑškeˑšši.* I surely would have hit that deer.
281. *paˑmaˑ ko ka-necciˑweʔaˑ.* You may scold him later on.
282. *kenoˑntuwaˑ na aw?* Do you hear him?
283. *kuwaˑpemaˑ na aw ekkweˑ?* Do you see that woman?
284. *kekiˑ-waˑpemaˑ na?* Have you seen him?
285. *paˑmaˑ ko naˑ ka-eššamaˑ.* You may feed him later on.
286. *paˑmaˑ naˑkac ka-pešši·penaˑ.* Later on, after a while, you may skin him.
287. *nuwaˑpemaˑk kepašekkiˑmuwaˑk.* I see your (pl.) cows.
288. *nenkiˑ-peškopenaˑk miˑkunan aw šiˑššiˑpẽ.* I have plucked the feathers from that duck.
289. *nenkiˑ-penakekkonaˑk uppiniˑk.* I have peeled the potatoes.

290. *nenki·-menwa·peme·wis, ni·puwa nenki·-nessa·k ki·ko·nyak.* I have had good luck; I have caught lots of fish.
291. *nenkossa·k enimo·k.* I am afraid of the dogs.
292. *nenki·-ki·škešwa·k neškanši·k.* I have cut my nails.
293. *keno·ntuwa·k na ekiw?* Do you hear them there?
294. *use·keʔa·n ukittesi·man.* He frightened his parents.
295. *uki·-pi·neʔa·n ši·šši·pan.* He cleaned the duck.
296. *upa·tti·neʔa·n esse·ma·n.* He has lots of tobacco.
297. *uki·-necci·weʔa·n eniw kwi·wesse·nsan.* He scolded that boy.
298. *uki·-wa·pema·n enimo·n.* He saw the dog.
299. *utaššema·n epino·ci·nyan.* He is feeding the child.
300. *uki·-wi·teke·ma·n ni·tta·wessan.* He married my cousin.
301. *uki·-pi·kuššima·n utakkekko·n.* He broke his kettle.
302. *ni·šink uki·-nentoma·n.* He called him twice.
303. *uki·-nenkana·n unaʔa·nkešši·man ema· menišše·nʔink.* He abandoned his son-in-law there on the island.
304. *uto·ta·pa·nan una·na·n.* He is fetching his wagon.
305. *uki·-si·nena·n pešikkuwan.* He milked the cow.
306. *uki·-peškopena·n ši·šši·pe·nyan.* She plucked the duck.
307. *uki·-uta·ppena·n utakkekko·n.* She picked up her kettle.
308. *ekkikko·n uki·-ki·we·wena·n.* He took the kettle home with him.
309. *ki·ko·nsan uki·-ki·we·wena·n.* He took the little fish home.
310. *uki·-ši·kuna·n ekkikko·n.* She emptied the kettle.
311. *upanekikkuna·n uppini·n.* She is peeling potatoes.
312. *uki·-eko·na·n ekkikko·n.* She hung up the kettle.
313. *uni·ca·nessan uno·na·n, no·na·wesso.* She is suckling her child; she is nursing.
314. *utassa·n eniw ka·weyan umakkesinink.* She is placing those quills on her moccasins.
315. *uki·-nessa·n šeka·kon.* He has killed a skunk.
316. *uki·-nessa·n wa·wa·ške·ššuwan.* He has killed a deer.
317. *uki·-nessa·n utayan.* He has killed his dog.
318. *nentawe·ma· uki·-nessa·n wa·wa·ške·ššuwan.* My brother (woman speaking) has killed a deer.
319. *nesswi uki·-nessa·n ki·ko·nyan.* He has caught three fish.
320. *una·temawa·n no·ssena·n.* He is helping our (exc.) father.
321. *uki·-ma·ci·tuwa·n uwi·teke·ma·kenan umasenaʔekan.* He took his wife's book away with him.
322. *uniška·tesi·ttuwa·n uwi·teke·ma·kenan.* He is angry at his wife.

323. *uki·-wi·ci·wa·n wi·tta·n.* He went with his brother-in-law.
324. *uki·-ta·škekawa·n mettiko·n.* He split the tree with his axe.
325. *umo·nuwa·n uppini·n.* He is digging potatoes.
326. *nenkwaci· utišuwe·puwa·n ko·nan.* He is sweeping away the snow.
327. *uki·-pecipuwa·n ki·ko·nyan.* He speared the fish.
328. *uki·-nenkwawa·n uko·kko·ššeman.* He buried his pig.
329. *uppini·n utamwa·n.* He is eating potatoes.
330. *uki·-emwa·n wa·po·so·n.* He ate a rabbit.
331. *uki·-menoswa·n ši·šši·pe·nyan.* She cooked the duck.
332. *etta·tuwak mesineʔika·nsan, pe·šik etašš ki·-pekkinuwa·.* They played cards, and one of them lost.
333. *kuta·cema·wak mekko·nsak.* The bear cubs are being tested in the cold (i.e., it is very cold weather.)
334. *neme· nuwi·-pecipuwa·na·n.* We (exc.) are going to spear sturgeon.
335. *nenki·-na·pekwe·ppena·na·n pešikki·ns, nenki·-wi·kkupina·na·n pi·nci·yeʔi· uta·pa·nink.* We (exc.) roped the calf, and we pulled it into the wagon.
336. *peššiššik ko ki·koʰ nuwi·-emwa·na·n.* We (exc.) shall eat nothing but fish.
337. *keno·ntuwa·wa· na aw?* Do you (pl.) hear him there?
338. *keno·ntuwa·wa·k na ekiw?* Do you (pl.) hear them there?
339. *nenki·-pi·ni·nta·ʔik šo·neya·.* He sent me some money.
340. *utayan nenki·-se·keʔik.* His dog frightened me.
341. *a·ši nenki·-ki·ʔik.* He has got away from me.
342. *no·kkumiss nenki·-eššamik.* My grandmother gave me food.
343. *uwi·teke·ma·kenan nuwi·-eššamik.* His wife will give me food.
344. *neno·ppenanik ki·siss.* The sun is following me.
345. *nenki·-ema·cwe·penik ni·teke·ma·kan.* My wife woke me up.
346. *nemiššo·miss nenki·-mi·nik esse·ma·n.* My grandfather gave me some tobacco.
347. *nenki·-pekkiketo·ne·ʔok, nenki·-pekkitte·ʔok nento·nink.* He hit me on my mouth; he gave me a blow on my mouth.
348. *kenapac nenka-emok.* I guess he means to eat me up.
349. *nenki·-mo·nšok, ke· wi· kwa uki·-mo·nšwa·n epino·ci·nyan.* He cut my hair, and he cut the child's hair too.
350. *nenki·-pekitenama·k aw enini upa·škesikan.* That man let me have his gun.

351. *nenki·-na·tema·k aw enini kecci·na·kwa.* That man helped me yesterday.
352. *nenki·-ma·ci·tema·k nento·neme·man.* He took my sturgeon away.
353. *nenki·-ma·ci·tema·k nento·šepi·ʔeka·ns.* He took my pencil away.
354. *nenki·-ki·škešama·k neškanši·n.* He cut my nails for me.
355. *a·ši nenki·-to·kkuntama·k.* Already one is biting at my hook.
356. *aw ekkwe· nentašettama·k nempapekiweya·n.* That woman is making a shirt for me.
357. *kekkina nenki·-pekkina·k iw nešo·neya·m, ka· tašš ke·ko· no·nkwa šo·neya·.* He won all my money from me, and now I have no money left.
358. *a·ppeci tašš uki·-sa·keʔiko·n.* Also the other loved him very much.
359. *uki·-wa·pema·n kene·peko·n, wi·cekkiwe·nyan tašš ka· wi·n. wi·cekkiwe·nyan uki·-tekkameko·n eniw kene·peko·n.* He saw the snake, but his friend did not. That snake bit his friend.
360. *uki·-no·nta·ko·n uwi·teke·ma·kenan.* His wife heard him.
361. *neno·ppenanekona·n kwi·wesse·ns.* The boy is following us (exc.).
362. *nenki·-wi·ntema·kuna·n, usa·m wi·kka· nenki·-pi-eya·mi.* He told us (exc.) that we had come too late.
363. *kekkina keki·-wa·pemikuna·n.* He has seen us (inc.) all.
364. *kunima· aw mentimo·yẽ ka-ššamekona·n.* Perhaps that old woman will give us (inc.) something to eat.
365. *kenapac keminta·še·nemikuna·n.* Maybe he has taken a liking to us (inc.).
366. *usa·m ni·pena keki·-mi·š.* You have given me too much.
367. *pa·ma· na·kac ka-mi·š ci-pi·nta·kkwe·ya·n.* Later on you may give me a smoke.
368. *keki·-wa·pam na?* Did you see me?
369. *keki·-wa·pemim ena?* Did you (pl.) see me?
370. *ni·pena teccink keki·-nentomin.* I called you many times.
371. *kemi·nin ma·pa esse·ma·.* I give you this tobacco.
372. *ni·n ssa wi· kwa keta·-wi·ci·win.* Let me be the one to go with you.
373. *keta·-na·temo·n na?* Shall I help you?
374. *pa·ma· ka-ni-etimene·wenim.* After a while I will catch up with you (pl.).
375. *nenki·-pa·škeci·ʔa·n wa·wan.* I have broken open an egg.

376. *nenki·-ušipi·ʔa·n etto·wak.* I have made a drawing of a human ear.
377. *ke·ššuwa·kkussin, a·ši kwa nenki·-so·nka·kkuʔa·n.* It was loose where it is attached, but now I have tightened it.
378. *ušipi·ʔeka·ns nenki·-mekka·n.* I have found a pencil.
379. *pe·šik e·tta nenki·-mekka·n wa·wan.* I found only one egg.
380. *nenki·-mekka·n upakkwakk.* I have found his arrow.
381. *nenki·-a·tte·ška·n eškote·.* I stamped out the fire.
382. *nenki·-pekicwe·pena·n, ki·-pa·škessin tašš iw wa·wan.* I dropped the egg and it broke.
383. *nenki·-kuttikwe·pena·n una·ka·ns.* I turned the dish face down.
384. *nenki·-si·kwe·pena·n nempi·šš.* I poured away the water.
385. *eto·ppuwinink nenki·-untina·n.* I picked it up from the table.
386. *nenki·-ca·kesa·n nenkipo·ssene͂.* I burned a hole in my trousers.
387. *a·pettaweyaʔi· nenki·-pa·škesa·n.* I shot it right through its center.
388. *una·ka·ns nento·nsa·n.* I am bringing the vessel to a boil.
389. *wa·pi-meno·min nenitta·-menosa·n.* I know how to cook rice.
390. *nenki·-ni-kepikka·ta·n tašš kecci-essin.* Also I passed the big rock.
391. *nuwa·penta·n uwi·kuwa·muwa·.* I see their house.
392. *nuwa·penta·n uci·ma·nuwa·.* I see their canoe.
393. *eškote· nempi·cema·nta·n.* I smell fire.
394. *nempo·p nenka-kuta·kuma·nta·n.* I shall taste the soup.
395. *nenki·-kunta·n wi·ya·ss.* I have swallowed the meat.
396. *keka·ta·n na e·ššo͂?* Are you planting cabbage?
397. *uki·-ki·škekaʔa·n mettiko·ns.* He chopped through the stick.
398. *uci·ketaʔa·n iw wi·kuwa·m aw ekkwe·.* That woman is sweeping out that house.
399. *uki·-ki·ssekka·n upi·ssekkawa·kan.* He took off his coat.
400. *uki·ssekka·n ukiccepisuwin.* He takes off his belt.
401. *upi·ssekkawa·kan usi·neška·n, usa·m eka·cci·ketini.* He has a tight fit of his coat; it is too small.
402. *utatessa·n mencikekkan.* He is painting the fence.
403. *uki·-meskwatessa·n mencikekkan.* He painted the fence red.
404. *uki·-wa·peškitessa·n mencikekkan.* He painted the fence white.
405. *emikk uki·-ki·škenta·n.* A beaver has gnawed it through.
406. *nempwa·kka·, ni·pena ke·ko· ukikke·nta·n.* He is wise; he knows many things.
407. *mo·kkuma·ne·ns uki·-ki·škekkota·n mettiko·ns.* With his pocket-knife he whittled through the stick.

408. *a·nint e·tta nenki·-mekka·nan.* I found only some few of them.
409. *nenki·-no·nta·nan kwa ša·ši.* I heard those things long ago.
410. *ni·š wi·wekkwa·nan nentaya·nan.* I have two hats.
411. *ni·š nenka-eya·nan epwi·n.* I shall have two paddles.
412. *keka·ta·nan na e·ššo·nyan?* Are you planting cabbages?
413. *uki·-mekka·nan ekwiwenan.* He found some clothes.
414. *kekkina uki·-mekka·nan ekwiwenan.* He found all the clothes.
415. *uwaya uki·-mekka·nan nentakuwinan.* Someone found my clothes.
416. *uwaya uki·-mekka·nan wi·n utakuwinan.* Someone found his clothes.
417. *uki·-mekka·nan uwaya utakuwinan.* He found someone's clothes.
418. *upi·ssekka·nan umakkesinan.* He put on his moccasins.
419. *uki·ssekka·nan umakkesinan.* He took off his moccasins.
420. *uki·ssekka·nan utakuwinan.* He took off his clothes.
421. *uki·-pi·meskwa·pi·kena·nan mettikonk unakeši·n, uki·-peswa·pi·sseto·nan.* He wound his entrails round a tree; he threw them so as to wind around.
422. *kekkina uki·-tekona·nan meškikkuwan.* He mixed all the herbal ingredients together.
423. *kenantuwa·penta·na·n wa·weno·n.* We (inc.) are looking for eggs.
424. *pa·ma· na·kac ka-tešinta·na·n.* We (inc.) will talk about it later.
425. *ne·yi·š uki·-wi·wekkwe·na·na·wa·n.* They wrapped them both up.
426. *ka· wi· nenkoci ni·-eša·ssi·.* I shall not go off anywhere.
427. *ka· wi· nempakkete·ssi·, ki· na e·tta?* — *a·ppeci kwa nempakkete·.* I am not hungry; are you? — I am very hungry.
428. *ketaye·kkos ena?* — *ka·, ka· wi· nentaye·kkusissi·.* Are you tired? — No, I am not tired.
429. *ka· wi· we·we·ni ketikketossi·.* You do not say it right.
430. *ka· kenapac ta-pi-eša·ssi· aw uškeni·kekkwe·.* I guess that young woman is not going to come.
431. *ka· wi·kka· ta-pi-eya·ssi·.* She will never come.
432. *ka· wi·kka· ki·wusse·ssi·, kettimeški.* He never goes hunting; he is lazy.
433. *ka· wi· te·pwe·ssi· aw enini.* That man is not telling the truth.
434. *ka· wi·kka· ni·messi·.* He never dances.
435. *ka· wi·n a·kkusissi· ki·kka·nessina·n, ki·-ki·weškwe·pi· e·tta tepikkonk.* Our (inc.) friend is not ill; he was just drunk last night.
436. *ka· wi·kka· pekisussi·.* He never goes swimming.

437. *ka· wi· kwa na· ka-eša·ssi·mi·* We (inc.) shall certainly not go there.
438. *ka· wi· ma·meppi· keta·-eya·ssi·mi.* We (inc.) must not stay here.
439. *nentawa· ka· wi· ka-pi·nta·kkwe·ssi·mi.* We (inc.) shall have to refrain from smoking.
440. *ka· wi· kwa na· ka-wi·ssenissi·mi.* We (inc.) shall not eat at all.
441. *ka· wi·kka· pekisussi·wak.* They never go swimming.
442. *ka· wi· kwa na· we·wi·pe·nta·kussino·n.* There is no hurry at all.
443. *ka· wi· nuwa·pema·ssi·, nuwa·pentamuwa· tašš wi· kwa uto·ppwa·-kenan.* I do not see him, but I see his pipe.
444. *ka· wi· nenissetottuwa·ssi· po·te·wa·temi·.* I do not understand Potawatomi.
445. *ka· wi·n kuyakk kekanuwe·nema·ssi·.* You are not taking proper care of him.
446. *ka· wi·n nentawa· ka-mi·na·ssi· uta·pa·nan.* You had better not give him the wagon.
447. *ni·pena teccink nenki·-no·nta·kos, ka· wi·n etašš nenki·-no·nta·kussi·.* I called out many times, but he did not hear me.
448. *ka· wi· keta·-tekkamekossi· aw enimošš.* That dog will not bite you.
449. *nenki·-ena·na·n ka· wi· keta·-wi·ci·wessi·mi.* We (exc.) told him, "You can't go with us."
450. *ka· wi· neminwa·kemippetansi·n ma·nlu nempo·p.* I do not like the taste of this soup.
451. *nemišso·messina·nik ka· wi· uki·-eya·nsi·na·wa·n pa·škesikenan.* Our (exc.) grandfathers did not have guns.
452. *ka· wi·n kenapac, ka· wi· nentine·ntansi·.* I guess not; I do not think so.
453. *kenapac uwaya pi-eya·tik, kunima· ni·kka·niss.* Someone seems to be coming here, perhaps my friend.
454. *kenapac ki·koˉ pena·tesitik.* Perhaps the fish is spoiled.
455. *kenapac eye·kkusitik.* Maybe he is tired.
456. *kenapac šo·pi·tik.* I guess he must be a bit drunk.
457. *kenapac ke· wi· uškinuwe· ki·weškwe·pi·tik.* It seems that the young man is drunk too.
458. *kenapac ki·-nenkamutik.* It seems that he sang.
459. *pepa·-ki·wusse·teke·nak kenapac.* Probably they are off hunting.
460. *kenapac ke·uškinuwe·k ki·weškwe·pi·teke·nak, enišša·na·ntekosuwak.* The young men must be drunk; they are carrying on in a rough way for no apparent reason.

461. *kenapac ke· wi· utakkuwe·nsi·nᵓeman ki·weškwe·pi·teke·nan.* It seems that her old man is drunk too.
462. *kenapac keki·-kemo·tena·tik iw wa·ka·kkuto·ns.* It looks as if you must have stolen that hatchet.
463. *kenapac wi·ya·ss pena·tessintik.* It seems that the meat is spoiled.
464. *kenapac ni·pena uki·-nessa·teke·nan eninuwan.* He must have killed many men.
465. *kenapac kenantuwa·pemikumina·tik.* He must be looking for us (inc.).
466. *kunima· ka· wi· enokki·ssi·tik.* It appears that he is not working.
467. *kunima· ka· wi· uwi·teke·ma·kenan enokki·ssi·teke·nan.* It appears that his wife is not working.
468. *ka· wi· kenapac uki·-nessa·ssi·teke·nan.* Perhaps he did not kill him.
469. *kecci-ša·ši kwa ki·-nempopan nemiššo·miss.* My grandfather died very long ago.
470. *ki·-ekkiwe·nsi·nᵓuwi, ša·ši kwa ki·-nempopan.* He was an old man; he died long ago.
471. *a·ppeci kena·cuwikupan uškinuwe·.* The young man must have been very handsome.
472. *usa·m wi·kka· nenki·-tekoššin, a·ši tašš ki·-ma·ci·pesokupa aw eškote·ta·pa·n.* I got there too late; it appeared that the train had already departed.
473. *ki·špin enokki·yan ka-tepaᵓemo·n.* If you work I will pay you.
474. *ki·špin uta·ppeškate·penikuya·n nemiššo·miss nenka-nena·ntuwiᵓik.* If I get cramps my grandfather will doctor me.
475. *ki·špin muwit uta·ppin.* If he cries pick him up.
476. *ki·špin pwa·-pi·eya·t ka· wi· ko na· ka·pa·pi·ᵓa·ssi·na·n.* If he does not come we (inc.) will not wait for him.
477. *ki·špin no·nta·kot uwi·teke·ma·kenan uka-necci·weᵓiko·n.* If his wife hears him she will scold him.
478. *ki·špin ke·ko· eššameyamenkit.* If he gives us (exc.) anything to eat.
479. *ki·špin ke·ko· eššamenank.* If he gives us (inc.) anything to eat.
480. *ki·špin pwa·-uniška·t ka· wi·n ta-wi·ssenissi·.* If he does not get up he shall not eat.
481. *mi· šekwa wi·-ni·ma·ca·ya·n.* Now I must leave right away.

482. *ni·kka·ne⁻ nenki·-ka·nte ʔok, mi· tašš ki·-pekkopi·sse·ya·n.* My brother gave me a push, and then I fell into the water.
483. *ci-pwa·-nempa·ya·n kwa nenakkuwe·-pi·nta·kkwe·. ki·-eškwa·--pi·nta·kkwe·ya·n mi·šš tašš a-nempa·ya·n.* Before I go to bed I shall first have a smoke. After I have smoked then I shall go to bed.
484. *neni·puwina·pan essini·nk, mi· tašš ki·-šo·škuššina·n, keye· kwa mi· ki·-pekkopi·sse·ya·n.* I was standing on a stone; and then I slipped and fell into the water.
485. *mi· na wi·-po·netta·yank?* Is this when we (inc.) stop working?
486. *mi· ko a·ši kwa we·pi-kemiwank.* Then it started to rain.
487. *nenki·-peškonuwa·. mi·nuwa· nenki·-pa·škeswa·, mi· tašš ki·--mešwak.* I missed him with my shot. Then I shot at him again, and this time I hit him.
488. *uki·-ekwa·ššema·n ši·šši·pe·nyan, mi· tašš ki·-pekaškešwa·t.* She took the duck out of the kettle, and then she carved it up.
489. *ki·špin na·temaweyan mi· ko ci-ki·ši·tta·ya·n mo·nuwakwa· kekkina ekiw uppeni·k.* If you help me I may get done digging up all those potatoes.
490. *eppi· ki·-pi-tekoššink nenka-kekwe·cema·.* When he has arrived here I shall ask him.
491. *a·ppi·šš ki·-mekkaman ušipi·ʔeka·ns?* — *mi·kka·nsink nenki·--untina·n.* Where did you find the pencil? — I picked it up on the path.
492. *a·ppi·šš ki·-wa·pentaman ma·nta?* Where did you see this?
493. *e·ntekwe·n ta-wi·-nentawa·peminank.* I wonder whether he will be looking for us (inc.).
494. *e·ntekwe·n ta-wi·-wa·peminank.* I wonder whether he will see us (inc.).
495. *e·ntekwe·n ta-ki·-wa·peminank.* I wonder whether he has seen us (inc.).
496. *empe·kišš nentawa· pepa·-ki·wusse·t.* I wish he would go and hunt.
497. *una·kuššik nenka-pi-tekoššin.* I shall get here in the evening.
498. *una·kuššik ka· wi·n ma·meppi· nuwi·-wi·ssenissi·.* This evening I shall not be eating here.
499. *wa·pank nenka -wa-enokki· o·te·na·nk.* Tomorrow I shall go to work in Detroit.
500. *nenka-wa·pema· wa·pank.* I shall see him tomorrow.
501. *ta-enokki· wa·pank.* He will work tomorrow.

502. *nenka-pi·to·n wa·pank.* I shall bring it tomorrow.
503. *nenka-pi·na· wa·pank.* I shall bring him tomorrow.
504. *wa·pank ka-pi·to·n.* Tomorrow you are to bring it.
505. *ka-pi·to·n wa·pank.* You are to bring it tomorrow.
506. *ka-wi·-eta·wemin kuwe·ppecika·ns, pa·ma· nenka-pi·to·n wa·pank.* I want to borrow your hammer; I will bring it back tomorrow.
507. *ka-wa·pemin wa·pank.* I will see you tomorrow.
508. *ki·špin kemiwank wa·pank ka· wi· nenka-eša·ssi·.* If it rains tomorrow I shall not go there.
509. *ni·-ni-ma·ca· ki·-eškwa·-na·wekkwe·k.* I shall leave after noon.
510. *pa·ma· ki·-eškwa·-una·kušši-wi·sseniya·nk nenka-ni-ma·ca·mi.* After we (exc.) have eaten the evening meal we shall leave.
511. *nessokunakakk ta-pi-peska·pi· aw ekkwe·.* In three days that woman will be back.
512. *wi·-ni·muwak no·nkwa tepikkakk.* They are going to dance tonight.
513. *wi·-kessina·mekat no·nkwa tepikkakk, ni·š etašš nentawe·nta·kuto·n wa·po·weya·nan.* It is going to get cold tonight; one will need two blankets.
514. *a·petik ka-pi-ki·we· ta-pwa·-tepikkakk.* You will have to get back home before nightfall.
515. *ni·teke·ma·kan wi·-pi-tekoššin ma·meppi· na·neki·šekakk, una·-kuššinik ta-pi-tekoššin.* My wife will get here on Friday; she will get here in the evening.
516. *nenkikke·nema ešiya·t.* I know where he is.
517. *nenki·-wa·pema· pi-eya·t, nenki·-pesa·ni-eya· tašš.* I saw him coming, and so I stayed quiet.
518. *nenki·-wi·ntema·k a·kkusit.* He told me he was ill.
519. *uwi·kka·ne·nyan uki·-pa·tta·meko·n iw ki·-kemo·tit wa·ka·kkuto·ns.* His brother accused him of having stolen the hatchet.
520. *nenki·-wi·ntemawa· wi·-ni-ma·ca·ya·n.* I told him I was going away.
521. *nenki·-no·nta·n wi·-pepa·ma·tesiyan.* I heard you were going on a journey.
522. *nuwi·-wi·ntemawa·k a·ši kwa tepiško·sse· ta-ni-ma·ca·ya·nk.* I shall tell them it is time now for us (exc.) to leave.
523. *nenki·-wi·ntema·k uwi·teke·ma·kenan a·kkusinit.* He told me his wife was ill.

524. *nenki·-wi·ntema·kuna·n neška·tesi·ttuwiyeminkit.* He told us (exc.) that he was angry at us.
525. *nenki·-wi·ntema·k ki·-mekkank keci·ma·n.* He told me he had found your canoe.
526. *kecci-enokki· aw mentimo·ye͞ pi·neccike·t ema· ka·wetta·kemik.* That old woman works hard cleaning up all over the house.
527. *umettikwa·pi·n uki·-ma·ci·na·n pepa·-ki·wusse·t.* He took along his bow and went about hunting.
528. *kekkina nenki·-ki·ši·tta· menose·kkwe·ya·n.* I have finished all my cooking.
528a. *uki·-na·temawa·n pepa·-ki·wusse·wa·t.* He helped him as they went about hunting.
528b. *ki·-ni-ma·ca· ci-pwa·-tepikketinik.* He left before nightfall.
529. *ki·-mi·ka·so ki·-mi·ka·tink.* He fought in the war.
530. *keša·tte·mekat no·nko ki·šekakk.* It is hot weather today.
531. *kessina·mekat pepo·nk.* It is cold in winter.
532. *nenana·metapemi ema· mi·šeško·nsekka·k, neno·ntuwa·na·nik etašš pene·šši·nyak nenkamuwa·t.* We (exc.) sat a while there in the grass, and we heard the birds singing.
533. *nenantuwa·pema·na·n wa·po·so͞, ma·meppi· tašš eya· na·meyaʔi· mi·šeško·nsekka·k.* We (exc.) are looking for the rabbit, and here he is, under the grass.
534. *unci·ye͞ nenki·-nematap a-nematepit.* I sat next to him where he sat.
535. *keša·tte·mekat ma·meppi· a-nematepiya·n. — ka-a·ntap.* The sun shines hot here where I am sitting. — You had better change your seat.
536. *ni·šink ekkossink mettiko·n, ni·šink ekkossink messan.* Two cords of wood; two cords of firewood.
537. *nenkwatink ekkossink.* One cord.
538. *nenkwatink tepa·kkussink.* One spool of thread.
539. *ma·nta ketipeʔamo·n ki·-nena·ntuwiʔeyan.* I am paying you this for doctoring me.
540. *pi-entasso-ki·we·t unicci·weʔiko·n.* Every time he comes home she scolds him.
541. *nentano·na· kwi·wesse·ns ke·ko· wi·-na·tit.* I am commissioning the boy to fetch something.
542. *nentipeninci·pesowin nenki·-mi·nik keta·-eya·ma·n.* He gave me a ring to have as my own.

543. *pa·ma· ko na· na·kac ka-mi·š ci-pi·nta·kkwe·ya·n.* After a while you may give me a smoke.
544. *nenki·-wi·kkumiko·k ci-wi·to·ppumakwa·.* They have invited me to eat with them.
545. *ni·-enokki·nan wi·-nena·ʔeccika·te·k.* I am going to have the things repaired.
546. *tepiško·sse· ta-ma·ca·yank.* It is time for us (inc.) to go.
547. *senaketto·wak wi·-nessituttamuwa·t.* They have a hard time understanding it.
548. *ketaka·wa·na· na wi·-pi·nta·kkwe·yan?* Are you hankering for tobacco to smoke?
549. *kenantuwe·nemin ta-mi·ceyan.* I want you to eat it.
550. *nento·ne·nema· wi·-uttamak.* I am forgetting to draw at my pipe.
551. *menwa·peme·wesiwin ta-wi·ci·wekoya·nk ni·ka·n ki·šekato·n.* That we (exc.) may be accompanied by good fortune in the days to come.
552. *kenapac sekime͂ nenki·-petakkeʔokutik, nenkiši·pi· ka·-enamit.* A mosquito must have stung me; I am itching where he bit me.
553. *ni·n ka·-ešiwe·pesiya·n.* The way I fared and did.
554. *a·ni·šš e·ši-eya·yan?* What is ailing you?
555. *a·ni·šš ka·-ešiwe·pesiyan? kekkina kenimpi·wa·kkos. — nenki·-kunipeška·.* What has happened to you? You are all drenched — I fell out of the boat.
556. *a·ni·šš e·ši-pema·tesiyan?* How are you?
557. *a·ni·šš e·šinekka·suyan?* What is your name?
558. *a·ni·šš ka·-ekkituyan?* What did you say?
559. *a·ni·ppi·šš e·ša·t?* Where is he going?
560. *mi· ko na· iw eppane· e·ši-eya·t.* That is the way he always is.
561. *na·ssa·p ke· ni· nenka-ešicceke· e·šeccike·t.* I shall do exactly as he does.
562. *a·ni·šš na· e·ši-pema·tesit?* How is he?
563. *a·ni·šš ko·ss e·ši-pema·tesit?* How is your father?
564. —
565. *mi· e·šenikka·sot ca·n.* That is his name, John.
566. *a·ni·šš ka·-ekkitot?* What did he say?
567. *mi· iw ka·-ekkitot.* That is what he said.
568. *mi· ma·nta ka·-ešisseto·t.* This is the way he placed it.
569. *ša·ši kwa ka·-ena·kkunike·wa·t.* The way they did things in times past.

570. *a·ppi·šš ma·nta e·nemok mi·kkan?* Where does this road lead to?
571. *a·ni·šš e·šeccika·teman ešitto·yan?* How do you make it?
572. *uwiti e·nteʔipi·ya·nk.* Over there where we (exc.) draw our water.
573. *we·kune·šš we·šetto·yan?* What are you doing (making)?
574. *nenki·-pa·škeswa· ecitemõ, mi· kwa na· ma·meppi· ka·-unta·kkwi·-ya·n.* I have shot a squirrel; I shot from right here.
575. *we·kune·šš nenkwaci· ka·-unci-eša·yan?* Why did you go off somewhere?
576. *we·kune·šš we·nci-ešicceke·yan?* Why do you do that?
577. *we·kune·šš e·ni-unci-ma·ca·t?* Why is he leaving?
578. *ni·cekkiwẽ nenki·-nematepimi e·nteši-pekisuwa·t.* My friend and I sat at the bathing beach.
579. *kecci-mema·nka·ška· e·nteši-pekisuwa·t.* The water is very rough at the bathing beach.
580. *wa·ssa e·nta·ya·n.* It is far to where I live.
581. *pe·ššo e·nta·ya·n.* It is near [from here] to where I live.
582. *pe·ššo eya·mekat ma·meppi· e·nta·ya·n.* The place where I live is close by here.
583. *wa·ssa eya·mekat ma·meppi· e·nta·ya·n.* The place where I live is far from here.
584. *ka· wi· nenki·-eya·ssi· e·nta·ya·n.* I was not at home.
585. *a·ppi·šš e·nta·yan?* Where do you live?
586. *a·ppi· tašš ki·n e·nta·yan?* And you, where do you live?
587. *mi· nenkwana ema· e·nta·yan.* And so this is where you live!
588. *nenki·-a·nci-kusimi e·nta·ya·nk.* We (exc.) moved [our residence].
589. *nenkwissẽ ki·-ni-ma·ca· ema· e·nta·ya·nk.* My son went out of our (exc.) house.
590. *wa·ssa e·nta·ya·nk.* We (exc.) live far from here.
591. *mi· na ema· e·nta·ye·k?* Is it there that you (pl.) live?
592. *wi·n e·nta·t.* Where he lives.
593. *eniššena·pe· e·nta·t.* The Indian's dwelling (name of a brand of tobacco).
594. *emikk e·nta·t.* The beaver's lodge.
595. *pene·šši̵ e·nta·t.* A birdhouse.
596. *pi·nette·ni e·nta·t aw ekkwe·, ka· wi· uwaya ekko·ci·ššan.* That woman's house is clean; there are no lice.
597. *ma·pa ekkwe· e·nta·t necci·wette·ni.* This woman's house is in disorder.
598. *eša·weškwa·nte·ni e·nta·t.* He lives in a green house.

599. *mi· ssa ma·meppi· e·nta·t.* Right here is where he lives.
600. *na·mekkamik e·nta·t.* He lives underground.
601. *wi·nuwa· e·nta·wa·t.* Where they dwell.
602. *nenki·-wi·kkumiko·k ci-eša·ya·n e·nta·wa·t.* They have invited me to their house.
603. *e·ntesso-tekoššink unicci·weʔiko·n eniw ekkwe·wan.* Every time he comes that woman scolds him.
604. *e·ntesso-tekoššink nemi·na· esse·ma·n.* Every time he comes I give him tobacco.
605. *a·ni·šš e·ntessotepaʔekane·k?* What time is it?
606. *e·ntesso-wa·peminank ma·pa ekkwe· kepa·ppeʔikuna·n.* Every time this woman sees us (inc.) she laughs at us.
607. *ki·-kecci-kemiwan eppane· me·no·kkemik.* It rained hard all last spring.
608. *nemiššo·miss kkwa nenki·-na·tema·k me·kwa· pe·ma·tesit.* My grandfather used to help me when he was living.
609. *eppi· eya·pentisot ki·-nempokupa.* When he saw himself he must have died.
610. *pa·ma· wa·pank nenka-ni-ma·ca·. — a·ni· tašš eppi· ke·-peska·pi·-yan?* Tomorrow I shall leave. — And when are you coming back?
611. *eppi· eye·pi-kemiwank nenki·-peska·pi·mi ki·-ni-ki·we·ya·nk.* When it started to rain we (exc.) turned about and went home.
612. *eppi· eye·pi-kemiwank mi· ki·-ki·we·ya·nk.* When it started to rain we (exc.) went home.
613. *eppi· ke·muwank.* When it rained.
614. *ka· wi· uki·-nessituwina·kussi·n eniw ukaššuwan eppi· pe·ska·pi·t, eppi· tašš ka·-nessituwinuwa·t uki·-a·kukwe·na·n, mi· tašš ki·-uci·-ma·t.* His mother did not recognize him when he came back, but when she did recognize him she embraced him and kissed him.
615. *a·ni·špi·cc ka·-pi-peska·pi·yan?* When did you come back?
616. *a·ni·špi·cc ke·-pi-tekoššink?* When will he arrive here?
617. *a·ni·ppi·šš ki·-wa·pemat?* Where did you see him?
618. *a·ppi·šš ki·-wa·pemat?* Where did you see him?
619. *a·ni·šš menikk e·ya·nk ci·ma·nan?* How many canoes has he?
620. *ke·ka· ka·-a·šekiteko·cenan.* You almost tumbled backwards.
621. *kecci-ki·ko͞ nenki·-kuntamo·na·, mi· tašš ki·-wi·kkupišit nempi·nk, ke·ka· tašš ka·-kunta·ppene·ya·n.* I got a big fish on my line, and it pulled me into the water, and I almost got drowned.
622. *ke·ko· ni·-ki·špenato·na·pan eta·we·wekamekonk, usa·m tašš wi·kka·*

nenki·-ni-tekoššin, a·ši tašš ki·-kepa·kku ͻika·te·kupan eta·we·-wekamik. mi· tašš ka·-eši-ki·we·ya·n pe·pešiššak, no·ss etašš nenki·-necci·we ͻik. I was going to buy something at the store, but I got there too late, and the store was already closed. So then I went back empty-handed, and my father scolded me.

623. *ka· kenake· pi-peska·pi·ssi·. nempa·pi· ͻa·na·n. kenapac ki·--weniššena·tik. ukikke·nta·n ke·-pi-eša·t. ki·-we·wi·peška· kwa ša·ši.* He is not coming back at all. We (exc.) are waiting for him. Perhaps he has got lost. He knows the way here. He always made the trip quickly before.

624. —

625. *ka· nenkikke·nema·ssi· ke·na·temo·nank.* I do not know whether he will help us (inc.).

626. *e·ntekwe·n ta·wi·-na·temo·nank.* I wonder whether he will help us (inc.).

627. *we·we·ni ka·-eššameyan.* Thank you for giving me food.

628. *we·we·ni ka·-eššameya·nk.* Thank you for giving us food.

629. *uwiti e·ya·t kecci-ki·ko͞ na·mi-mekkom.* There is a big fish there under the ice.

630. *utašettamuwa·n wa·-ekwinit.* She makes clothes for him.

631. *eya·pesot nentaya·wa· mešši·min.* I have a ripe apple.

632. *aw ne·nkemot.* The one who is singing.

633. *aw wa·-nenkamot.* The one who is going to sing.

634. *aw epino·ci͞ e·-pwa·-wi·ssenit a·ppeci ta-pekkate·.* The child that does not eat will be very hungry.

635. *ni·n ssa aw ka·-ni·mit.* I am the one who danced.

636. *ki·n ssa aw ka·-ni·mit.* You are the one who danced.

637. *ma·pa kenapac ka·-ni·mit.* This one perhaps is the one who danced.

638. *ni·š nenki·-eya·wa·na·nik te·we· ͻekanak, pe·šik kecci-te·we· ͻekan keye· kwa pe·šik e·ka·cci·n ͻit.* We (exc.) had two drums, one big drum and one little one.

639. *aw eškwa·ya·c ka·-pi-eša·t nenki·-mi·na· šo·neya·.* I gave some money to the one who came last.

640. *nettam ke·-pi-eya·t nenka-mi·na·. esse·ma·n.* I shall give some tobacco to the one who comes here first.

641. *ni·n aw ka·-wa·pema·t wa·wa·ške·ššuwan.* I am the one who saw the deer.

642. *e·sa·wa·k wa·wan pi·nci·ye ͻi·.* The yolk of an egg.

643. *uki·-pekkipeto·nan e·sa·wa·nik.* She picked yellow ones.
644. *uki·-pekkipeto·nan e·ša·weškwa·nik.* She picked blue ones.
645. *uwe·ne· tašš aw e·-ki·wusse·t?* Who is the one hunting?
646. *uwe·ne·šš ka·-uta·ppenank nemo·kkuma·ne·ns?* Who picked up my knife?
647. *uwe·ne·šš ma·nta te·pe·ntank ušipi·ʔeka·ns?* Whose pencil is this?
648. *we·kune·šš ke·-pi·tuwiyan?* What are you going to bring me?
649. *we·kune·šš ka·-mi·nikk?* What did he give you?
650. *ekiw e·tta e·-ni·mecik ta-wi·sseniwak.* Only those who dance shall eat.
651. *ki·nuwa· ko šša ekiwi ka·-ni·mecik.* You are the ones who danced.
652. *ekiw epino·ci·k e·-pwa·-wi·ssenicik a·ppeci ta-pekkate·wak.* The children who do not eat will be very hungry.
653. *ki·-pa·tti·nuwak pe·ma·tesicik.* There were many people.
654. *ekiw e·tta e·nukki·cik ta-wi·sseniwak.* Only those who work shall eat.
655. *ekiw e·tta e·-nenkamucik ta-wi·sseniwak.* Only those who sing shall eat.
656. *ekiw epino·ci·nyak e·-pwa·-na·temawecik ka· wi·n nenka-mi·na·ssi·k si·sepa·kkuto·nsan.* I shall not give any candy to the children who do not help me.
657. *ma·pa kwi·wesse·ns ukossa·n uwe·kwe·n pi-eya·necin.* This boy is afraid of everyone who comes here.
658. *sekime·nyak utamwa·wa·n pe·ma·tesinecin.* Mosquitoes eat human beings.
659. *nenki·-ne·kussito·nan eniw nentaneka·suwinan wa·-pepa·-eya·ma·nin wi·-pepa·-ki·wusse·ya·n.* I stuck under my belt the implements I was going to take along as I went hunting.
660. *kekkina te·pe·ntema·nin.* All the things I own.
661. *eppi· nenkwisse͂ me·no-ešiwe·pesicin si·sepa·kkuto·ns kkwa nenta-ššema·.* When my little son behaves well I give him candy.
662. *ki·špin ke·muwankin e·nta·yank ketaya·mi.* Whenever it rains we (inc.) stay home.
663. *eppi· kko ke·muwankin mi· kkwa ki·-ki·we·ya·nk.* Whenever it rained we (exc.) went home.
664. *eppi· ušišše·nyan e·ššemikucin si·sepa·kkuto·ns mi· kwe·cc utina·n. mi· tašš e·na·t mi· kwe·cc.* Whenever his uncle gives him candy he thanks him. Then he says to him, "Thank you."

665. *ki·-se·kesi kekke·nema·ssik iw no·ss nemanci ke·-ekkitukwe·n.* She was frightened because she did not know what my father might say.
666. *ki·špin no·ntuwa·ssuwak.* If I do not hear him.
667. *ki·špin na·temo·ssuwan.* If you do not help me.
668. *nenkašši ki·-pi-eša· ema· a-nempa·ya·n ki·-pi-wa·pemit ne·mpa·wa·ne·n.* My mother came to where I was sleeping to see whether I was asleep.
669. *nempi-eša· e·nta·ye·k ki·špin e·ya·we·kwe·n.* I came to your (pl.) house [to see] if you (pl.) were there.
670. *nenki·-eša· e·nta·wa·t ki·špin e·ya·wa·kwe·n.* I went to their house [to see] if they were there.
671. *ecitemo͞ pepa·ma·ntuwe·petto· pepa·-wa·pentank peka·nan ki·špin eya·pete·nekwe·n.* The squirrel is running about on the branches looking to see whether the nuts are ripe.
672. *uta·nessan ta-ešicceke·wan we·kutakwe·n e·na·kwe·n.* His daughter will do whatever he tells her.
673. *e·ntekwe·n ka·-pepa·-ki·wusse·kwe·n.* I wonder if he went hunting.
674. *e·ntekwe·n ke·-pepa·-ki·wusse·kwe·n.* I wonder whether he will go hunting.
675. *e·ntekwe·n wi·kka· ka·wusse·kwe·n.* I wonder if he ever goes hunting.
676. *e·ntekwe·n ka·-nenkamukwe·n.* I wonder whether he sang.
677. *e·ntekwe·n ke·-una·c-wa·pentisukwe·n.* I wonder whether he will like his own looks.
678. *e·ntekwe·n ka·wusse·wa·kwe·n.* I wonder whether they are hunting.
679. *e·ntekwe·n ke·ke·tt ke·temiškenikwe·n uwi·teke·ma·kenan.* I wonder whether his wife really is lazy.
680. *e·ntekwe·n uwi·teke·ma·kenan e·nukki·nekwe·n.* I wonder whether his wife works.
681. *e·ntekwe·n uwi·teke·ma·kenan ka·-enokki·nekwe·n ci·na·kwa.* I wonder whether his wife worked yesterday.
682. *e·ntekwe·n ke·muwanukwe·n uwiti menišše·nᵖink.* I wonder if it is raining over on the island.
683. *e·ntekwe·n ta-etimene·wa·wete·n.* I wonder whether you will catch up to him.
684. *e·ntekwe·n wi·kka· ma·pa nemiššo·miss ka·-nessa·kwe·n eninuwan.* I wonder whether this grandfather of mine ever killed a man.

685. e·ntekwe·n ta-wi·-na·temawekwe·n. I wonder if he will help me.
686. e·ntekwe·n ke·-na·temawuwane·n. I wonder whether you will help me.
687. e·ntekwe·n ke·-na·temawuwa·nke·n. I wonder if you will help us.
688. e·ntekwe·n ke·-na·temawuwe·kwe·n. I wonder whether you (pl.) will help me.
689. e·ntekwe·n ka·-mekkamuwa·kwe·n. I wonder whether they have found it.
690. e·ntekwe·n uwi·teke·ma·kenan e·nukki·ssi·nekwe·n. I wonder whether his wife is not working.
691. ki·špin pwa·-untametta·ya·mpa· nenta·-ki·-eša·. If I were not busy I would go there.
692. ki·špin pa·tti·netto·ya·mpa·n šo·neya· nenta·-ki·-ki·špenato·n ma·nta wi·kuwa·m. If I had lots of money I would buy this house.
693. ki·špin eya·ppan aw no·ss ma·meppi· keta·-ki·-na·tema·kuna·n. If my father were here he would help us (inc.).
694. ki·špin tekke·ya·kupa nenta·-ki·-enokki·. If the weather were cool I should work.
695. ki·špin eya·wekipa· esse·ma· nenta·-ki·-pi·nta·kkwe·. If I had any tobacco I should smoke.
696. ki·špin nessa·ppa ki·ko·nyan meno-menikk nenta·-ki·-emwa·na·n ki·ko·nyan. If he caught any fish we (exc.) would have enough fish to eat.
697. ki·špin wi·ntemaweyampa keta·-ki·-na·temo·n. If you had told me I should have helped you.
698. ki·špin pwa·-wa·pemippa mi· ko ta·-ki·-ki·ʔekipan. If he had not seen me I should have got away from him.
699. ki·špin wa·pemippan nenta·-ki·-kepa·kkuʔok. If he had seen me he would have jailed me.
700. ki·špin wa·pemiwa·ppan ke· ni·n nenta·-ki·-kepa·kkuʔoko·k. If they had seen me they would have put me, too, in jail.
701. ki·špin wa·pemikkupa keta·-ki·-kepa·kkuʔok. If he had seen you he would have jailed you.
702. ke· ki· ki·špin wa·pemikkwa·pan ke· ki· keta·-ki·-kepa·kkuʔoko·k. If they had seen you, too, they would have jailed you as well.
703. ki·špin wa·peminankupa keta·-ki·-kepa·kkuʔokuna·n. If he had seen us (inc.) he would have jailed us.
704. ki·špin na·temo·nenankupa keta·-ki·-ki·ši·tta·mi. If he had helped us (inc.) we should have finished our work.

705. *ki·špin wa·pemina·mpa·n keta·-ki·-wi·ntemo·n.* If I had seen you I would have told you.
706. *ki·špin eya·ma·mpa· šo·neya· nenta·-ki·-eya·muwa· uwi·wekkwa·n.* If I had money I would buy his hat from him.
707. *wa·wa·ške·šši nenki·-wa·pema· uwiti me·kuya·k. ki·špin eya·ma·mpa· pa·škesikan nenta·-ki·-pa·škeswa·.* I saw a deer over in the woods. If I had had a gun I should have shot him.
708. *me·yo·ša ki·-no·ntema·mpa·.* I heard it a long time ago.
709. *neme·tto· ssa wi· kwa ka·-pi-eša·kupane·n.* He has left traces which show that he must have come here.
710. *neme·tto·wak ka·-pi-eša·kupane·nak.* They have left traces which show that they must have come here.
711. *neme·tto·wan ka·-pi-ešakupane·nan uwi·teke·ma·kenan.* There are traces indicating that his wife must have come here.
712. *e·ntekwe·n ka·-nenkamukopene·n.* I wonder whether he sang.
713. *e·ntekwe·n ta-ki·-mešwa·wetipene·n. kenapac keta·-ki·-peškonuwa·.* I wonder whether you would have hit him. I daresay you would have missed him with your shot.
714. *e·ntekwe·n ke·-na·temawekopene·n.* I wonder whether he would have helped me.
715. *ma·ca·n ma·meppi·.* Come here.
716. *a·mpe· wi·-uniška·n.* Do please get up (from lying).
717. *no·šešše̅, pi-eša·n ma·meppi·.* Come here, grandchild.
718. *ma·meppi· pi-eša·n.* Come here.
719. *e·ši-keccinekka·yan eni-eša·n.* Go to your right.
720. *e·ši-nemancenikka·yan eni-eša·n.* Go to your left.
721. *ekwaci·nk eša·n.* Go out of doors.
722. *po·netta·n iw keki·pa·tesiyan.* Stop being so bad.
723. *we·wi·petta·n enokki·yan.* Hurry up your work.
724. *pe·kka· ema· eya·n.* Stay there and don't budge.
725. *pesa·n eya·n.* Stay quiet.
726. *kwa eya·n ma·meppi·.* Go away from here.
727. *ešicceke·n ke· ki· e·šeccike·t.* Do the way he does.
728. *we·we·ni nentošše·n.* Listen attentively.
729. *ekwaci·nk pi·nta·kkwe·n.* Smoke out of doors.
730. *we·wi·p menikkwe·n.* Drink it up fast.
731. *e·ka·c menikkwe·n.* Drink it slowly.
732. *ecina e·tta ni·min, mi· tašš ci-enwe·peyan.* Dance only a short time, so that you get a rest then.

733. *we·wi·p nematepin.* Sit down at once.
734. *a·ssena· we·we·ni ena·pin.* Be sure to look carefully.
735. *ni·šink no·nta·kusin.* Call out twice.
736. *nessink no·nta·kusin.* Call out three times.
737. *nenkwatink no·nta·kusin.* Call out once.
738. *mi·nuwa· no·nta·kusin.* Give another call.
739. *ma·meppi· teši-enokki·n nena·š ci-na·wekkwe·k.* Work here until noon.
740. *ekwaneʾoteson wa·po·weya·n.* Cover yourself with the blanket.
741. *ke·ttin ki·keton.* Speak the truth.
742. *e·ka·c ki·keton.* Speak slowly.
743. *nesswi ki·špenato·n.* Buy three of them.
744. *pe·ššo pi-ešipeto·n.* Pull it up close here.
745. *šeya·w wi·kkupito·n.* Pull it straight to you.
746. *a·petta po·kkupito·n.* Break it in half with your hand.
747. *nempi·nk eppito·n.* Pull it into the water.
748. *nenkoci· wa·ssa ešiweto·n.* Take it far off with you somewhere.
749. *pi·to·n nemasenaʾekan.* Bring my book.
750. *pi·to·n nenci·ma·n.* Bring my canoe.
751. *pi·to·n nentapwi.* Bring my paddle.
752. *pi·to·n e·ššoˉ.* Bring some cabbage.
753. *pi·to·n mettiko·n.* Bring some sticks.
754. *pi·to·n kepa·škesikan.* Bring your gun.
755. *pi·to·n kemo·kkuma·n.* Bring your knife.
756. *we·wi·p pi·to·n.* Bring it quickly.
757. *pe·šik pi·to·n.* Bring one of them.
758. *mi·kka·ns na·keʾatto·n.* Follow the path.
759. *eškote· ušitto·n.* Make a fire.
760. *šenkiššenin eto·ppuwinink.* Lie down on the table.
761. *ekici-eto·ppuwin šenkiššenin.* Lie down on top of the table.
762. *na·meyaʾi· šenkiššenin.* Lie down under it.
763. *a·, wi·-wi·ssenik.* Come on, eat (ye)!
764. *aʾa·w, mi·nuwa· wi·ssenik.* Well, eat (ye) some more.
765. *we·wi·p kwa·škunik.* Disembark (ye) quickly.
766. *po·sik nenci·ma·nink.* Get (ye) into my canoe.
767. *po·sik nento·ta·pa·nink.* Get (ye) into my wagon.
768. *ekwaci·nk wi·-ni-eša·ta·.* Let us go out of doors.
769. *pe·kka· eya·ta· ma·meppi·.* Let us stay right here.
770. *a·mpe· pi·nteke·ta·.* Do let us go in.

771. *a·mpe· wi·-ni·ssa·ntuwe·ta·.* Do let us go downstairs.
772. *a·mpe· wi·-ki·we·ta· e·nta·yank.* Do let us go back home.
773. *a·w tašš wi·ssenita·.* Well, let us eat.
774. *ma·meppi· nematepita·.* Let us sit here.
775. *ma·no·ko necci·wiˀ.* Just scold him.
776. *wa·pam epino·cĩ.* Look at the child.
777. *wa·pam ekkikk.* Look at the kettle.
778. *wa·pam aw emikk.* Look at that beaver.
779. *eššam epino·cĩ.* Feed the child.
780. *kenawe·nim kepe·-pepo·n.* Take care of him through the winter.
781. *eni-tekkon epino·cĩ.* Hold the child.
782. *pekitin epino·cĩ.* Set the child down.
783. *menta·min na·š ka·ši·nkwe·t.* Fetch ripe corn.
784. *ma·pa tenawa pi·nta·kkwa·š.* Smoke this kind of tobacco.
785. *keta·-tekkopena· ema· tekkina·kenink. tekkopiš nentawa·, ta-nempa· tašš.* You had better tie him on the cradle board. Just tie him fast, then he will sleep.
786. *aw na· ko na· ma·no· mi·š.* Oh, do give it to him anyway!
787. *pi·š kwi·wesse·ns.* Bring the boy.
788. *pi·š enimošš.* Bring the dog.
789. *pi·š pa·keˀa·kkwa·n.* Bring the chicken here.
790. *pi·š pe·šeko·keši·.* Bring the horse.
791. *pi·š ekkikk.* Bring the kettle here.
792. *pi·taw umo·kkuma·n.* Bring him his knife.
793. *a·mpe· ssa ki·škaw ma·pa mettik.* Please chop through this tree.
794. *a·paw aw pe·šeko·keši·.* Untie that horse.
795. *uppikkuna·nk we·ppetaw.* Beat him on his back.
796. *uninci·nk pekkitte·w.* Hit him on his hand.
797. *a·mpe· ssa kuwaw ma·pa mettik.* Please fell this tree.
798. *teka kuwaw aw mettik.* Come, fell that tree.
799. *ni·š šeka·kuwi·nši·k tekos.* Cook two onions along with the rest.
800. *mi·šekon na· iw uwi·wekkwa·n.* Do (ye) give him his hat!
801. *nempi·šš menaˀeššin.* Give me a drink of water.
802. *nekkwe·ttuwiššin. a·ni·šš pwa·-nekkwe·ttuwiyan?* Answer me. Why don't you answer me?
803. *mi·šeššik nuwi·wekkwa·n.* Give (ye) me my hat.
804. *eni-kenawe·nemiššena·nk ni·ka·n ki·šekato·n.* Do Thou watch over us in the days to come.

805. *a·mpe· wi·-po·nemiššena·nk.* Please stop bothering us with talk!
806. *nekkwe·ttuwiššena·nk. a·ni·šš na· pwa·-nekkwe·ttuwiya·nk?* Answer us. Why don't you answer us?
807. *keška·pekka ʔan eškwa·nte·m.* Lock the door.
808. *ci·cci·kkeše· ʔan eškote·.* Poke up the fire.
809. *a·tte· ʔan eškote·.* Put out the fire.
810. *kepa·kku ʔan eškwa·nte·m.* Shut the door.
811. *we·we·ni kesi·pi·kenan.* Wash them carefully.
812. *ke·sepi·kenan wa·po·weya·n.* Fold up the blanket.
813. *ka·ncwe·penan nempi·nk.* Push it into the water.
814. *e·ka·c umpinan.* Lift it slowly.
815. *kekkina kekwe·ceci·nan.* Feel it all over with your hand.
816. *nessa·kkunan eškwa·nte·m.* Open the door.
817. *e·ka·c nessa·kkunan.* Open it slowly.
818. *ni·šo-tepaʔeka·ns tenisan.* Cook it for two hours.
819. *nesso-tepaʔeka·ns tenisan.* Cook it for three hours.
820. *po·ta·tan eškote·.* Blow up the fire.
821. *šeya·w eppaketan.* Throw it straight.
822. *wa·pentan eškote·.* Look at the fire.
823. *wap·entan mesineʔikan.* Read the book.
824. *we·we·ni pi·cema·ntan.* Take a good smell of it.
825. *a·w, tašš wi· ekintan.* Come now, count them.
826. *a·ssena· we·we·ni ekintan.* Be sure to read it (to count them) carefully.
827. *e·ka·c ekintan.* Read it slowly.
828. *pa·ma· wa·pank pi-eša·kkan, mi· tašš ta-wi·ci·wena·n.* Come tomorrow, then I will go with you.
829. *pa·ma· pi·to·kkan.* Bring it later on.
830. *pa·ma·ko na· wi·ntemaweššikkan.* Tell me about it later on.
831. *ke·ko wi· ki· pi-eša·kke·n ma·meppi·.* Don't you come here!
832. *ke·kwa ešicceke·kke·n iw.* Don't do that.
833. *ke·kwa ma·nta ešicceke·kke·kon.* Do (ye) not do this.
834. *ke·kwa ma·meppi· ni·mekke·n.* Do not dance here.
835. *ke·ko pi·to·kke·n nentapwi.* Do not bring my paddle.
836. *ke·ko wi· ema· nematepikke·kon, kesa·ka·ssom. eka·wa·kkwa·k eša·k. wi·kuwa·mink eša·k.* Do (ye) not sit here; you are right in the sun. Go where it is shady. Go inside the house.
837. *ke·kwa wi·kka· pekisukke·kon.* Do (ye) not ever go swimming.
838. *ke·ko eššama·kke·n pe·šeko·keši·.* Do not feed the horse.

839. *ke·ko wi·kka· eššama·kke·n pe·šeko·keši·.* Do not ever feed the horse.
840. *ke·kwa we·pena·kke·n nento·ppwa·kan.* Don't throw away my pipe.
841. *ke·ko wi·n kwa na· mi·na·kke·n.* Do not give it to him, of all people.
842. *ke·ko wi·kka· nessa·kke·n aw e·nekoˉ.* Don't ever kill ants.
843. *ke·ko wi·-kussa·kke·n ekiw enimo·k. ka· wi· ke·ko· keta·-to·ta·-kussi·k.* Don't be afraid of those dogs; they won't do anything to you.
844. *ke·ko wi·n kwa na· ni·n mi·šeššikke·n.* Do not give it to me, of all people.
845. *ke·ko wi·n kwa na· mi·šeššikka·nke·n.* Do not give it to us.
846. *ke·kwa pa·škeʾanke·n wa·wan.* Do not break the egg.
847. *ke·kwa nessa·kkunanke·n wa·sse·ccekan.* Do not open the window.
848. *ke·kwa nessa·kkunanke·kon eškwa·nte·m.* Do (ye) not open the door.
849. *po·šo· no·kko·.* Good day, grandmother.
850. *po·šo· nemiššo·.* Good day, grandfather.
851. *nenka-wi·-nekkawe·-ši·šši·k.* — *mi· na a·ši?* I must first go and urinate. — Have you done now?
852. *ma·nta ssa una·ka·ns.* Here's a dish for you.
853. *a·ppi· tašš kı·n kuwi·wekkwa·n?* And you, where is your hat?
854. *a·ni·ppi·šš epino·ci·nyak?* Where are the children?
855. *a·ni·ppi·šš nento·ppwa·kan?* Where is my pipe?
856. *a·ni·ppi·šš nemasenaʾekan?* Where is my paper?
857. *uwe·ne·šš tenawa pene·šši˜?* What sort of bird is it?
858. *we·kune·šš iw?* What is that?
859. *a·nı·šš e·šenikka·te·k?* What is it called?
860. *ni·n ssa aw.* It's me.
861. *ni·kka·ne˜ kecci-enini.* My brother is a big man.
862. *kekkina kuyakk eninuwak.* They are all good men.
863. *uwi·kuwa·muwa· essini·-wi·kuwa·m.* Their house is a stone house.
864. *usa·m wi·pa.* It's too early.
865. *a·ppeci meno-eppı·.* Just at the right time.
866. *uwaya ukka·t.* Somebody's leg.
867. *wi·nuwa· utaškwa·nte·muwa·.* Their door.
868. *wi·nuwa· ukwi·wesse·nsemiwa·n.* Their boy.

869. *wi·nuwa· utaye ʾa·muwa·n.*   Their horse.
870. *uwiti pi·nci·ye ʾi· wa·nekka·nink.*   Down there in the pit.
871. *na·meya ʾi· mekkomi·nk.*   Under the ice.
872. *ni·sseya· ʾi· ekkwa·ntuwa·kenink.*   Down the stairs.
873. *ma·nta wa·po·weya·n kekkina ma·netta·nešši·ye ʾi·.*   This blanket is all wool.
874. *ma·pa enini.*   This man.
875. *ekonta eninuwak*   These men.
876. *aw uppwa·kan.*   That pipe.
877. *uwe·ti enini.*   That man yonder.
878. *ekiwe·ti eninuwak.*   Those men yonder.
879. *ma·nta eto·ppuwin.*   This table.
880. *uwe·ti eto·ppuwin.*   That table yonder.
881. *eniwe·ti eto·ppuwinan.*   Those tables yonder.
882. *pe·šik mi·kwan.*   One feather.
883. *ni·š ekkikko·k.*   Two kettles.
884. *ni·š šenin.*   Two (York) shillings (25 cents).
885. *ni·win šenin.*   Four shillings (50 cents).
886. *nenkotwa·sso-šenin.*   Six shillings (75 cents).
887. *pe·šik keye· ni·š.*   One and two.
888. *ki·n keye· ni·n.*   You and I.

PART III
TEXTS

TEXTS

1. DIALECTS

e·ški-tekoššena·n ema· Walpole Island iw e·nwe·ya·n nenki·-unci--nempašša·pe?iko·k. ka· wi· iw nenki·-enwe·ssi· e·nwe·wa·t. iw ki·--a·pecitto·wa·t enwe·win wi·nuwa· "ya·n" enwe·win, ke· ni·nuwi tašš ka·-pi-uncipa·ya·n na·ssa·p ekwa iw ekkituwin "ya·n" e·šenikka·te·k ke· ni·nuwi nentišenikka·ta·na· "ya˜." ke· wi·nuwa· e·šenikka·temowa·t "e·nta·ya·n" ke· ni·nuwi tašš "e·nta·ya˜."

When I first came to Walpole Island they made fun of me on account of the way I spoke. I did not pronounce the way they did. Where they used the pronunciation "ya·n," there we, where I came from, for that same speech form which is spoken "ya·n," we used the pronunciation "ya˜." Where they said "e·nta·ya·n" [where I dwell], there we said "e·nta·ya˜."

2. GRANDMOTHER

no·kkumiss ute·-kekke·nta·n ki·-pe·šekonk e·tta eta·we·wekamik ema· sa·ki·na·nk. ki·-ša·nkessimetana-ešši-ni·win ki·-tessopepo·nekisi [1] aw no·kkumiss eppi· ne·mpot.
nenki·-sa·ke?a· no·kkumiss keye· kwa aw nemišso·miss. eppane·ko e·nta·wa·t nenki·-tenis.

My grandmother remembered the time when there was only one store there in Saginaw. My grandmother was ninety-four years old when she died.

I loved my grandmother and my grandfather. I was always staying at their house.

3. THE WHITE MAN

e·ški-wa·pemak aw kecci-mo·kkuma·n ema· tepe·w si·pi·nk nenki·--se·ke?ik. tepe·w etašš nenki·-eni-eppatto· eni-ki·we·petto·ya·n. nenki·-eni-a·pena·p kuma·ppi· e·ni-eya·ya·n.

---

[1] Speaker begins by including the number phrase between preverb and verb, but then uses the preverb over again.

"nenki·-no·ppenanik" nenki·-ene·ntam.
mi· tašš ki·-ki·we·petto·ya·n ki·-wi·ntemawak aw nenkašše·.
mi· tašš ka·-ešit "ka· wi· keta·-eya·wekossi·. kunima· o·te·ttɔ·tik" nenki·-ik.
mi· tašš ma· ki·-po·ne·ntema·n.
nenki·-kecci-kwi·wesse·nsiw ekwa na· ci-pwa·-kecci-mo·kkuma·-nemoya·n.

The first time I saw a white man there by the bank of the river, he frightened me. I ran along the bank of the river and made for home. When I had run a ways, I turned and looked back.
"He was pursuing me," I thought.
Then I ran home and told my mother about it.
What she said to me was, "He won't do anything to you. He is probably going to town," she said to me.
So then I dismissed it from my mind.
I was quite a big boy before I spoke any English.

4. FALLING IN THE WATER (*First Dictation*)

ša·ši kwa me·kwa· epino·ci·n ʔuwiya·n nenki·-ma·ci·nik aw nenkašši keye· pe·šik ekkwe· ki·-uwa-eya·muwa·t iw pekwaci-meno·min. ci·-ma·nink ki·-pemiška·wak wa·-teši-puwa ʔemowa·t iw pekwaci-meno·-min. a·no tašš ekwa nenki·-ekkawa·pemik aw nenkašši wi·-pwa·-pekkopi·sse·ya·n. nenkwatink tašš ekko na· e·na·pit eškwe·ya·nk nenki·-wa·pemik a·ši kwa ki·pekkopi·sse·ya·n. eka·wa· tašš nenki·-te·penik keye· ki·-ekwa·pi·kenit. we·wi·p etašš nenki·ssekkoneye·penik aw nenkašše· keye· ki·-wi·wekkwe·ci·nit a·nint iw utakuwin.
ki·-we·wi·petta·wak etašš penki· mi·nuwa· ki·-puwa ʔemowa·t iw pekwaci-meno·min. mi· tašš nentawa· ki·-ki·we·wa·t. a·ppeci ki·-se·-kesi ma·pa nenkašše·. ka· ukikke·nema·ssi·n nemanc ke·-ekkitukwe·n ma·pa no·ss.

Long ago, when I was a little child, my mother and another woman took me along as they went to get wild rice. They went in a canoe to the place where they knocked down that wild rice. To be sure, my mother did keep watch over me that I should not fall into the water. But once as she looked behind her, she saw me already fallen into the water. With difficulty she got hold of me and drew me out of the water. She hurriedly pulled off my clothes and wrapped me in some garment of her own.

Then hastily they gathered a little more of the wild rice. Then they were compelled to go home. My mother was badly frightened. She did not know what my father would say.

5. FALLING IN THE WATER (*Second Dictation*)

me·kwa· ki·-epino·ci·n²uwiya·n te·kwa·kik nenki·-pepa·-ma·ci·nik aw nenkašši. ci·ma·nink nenki·-po·semi, mi·nuwa· pe·šik ekkwe·, ki·-pepa·-eya·muwa·t pekwaci-meno·min uwiti wa·peškokki·nk.

me·kwa· tašš ekwa puwa²emowa·t iw meno·min a·no kwa nenki·--kenawa·pemik aw nenkašši wi·-pwa·-pekkopi·sse·ya·n. nenkwatink tašš ekwa na· ena·pit eškwe·ya·nk aw nenkašši nenki·-wa·pemik a·ši kwa ki·-pekkopi·sse·wa·mpa·. eka·wa· tašš nenki·-te·pepinik. mi· tašš ki·-ekwa·pi·kenit. keye· kwa nenki·-ki·ssekkoneye·penik. mi· tašš pe·kka·nakk ki·-wi·weci·nit.

ecina tašš e·tta mi·nuwa· uki·-eya·na·wa· penki· iw meno·min. mi· tašš ki·-ki·we·ya·nk. ki·-se·kesi tašš aw nenkašše·. ka· wi· uki·--kekke·nema·ssi·n nemanc ke·-ekkitukwe·n aw no·ss.

When I was a child, one autumn my mother took me about with her. We went in a canoe, along with another woman, and they went about gathering wild rice there in the marsh.

While they were knocking down that rice, my mother, to be sure, watched me so that I should not fall into the water. But at one time as my mother looked back, she saw that I had indeed fallen into the water. With difficulty she seized hold of me. Then she took me out of the water. She pulled off my clothes. Then she wrapped me in something else.

Just for a short time then they gathered a little more of the rice. Then we went home. My mother was frightened. She did not know what my father would say.

6. FALLING IN THE WATER (*Phonograph Record*)

ša·si kwa me·kwa· epino·ci·n²uwiya·n nenki·-pepa·-ma·ci·nik aw nenkašši pepa·-puwa²emowa·t iw meno·min ema· wa·peškokki·nk. a·no tašš eko nenki·-ekkawa·pemiko·k iw eppi· enakkemikesiwa·t pe·kkišš essa puwa²emowa·t ma·nta meno·min, nenkwatink etašš ko na· ma·nta eši-kuttikuška·k ma·nta ci·ma·n, mi· ki·-a·ppecipesoya·n keye· kwa uwiti nempi·nk ki·-penkiššena·n. mi· tašš ki·-wa·pemit ma·pa nenkašši. eka·wa· tašš nenki·-te·penik iw ki·-nuwatenit [1] ki·-ekwa·pi·kenit ne·ya·p ci·ma·nink ki·-pekitenit.

a·ppeci tašš ki·-se·kesi. we·wi·p etašš nenki·-ki·ssekkoneye·penik keye· tašš iw e·kwit a·nint nenki·-wi·weci·nik wi·-pwa·-tekkaceya·n.

ki·-we·wi·petta· etašš ekwa iw penki· ki·-puwaʔemowa·t ma·nta ssa pekwaci-meno·min. ka·-ki·ši·tta·wa·t tašš mi· ne·ya·p mi·nuwa· ki·-ki·we·ya·nk, keye· ka· uki·-kekke·nema·ssi·n nemanci-i·tik ke·- -ekkitukwe·n essa no·ss. a·ppeci ki·-se·kesi aw ssa nenkašši unci iw ki·-pešiššene·ya·n ta-ki·-ta·ppene·ya·mpa·n.

a·ppeci tašš ekwa ni·pena usakekkina·na·wa· iw meno·min ekonta eniššena·pe·k te·kwa·keninekin sekakkenamuwa·t iw meno·min pepo·- nenik wa·-ma·mi·cuwa·t tepiško· ko na· e·ši-sekakkenike·t ma·pa ecitemo͞ e·šenikka·sot.

mi· iw menikk e·kketoya·n.

Long ago, when I was a child, my mother took me along as they went about gathering rice in the marsh. Although they kept an eye on me as they were busy, at the same time, gathering the rice, still at one time, when the canoe tipped to one side like this, I fell out and tumbled into the water. Then my mother saw me. She just managed to get hold of me and grabbed me up and pulled me out of the water and set me down back in the canoe.

She was very much frightened. Quickly she pulled off my clothes and wrapped me up in some of her garments so that I might not catch cold.

Then she hurried and they gathered a little more of the wild rice. When they were done we went back home. She did not know what my father would say. My mother was very much frightened because when I fell out of the canoe I might well have got drowned.

These Indians collected very much rice, collecting it in the autumn so as to have it to eat in the winter, just as that creature who is called a squirrel gathers his store.

This is as much as I have to say.

---

[1] Not clear; perhaps end of word was slurred with view to replacement by the next word.

7. FISHING

me·kwa· ki·-kwi·wesse·nsuwiya·n eppane· ekwa nenki·-kuntamo·ceke·. ki·-pa·tti·nuwak ekwa ki·ko·nyak iw eppi·, ko·ta·šši·nyak, eššikenak, neme·pene·nyak, keno·še·k, ešikume·kok, keye· ekiw ekwa·peke·ssuwak.

nenkwatink nenki·-kuntamo·na·pa aw kecci-ekwa·peke·ssi ke·ka· ekwa na· ka·-pekkopi·ta·pa·šit. nenki·-na·tema·k kwi·wesse·ns pe·pa·-wi·ci·wak. eka·wa· tašš ekwa na· nenki·-unci-ma·šeʔa·na·n a·ppeci ko kecci-ki·koˇ. aw etašš kwi·wesse·ns wi·n uki·-nuwatena·n a·petta·wena. mi· tašš na· ki·-ekwa·wena·t.

When I was a boy I was always fishing. There were many fish then: rock bass, black bass, suckers, pike, dogfish, and mullets too. Once I had a big mullet on my hook, and it almost dragged me down into the water. The boy I was going with helped me. We barely managed to get the better of that very big fish. That boy grabbed it round its body and so pulled it out of the water.

8. CARLISLE INDIAN SCHOOL (*Dictation*)

nenkwatink me·kwa· uškinuwe·wcya·n ki·-tekoššin pe·pa·-na·na·t wa·-kekkino·ʔema·kusinecin uwiti ka·-pi-uncipa·t Carlisle Indian School. nenki·-kekwe·cemik keye· ni· ke·-eša·wa·mpa·ne·n. nenki·-nekkwe·ttuwa· tašš ci-eša·ya·mpa· ki·špin pekiteniwa·t nenkittesi·mak. uki·-kekwe·cema·n etašš eniw nenkittesi·man ma·pa kecci-mo·kkuma·n. nenki·-pekiteniko·k etašš ekiw nenkittesi·mak. mi· ssa ki·-ušipi· ʔank ema· mesineʔikeninink iw nentano·suwin, keye· kwa mi· ki·-tepa·cemot eppi· ke·-ma·ca·ya·n.

eppi· tašš te·peško·sse·k nenki·-eša·mi uwiti a·-pemi-no·kepisot aw meškote·ta·pa·n. eppi· tašš pe·kemipesot ki·-pi-kwa·škuni aw enini keye· kwa ekiw a·nint epino·ci·nyak wa·-eša·cik uwiti kekkino·ʔema·ti·wekamekonk. mi· tašš ke· ni· ki·-po·seya·n.

kepe·-tepikk ki·-pemipeso aw meškote·ta·pa·n keye· kwa kepe·-ki·šik, mi·nuwa· kwa kepe·-tepikk. mi· tašš ki·-tekoššena·nk uwiti o·te·naw Carlisle e·šenikka·te·k kekiše·p.

mi· ˈtašš ki·-ma·ca·ya·nk ki·-eša·ya·nk uwiti school. keye· kwa mi· ki·-a·nsekkama·nk nentakuwinena·nin. keye· kwa mi· ki·-mi·neko·ya·nk rooms wa·-teniseya·nk.

ka·-wa·pank mi· ki·-ešiweniko·ya·nk wa·-teši-enokki·ya·nk. ke· ni·ekwiwenan e·nteši-ušicceka·te·k nenki·-ešiweniko·. ka· tašš iw tenawa enokki·win nenki·-nentawe·ntensi·n.

mi·nuwa· tašš nenki·-kekwe·cemiko· "a·ni· tašš ke·-ene·ntemampa carpenter shop?"

nenki·-nekkwe·ttuwa· tašš "mi· iw tenawa keye· ni· ka·-messawe·ntema·n ci-enanukki·ya·mpa·."

a·ppeci ki·-keša·tte· iw eppi·. mi· tašš ki·-we·petta·ya·n ki·-na·tema·ke·ya·n ema· e·nteši-ešitto·wa·t iw mi·šeškokemik. pessaka·kkok nenki·-a·wena·na·nik. e·škam tašš nenki·-eni-nessitutta·n iw enokki·win. ki·špin e·ya·kin wa·-enanukki·nk uwiti Girls' Quarters mi· ko ni·n uwiti e·šena·šekka·kuya·n ci-wa·pentama·n we·kutakwe·n i·tik ne·ntuwe·nta·kutokwe·n.

ni·cekkiwe˜ nenki·-wi·ntema·k nenkwatink pe·šik uškeni·kekkwe· Menomini girl nessituttawa·t eniw ucipwe·n.

mi· tašš ka·-ene·ntema·n "eppi· kwa neššikke· wa·pemak nenka·-ucipwe·muttawa·." nenki·-ene·ntam.

nenkwatink etašš mi·nuwa· ki·-pi-eya·mekat order . nenki·-mi·nik etašš aw ema· ne·mpa·ssuwit carpenter shop ki·-ešit "uwa-wa·pentan we·kutakwe·n ne·ntuwe·nta·kutokwe·n." nenki·-mi·nik etašš iw order.

nenki·-ma·ca· tašš ki·-eša·ya·n uwiti Girls' Quarters. mi· tašš ki·-wa·pemak ma·pa Menomini girl teši-kesi·pi·kenank wa·sse·ccekanan. mi· tašš pe·ššo e·ni-eya·ya·n ema· e·ntenakkemikesit. ka· uwaya e·kkuwa·pit nuwa·pema·ssi·. mi· tašš ki·-keno·nak.

"me·kwa· ssa kekisi·pi·kessakenike·!"

mi· tašš ki·-nekkwe·ttuwit.

"e·, me·kwa·." ekkito.

At one time when I was a young boy, there arrived a man who went about fetching those who were to go to school at the place from which he came, the Carlisle Indian School. He asked me, too, whether I should care to go there. I answered him that I would go if my parents permitted me. Then he asked my parents, that white American. My parents allowed me to go. So then he wrote my name in his book and told when I was to leave.

When the time came we went to the railway station. When the train arrived, that man got off, and also several children who were to go to that school. So then I, too, got on board the train.

The train went all night and all day and all the next night. Then we arrived, in the morning, at that town which is called Carlisle.

Then we set out and went to the school. Then we changed our clothes. And then we were given rooms in which we were to stay.

The next morning we were conducted to the places where we were to work. As for me, I was taken to the place where clothes were made. That was not the kind of work I wanted.

Then, on another occasion, I was asked, "Now, how would you like the carpenter shop?"

I answered him, "That is the kind of work I would like to do."

It was very hot weather then. Then I began to help where they were building a barn. We were hauling boards. Gradually, as time went on, I learned to understand that work. Whenever there was any work to be done over in Girls' Quarters, I was the one to be sent there to see what it might be that was wanted.

My friend once told me that a certain Menomini girl understood Ojibwa.

Then I thought, "If at any time I see her alone, I shall speak to her in Ojibwa," I thought.

Then again at one time there came an order. The instructor in the carpenter shop gave it to me, saying, "Go see what is wanted", and he gave me the order slip.

So I started off and went over to Girls' Quarters. There I saw this Menomini girl washing windows. Then I got near to where she was working. I did not see anyone keeping watch. So then I spoke to her.

"I see you're washing woodwork!"

Then she answered me.

"Yes, so I am," she said.

9. CARLISLE INDIAN SCHOOL (*Phonograph Record*)

nenkwatink me·kwa· uškinuwe·weya·n ki·-pi-eya· aw kecci-mo·kkuma·n pe·pa·-nentawa·pema·t wa·-kekkino·ʔema·kusinecin. keye·ni· tašš nenki·-kekwe·cemik ke·-eša·wa·mpa·ne·n. nenki·-nekkwe·ttuwa· tašš ta-eša·ya·mpa·n ki·špin pekiteniwa·t ekiw nenkittesi·mak. mi·nuwa· tašš uki·-kekwe·cema·n eniw nenkittesi·man. nenki·- pekiteniko·k tašš ta-eša·ya·n. mi· tašš ma·pa enini ki·-ušipi·ʔank iw nentano·suwin ema· mesineʔikenink, keye· kwa mi· iw ki·-tepa·cemot eppi·mi·nuwa· ke·-pi-tekoššink ema· a-pemi-no·kesse·t aw eškote·ta·pa·n.

eppi· tašš te·peško·sse·k nenki·-eša·, nenki·-eša·mi, uwiti a-pemi-

-no·kesse·t aw eškote·ta·pa·n. ki·-pi-pekamepiso tašš aw eškote·ta·-pa·n. keye· kwa ki·-pi-kwa·škuni ma·pa enini keye· kwa a·nint epino·ci·nyak wa·-eša·cik uwiti kekkino·ˀema·ti·wekamekonk. mi· tašš ki·- po·seya·n. mi· tašš ki·-po·seya·n, ka·-eškwa·-ki·špenato·t iw mesineˀikan ke· ni· wa·-ni-a·pecitto·ya·n ci-pemita·pa·nekoya·n eškote·ta·pa·nink.

kepe·-tepikk ki·-pemipeso aw eškote·ta·pa·n, keye· kwa mi·nuwa· ka·-wa·pank kepe·-ki·šik, mi·nuwa· kwa kepe·-tepikk. mi·nuwa· ke·keše·pa·wekakk mi· ki·-tekoššena·nk o·te·naw e·šenikka·te·k Carlisle.

mi· tašš mi·nuwa· ki·-ma·ca·ya·nk ki·-eša·ya·nk uwiti school. keye· kwa mi· ki·-a·nsekkoneye·ya·nk, keye· kwa mi· ki·-mi·neko·ya·nk eniw rooms wa·teniseya·nk.

ka·-a·šo·-wa·pank mi· e·-ki·-ešiweniko·ya·nk wa·-teši-enokki·ya·nk. keye· ni· nenki·-ešina·šeˀoko. ema· e·nteši-ušicceka·te·k eniw ekwi-wenan. ka· tašš iw tenawa enokki·win nenki·-menta·kwe·ntensi·n.

mi·nuwa· tašš nenki·-eko·k "a·ni·šš ke·-ene·ntemampa carpenter shop?"

nenki·-nekkwe·ttuwa·k tašš ta-enanukki·ya·n iw. mi· tašš ki·-we·petta·ya·n ki·-enokki·ya·n ema· carpenter shop.

a·pecci tašš ki·-keša·tte·. keye· tašš nenki·-a·wena·na·nik ekiw pessaka·kkok e·ntesso-ki·šekakk ki·-ešitto·ya·nk iw mi·šeškokemik.

e·škam etašš nenki·-nessitutta·n ke· ni· iw essa enokki·win. eppi· ke·ko· essa e·ya·kin enokki·win up in Girls' Quarters mi· kwa ni·n uwiti e·šena·šekka·ko·ya·n uwicuwak [1] eni-nento-kekke·ntema·n we·kutakwe·n ne·ntuwe·nta·kutakwe·n.

nenkotink tašš aw ni·cekkiwe⁻ nenki·-wi·ntema·k aw pe·šik uškeni·kekkwe· nessituttawa·t eniw ucipwe·n. mi· tašš ka·-ene·ntema·n "eppi· kwa neššikke· ci-wa·pema·weke·n nenka-ucipwe·muttawa·" nenki·-ene·ntam.

nenkotink tašš kekišep· ki·-pi-eya·mekat iw order. mi· tašš ki·-ešina·šeˀot ma·pa ne·mpa·ssuwit ema· carpenter shop ci-wa·pentama·n we·kutakwe·n ne·ntuwe·nta·kutakwe·n uwiti Girls' Quarters. nenki·-mi·nik etašš iw order. nenki·-eša· tašš uwiti ki·-uwa-nentawa·-nento-kekke·ntema·n we·kutakwe·n i·tik ne·ntuwe·nta·kutakwe·n. nenki·-wa·pema· ma·pa Menomini girl teši-kesi·pi·kenank wa·sse·ccekanan uwiti wa·-eni-eša·ya·n.

---

[1] Hearing error?

miˑ tašš kaˑ-eneˑntemaˑn "miˑ ssa noˑnkwa ssa ucipweˑmuttawak" nenkiˑ-eneˑntam.

eˑni-tekoššenaˑn tašš peˑššo miˑ kiˑ-kenoˑnak.

miˑ tašš kaˑ-enak "meˑkwaˑ ssa kekisiˑpiˑkessakenikeˑ!"

miˑ tašš kiˑ-nekkweˑttuwit "eˑ, meˑkwaˑ nenkisiˑpiˑkenaˑnan."

miˑ tašš kiˑ-neʔeˑntemaˑn iw kiˑ-kekkeˑnemak keˑkeˑtt iw nessituttank. eppaneˑ tašš ekwa eˑntesso-waˑpemak nenkiˑ-kenoˑnaˑ kiˑ--enissena·pe·muttawak ucipweˑ-enweˑwin. miˑnuwaˑ tašš eko kaˑkuneˑnkim¹ nenkiˑ-unci-waˑpemaˑssiˑ. kumappi miˑnuwaˑ nenkiˑ--waˑpemaˑ. miˑ tašš miˑnuwaˑ essa nenkiˑ-enissena·pe·muttawaˑ maˑpa Menomini girl. miˑ tašš neʔeˑntemaˑn keˑkeˑtt essa kiˑ-kekkeˑnemak essa ucipweˑmot.

miˑ iw menikk eˑkketoyaˑn.

At one time, when I was a young boy, there came that white American who went about looking for those who wanted to attend school. He asked me, too, whether I would go. I answered him that I would go if my parents permitted me. So then he again asked my parents. They permitted me to go. So then that man wrote my name in a book and told when he would come again to the railway station.

When the time came, I went, we went, to the railway station. The train arrived and that man got off, as well as a number of children who were going to that school. Then I boarded the train. I boarded the train, that is, after he had bought the ticket which I was to use when I traveled on the train.

All night long the train went and the next day all day and again all night. The next morning we arrived at the town that is named Carlisle.

Then we set out again and went over to the school. Then we changed our clothes and we were given the rooms in which we were to stay.

On the next morning we were conducted to the places where we were to work. As for me, I was sent to the place where clothes were being made. I did not find pleasure in this kind of work.

Then at another time they asked me, "How would you like the carpenter shop?"

---

¹ So it sounds; unknown word.

I answered them that I would do that kind of work. So then I began to work in the carpenter shop.

It was very hot weather. Every day we hauled boards, for we were building a barn.

Gradually I came to understand that work. Whenever there was any work to be done up in Girls' Quarters, I was the one to be sent there to find out what was wanted.

Then at one time my chum told me that one of those young women understood Ojibwa. Then I thought, "If by any chance I should see her alone, I shall talk to her in Ojibwa," thought I.

Then one morning there came an order. Then the instructor in the carpenter shop sent me to see what was wanted there in Girls' Quarters, and he gave me the order slip. So I went there to find out, as was necessary, what it was that was wanted. Then I saw this Menomini girl washing windows there where I had to go past.

So then I thought, "Now is the time I'll speak to her in Ojibwa," I thought.

When I got near her I spoke to her.

I said to her, "You're washing woodwork, I see!"

Then she answered me, "Yes, I'm just now washing it".

So now I felt sure that I knew that she did really understand it. Always then whenever I saw her I addressed her in the Indian language, in Ojibwa. I did not see her again for a long time. Finally I did see her again; so then again I spoke Indian to this Menomini girl. I was certain now that I knew she spoke Ojibwa.

This is all I have to tell.

10. SPRING THUNDERSTORM

nenkwatink nenki·-enokki·na·pa ki·we·tenunk kepe·-pepo·n. eppi·tašš me·no·kkemik, si·sepa·kkutokke·-ki·siss e·ko·cink, ki·-kessina·mekat. ki·-ešpa·kunaka·. nessink e·kko·sete·nk ki·-eppi·tta·kunaka·. kekiše·p etašš nenki·-na·tin nempi·šš. ema· tašš e·nteʔama·nk tekkipi a·pettaweta·kki eya·mekat, pe·ššo eya·k nempiss.[1] e·ni-tekoššena·n wi·na·kemi iw nempi·šš e·nteʔama·nk. keye· ko tepi uncicuwank ke·wi· kwa pekkwe·pi·kemi. ma·no· tašš ko na· penki· a·petto·škin ni·mepa·keninik nenki·-kwa·peʔa·n. nenki·-ma·ci·to·n e·nta·ya·nk.

---

[1] The syntax seems queer; no doubt the sentence was incorrectly recorded.

nenki·-wi·ntemawa·k "kenapac we yak[1] uwe·ssi" eya·tik ema·enta ʔepa·nink."
  aw tašš ekkiwe·nsi" ki·-ki·keto "a·ni· tašš?"
  mi· tašš ka·-enak "wa·pentamok o·w[1] nempi·šš e·šena·kwakk."
  "a· ni· nenka-wa·penta·n" ekkito tašš aw ekkiwe·nsi".
  uki·-wa·penta·n etašš.
  mi· tašš e·kketot "ci-pwa·-ni·šukonekakk wi·-pi-kecci-enimekki·kka·."
  nenki·-ma·ca· tašš ke·-enokki·ya·n. mi·nuwa· ka·-wa·pank e·škam ki·-a·puwa·. mi· tašš e·na·kuššik e·škam ki·-kecci-a·puwa·k, keye·kwa mi· ki·-wa·pentama·n wa·ssemowa·t ekiw enimekki·k. e·ni-tepikkakk mi· ki·-no·ntuwanketwa· enimekki·k, keye· ko ki·-kecci-enimekki·kka·k. ke·keše·pa·wekakk eko·n kekkina ki·-nekka·pa·we·. mi· e·tta nempi·šš ka·-pemicuwank ke·keše·pa·wekakk.

Once I was working in the North all winter. Then when spring was at hand, in the month of March, there was cold weather. There was deep snow. The snow was three feet deep. In the morning I fetched water. The spring from which we got water was halfway up a hill, near a lake. When I got there the water in our spring was dirty. Also, the place from which it flowed had muddied water. Nevertheless I dipped up a little, half a filling, in the pail. I took it to our house.

  I said to them, "It seems as if there may be some creature in the spring from which we get water."

  Then the old man spoke: "How is that?"

  I said to him, "Look at the way this water looks."

  "Well, let me take a look at it," said the old man.

  Then he looked at it.

  This was what he said: "Before two days have passed there will be a big thunderstorm."

  Then I went off to work. The next day the weather was getting warmer. Then in the evening it began to get very warm, and then I saw lightning. When night came we heard the Thunderers, and there was a great thunderstorm. By morning all the snow had melted away. Only then did the water flow, in the morning.

---

[1] Error of record?

11. A VISIT HOME (*Dictation*)

menta·kukkwe·tok keye· menta·kuninuwitok!

uwe·ti ka·-pi-pemisse·k nenki·-ki·we· uwiti Walpole Island ka·-pi--uncipa·ya·n. kekkina ke·ko· nenki·-mekka·n meno-eya·k kuyakk eši-eya·k e·nta·ya·n. mi·nuwa· tašš nenki·-nena·ʔetto·n iw mencikekkan e·nteniseya·n. mi·nuwa· nenki·-pi-peska·pi· ne·ya·p ema· e·nteši-enokki·ya·n Ann Arbor. nenki·-mekkawa·k kekkina meno--pema·tesiwa·t ekiw wa·cenokki·mekik.

mi·nuwa· tašš kenapac pe·ššo ci-po·netta·ya·nk. mi· tašš ci-ki·-we·ya·n ka·-pi-uncipa·ya·n. ke· wi·n ma·pa ni·kka·niss wa·cenokki·mak ta-ki·we· eniwe·ti ka·-pi-uncipa·t ki·we·tenonk, ke· wi· ta-ki·we·t ne·ya·p ka·-pi-uncipa·t .

eni-kenawe·nemiššena·nk ni·ka·n ki·šekato·n!

Ladies and gentlemen!
This last week I went home to Walpole Island where I come from. I found everything in good shape and my house in proper condition. I repaired the fence on my place. Then I came back here to Ann Arbor, where I am working. I found all my fellow workers in good health.

But I daresay the time is near when we shall stop working. Then I shall go back where I came from. And also this friend of mine here, my fellow worker [Charles Snow, Hidatsa informant], will go back to the north, whence he came, so that he, too, will return to the place from which he came here.

Continue Thou to keep us in Thy care through the days to come!

12. A VISIT HOME (*Phonograph Record*)

uwe·ti ka·-pi-pemisse·k nenki·-ki·we· uwiti Walpole Island. kekkina ke·ko· nenki·-mekka·n essa kuyakk ki·-eya·k ema· e·nta·ya·n. mi·nuwa· nenki·-nena·ʔetto·n essa mencikekkan essa e·nteniseya·n. mi·nuwa· nenki·-peska·pi· ne·ya·p ma·meppi· e·nteši-enokki·ya·n Ann Arbor. nenki·-mekkawa·k etašš kekkina meno-pema·tesiwa·t ekonta wa·cenokki·mekik.

mi·nuwa· tašš ssa ko kenapac pe·ššo essa neka-po·netta·min etašš ci-ki·we·ya·n ka·-pi-uncipa·ya·n. keye· wi·n ma·pa ni·kka·niss wa·--

cenokki·mak kecci-wa·ssa ki·-ssa-uncipa· uwiti ki·we·tenonk, ke· wi·
ta-ki·we·t ne·ya·p mi·nuwa· ci-wa·pentank ema· ssa ke· wi· ka·-pi-
-unci-ma·ca·t.

šuwe·nemiššena·nk etašš ema·nena·nk.[1] ni·ka·n essa ma·no· nenti-
ši-pekosse·nta·min essa keminwa·peme·weʔiwe·win ci-wi·ci·wekoya·nk.

This last week I went home to Walpole Island. I found everything
in good shape at my house. I repaired the fence on my place. Then
I came back here again to Ann Arbor, where I am working. I found
my fellow workers here all in good health.

But now I daresay the time is near when we shall stop working
and when I am to go back where I came from. My friend here, too,
my fellow worker, has come from far away in the north, and he, too,
will now go back home and see the place from which he set out to come
here.

Have Thou pity on us now Who art Lord of us all. In the future
we hope that Thy blessing will accompany us.

13. END OF THE SUMMER'S WORK (*Phonograph Record*)

no·nkwa kekiše·p nenki·-wi·ntema·ko·mi iw eppi· i·tik essa wa·-
-ka·ki·we·ya·nk ci-ki·ši·tta·ya·nk iw ssa menikk wa·-enanukki·ya·nk.
keye· kwa ma·pa ni·kka·niss kecci-wa·ssa ka·-pi-uncipa·t Mister Snow
uwiti wa·ssa ki·we·tenonk ke· wi· ci-eši-ki·we·t nentawa·pentank
ne·ya·p mi·nuwa· uwiti ka·-pi-unci-ma·ca·t. keye· ni· kwa ci-ki·-
we·ya·n keye· ekonta ni·kka·nessak ce·ci·pa·n ka·-pi-uncipa·cik, a·nint
uwiti Indiana, keye· kwa ma·pa pe·šik Philadelphia ki·-pi-uncipa·,
keye· wi· ci-wa·pentank iw ssa ka·-pi-uncipa·t. a·ppeci tašš ko ke· ni·
a·ši kwa nuwe·wi·pe·ntam essa ci-ki·we·ya·n keye· kwa ci-wa·pemakwa·
kekkina ekiw ko ka·-wa·pemakik ema· Walpole Island.

This morning we were told when we should all go home, having
finished the amount of work which we were to do. And my friend
Mr. Snow here, who comes from very far in the north, he, too, then
is to go home and seek again the place from which he set out to come
here. And for me, too, it will be time to go home and for these

---

[1] Record is blurred, and transcription is surely wrong; one expects something
like *te·pe·nemina·nk* 'our Lord'.

friends of mine who have come from various places, some from Indiana, and this one comes from Philadelphia and he, too, will now see the place from which he came. I, too, am by this time very eager to see all those whom I saw on Walpole Island.

14. THE FISH TRAP

eppi· ko me·no·kkemikin kecci-mo·ške?an iw si·pi·we͞ e·nta·ya·n. mi· tašš kwa ema· ekote ?owa·t ekiw keno·še·k keye· kwa ekiw ešikume·-kok. nentatto·n tašš kwa iw pi·wa·pekko·ns menka·we·penakwa·wi·-pwa·-ša·pekkošuwa·t ekiw keno·še·k keye· ešikume·kok. pi·cin tašš ekwa nentawa-ena·p ema· si·pi·we·n?ink e·ya·mekakk iw nentasso·-na·kan. nuwa·penta·n kwa kuma·ppi·cc iw mema·sekka·k iw pi·wa·pekko·ns. mi· a·ši ki·-tekoššink aw ki·ko͞. mi· tašš eša·ya·n keye· kwa mi· nena·?etta·ppenama·n iw nentanitt. mi· tašš pecipuwak aw ki·ko͞. na·nenkotenonk ni·š nente·-pecipuwa·k ci-pwa·-kekkina·-kencipe?iwe·wa·t.

In springtime the creek near my house runs very deep. Then the pike and dogfish swim upstream there. Then I put wire netting there to keep the pike and dogfish from swimming through. At frequent intervals I go and look there in the creek where my trap is placed. In time I see the wire moving. That is when the fish have arrived. Then I go and tie fast my fish spear. Then I spear those fish. Sometimes I manage to spear two of them before they all get away.

15. MEANS OF LIVELIHOOD

ekiw enišsena·pe·k ema· Walpole Island eno·c enanukki·wak wi·-keškitto·wa·t iw šo·neya· wa·-unci-meno-eya·wa·t. a·nint kuntamo·ceke·wak, keye· kwa a·nint ekkokkupina·kenikke·wak, keye· kwa a·nint wa·ka·kkuta·ttekokke·wak, keye· kwa souvenir uto·šetto·na·wa·n, mettikwa·pi·nsan, wa·ka·kkuto·nsan, epwi·nsan. kekkina tašš eniw utata·we·na·wa·n. mi· tašš šo·neya· keškitto·wa·t. a·nint kettika·nink enokki·wak ma·ci·ketto·wa·t wa·-mi·cuwa·t, uppini·n, e·ššo·nyan, meskoti·sseminan, ekkwassema·nan, e·šketamo·nyan, e·ssa·-wa·nyan, keye· menta·menan, pekkwe·šeka·ns, menici·min. keye· a·nint pe·po·nkin ki·wusse·wak. eššaško·nyan keye· ša·nkwe·ššuwan unissa·wa·n eta·we·wa·t. šo·neya· ukašketto·na·wa·, keye· kwa mi·

iw ki·špenato·wa·t na·ppa·ni·. kekkina pe·pekka·n enanukki·wak
eniššena·pe·k wi·-te·penamuwa·t šo·neya·.

keye· kwa mettiko·n uki·škepo·to·na·wa·n, mi· tašš eta·we·wa·t
o·te·na·nk keye· kwa ema· Island. penki·šše˜ ke· ni· nentaya·n
mettikwa·kki·ns ema· e·nta·ya·n. a·ppeci tašš ekwa nesa·ketto·n.
ka· wi· nento·ki·ške?ansi·n a·ppeci ke·ko·. pa·ma· ni·ka·n wi·-a·-
pecitto·ya·n keye· ušo·neya·messiwa·n ci-ki·špenato·ya·mpa· iw mettik,
mi· pa·ma· iw ta-ki·škuwak aw mettik. e·škam senakat wi·-te·pena-
mink iw wa·-po·tuwe·nk. uca·keka?a·na·wa· ni·pena utakki·muwa·n
ekiw eniššena·pe·k. keye· kwa e·škam ni·pena enakente·no·n metti-
ko·n.

The Indians on Walpole Island do various kinds of work to earn
money for their living. Some catch fish and some make baskets and
some make axe handles, and they make souvenirs: miniature bows,
axes, and canoe paddles. All these things they sell, and thus earn
money. Some work on farms, raising their food: potatoes, cabbages,
beans, pumpkins, watermelons, muskmelons, and Indian corn, wheat,
pease. And some in winter go hunting. They kill muskrats and mink
and sell them. They earn money and with it buy flour. All the Indians do one or another kind of work to earn money.

Also they saw wood and sell it in Detroit or on the Island. I too
have a small plot of wooded land there where I dwell. But I am very
chary of using it. I do not cut down anything at all, since I mean to
make use of it later on in the future, selling that wood in case I should
run out of money. Then, later on, I shall cut down those trees. It is
getting harder and harder to obtain firewood. Those Indians are
clearing much of their land. And wood is becoming dearer all the time.

16. THE WALPOLE ISLAND FAIR (*First Dictation*)

menta·kukkwe·tik keye· menta·kuninuwitok!

no·nko ki·šekakk nentipa·cim a·ši pe·ššo wi·-eya·muwa·t iw fair
ema· wa·pow Island nenko-ename?e·-ki·šik no·nkwa unci. me·kwa·
tašš ekiw Fair Company uši·tta·wak. na·pekkwa·nan wi·-pekame-
pite·no·n wa·-pi·uncikka·mekakkin ema· Sandusky keye· kwa ema·
Cleveland keye· kwa ema· Port Huron keye· kwa wenina wa·-pi·uncipa·-
cik etamo·pi·link wa·-pi·eya·cik. kekkina tašš ke·ko· eši-uši·tta·wak
ekonta Fair Company ke·-eši-meno·eya·wa·t wa·-pi·eša·cik. kekkina

ke·ko· wi·-eya·mekato·n eniw games, wa·-kekwe·cekkaneticik pe·-šeko·keši·k ke·ši·kka·petto·cik. ekiw etašš wa·-pemo·mekocik uwi·--pi·ssekka·na·wa·n eniw Indian costume. keye· wi·nuwa· ekiw wa·--pekkwa·kkutwe·cik wi·-pi·eša·wan wa·-pi·etta·kuwa·cin.

me·kwa· tašš unana·ʔetto·na·wa· ma·nta exhibit hall keye· kwa iw wa·-teši-ni·muwa·t. kekkina tašš ke·ko· wi·-wa·pentaʔuwe·wak ekiw eniššena·pe·k ema· wa·pow Island we·šetto·wa·t, ekwi·tepiwenan, eto·ppuwinan, wa·ka·kkuta·tteko·n, mettikwa·pi·k, ekkokkupina·kenan, kesi·sete·ššemowenan, keye· ekiw ekkwe·wak we·šetto·wa·t, wa·po·weya·nan, menciko·te·nyan, pepakuwiya·nan, mekkisenan, keye· iw ke·pa·kku ʔika·te·k eno·ci·ke·ko· e·ppukwakk, meskomenak, utatteka·kuminak, mešši·menak. we·kutakwe·n ke·-nentawe·ntemo·kwe·n wi·-wa·pentank aw ke·-pi·eša·t mi· kwa ema·ci·ette·mekakk. ekkwassema·nan a·ppeci me·ma·cca·kin ta·ette·no·n. kekkina ke·ko· ta·ette·mekat ne·tta·wekink, ci·ssan, e·ššo·nyan, meskoti·sseminak, uppeni·k, menta·menak, penakesikenak, enici·min.

me·kwa· tašš uto·šetto·na·wa· iw ni·me ʔiti·wekamik wa·-teši-ni·-muwa·t ekiw wa·-pi·eša·cik. kepe·-ki·šik ta·ni·muwak keye· kwa enikwa a·petta·tepikk.

Ladies and gentlemen!

Today I am telling about the fair they are going to hold very soon now on Walpole Island, a week from today. The Fair Company is even now preparing for it. Ships will come sailing from Sandusky, Cleveland, and Port Huron, and from everywhere people will come by automobile. The Fair Company are doing everything possible for the convenience of those who come. There will be everything in the way of games, including racing of fast horses. Those who ride the horses will wear Indian costumes. Also, a team will come to play against the baseball team.

At present they are preparing the exhibit hall and the place for dancing. The Indians of Walpole Island will exhibit everything they make: chairs, tables, axe handles, bows, baskets, door mats, and the things which the women make: blankets, dresses, shirts, moccasins, and canned preserves of every sort: raspberries, blackberries, apples. Everything the visitor may want to see will be there. There will be very large pumpkins. There will be everything that is raised: turnips, cabbages, beans, potatoes, Indian corn, hard-shell corn, pease.

At present they are preparing the dance hall where the visitors will dance. There will be dancing all day and until midnight.

17. THE WALPOLE ISLAND FAIR (*Second Dictation*)

uwe·ti wa·-ni-pemisse·k mi· iw fair wi·-eya·muwa·t ekiw eniššena·pe·k ema· wa·pow Island. kekkina ekiw Fair Company me·kwa·uši·tta·wak. keye· ni·meʔiti·wekamik umicca·tto·na·wa·, iw etašš wa·-ni·mecik we·we·no·k ci-ni·muwa·t. kekkina ke·ko· wi·-wa·penta·ʔetim we·šetto·t aw eniššena·pe·, eto·ppuwinan, ekwi·tepiwenan, wa·-ka·kkuta·tteko·n, peššanše·ʔekane·ya·tteko·n keye· ekkwe·wak we·šetto·wa·t, ekkokkupina·kenan, wa·po·weya·nan, menciko·te·nyan, pepakuwiya·nan, kepo·ssene·nyan; ke· wi· eninuwak ne·tta·wekitto·wa·t, uppini·k, menta·menak, meskoti·sseminak, ekkwassema·nan, e·ššo·nyan, messimene·ns, meno·min, menici·min, e·ša·wa·nyan, keye· e·šketamo·nyan.

keye· kwa games wi·-eya·no·n, kekwe·cekkanetiwenan. pe·šeko·keši·k wi·-kekwe·cekkanetiwak. ekiw uškinuwe·k wa·-pemo·mekocik uwi·-pi·ssekka·na·wa·n eniw Indian costume. keye· kwa wa·-pekkwa·kkutwe·cik nenkwaci wi·-pi-uncipa·wan wa·-pi-etta·kuwa·cin ekiw eniššena·pe·k pe·kkwa·kkutwe·cik ema· wa·pow Island. aw e·ppekitank pekkwa·kkwat c·šcnikka·sot Wellington ša·kena·šš, mi· aw ne·tta·-eppakitank pekkwa·kkwat ema· wa·pow Island. kekkina ke·ko· wi·-eya·mekat, keye· kwa e·nteši-wi·sseniwa·t keye· kwa souvenir stands. keye· kwa wa·pow Island Indian Band wi·-mentwe·cceke·wak. uwi·-pi·ssekka·na·wa·n ke· wi·nuwa· eniw Indian costume. eppi· pekamepite·k iw excursion boat utawa-nekkwe·škuwa·wa·n eniw wa·-kwa·škuninecin. wa·-pi-uncipete·k etašš eniw ci·ma·nan uwiti Sandusky, Cleveland, keye· kwa Port Huron.

Next week the Indians on Walpole Island are going to hold a fair. The Fair Company is now preparing everything. They are enlarging the dance hall so that those who dance may have plenty of room. Everything that the Indian produces will be exhibited: tables, chairs, axe handles, whipstocks; and the things the women make: baskets, blankets, dresses, shirts, trousers; and the things the men raise in the way of crops: potatoes, Indian corn, beans, pumpkins, cabbages, wheat, oats, pease, muskmelons, and watermelons.

Also, there will be games and races. There will be horse races.

The young men who ride the horses will put on Indian costumes. And for the baseball game, from somewhere a team will come to play against the Indian baseball players there on Walpole Island. The pitcher is named Wellington Shaganash [Englishman]; he is the best pitcher there on Walpole Island. Everything will be there, places where one eats and souvenir stands. The Walpole Island Indian Band will play. They too will put on Indian costumes. When the excursion boat arrives they will go and welcome the people who disembark. Those boats will sail from Sandusky, Cleveland, and Port Huron.

18. THE WALPOLE ISLAND FAIR (*Phonograph Record*)

menta·kukkwe·tik keye· ki·nuwa· menta·kuninuwitok!

no·nkwa ki·šekakk nuwi·-tepa·cim iw eniššena·pe·k ema· wa·pow Island fair wi·-eya·muwa·t. nenko-ename ʔe·-ki·šekakk no·nko ma·nta ki·šekakk mi· wi·-we·pekkamekakk. kekkina tašš ke·ko· eši-uši·tta·-wak ekonta Fair Company ke·-eši-meno-eya·wa·t ekiw wa·-pi-eša·cik. wi·-pi-uncipete·no·n ci·ma·nan uwiti Sandusky, keye· kwa uwiti Cleveland, keye· kwa uwiti Port Huron, keye· kwa wenina wi·-pi-uncipa·-wak etamo·pi·link wa·-pi-eya·cik wi·-pi-wa·pentamuwa·t keye· wi·-nuwa· iw e·nenokki·t aw eniššena·pe· ema· wa·pow Island. kekkina tašš kenantumiko·m ta-pi-eša·ye·k menikk ke·-keškitto·ye·k ci-pi-wa·-pentame·k ke· wi· e·nenokki·t aw eniššena·pe· ema· utanekki·wenink.

kekkina ke·ko· essa wi·-eya·mekat eniw games, keye· kwa pe·šeko-keši·k wi·-kekwe·cekkanetiwak ke·ši·kka·petto·cik. eniššena·pe·k u-škinuwe·k wi·-pemo·mekowak, keye· uwi·-a·pecitto·na·wa·n eniw Indian costume. keye· kwa ekiw essa wa·-pekkwa·kkutwe·cik ke· wi·nuwa· essa wi·-pi-tekoššeno·n eniw wa·-pi-etta·kuwa·cin. aw ke· wi·nuwa· uwiti wa·pow Island ne·tta·-eppaketank iw pekkwa·kkwat mi· e·-šenikka·sot, ša·kena·šš.

mi·nuwa· tašš kekkina ke·ko· wi·-pa·tti·nat essa ke·-wa·pentamuwa·t ekiw ke·-pi-eša·cik. me·kwa· no·nko ssa ma·nta eppi· unana·ʔetto·-na·wa· iw exhibit hall. kekkina ke·ko· uto·šetto·na·wa· ekiw eniššena·-pe·k ke·-wa·pentamuwa·t ekiw wa·-pi-eša·cik. ekwi·tepiwenan, uta·-šetto·na·wa·n, keye· kwa eto·ppuwinan. keye· kwa ne·tta·wekitto·-wa·t kekkina ke·ko· wi·-ette·mekat, ci·ssan, uppini·k, menta·menak, meskoti·sseminak, keye· kwa iw pekkwe·šeka·ns, keye· kwa meno·min, menici·min, penakesikenak, keye· kwa ke·pa·kkuʔika·te·k kekkina

ke·ko·. we·kutakwe·n ... ci-wa·wa·pentamukwe·n ... kepa·kku-
ʔika·te·k¹ ta-ette·mekat eko ema·, keye· kwa we·šetto·wa·t ekiw enišše-
na·pe·k ekkwe·wak, wa·po·weya·nan, menciko·te·nyan, kepo·ssene·-
nyan, keye· kwa mekkisenan. kekkina ke·ko· uto·šetto·na·wa· ekiw
essa enišsena·pe·k, wi·-wa·pentaʔuwe·wa·n, mettikwa·pi·k, wa·ka·-
kkuta·tteko·n, peššanše·ʔekane·ya·tteko·n. mi· ma·nta essa ke·-
-wa·pentame·k ki·nuwa· wa·-pi-eša·ye·k. me·kwa·c unana·ʔetto·na·wa·
ma·nta ssa ni·meʔiti·wekamik ke·-teši-ni·muwa·t ekiw wa·-pi-eša·cik.
kepe·-ki·šik ta-ni·muwak keye· kwa nena·š ci-a·petta·tepikkakk.
  mi· ma·nta penki· essa e·ši-tepa·cemoya·n iw no·nko ki·šekakk.

  Ladies and you, gentlemen!
  Today I am going to tell of the fact that the Indians on Walpole
Island are going to have a fair. A week from today is when it will
begin. The Fair Company is doing everything for the convenience
of those who will come. Boats will sail from Sandusky and from
Cleveland and from Port Huron, and from everywhere will come
those who travel in automobiles to see the ways of the Indian there
on Walpole Island. You are all invited, as many of you as will be
able, to come and see the ways of the Indian there on his reservation.
  There will be everything in the way of games, and there will be
racing of fast horses. Young Indian men will ride the horses and
they will use Indian costumes. Also a team will come to play against
the baseball players there. The best pitcher among those players
there on Walpole Island is named Shaganash [Englishman].
  Moreover, every sort of thing will be in plenty there for the visitors
to see. Right now, at this very time, they are putting the exhibit
hall into shape. The Indians are preparing everything for the
visitors to see. They are building chairs and tables. Also everything that they raise in the way of crops will be there: turnips, potatoes,
Indian corn, beans, and wheat and oats, pease, hard-shell corn,
and every kind of preserves. Whatever one may want to see in the
way of preserves will be there, as well as the things which the Indian
women make: blankets, dresses, trousers, and moccasins. The Indians
are making everything, and it will be exhibited, such as bows, axe
handles, whipstocks. Such are the things you will see, you who will
come there. At present they are putting in shape the dance hall where

---

¹ Short blurs in the record; probably no words missing.

the visitors will dance. There will be dancing all day and until midnight.

This then is what little I have to say today.

19. THE SWEATING CURE (*First Dictation*)

nenkwatink pe·šik enini ki·-pepa·ma·tesi ki·we·tenonk. mi· tašš ki·-pemi-tekkacit. ekiw etašš enišsena·pe·k uki·-nena·ntuwi ʔa·wa·n. mi· tašš ki·-ušitto·wa·t iw meškikkuwa·po· wa·-a·pecitto·wa·t. mi· tašš ki·-pi·nteke·yo·te·t ema· mento·to·wekamekonk, keye· kwa ki·--ettamuwa· mento·to·-essini·n ema· pi·nci·yeʔi·nk, keye· kwa iw meškikkuwa·po· ka·-a·pecitto·wa·t.

mi· tašš ka·-ena·wa·t "pi·ntik ko ma·no· ta-eya·yan e·kko-keški ʔe·wesiyan."

eppi· tašš ka·-uwe·nepit eniw eya·nik eniw essini·n uki·-si·kena·na·wa· iw meškikkuwa·po· ema· mento·to·-essini·nk. mi· tašš ki·--umpa·pette·k iw meškikkuwa·po·. a·ppeci tašš ki·-kecci-epwe·so.

mi· tašš ka·-ena·wa·t "ma·no· kwa eya·n ema· pi·nci·yeʔi· e·kko--keški ʔe·wesiyan."

mi· tašš ki·-sa·keto·te·t kuma·ppi·. keye· kwa mi· ki·-pe·nkuše·ʔot. mi· tašš ki·-pi·ssekkank neya·nkeninekin ekwiwenan. ke·keše·pa·wekakk mi· ki·-uniška·t. a·ppeci tašš ki·-meno-pema·tesi, keye· kwa kekkina ki·-ma·ca·mekateni utakkeciwin.

Once a certain man was traveling in the North. Then he caught a cold. The Indians there doctored him. They made the liquid medicine which they were going to use. Then he crawled into the sweating lodge, and the stones for the steam bath were placed inside there for him, and the liquid medicine which they used.

Then they told him, "Be sure to stay in there as long as you can stand it."

When he had seated himself in place, then on those stones which were there they poured that liquid medicine, on those stones for the steam bath. Then that liquid medicine went up in steam. He felt extremely hot.

This is what they said to him: "Stay inside there just the same, as long as you can stand it."

Then finally he crawled out. Then he dried himself. Then he put on light garments. The next morning he got up. He felt very well and all his cold had gone away.

20. THE SWEATING CURE (*Second Dictation*)

pe·šik enini ki·-pepa·ma·tesi ki·we·tenonk. ki·-kessina·mekat tašš, keye· kwa mi· ki·-pemi-tekkacit. mi· tašš ki·-nena·ntuwi ʔa·wa·t. uki·-pi·ntekana·wa·n tašš ema· mento·to·wekamekonk. a·ppeci tašš ki·-kecci-epwe·so.

mi· tašš ka·-ena·wa·t "ma·no· kwa eya·n ema· pi·nci·ye ʔi·."

mi· tašš ki·-eya·t pi·nci·ye ʔi· ema· mento·to·wekamekonk. ki·-pi--keto·te·tašš kuma·ppi·. mi· tašš ki·-pe·nkuše·ʔutisot, ki·-pi·ssekkank neya·nkeninekin ekwiwenan. nempa·kenink etašš ki·-eya· kepe·--tepikk. ke·keše·pa·wekakk ki·-uniška·, keye· kwa mi· iw ki·-meno--pema·tesit, ki·-ma·ca·mekatenik uta·kkusiwin.

A certain man was traveling in the North. The weather was very cold, and he caught cold. Then they doctored him. They put him inside the sweating lodge. He felt extremely hot.

Then they said to him, "Just the same, do you stay inside there."

So then he was in there, in the sweating lodge. At last he came crawling out. Then he dried himself all over and put on light-weight garments. He stayed in bed all that night. When morning came he got up, and now he felt well and his illness had gone away.

21. THE SWEATING CURE (*Phonograph Record*)

nenkotink ki·šekakk enini ki·-pepa·ma·tesi uwiti ki·we·tenonk. ki·-kessina·mekateni tašš uwiti ka·-pepa·tenisit. keye· kwa mi· ki·--pemi-tekkacit uwiti ka·-tenisit, ki·-a·kkusit tašš.

wi·nuwa· tašš wi·nuwa· ssa eniššena·pe·k e·ya·cik unana·-ntuwiʔekawa·wa·n. mi· tašš ki·-ušitto·wa·t iw ssa mento·to·wekamik keye· kwa essini·n ki·-keša·pekkisemowa·t. meškikkuwa·po· keye· uki·-ušitto·na·wa· wa·-a·pecitto·wa·t. mi· tašš ki·-si·kenamuwa·t ka·--pi·nteke·yo·te·t ema· mento·to·wekamekonk iw meškikkuwa·po· wi·--umpa·pette·k. a·ppeci tašš ki·-kecci-epwe·so.

keye· kwa uki·-ena·wa·n "ma·no· kwa eya·n e·kko-keškisuyan ema· pi·nci·ye ʔi·."

mi· tašš ka·-ešicceke·t. a·no wi·-keto·te·.

"usa·m kešite· mi· ema· pi·nci·ye ʔi·nk."

"ma·no· kwa eya·n" uki·-ena·wa·n.

mi· tašš ka·-ešicceke·t. ma·no· mi·nuwa· ecina ki·-eya·. kuma·ppi· tašš ki·-pi·keto·te· keye· ki·-pe·nkuše· ʔutisot, keye· ki·-pi·ssekkank pe·kka·netinekin eniw ssa ekwiwenan. mi·nuwa· tašš nempa·kenink ki·-kuwiššemo. keye· kekiše·p ki·-uniška·. a·ppeci ki·-meno-pema·tesi, keye· kekkina iw ssa uta·kkusiwin ki·-ma·ca·mekateni.

mi· ssa ma·nta ka·-ešicceke·wa·t ekiw enissena·pe·k ša·ši kwa. uwaya eya·kkusicin mi· ko ki·-mento·to· ʔint ema· mento·to·wekamekonk. keye· kwa mi· ko meno-pema·tesit essa ka·-eškwa·-mento·to·cin. ema· tašš nempa·kenink ekkawe·-ki·šo·ššin ka·-eškwa·-mento·to·cin.

Once a man was traveling in the North. It was cold there where he was staying about. Then he caught a cold there where he was staying, and he fell ill.

The people who were there gave him medical treatment. They built a lodge for the steam bath and heated some stones. They prepared an infusion of herbs which they were going to use. Then, when he had crawled inside that bath tent, they poured the infusion which was to form steam. He felt extremely hot.

They said to him, "Stay inside there as long as you can."

That was what he did. To be sure, he wanted to crawl out.

"It is too hot in here."

"Stay just the same," they said to him.

Then he did so. He did stay a little longer. Finally he came crawling out and dried himself and put on other clothes. Then he lay down on a bed. The next morning he got up. He felt very good, and his illness was entirely gone.

This was what those Indians did of old. When anyone fell ill he was given a steam bath there in the sweating lodge. Then he would be well, after he had taken the steam bath. He would first lie warmly covered a while in bed, after he had taken the steam bath.

22. FASTING (*Dictation*)

mi· tašš e·na·t eniw ukwissan "ki·špin pi-eša·t aw a·ppeci kwa menta·kunini ci-pi-kekwe·cemikk ci-šuwe·nemikk, ka· wi· ka-te·pwe·ttuwa·ssi·. ketima·kesi eppane· aw enini."

uwe·še ʔo keye· kekkiše·. enake·kkukameko·ns ušittemawa· wa·-teši-mekkate·kke·t. e·ntesso-kekiše·p etašš eša· ma·pa ekkiwe·nsi" uwa-kekwe·cema·t uto·škenawe·man a·ni· ka·-ena·pentamenit.

"a·ni· ka·-ena·pentaman?"

pa·ma· tašš šekwa ne·ntuwe·nema·cin aw ekkiwe·nsi͂ ki·-puwa·-na·nit, mi· iw ci-eššama·t eniw ukwissan.

And this was what he said to that son of his: "If that very elegant man comes and offers to bless you, you will not believe him. That man is always in want."

He painted himself with charcoal. A bark hut was built for him in which he was to fast. Every morning this old man went to ask his young man what he had seen in a vision.

"What have you seen in your vision?"

Finally, when the other had dreamt of that being which the old man desired, then he would give his son something to eat.

23. FASTING (*Phonograph Record*)

me·kwa· kwa me·kkete·kke·wa·t ekiw eniššena·pe·k ki·-nento-
-kekke·ntemowa·t ke·ko·. iw tepiško· ko na· no·nkwa essa e·šeccike·-
wa·t ekiw ke·kkeno·ʔema·kusicik iw eppi· ki·-mekkate·kke·wak ekiw
uškinuwe·k keye· kwa ekiw ssa ekkwe·wak iw ke·ko· wi·-kekke·-
-ntemowa·t iw ni·ka·n wa·-ni-meno-a·pecitto·wa·t. ušittemawa·wak
ekiw wa·-teši-mekkate·kke·wa·t wi·kuwa·mink. keye· kwa ušipi·-
ʔeka·suwak ema· ute·nkuyiwa·nk iw wi·-kekke·nta·kusit aw me·kkete·-
kke·t. a·ppeci tašš ki·-mekkate·kke·wak na·nenkotenonk ekiw tašš
uškinuwe·k keye· kwa uškeni·kekkwe·k iw ke·ko· wi·-kekke·ntemowa·t
iw wa·-puwa·temowa·t. ena·pentamuwin uki·-a·pecitto·na·wa·. ki·-
-ena·pentamuwa·t tašš ke·ko· mi· iw ki·špin uta·ppena·wa·t eniw ssa
wa·-šuwe·nemikuwa·cin.

e·ntesso-kekiše·p ki·-eša· ma·pa ekkiwe·nsi͂ ema· ssa eniw e·nteši-
-mekkate·kke·nit eniw ssa uto·škeni·ki·man uwa-kekwe·cema·t iw
nemanci [1] ka·-ena·pentamenikwe·n uwe·kwe·ni [1] keye· ka·-puwa·-
na·kwe·n. mi· ma·nta ka·-ešiwe·pakk essa eškwe·ya·nk ke·-ki·šekakk
ke· wi·nuwa· ekiw ssa uškinuwe·k wi·-kekke·ntemowa·t ke·ko· keye·
kwa iw wa·-meno-a·pecitto·wa·t.

pe·šik etašš ekwa uwe·ssi͂ essa uki·-ši·nkwe·nema·wa·n essa ekiw
ke·ttesicik ci·šuwe·nema·nit eniw ssa uto·škeni·ki·muwa·n.

"menta·kunini ta-pi-eya·." uki·-ena·wa·n eko eniw we·ški-pema·-
tesinecin eppi· me·kkete·kke·necin, "menta·kunini ta-pi-eya·."

mi· tašš ka·-ena·t aw ke·ttesit ka· wi·n aw menta·kunini ta-uta·-

---

[1] The record seems to have final *i*; hearing error?

ppena·ssik essa ešša wa·-wi·ntema·kot. aw ma· menta·kunini mi·ma·pa aw ssa ci·nti·ssi" e·šenikka·sot. ka·keke· pema·ntam eko ma·eko na· ke· wi· aw ci·nti·ssi". ka· ke·ko· keški ʔe·wesiwin utaya·nsi·n.

"mi· ko na· e·tta ekkona·šuwat. mi· ko na· e·tta ke· wi· essa e·ši-keški ʔe·wesit."

mi· tašš eniw ka·-kena ʔemawa·wa·cin ekiw ke·ttesicik eniw ssa uto·škeni·ki·muwa·n ci-uta·ppena·ssenik.

nešwina·[1] a·nint kwe·tta·mekosenicin meššipeši·n ma·ke· ma·ke· mešši-kene·peko·n uwaya ko na· eninta kecci-uwe·ssi·n kwe·tta·-mekosenicin ma·ke· enimekki·n a·nint essa uki·-uta·ppena·wa·n essa ci-šuwe·nemikuwa·t. mi· ma·nta ka·-ešiwe·pakk ša·ši kwa essa ki·--pi-mekkate·kke·wa·t ekiw enišsena·pe·k. ki·-pi-senaketto·wak ke·wi·nuwa· essa ke·ko· ci-kekke·ntemowa·t ke·[2] essa wa·-meno-pema·tesiwa·t. mi· ma·nta ka·-unci-mekkate·kke·wa·t ekonta ssa pema·tesicik.

a·ppeci tašš a·nint enišsena·pe·k ki·-kutta·mekosuwak, keye· kwa uki·-kekke·nta·na·wa· ke·ko·, keye· kwa uki·-kekke·nta·na·wa· essa wa·-pi-tekoššeno·mekatenik ni·ka·n. wa·ssa ki·-ekkawa·pi essa wa·-pi-tekoššeninecin wa·-pi-nessikuwa·cin. keye· uki·-kekke·nema·wa·n eniw ssa wi·ci-enišsena·pe·wa·n. mi· ma· ša·ši kwa ekiw pe·ma·tesicik nento-nessa·wa·t eniw ssa enišsena·pe·n pekka·n e·nwe·necin. uwiti ki·we·tenonk keye· kwa e·-penkiššemok ki·-pi--uncipa·wak ekiw na·tuwe·ssuwak ka·-pi-muwine·wa·cik eniw ucipwe·n ma·meppi· enikke·kkemik.

How the Indians fasted to obtain knowledge. Just as now they do who receive schooling, so at that time the young men and women used to fast in order to obtain knowledge which they would use in the later course of their lives. Something was prepared for them where they were to fast in a wigwam. And they were painted on their faces with the marking by which a person who fasted was known. Sometimes they fasted very much, those young men and young women, in order to obtain that knowledge which they were to get in a dream. They made use of dream visions. When they had dreamt anything, the question was whether they would accept that being which offered to bless them.

Every morning that old man would come to where his young person

---

[1] Unknown word, perhaps wrongly heard.
[2] Doubtless wrongly heard.

was fasting and ask him what vision he had seen and of what being he had dreamt. This happened so that in the days to come the young men also might have some knowledge and something of which they could make good use.

And one creature there was whom those old people hated to bless their young persons.

"A fine gentleman will come", they would tell those young persons who were fasting, "A fine gentleman will come."

And the old person would tell him not to accept that fine gentleman and what he would tell him. This fine gentleman, you must know, is the one who is called the bluejay. He is always in want, that bluejay. He has no power at all.

"You must simply drive him away. That is the extent of his power.'

That is the way those old people warned the young people not to accept that creature.

But some would accept the blessing of a frightful Great Lynx, and some of a Great Serpent, and some of some other frightful great creature, and some of a Thunderer. That is the way it was of old when those Indians fasted in the hither course of time. They too went to great pains that they might obtain knowledge and lead a good life. This was why these people used to fast.

Some Indians were very formidable and knew much and knew what was to arrive in the future. From a long ways off he would observe those who were coming to kill him. And they had knowledge of their fellow Indian. For in the old time those people tried to kill the Indian of other tongue. From the North and from the West came those Iroquois to attack the Ojibwa here in this part of the country.

24. BURIAL RITES (*Phonograph Record*)

ša·ši kwa ka·-ešicceke·wa·t ke· wi·nuwa· ekiw ki·-pekite·ntuwa·t ci-pwa·-tekoššink aw eya·peški·we·t.

keye· wi·n aw ssa no·ss eppi· ka·-nempot ke· wi· ki·-pekite·nema·. ma·pa essa pe·kete·nema·t eniw ssa e·ni-nemponecin, tepiško· na· no·-nkwa essa me·kkete·wekkoneye· e·šeccike·t, mesine ʔikan utakenta·n eninta ssa pekite·nema·t ka·-nemponecin. ke· wi·n etašš ša·ši kwa ekiw ka·-pi-nempocik ka· wi· ke·ko· mesine ʔikan uki·-eya·sseno·n. uki·--kekke·nta·na·wa· essa wa·-eši-keno·na·wa·t eninta ssa ka·-nemponecin.

ma·pa tašš no·ss ke· wi· ki·-nempot kekkina ke·ko· essa ki·-uwe·še ʔa·

iw ka·kuma·[1] ute·nkuyink. keye· kwa uki·-keki·kkema·n ma·pa aw e·-pekite·nema·t eninta ssa no·ssan ki·-wi·ntemawa·t ka· wi·n ta-a·pena·pessinik ka·-pi-uncipa·nit, pa·ma· ko ni·ka·n ci-ena·penit uwiti e·ša·nit nena·š tašš eko ci-tekoššenit uwiti ssa e·ša·nit.

mi·nuwa· uki·-no·kko·na·wa·n [1] ni·šena ssa pekkwe·šeka·nsan pe·-pi·wa·kin ekwaci·nk e·ntenite·kin. keye· kwa nenkotwe·wa·n eniw mekkisenan a·kuwi·tta mi·nuwa· ki·-ettamuwa· ko ma· mekkakkonk, ki·špin ni-no·nte·-pi·kussito·t eniw umakkesinan ci-pwa·-tekoššink uwiti e·ša·t e·-penkiššemok, ci-uncipeto·t ne·ya·p mi·nuwa· ci-pi·-ssekkank eniwi mekkisenan.

mi· ma·nta ka·-ešicceke·wa·t ša·ši kwa ekiw ssa pe·ma·tesicik.

The way they did when they held burial rites before the white man came.

When my father died they held these burial rites for him. This person who performed the burial rites over those who died in the course of time, just as the priest does now, he read from a book when he performed the rites over one who had died. Only when they died in ancient time he had no book. They knew by heart that which they would say in addressing the one who had died.

When my father died he was adorned in every way and painted on his face. And he who held the burial rites for my father exhorted him, telling him not to look back whence he had come, but to look forward toward the place to which he was going until he should arrive at the place to which he was going.

They placed for him two small loaves of bread that had been baked out of doors. Also an extra pair of moccasins was placed in the coffin with him, so that if he wore out his moccasins before he arrived whither he was bound in the West, he might take them out and put on these other moccasins.

This is the way those people did of old.

25. INDIAN BREAD (*Dictation*)

pe·šik uškeni·kekkwe· utaya·n mettiko-una·kan keye· kwa iw metti-ko-e·mekkwa·n. mi· tašš ušitto·t iw pekkwe·šekan. na·ppa·ni· tašš utatto·n ema· mettiko-una·kenink keye· kekkina e·ši-tekoneke·t.

---

[1] Unknown word, perhaps wrongly transcribed; the translation is a guess.

mi· tašš mi·nuwa· nempi·šš nenka·pa·weto·t kekkina iw na·ppa·ni·,
mi·nuwa· kekkina ki·-ki·ši·tta·t enatenank. mi· tašš ena·wenka^ʔank
ema· wa·-teši-menosank. mi· tašš pekitenank ema· me·kwe·-eškote·nk.
keye· kwa mi· a-nenkwa^ʔank. ecina tašš e·tta ette·ni ema· eškote·nk.
mi· tašš kwe·kkussito·t. mi· tašš ki·-menote·k ekwa·we·pe^ʔank.
mettiko·ns etašš uta·pecitto·n iw peššanše·^ʔank iw pekkwe·šekan.
mi·nuwa· tašš uka·ka·škeci·^ʔa·n. ki·-eši-ka·ka·škeci·^ʔank etašš mi·-
nuwa· upaššenše· ^ʔa·n. mi· tašš wi·wekkwe·ci·nank pepakuwiya·-
ne·n^ʔink ne·mpi·we·kakk we·nepikk. mi· tašš a·pi·kenank keye·
kwa mi· iw ki·kki·škekkotank. mi· tašš ki·ši·tta·mekakk a·ši ci-mi·-
cink iw pekkwe·šekan.

A young woman has a wooden dish and a wooden ladle. Then
she prepares that bread. She has flour in the wooden bowl and
all the things which she mixes with it. Then she moistens all that
flour with water, and when she has done that she kneads it. Then
she shapes the ashes in which she is going to bake it. Then she sets
it down there, right in the fire. There she covers it with ashes. Only
for a short time is it there in the fire. Then she turns it over. Then
when it is baked done she takes it out of the fire. She uses a switch
with which she whips that bread. Then she scrapes it clean. When
she has scraped it she whips it again. Then she wraps it up for a
while in a wet piece of cotton cloth. Then she unwraps it and slices it.
Then that bread is done and ready to eat.

26. INDIAN BREAD (*Phonograph Record*)

uškini·kekkwe· uki·-eya·n iw mettikuna·kan keye· iw mettiko-e·-
mekkwa·n wa·-teši-ušitto·t iw pekkwe·šekan. kekkina tašš ke·ko·
uki·-etto·n na·ppa·ni· ema· una·kenink keye· iw wa·-teši-tekoneke·t.
mi·nuwa· tašš nempi·šš uki·-etto·n, kekkina tašš ki·-nekka·pa·weto·t,
keye· ki·-enatenank iw na·ppa·ni·. kekkina tašš ka·-ki·šetto·t ke·ko·,
mi· tašš mi·nuwa· ki·-ena·wenka^ʔank ema· eškote·nk wa·-teši-menote·k
iw pekkwe·šekan. mi·nuwa· tašš uki·-etto·n iw pekkwe·šekan keye·
kwa uki·-nenkwa^ʔa·n. ecina tašš e·tta ki·-ette·ni ema· eškote·nk
mi·nuwa· ki·-kwe·kkussito·t. mi·nuwa· ko uki·-nenkwa ^ʔa·n. ecina
tašš ki·-ette·ni. mi· tašš ki·-ekwa·we·pe^ʔank. mi·nuwa· mettiko·ns
uki·-enakka·sa·n [1] ki·-peššanše·^ʔank iw pekkwe·šekan me·nuppo-

---

[1] Unknown word, perhaps wrongly transcribed.

kwakk, keye· kwa ki·-ka·ka·škeci·ʔank. mi·nuwa· uki·-peššanše·ʔa·n
keye· kwa mi·nuwa· uki·-wi·wekkwe·ci·na·n iw ne·mpi·we·ketinik
pepakuwiya·ne͞·. mi· tašš ki·-ki·šetto·t. mi· tašš e·šenikka·te·k
ma·nta pekkwe·šekan po·ci·nkwe·ʔekan.

A young woman had a wooden bowl and a wooden ladle in which to make that bread. She put all the things into that bowl, the flour and that which she mixed with it. Then she put in water, wetting it all, and kneaded the flour. When she had made ready all this, then she shaped out the ashes of the fire to make a place in which to bake that bread. Then she put the bread there and covered it with ashes. It was in there only a little while when she turned it over. Again she covered it with ashes. It was there a little while. Then she took it out of the fire. Then she charred a switch and whipped that tasty bread and scraped it clean. She whipped it again and wrapped it in a damp piece of cotton cloth. Then she had finished it. This bread is called Indian bread.

27. CATS' EYES

ka· wi· uki·-eya·wa·ssi·wa·n tepaʔeki·sesswa·nan ša·ši kwa eniššena·-pe·k. mi· tašš na· eniw ka·šeke·nsan ka·-utapeʔaki·sesswa·nuwa·cin. aw ma· ka·šeke·ns wa·weye·ya·ni ke· wi· umakkete·weški·nšekwa·n. eppi· tašš ekwa na·wekkwe·k eka·wa· pe·šša·pi·kemoni iw umakkete·-weški·nšekwa·n. mi· tašš e·kketowa·t ekiw enissena·pe·k "na·wekkwe·-ya·kemi·nkwe· aw ka·šeke·ns."

The Indians of old had no clocks or watches. So then they used the cat for a clock. The pupil of the cat's eye is round. But when it is noon, his pupil is only a very narrow line. Then the Indians say, "The cat's eyes are in the noonday state."

28. LOVE MEDICINE (*Dictation*)

nenkwatink ekkiwe·nsi͞· nenki·-no·ntuwa·pa a-tepa·cemot uškeni·-kekkwe·n ki·-nentotema·kot iw wi·kkwe·pecikan. uki·-messawe·-nema·n eniw uškinuwe·n. mi· tašš eniw ekkiwe·nsi·nyan ki·-nentote·mawa·t iw wi·kkwe·pecikan, keye· kwa uki·-tepaʔemawa·n. mi· tašš ki·-a·pecitto·t ma·pa uškini·kekkwe· iw meškikki ka·-ki·špenato·t.

mi· tašš ma·pa uškinuwe· ka·-eši-kecci-sa·ke ?a·t eniw uškini·kekkwe·n.
keye· kwa mi· ki·-wi·teke·ma·t. keye· kwa mi· wi·pa ki·-eya·wa·wa·t
epino·ci·nyan. a·ppeci kwa ki·-sa·ke ?ituwak keye· kwa ki·-ma·ci·-
ška·wak.

Once I heard an old man tell of how a young woman asked him for
love medicine. She was in love with a young man. So then she asked
that old man for the love medicine, and she paid him for it. Then the
young woman used that medicine which she had bought. Then this
young man accordingly very much loved that young woman. Then
he married her. Very soon they had children. They loved each
other very much and they fared very well.

29. LOVE MEDICINE (*Phonograph Record*)

wi·kkwe·pecikan e·šenikka·te·k no·nkwa ekiw eniššena·pe·k ni·pena
eya·pecitto·wa·t me·nteke· essa we·ški-pema·tesicik.
nenki·-no·ntuwa·pa aw pe·šik ekkiwe·nsi͂ iw tepa·cetank keye·
wi· essa ke·kke·ntank wi·kkwe·pecikan e·ši-kutta·mekotenik. keye·
kwa uki·-tepa·cema·n eniw uškini·kekkwe·n ka·-messawe·nema·cin
eniw uškinuwe·n. uki·-kekwe·cema·n eniw ekkiwe·nsi·nyan wi·-
-ki·špenatemawa·t iw wi·kkwe·pecikan mcnci ko ma·nta messawe·-
nema·t eniw uškinuwe·n menta·kuninuwan.
ma·pa tašš ekkiwe·nsi͂ uki·-ena·n "a·ppeci ko kutta·mekwat essa
ke·kke·ntema·n ma·nta wi·kkwe·pecikan kcye· kwa a·ppeci ko ka·-
-na·no·ce ?ik" uki·-ena·n eniw ssa uškini·kekkwe·n, "ke·ko tašš šekate·-
nema·kke·n ma·pa uškinuwe·. ki·n ema· ketišeccika·na· essa ci·-
-menta·kwe·nemikk."
mi· tašš ki·-a·pecitto·t ma·pa ssa uškini·kekkwe· ma·nta wi·kkwe·-
pecikan. keye· kwa mi· iw ka·-eši-menta·kwe·nemikot eninta ssa
uškini·kekkwe·n.[1] keye· kwa mi· iw ki·-wi·teke·ma·t ma·pa uškinuwe·
eninta ssa uškini·kekkwe·n, menci ko ma·nta e·ši-enokki·mekakk
ma·nta ssa wi·kkwe·pecikan. eno·ci-ke·ko· essa ki·-ešicceke· ma·pa
uškinuwe· essa ke·-eši-menta·kwe·nemikot eninta ssa uškini·kekkwe·n
wa·kkwe·penikucin. keye· kwa ki·-wi·nteke·ntuwak etašš kuma·ppi·cc.
a·ppeci tašš uki·-sa·ke ?a·n ma·pa uškinuwe· eninta ssa ekkwe·wan
eppi· ka·-wi·teke·ntuwa·t. keye· kwa mi· iw ki·-we·pi-eya·wa·wa·t

---

[1] Apparently, a slip of the tongue for *uškinuwe·n*.

eniw ssa epino·ci·nyan. ki·-ma·ci·ška·wak kekkina ke·ko· essa ki·-ni-...[2]
ni·ka·n essa ki·šekakk ki·-ni-pema·tesiwa·t. ki·-meno-eya·wak keye·
kwa ki·-ma·ci·ška·wak epino·ci·nyan e·škam ki·-pa·tti·nu ˀa·wa·t.

The Indians even now use a great deal of that which is called love medicine, especially the young people.

I once heard a certain old man tell of the love medicine for which he knew the formula, and of how powerful it was. He told also of a young woman who was in love with a young man. She asked that old man to let her buy that love medicine from him, since she was so very much in love with that young gentleman.

This old man told her, "This love medicine which I know is extremely powerful: he will be urgently after you all the time," said he to that young woman; "And do not be too impatient to have that young man. You will bring it about that he will be the one to desire you."

Then this young woman made use of this love medicine. Then this young man fell in love with her. Then the young man married this young woman, so well did this love medicine work. This young man did all kinds of things to gain the affection of this young woman who had put him under the love spell. Then soon they were married. This young man very much loved this woman when they were married. Then they started to have children. They fared well in every respect ... in the days they lived from then on. They lived happily and were fortunate and in the course of time had many children.

30. THE DOCTOR'S LOVE MEDICINE

nenkwatink uškinuwe·k ki·-kekkino· ˀema·kusiwak ni·š ema· kekkino· ˀema·ti·wekamekonk, pe·šik etašš aw kecci-mo·kkuma·ni·-uškinuwe· keye· pe·šik eniššena·pe·ns. ki·-uwi·cekkiwe·nˀentiwak nena·š ekwa ki·-ki·ši·tta·wa·t ema· kekkino· ˀema·ti·wekamekonk iw ka·--kekkino· ˀema·kusiwa·t neyi·š ta-meškikki·wenini·wuwa·t.

ka·-ki·ši·tta·wa·t tašš ema· kekkino· ˀema·ti·wekamekonk keye· wi· ma·pa eniššena·pe·ns uki·-kekkino·ˀemawa·n eniw kecci-mo·kkuma·-ne·nsan iw ke·kke·ntank wi·kkwe·pecikan. uki·-ešiwena·n uwiti me·kuya·k. uki·-ešino· ˀemawa·n sa·kekki·nik iw meškikki. mi· tašš ki·-wi·ntemawa·t e·šeccika·te·k eppi· wi·kkwe·penint aw wa·-wi·-

---

[1] Short blur in record.

kkwe·penint. "ta-ušicceka·te·k nempi·ššink ci-unsika·te·k ma·nta uci·pekke·ns. mi· tašš umo·te·nsink ta-eccika·te·k.
"eppi· wi·-a·pecitto·yan ma·nta wi·kkwe·pecikan mi· ta-si·kenaman ema· mo·šwe·ka·nsink. eppi· tašš wa·pemat aw wa·-wi·kkwe·penat mi· ci-keno·nat keye· kwa ta-uncika·puwiyan we·nta·nemakk. e--pekanta·nemakk ma·no· enakke·ya· ta-uncika·puwi aw wa·-wi·kkwe·penint. mi· tašš ta-pi·cema·ntank ma·nta meškikki. we·wi·p etašš ta-pi-pekamusse·."
pa·ma· tašš kuma·ppi·cc ma·pa meškikki·wenini e·nta·t uki·-eno·na·n pe·šik uškini·kekkwe·n wi·-enokki·tta·kot. mi· tašš ma·pa uškini·kekkwe· uki·-eya·wa·n wi·cekkiwe·nyan keye· uki·-sa·ke ?a·n eniw uškinuwe·n. kuma·ppi· tašš uki·-mekkama·ko·n pe·šik uškini·kekkwe·n eniw ukwi·wesse·nseman. a·ppeci tašš uki·-ki·ssa·te·nema·n. keye· kwa mi· aw uškinuwe· ki·-ena·t eniw pe·kka·nesinecin ta-wi·teke·ma·t. mi· tašš ma·pa uškini·kekkwe· ki·-nempo·te·wi-eya·t keye· kwa eto·ppuwinink ki·-nuwakekkwe·ššin. uki·-kekke·nema·n tašš ma·pa meškikki·wenini ke·ko· eši-eya·nit eniw uškeni·kekkwe·n.
mi· tašš ki·-kekwe·cema·t "a·ni·šš e·ši·-eya·yan?"
aw tašš uškini·kekkwe· uki·-wi·ntemawa·n iw mekkamekot pe·šik pe·kka·nesinecin uškini·kekkwe·n ukwi·wesse·nseman.
mi· tašš ka·-ena·t aw meškikki·wenini "ke·kwa ene·ntanke·n. ka--mi·nin meškikki ne·ya·p ci-te·penat aw kekwi·wesse·nsim."
uki·-mi·na·n tašš eniw uškini·kekkwe·n iw meškikki ema· umo·te·nsink, keye· kwa uki·-wi·ntemawa·n ke·-eši-a·pecitto·nit.
mi· tašš ki·-ma·ca·t ma·pa uškini·kekkwe· ki·-pepa·-nentone·škuwa·t. mi·kkena·nk uki·-wa·pema·n pi-eya·nit. mi· tašš ki·-nessa·pa·weto·t we·wi·p iw mo·šwe·ka·ns iw meškikki, keye· mi· ki·-keno·na·t eppi· ne·kkwe·škuwa·t ki·-uncika·puwit we·nta·nemate·nik, keye· kwa eniw uškinuwe·n e·-pekanta·nematenik. mi· tašš ki·-uta·ppenank iw umo·šwe·ka·ns ki·-pi·cene·sseto·t iw meškikki ma·pa uškinuwe·. keye· kwa ma·pa uškini·kekkwe· uki·-keno·na·n. kuma·ppi· tašš ki·-ni-ma·ca·wak. ke· wi· ma·pa uškini·kekkwe· ki·-ni-ki·we· uwiti e·nteši-enokki·t.
uki·-kekwe·cemiko·n eniw meškikki·weninuwan e·ntekwe·n ka·-wa·pema·kwe·n eniw uškinuwe·n.
"nenki·-wa·pema·" uki·-ena·n.
"keki·-ešicceke· na tašš iw ka·-eši-kekkino·?emo·na·n?"
uki·-ena·n tašš aw uškini·kekkwe· "mi· ssa ko iw ka·-esicceke·ya·n ka·-eši-kekkino·?emawiyan."

aw tašš meškikki·wenini uki·-ena·n eniw uškini·kekkwe·n "mi·
kwa wi·pa ci-pekamusse·t."

mi· ko ke·ke·tt wi·pa ki·-pekamusse·t ma·pa uškinuwe· ki·-pi-eša·t
eniw uškini·kekkwe·n ka·-we·pena·peni·n.

Once upon a time two young men studied there at the University,
one young white American and one young Indian. They were friends
together until they completed the medical course which they were
both taking at the University.

When they had finished their course of study at the University,
this young Indian taught that young white American the love medicine
which he knew. He took him into the woods and showed him where
that herb grew. Then he told him what is done when the one is
put under the spell who is to be charmed, and that "It is to be prepared
by boiling this little root in water. And then it is to be put in one's
pocket.

"When you are ready to use this love medicine, then you must
pour it on a handkerchief. When you see the person on whom you
want to put the spell, you will speak to him and you must stand on
the side from which the wind is blowing. By all means, the person
who is to be charmed must stand in the direction toward which the
wind is blowing. Then he will smell this medicine. He will quickly
come where you want him."

Some time later this physician, in his house where he lived, employed a young woman to work for him. This young woman had a
man friend and she loved that young man. In time, however, a
certain young woman took her young man away from her. She was
very miserable at the loss of him. That young man told that other
young woman that he would marry her. Then this young woman grew
melancholy and sat at the table with lowered head. The doctor knew
that there was something wrong with the young woman.

Then he asked her, "What is ailing you?"

Then the young woman told him that another young woman had
robbed her of her young man.

The doctor told her, "Do not feel that way about it. I will give
you medicine by means of which you will get back your young
man."

Then he gave that young woman that medicine to put in her pocket,
and told her how to use it.

So then the young woman went off to go about looking for him. She saw him coming on the road. Then she quickly moistened her handkerchief with that medicine and spoke to him, when she had met him, standing at the side from which the wind was blowing, with the young man at the side toward which it blew. Then she took her handkerchief and held it so that this young man breathed in that medicine. The young woman spoke to him. After a while they went away from there, and the young woman went back to the place where she was working.

The doctor asked her whether she had seen the young man.

"I have seen him," she said to him.

"Did you do the way I taught you?"

The young woman said to him, "I did exactly as you taught me."

The doctor told the young woman, "Now he will soon come into your power."

And really, soon this young man came where she wanted him, to the young woman whom earlier he had abandoned.

31. THE MIRROR VISION

pe·šik enini ki·-mekkate·kke·kupan, aw ekkiwe·nsi̴ ki·-ušitto·t wi·kuwa·me·ns wa·-teši-mekkate·kke·nit eniw ukwissan. ka·-ki·-šetto·t tašš mi· ki·-we·pi-mekkate·kke·t aw uškinuwe·. eppane· pi·ntik ki·-eya·, keye· kwa ki·-uwe·še ʔo kekkiše· uma·nuwa·nk. ni·pena tessokon ki·-eya· ema· wi·kuwa·me·nsink, ki·-pa·pi·tto·t iw ke·ko· ci·-ena·pentank. e·ntesso-kekiše·p etašš ki·-eša· ma·pa ekkiwe·nsi̴ ekko ki·-kekwe·cema·t eniw ukwissan nemanci-i·tik ka·-ena·pentamenikwe·n. uki·-kena ʔemawa·n eniw ukwissan ka· wi· nekkwe·ttuwa·ssik eniw pi-kekwe·cemikot menta·kuninuwan iw ci·šuwe·nemikot.

mi· tašš ekko eppane· e·ntesso-kekiše·pa·wekakk ki·-eša·t ma·pa ekkiwe·nsi̴ ki·-wa·pema·t eniw ukwissan, ki·-kekwe·cema·t "we·kune·šš ka·-puwa·teman?"

pa·ma· tašš nenkwatink tepikkakk ki·-pi·-eya·mekateni iw wa·wa·pemowin. uki·-ekon tašš iw ci·šuwe·nemikot keye· kwa ci·na·tema·kot nemanci-i·tik eppi· iw ke·-nentawe·ntemokwe·n ci·wi·to·kka·kot.

kekiše·p etašš ki·-pi·-tekoššin mi·nuwa· eniw o·ssan ki·-kekwe·cemikot mi·nuwa· "a·ni·šš ena· ka·-ena·pentaman?"

aw tašš uškinuwe· uki·-wi·ntemawa·n iw ka·-ena·pentank wa·wa·pemowin iw ka·-eši-wa·wi·ntemawa·t.

aw tašš ekkiwe·nsi" uki·-ena·n eniw ukwissan "keta·-nekkwe·ttuwa·
iw ci-ma·no·-ci-šuwe·nemikk. mi· ma·nta ni·ka·n ta-ni-ki·šekakk
ke·-meno-a·pecitto·yan.''

mi·nuwa· tašš eya·šo·-tepikkakk ki·-pi-eya· aw wa·wa·pemowin.
ma·pa tašš uškinuwe· uki·-nekkwe·ttuwa·n iw ci-šuwe·nemikot. ma·pa
tašš ekkiwe·nsi" uki·-ki·we·wena·n eniw ukwissan, keye· kwa mi·
ki·-eššama·t.

kuma·ppi· tašš ma·pa uškinuwe· ki·-wi·teke·. keye· kwa mi·
ki·-ma·ca·t wa·-teši-ki·wusse·t, ki·-ma·ci·na·t uwi·teke·ma·kenan keye·
pe·šik ušši·me·nyan. ma·pa tašš uškinuwe· uki·-puwa·ta·n wi·-pi-
-eya·nit meyaki-eniššena·pe·n wa·-pi-nessikuwa·cin. kunima· ni·wu·
kon uki·-kekke·nta·n wi·-pi-tekoššeninit. mi· tašš ki·-ušitto·t iw
pa·kentipe· ʔekan, keye· kwa ki·-eko·to·t iw ci-pa·tte·nik we·we·ni.

ukakwe·cemiko·n etašš eniw uwi·teke·ma·kenan "a·ni·šš wa·-ena·-
pecitto·yan iw pekama·kan ?"

uki·-wi·ntemawa·n etašš iw ka·-ena·pentank.

"kekiše·p wa·pank ka-ma·ca· ci-wi·ntemawetwa· ekiw eniššena·pe·k
ewiti ka·-pi-uncipa·yank ci-pi-na·temawuwa·t ci-mi·ka·nenkitwa· ekiw
me·yeki-eniššena·pe·k.''

kekiše·p etašš ki·-ma·ca· ma·pa ekkwe· ki·-ki·we·petto·t keye· kwa
ki·-tepa·cemot, ka·-tekoššink ewiti e·nta·wa·t. mi· tašš ki·-wi·
ntema·tuwa·t kekkina ekiw eninuwak e·ši-nentawe·ntank ma·pa enini
wi·-pi-nessikot eniw meyaki-eniššena·pe·n.

mi· tašš ke·-a·šo·-kekiše·pa·wekakk ma·pa enini ki·no·ntuwa·t a·ši
kwa pi-eya·nit eniw wa·-nessikucin. uki·-mekkwe·nta·n tašš iw
ena·pentankepa keye· kwa mi· ki·-nentotank iw wa·wa·pemowin
ci-wi·to·kka·kot a·ši ko wi·-mi·ka·sot.

mi· tašš a·ši ko ki·-pi-tekoššeninit eniw wa·-mi·ka·nekocin.

uki·-ena·n tašš eniw ušši·me·nyan "ke·ko wi·n se·kesikke·n. ena·-
meya ʔi· eya·n ema· nempa·keninik.''

mi· tašš ka·-ešicceke·t aw kwi·wesse·ns ki·-ne·ko·te·t ena·mi-nempa·-
kan.

mi· tašš ki·-mi·ka·sot ma·pa enini. ka· wi· tašš ki·-na·kusissi·.
mi· ko e·tta iw wa·wa·pemowin ki·-pe·ppe·šša·pi·kemok. ekonta tašš
ma·ka·na·cik ka· wi· uki·-wa·pema·ssi·wa·n. enišša· tašš uki·-pi-
centipe·wa·n. ke·ka· tašš ekwa kekkina e·ni-nessa·t mi· iw ki·-kencipe-
ʔiwe·nit. penki· tašš e·tta ma·no· ki·-ni-ma·ci·peʔiwe·wan ma·no·.

ki·-pi-tekošše·no·k etašš ekiw wa·-na·tema·kucin. a·ši tašš ke·ka·
kekkina uki·-nessa·n eppi· ekiw eninuwak te·kuššinuwa·t.

mi· tašš e·kot "a·ni·šš ena· ekiw wa·-mi·ka·nenkicik?"
mi· tašš ka·-ena·t "a·ši kwa kekkina ke·ka· ka·-nessakwa·. penki·
e·tta nenki·-eškonena·k. ki·-kencipe ʔiwe·wak. ke· ki·nuwa· wi·-
-essa·nwe·seye·k nenki·-eškonena·k."
ki·-no·ppenanuwa·n tašš ekiw neya·tema·kucin, keye· kwa mi· iw
kekkina ekiw ka·-nessa·wa·t. pe·šik etašš e·tta uki·-pi·na·wa·n.
mi· tašš ki·-keno·na·wa·t "mi·nuwa· ma·nta ta-ešicceke·ssekwa·
uwa-wi·ntemaw ekiw enišsena·pe·k ka·-pi-uncipa·yan, mi·nuwa· ta-
-ešicceke·ssekwa· wi·kka· ma·nta."

Once upon a time a certain man fasted; that old man had built a hut in which that son of his was to fast. When he had finished building it, then the young man began his fast. He always stayed in the hut, and he painted his cheeks with charcoal. Many days he stayed there in the hut, waiting for that which he should see in a vision. Every morning this old man would come and ask his son what sort of a vision he had had. He warned his son not to accept the elegant man if he should come and offer to bless him.

Then always, every morning, this old man went there and saw his son and asked him, "What have you dreamt?"

Finally then one night there came that mirror. It told him that it would bless him and that it would help him at any time whatever when he might want it to help him.

In the morning his father again came there and again asked him, "What kind of a vision have you seen?"

Then the young man told him that he had had a vision of a mirror, for that was what he called it.

The old man said to his son, "You must accept the offer of this being to bless you. In days to come you will have good use of this."

The next night that Mirror Being came again. The young man accepted his blessing. Then this old man led his son home and gave him food to eat.

In time this young man married. Then he went hunting, taking along his wife and a younger brother of his. Now the young man dreamt that men of a different tribe were coming to kill him. He knew that they were going to come in four days. So then he made that war club and hung it up to dry properly.

Then his wife asked him, "What are you going to use that club on?"

Then he told her what he had seen in his vision.

"Tomorrow morning you must go and tell those people there where we came from to come and help me fight those men of a foreign tribe."

On the next morning this woman went off and ran home and told her message, when she had arrived where they dwelt. Then all those people told each other what this man wanted who was going to be sought out and killed by those foreign people.

When the next morning came, this man heard them come who were coming to kill him. He remembered the vision which he had seen long ago, and he now willed that that mirror should stand by him now as he was about to fight.

Now they arrived who were going to fight him.

Then he said to his young brother, "Do not be afraid. Stay there under the bed."

That was what that boy did: he crawled under the bed.

Then this man fought. He was not visible. There was just that mirror flashing the bright sunlight. Those men who were fighting him could not see him. He simply smashed their skulls. When he had killed nearly all of them they fled. Only a few of them were able to run away.

Then they arrived who were to help him. He had killed almost all of those others when those men arrived.

They said to him, "Where are those people whom we are to fight?"

He told them, "By this time I have killed almost all of them. I have just spared a few. They have run away. I spared them so that you, too, might have some amusement."

Then those who were helping him went in pursuit and then they killed all of them. Only one they brought back with them.

Then they spoke to him: "Go tell those people at the place whence you have come that they are not to do this way again, that they must never do this thing again."

32. FIGHTING (*Phonograph Record*)

me·ntake· ko sa·sepa·kkutokke·cin aw ucipwe·, mi· iw eppi· ekiw na·tuwe·ssuwak uwiti ki·-pi-enta ?[1] ki·-pi-eša·wa·t ma·meppi· enikke·kkemik ki·-pi-mekkama·wa·t eniw sa·sepa·kkutokke·necin iw ssa usi·sepa·kkutomeni. na·nekotenonk ka· wi· eya·ssi· aw enini pepa·-

---

[1] Word was broken off, or this is a hearing error.

-nentawe·ncike·t nenkoci pekwatekkamik. eniw etašš ke·ša·teke·necin ekkwe·wan neššikke· epinit mi· ko ki·-a·muwa·wa·t ki·-sa·kecina·šekkawa·wa·t ekonta na·tuwe·ssuwak. keye· tašš mi· kekkina ki·-ma·ci·tuwa·wa·t iw usi·sepa·kkutomeni.

ki·-neška·tesiwak etašš ko na·nenkotenonk ekonta ssa enišsena·pe·k. mi· tašš iw ka·-unci-muwine·wa·wa·t eniw na·tuwe·ssuwan keye· kwa ni·pena essa ki·-nessa·wa·t eniw na·tuwe·ssuwan, menci ko ma·nta essa keki·pa·tesinit essa pepa·-mekkantwe·nit iw si·sepa·kkwat ma·meppi· enikke·kkemik.

mi·nuwa· kwa iw eppi· kecci-mi·ka·tuwak kepe·ye ʔi·. iw essa ki·-nessituwa·t mi· ko ma·nta ka·-uncinenituwa·t essa ki·-pi-keki·pa·tesiwa·t ma·meppi· enikke·kkemik. na·nenkotenonk ke· wi·nuwa· mi·nuwa· ki·-peska·pi·wak ekiw ssa na·tuwe·ssuwak iw tašš kecci-mi·ka·tuwa·t ema· e·ntenakki·wa·t ekiw ssa ucipwe·k.

ekiw na·tuwe·ssuwak ema· Walpole Island no·nkwa menkwakkemikeššino·k. mi· ko ekiw na·tuwe·ssuwak ki·-mi·ka·suwa·t mi· ema· ki·-ni-menkwakkemikuwa·wa·t eniw na·tuwe·ssuwan. no·nkwa tašš we·nceta no·nko menkwakkemikessink ni·pena ema· High Bank Walpole Island ki·-nenkwaʔeka·suwa·t ekiw na·tuwe·ssuwak ka·-mi·ka·sukopene·nak iw eppi·.

Especially when the Ojibwa were making sugar, that was when those Hurons would come over to this side of the water to rob the sugar makers of their sugar. Sometimes the man of the family would not be at home, having gone off hunting somewhere in the wilds. Then these Hurons would drive off the woman who was keeping the house alone, chasing her away from the place. And then they would take all their sugar away from them.

But sometimes these Indians would get angry. That was why they would attack the Hurons and kill many of them, seeing how troublesome they were, going about robbing people of sugar here on this side of the water.

Then they fought for a long time. When they killed one another the cause of the mutual slaughter was that they came and did evil here on this side of the water. Sometimes those Hurons would come back here and fight fiercely where the Ojibwa dwelt.

Those Hurons now lie buried in mounds there on Walpole Island. Those Hurons when they fought, it was there that they buried the Hurons in grave mounds. Today truly there are grave mounds there on High Bank Walpole Island where the Hurons are buried who fought long ago.

33. RABBIT (*Dictation*)

nenkašši uta·sso·kka·nan ki·we͞ ki·-ta·, wa·po·so͞ ki·-ešinekka·so. ki·-kekwe·cema· we·kutakwe·n we·nci-wa·peškisekwe·n.
"wa·po·weya·ne·ns eya·peška·k eppane· nenki·-ekwin."
"we·kune·šš we·nci-ni·šo·tto·ke·yan?"
"eppane· nenki·-a·pecitto·n wi·wekkwa·ne·ns. mi· tašš ka·-unci-ni·šo·tto·ke·ya·n."
"wa·po·so͞, we·kune·šš we·nci-kekki·ci·nkwe·yan?"
"eškote·wa·po· eppane· nenki·-menikkwe·n."
"wa·po·so͞, we·kune·šš we·nci-wa·weye·mo·we·yan?"
"a·nekkona·nyan eppane· nenki·-mi·cenan. mi· tašš ka·-eši-wa·-weye·mo·we·ya·n."
"wa·po·so͞, we·kune·šš we·nci-esa·wesite·yan?"
"nešišše͞ kwa nenki·-mi·nik esse·ma·n, nenki·-tetakkukka·na· tašš ekkwa. mi· tašš we·nci-esa·wesite·ya·n."
mi· iw e·kko·sit.

According to my mother's Sacred Story, there was a creature and Rabbit was his name.

He was asked why he was white of color.
"I always wore a little white blanket robe."
"Why have you two ears?"
"I always used a little hat. That is why I have two ears."
"Rabbit, why have you sore eyes?"
"I always drank whiskey."
"Rabbit, why are your droppings round?"
"I always ate crackers. That is why my droppings are round."
"Rabbit, why have you brown feet?"
"My uncle gave me tobacco, and I always used to walk about on it. That is why I have brown feet."
This is the end of the Sacred Story.

34. RABBIT (*Phonograph Record*)

nenkašši uta·sso·kka·nan.

wa·po·so˜ ki·-kekwe·cema· tepa?[1] we·kutakwe·n we·nci-wa·-peš-kisekwe·n.

ki·-tepa·cemo tašš "wa·po·weya·ne·ns eya·peška·k eppane· nenki·--ekwin. mi· tašš ke·keppi· ka·-eši-wa·peška·k nentakuwin."

mi·nuwa· ki·-kekwe·cema· we·kutakwe·n we·nci-ni·šo·tto·ke·kwe·n. "wi·wekkwa·ne·ns eppane· nenki·-enakka·son[2]. mi· tašš no·nkwa we·nci-ni·šo·tto·ke·ya·n."

"wa·po·so˜, we·kune·šš we·nci-ki·ci·nkwe·yan?"

"nešišše˜ ko eppane· nenki·-mi·nik eškote·wa·po·. mi· tašš ke·keppi· ka·-eši-ki·ci·nkwe·ya·n."

"wa·po·so˜, we·kune·šš we·nci-wa·weye·mo·we·yan?"

"a·nekkona·nyan eppane· nenki·-mi·cenan. mi· tašš ka·-eši-wa·weye·ya·kin eniw nemo·wan."

"wa·po·so˜, we·kune·šš we·nci-esa·wesite·yan?"

"nešišše˜ eppane· nenki·-mi·nik esse·ma·n, nenki·-tetakkukka·na· tašš kkwa. mi· tašš ka·-eši-esa·wesite·ya·n."

mi· ssa e·kko·sit.

Mr. Bloomfield, ka· ke·ko· no·nkwa a·ppeci nentinenokki·ssi·. nento·šetto·n ma·nta record we·ški-pema·tesicik ci no·ntemowa·t.

My mother's Sacred Story.

Rabbit was asked why he was white of color.

He told this: "I always wore a little white blanket robe. So finally my clothing became white."

Again he was asked why he had two ears.

"I always wore a little hat. That is why now I have two ears."

"Rabbit, why have you sore eyes?"

"My uncle always gave me whiskey. So then finally I got sore eyes."

"Rabbit, why are your droppings round?"

"I always ate crackers. So then those droppings of mine grew round."

"Rabbit, why have you brown feet?"

"My uncle always gave me tobacco and I used to walk about on it. And so then I got brown feet."

---

[1] Hearing error?
[2] Unknown word.

This is the end of the Sacred Story.

Mr. Bloomfield, I am not doing anything at all now. I am making this record so that the young people may hear it.

35. NENABUSH AND THE PARTRIDGES (*Dictation*)

ne·nepoš ki·we˜ ki·-pemosse·kupan tepe·w. uki·-ni-wa·pema·n etašš pene·nsan ni·pete·ya·kkupinit. uki·-kekwe·cema·n tašš ne·nepoš eniw kecci-pene·nsan e·šenikka·sunit.

mi· tašš ka·-ena·t "menci·kkuwiss nentišenikka·s."

nena·š ekwa kekkina ki·-ni-kekwe·cema·t e·šenikka·sunit.

a·ppeci eškwa·c e·ka·cci·n ʔenicin "a·ni· tašš ki·n e·šenikka·suyan?" uki·-ena·n.

"kwe·šku ʔiwe·ssi."

mi· tašš aw ne·nepoš ki·-pa·šketiya·ma·t.[1]

mi· tašš ki·-ni-ma·ca·t e·šettikwe·ya·k iw si·pi.

ki·-pi-tekoššin aw kecci-pene·. uki·-wa·pema·n nemponit eniw pe·šik uni·ca·nessan.

"a·ni·šš ka·-eši-eya·t kešši·me·n ʔuwa·?" utina·n etašš eniw a·nint. "ne·nepoš ko šša ki·-pemi-eya·. mi· tašš aw ka·-pa·šketiya·ma·t."

a·ppeci tašš ki·-neška·tesi ma·pa kecci-pene·.

"a·ppi·šš ka·-eni-eša·t?"

uki·-ena·n tašš "tepe·w ki·-eni-eša·".

ki·-neška·tesi tašš ma·pa kecci-pene·. mi· tašš ki·-kessikke·t ki·-eppisot uwiti ka·-eni-eša·nit. uki·-wa·pema·n ne·nepošo·n tepe·w enimusse·nit. ki·-po·ni· tašš ema· tepe·w mettiko·nsekka·nik. eppi· tašš aw ne·nepoš pi-tekoššink mi· ki·-kessikke·t, keye· kwa umpi·kwe·we·ššema·t uninkwi· ʔekanan. ki·-se·kesi tašš aw ne·nepoš. ki·-umpi-kwa·škuni si·pi·nk enakke·ya·. ki·-penkiššin ema· ci·kepi·k, ke·ka· ka·-a·ppecišširk.

ki·-ena·pi tašš uwiti ka·-pi-uncipesot. uki·-wa·pema·n tašš wa·wa·ške·ššuwan ni·puwinit ekkita·kki. e·ka·c etašš uki·-uta·ppena·n umettikwa·pi·n, keye· kwa mi· ko ki·-pemwa·t, keye· kwa mi· ko ki·-meswa·t, keye· kwa mi· ko ki·-nessa·t.

mi· tašš ekotekkoni·si·t uwiti ka·-pi-uncipesot. mi· tašš ki·-pekkona·t eniw wa·wa·ške·ššuwan. keye· kwa mi· ki·-menoswa·t. kekkina tašš ka·-menoswa·t mi· peci·nak ki·-wi·ssenit.

---

[1] The meaning of this combination is not clear.

mettik etašš a·swa·kkuššin ema· pe·ššo. mi· tašš e·ši-kesi·pwe·we·ška·t. mi· tašš ki·-eša·t wi·-ekkawe·-ni·ssa·kkupina·t. ka· tašš kenake· uki·-keškipena·ssi·n, mi·nuwa· ki·-pi-ni·ssa·ntuwe·t.

mi·nuwa· ki·-we·pi-wi·sseni. mi·nuwa· ki·-mentwe·ška·wan eniw mettiko·n. mi·nuwa· ki·-ma·ci·ya·ntuwe·. we·we·ni tašš uki·-a·petto·ci·na·n eniw mettiko·n. uki·-ki·kka·kkupina·n tašš. ki·-tesso·so tašš unikka·nk.

mi· tašš ekiw me ʔi·nkenak ki·-pi-eya·wa·t, ki·-pi-mi·cuwa·t iw wi·ya·ss ka·-menosank aw ne·nepoš, keye· kwa kekkina ki·-ketamuwa·t.

mi· tašš na·nepe·n ki·-kɛškitto·t iw unikk, ki·-ni·ssa·ntuwe·t. ka· tašš ke·ko· wa·-mi·cit.

mi· ssa e·kko·sit nenta·sso·kka·n.

Once upon a time, the story goes, he was walking along the bank of a stream. He saw some nestling partridges sitting in a row on a bush. Then Nenabush asked the biggest of the young partridges what his name might be.

This was what he told him, "Eldest Brother is my name."

He asked all of them their names.

To the smallest one, in the end, he said, "And what is your name, you?"

"Little Winged Startler."

Then Nenabush burst him open at the rump.

Then he went off in the direction in which that river flowed.

The big partridge arrived. She saw that one of her young had died.

"What has happened to your little brother?" she asked those others.

"Why, Nenabush came by here. He was the one who burst him open at the rump."

The big partridge was very angry.

"Which way did he go from here?"

He told her, "Along the riverbank he went from here."

This big partridge was angry. She flew up and flew where the other had gone. She saw Nenabush walking along the bank of the stream. She alighted in a clump of bushes there by the river bank. Then, when that Nenabush came to that place, she flew up and moved her wings so as to make a whirring noise. That Nenabush was frightened. He leaped up in the direction of the river. He fell down there close to the water's edge and almost got killed in his fall.

He looked toward the place from which he had tumbled. He saw a deer standing there at the top of the bluff. Slowly he picked up his bow. Then he shot at it, and then he hit it, and then he killed it.

Then he scrambled up the slope to where he had tumbled from. Then he skinned that deer. And then he roasted it. When he had roasted it all, then at last he soon would eat.

There was a tree leaning against another tree close by there. It moved with a creaking noise as it rubbed against the other tree. So then he went over there to pull it loose before he ate. But he could not pull it loose at all, so he climbed down again.

Again he started to eat. Again that tree moved with noise. Again he climbed up. He got a good grip round that tree. He gave the tree a good hard pull. He got himself caught there by his hand.

Then those wolves came and ate up the meat which Nenabush had roasted. They gobbled up every bit of it.

Only then, when it was too late, did he get his hand free and climb down. There was nothing now for him to eat.

This is the end of my Sacred Story.

36. NENABUSH AND THE PARTRIDGES (*Phonograph Record*)

ne·nepoš ki·we" ki·-pemosse· tepe·w pepa·-nentawa·pentank ke·wi· wa·-unci-meno-eya·t. uki·-ni-wa·pema·n tašš uwiti pene·nsan ekkita·ttik nematepinit. mi· tašš eniw meya·muwi-mentitunicin pene·nsan ki·-kekwe·cema·t e·šenikka·sunit.

"menci·kkuwiss" mi· iw ka·-ešinekka·netisot aw pene·.

nena·š eko kekkina ki·-ni-kekwe·cema·t e·šenikka·sunit ema·ni·pete·ya·kkupinit.

eškwa·ya·c etašš eniw ka·-kekwe·cema·cin mi· ka·-ešinekka·netisunit "eškwe·ta·kan."

mi· tašš aw ne·nepoš ki·-pa·šketiya·ma·t.[1]

mi· tašš mi·nuwa· ki·-ni-ma·ca·t si·pi e·ni-ešittekwe·ya·nik.

ki·-pi-tekoššin tašš aw we·ni·ca·nessit eniw pene·nyan, pene·nsan.

"a·ni·šš ka·-eši-eya·t aw kešši·me·n ʔuwa·?" uki·-ena·n tašš eniwi meya·muwi-mentitunicin.

"ne·nepoš ko šša ki·-pemi-eya· ma·meppi·. uki·-pa·šketiya·ma·n tašš."

---

[1] The meaning of this combination is not clear.

mi· tašš ki·-neška·tesit ma·pa kecci-pene·.

"a·ni·ppi·šš ka·-ni-eša·t aw ne·nepoš?" uki·-eši-kekwe·cema·n.

"e·ni-ešittekwe·ya·k si·pi."

mi· tašš ki·-neška·tesit ma·pa pene·. mi· tašš ki·-kesotesse·t[1] ka·-uni·ca·nessit ki·-wa·pema·t eni-pemosse·nit tepe·w. mi· ssa ema· ki·-po·ni·t ema· ci·keya?i· ka·-uni·ca·nit me·kwa·-mettiko·nsekka·. eppi· tašš pe·ššo pi-eya·nit mi· ema· ka·-unci-kessikke·t ki·-mentwe·-nenkwi·ššink e·kko-keški ?e·wesit. ma·pa tašš ne·nepoš ki·-se·kesi. ka· ukikke·ntensi·n iw ki·-umpi-kwa·škunit. ki·pi·n[1] etašš enikke·-ya·wetakki·[1] ki·-penkiššin. mi· tašš ka· wi· uki·-kekke·ntensi·n nemanci-i·tik pi·wetaka·k[1] pekamepisukwe·n.

ki·-ta·ttekana·pit enakke·ya· ka·-pi-uncipesot, uki·-wa·pema·n uwiti wa·wa·ške·ššuwan ni·puwinit. ka· tašš ke·ko· wa·-ešicceke·t essa ci-pemwa·t. e·ka·c etašš ki·-uniššin keye· eniw umittekwa·pi·n ki·-uta·ppena·t. keye· kwa mi· ki·-pemwa·t, keye· kwa mi· ki·-nessa·t. mi· tašš ki·-kutakuni·si·t uwiti ekiceya?i· ki·-pekkona·t eniw wa·wa·ške·ššuwan, keye· kwa mi· kekkina ki·-menoswa·t. mi· tašš peci·nak ki·-wi·ssenit.

eniw tašš mettiko·n ki·-kesi·pwe·ška·wan me·kwa· eya·swa·kkušši·nenicin.

"nenka-wa-ekkawe·-ni·ssa·kkupina·" ki·-ene·ntam.

ka· tašš uki·-keškipena·ssi·n. nc·ya·p ki·-pi-ni·ssa·ntuwe·. mi·nu·wa· keye· ko wi·ssenit, mi·nuwa· ki·-mentwe·ška·wan.

"mi· ssa no·nkwa!"

ki·kki[1] tašš i·tik ki·ke·pctinit[1] ki·-a·petto·ci·na·t eniw mettiko·n ki·-ki·kka·kkupina·t, keye· ki·-tekkonekke·ško·sot. ka· ke·ko· wa·-ešicceke·t. mi· ko ema· ki·-pa·tta·ššink.

Nenabush, so goes the Sacred Story, was walking along the bank of a river, looking about for something on which to sustain himself. As he went along, he saw over there some young partridges sitting on a branch. So then he asked the biggest one of the young partridges what his name was.

"Eldest Brother," that partridge gave as his name.

In the end he asked them all their names one after another as they sat there in a row.

The one whom he asked last of all gave his name as "Last Born."

---

[1] Unknown word.

Then that Nenabush burst him open at the rump.

Then again he walked off in the direction in which the river flowed.

The mother of those young partridges arrived.

"What has happened to your little brother?" she asked that biggest one.

"Why, Nenabush came by here and burst him at the rump."

Then that big partridge was angry.

"Where did that Nenabush go?" she asked him.

"The way the river flows."

Now this partridge was angry. The mother partridge flew up and saw him walking along the bank of the river. Then the mother bird alighted close by there in a clump of bushes. Then, when he came near, she flew up, with all her might flapping her wings to make noise. This Nenabush got a fright. Without knowing it, he leaped up. Down he fell to the foot of the bluff. He did not know where he landed.

When he looked up to the place from which he had fallen, he saw a deer standing there. There was nothing he could do to shoot it. Slowly he adjusted himself as he lay and picked up his bow. Then he shot it and then he killed it. Then he scrambled up to the top of the bluff and skinned and cut up the deer and roasted it all. Now at last he had something to eat.

Then a tree made a creaking noise as it lay against another tree.

"I'll first go pull it free," he thought.

He did not succeed in pulling it. He climbed back down again. As he was again about to eat, again it moved with noise.

"Well this time surely!"

When it would not move easily, he got his arm round the whole girth of that tree to pull it from where it was wedged, and then he got his arm caught fast. There was nothing he could do. He lay caught there.

37. NENABUSH AND THE DUCKS (*Dictation*)

nenta·sso·kkka·n ki·we" ki·-ta·kupa ne·nepoš. ka· ke·ko· wa·-mi·cit. ki·-pekkate·. mi· tašš essapa·p ki·-uta·ppenank. tepe·w etašš ki·--eša· si·pi·nk. uki·-wa·pema·n ni·pena ekiw ši·šši·pan. mi· tašš ema·ka·-unci-ko·ki·t ki·-enakkušiwe·t uwiti eya·nit. mi· tašš ki·-pepa·--tekkopena·t eniw ši·šši·pan ukka·tenink kekkina e·kkwa·pi·kakk iw essapa·p. mi· tašš na·weya ʔi· ki·-mo·škemot.

a·ppeci tašš uki·-se·ke ʔa·n eniw ši·šši·pan. ki·-kessikke·wak ekiw ši·šši·pak ešpimink e·kko·suwa·t ekiw mettiko·k. keye· tašš mi· iw ki·-eni-pekka ʔemowa·t iw essapa·p ekiw ši·šši·pak. mi· tašš uwiti ka·-pi-uncipesot aw ne·nepoš ka·-pi·ntenakkesse·t ema· wi·mpenakketo·n ʔink.

uki·-no·ntuwa·n ekkwe·wan pi-tena·nekito·nenit.

pe·ššo tašš pi-eya·nit mi· iw ka·-ekkitot aw ne·nepoš "wa·peka·ko·!"[1]

pe·ššo tašš pi-eya·nit mi·nuwa· ki·-no·nta·kusi ki·-ekkitot "wa·peka·ko·!"

mi· tašš ka·-ekkituwa·t ekiw ekkwe·wak "ka·k ma·mpi·[2] eya· wi·mpenakketo·n ʔink."

mi· tašš aw pe·šik ki·-na·tit wa·ka·kkwat ki·-pekwanekka ʔeke·wa·t ema· ecikke·n ʔink. ki·-ekoski·wak wi·-sa·keto·te·nit. pe·šik etašš uki·-ki·ssekka·n umanceko·teˉ. mi·nuwa· nuwanc ni·pena ki·-pekokeʔike·wak. mi·nuwa· ko pe·šik uki·-ki·ssekka·n umanceko·teˉ. nuwanc etašš ni·pena ki·-pekoke ʔike·wak. mi· tašš meno-menikk ka·-pekokeʔike·wa·t ki·-sa·keto·te·petto·t aw ne·nepoš. keye· kwa mi· ki·-kencipettwa·tank eniw menciko·te·nyan.

mi· e·kko·sit nenta·sso·kka·n.

Once upon a time, so goes my Sacred Story, there dwelt Nenabush. There was nothing for him to eat. He was hungry. Then he took some cord. He went to the bank of the river. He saw many ducks. Then he dived from there and swam over to where they were. Then he went about tying those ducks by their legs along the whole length of that cord. Then right in the midst of them he came up from under water.

He gave those ducks a great fright. The ducks flew up in the air as high as the tops of the trees. And then, as those ducks flew along, they broke that cord. So then down fell that Nenabush and fell into a hollow tree.

He heard some women talking as they came toward where he was.

When they got quite near, Nenabush said, "White porcupi-i-ine!"

When they got nearer, again he called out, saying, "White porcupi-i-ine!"

---

[1] The form with final o· is apparently a special form for calling; cf. Word List. — CFH.

[2] Apparently for ma·meppi·. — CFH.

Then those women said, "There is a porcupine here in this hollow tree."

Then one of them fetched an axe and they chopped a hole in that dead tree. They were worried that he might crawl out. So one of them took off her skirt. Then they chopped some more, to make a larger opening. Then the other woman took of her skirt. They chopped the opening still bigger. And then, when they had chopped a big enough opening, that Nenabush came running out on all fours. And then he took the skirts with him as he ran away.

This is the end of my Sacred Story.

38. NENABUSH AND THE DUCKS (*Phonograph Record*)

a·sso·kka·n ki·we˜ ša·ši kwa ne·nepoš ka·-ešinekka·sot. ki·-pekkate·kuma·ppi·cc. ka· ke·ko· wa·-mi·cit. keye· tašš uki·-uta·ppena·n essapa·pi·n. ki·-eša· tepe·w si·pi·nk. uki·-wa·pema·n tašš eniw ši·šši·pan ni·pena pepa·-ekomunit. mi· tašš a·pettawena ki·-tekkopenitesot iw essapa·p. mi· tašš ki·-eša·t uwiti e·ši-ekomunit eniw ši·šši·pan ki·-pepa·-sekika·te·pena·t kekkina nena·š eko kekkina ki·-tekkopecike·t iw essapa·p. na·weya ʔi· tašš ki·-mo·škemo ema· eya·nit eniw ši·šši·pan.

mi· tašš ki·-se·ke ʔa·t, ki·-kessikke·wa·t ekiw ši·šši·pak. ešpimink e·kko·suwa·t ekiw mettiko·k ki·-ni-eppisuwak ekiw ši·šši·pak. keye· kwa mi· ki·-ni-pekka ʔemowa·t iw essapa·p. mi· tašš ki·-penkiššink ma·pa ne·nepo·šo· ema· ki·-pi·ntenakkesse·t wi·mpenakketo·n ʔink. mi·nuwa· tašš ka· ke·ko· wa·-ešicceke·t iw ci-sa·keto·te·t.

kuma·ppi· tašš uki·-no·ntuwa·n ni·š ekkwe·wan pi-te·petta·kusinit pi-ka·ki·ketonit.

pe·ššo pi-eya·nit nwa·ntuwa·t mi· iw ka·-ekkitot "wa·peka·ko·!"[1]

mi· tašš ka·-ekkituwa·t ekiw ekkwe·wak "ka·k ma·mpi·[1] eya· wi·-mpenakketo·n ʔink."

mi· tašš aw pe·šik ki·-na·tit we·wi·p iw ssa wa·ka·kkwat. mi· tašš ki·-pekoke ʔike·wa·t ema· mettikonk. keye· kwa wi·-pwa·-sa·kecisse·nit eniw ka·kon ki·-kepanekka ʔeke· pe·šik ma·pa iw umanceko·te˜. mi· tašš mi·nuwa· nuwanc ni·pena ki·-pekwawa·wa·t eniw mettiko·n. mi·nuwa· pe·šik uki·-ki·ssekka·n iw umanceko·te˜, sa·keto·te·petto· tašš aw ne·nepoš keye· kwa ki·-kencipettwa·tank eniw menciko·te·nyan.

mi· ssa ko na· iw e·kko·sit nenta·sso·kka·n.

---

[1] See comment on same form in T 37. — CFH.

This Sacred Story is about him long ago who was called Nenabush. He had been hungry for some time. There was nothing for him to eat. So then he took some cord. He went to the bank of the river. There he saw many ducks swimming about. Then he tied that cord round his waist. Then he went where those ducks were swimming and went about tying them all by the legs until he had used the whole cord in tying them. He came up from under water right in the midst of those ducks.

He frightened the ducks and they flew up. The ducks flew up in the air as high as the trees. And on the way they broke that cord. Then this poor Nenabush fell and landed inside a hollow tree. There was nothing he could do to crawl out.

At last he heard two women who came within hearing as they talked.

When he heard that they had come near, what he said was, "White porcupi-i-ine!"

Then those women said, "There is a porcupine here in this hollow tree."

Then one of them quickly fetched an axe. Then they chopped a hole in the tree. To keep the porcupine from running out, one of them stopped up the hole with her skirt. Then again they made larger the hole in that tree. The other one took off her skirt. Out ran that Nenabush on all fours and carried off those skirts as he fled.

And this is the end of my Sacred Story.

PART IV
WORD LIST

WORD LIST

The arrangement is alphabetical, save that dependent stems are given first. The order of the dependent stems is alphabetical by the first sound of the stem. For convenience, a hyphen is inserted between the prefix and the dependent stem; this hyphen is not functional and does not imply that the word is a compound.

Transitive and pseudo-transitive verbs are entered in the conjunct indicative form for third person singular actor; other verbs, as far as possible, in the equivalent form of the independent indicative.

The abbrevations are those used in the grammar (see p. xi). In a few instances, where the form of a verb used as entry conceals the basic shape of its stem, brief parenthetical indication of that basic shape is given. Thus in

$a·muwa·t$ 'he drives him off' ($^{\prime}w$)

the parenthesized $^{\prime}w$ means that the stem of the verb ends basically with these sounds (3.37).

DEPENDENT STEMS

nen-ca·š 'my nose'; *eca·š* 'a nose'
nen-ci·nkwan 'my thigh'
n-i·cekkiwe·nsi͂, *n-i·cekkiwe͂* 'my male friend'
n-i·ci prenoun 'my fellow-':
 ni·ci-eniššena·pe· 'my fellow Indian'
n-i·kka·n 'my brother' (man speaking)
n-i·kka·niss 'my brother, my male friend' (man speaking)
n-i·n 'I'; *wi·n* 'he, she ,it; however'; *ni·nuwi* 'we (exc.)'; *ki·nuwi* 'we (inc.)'; *ki·nuwa·* 'ye'; *wi·nuwa·* 'they'.
n-i·nemokka·n 'my sister-in-law' (man speaking), 'my brother-in-law' (woman speaking)
n-i·nentip 'my brain'
n-i·nessiss 'my (single) hair (of head)'
n-i·nim 'my sister-in-law' (man speaking), 'my brother-in-law' (woman speaking); pl. *-o·k*
n-i·pit 'my tooth'; pl. *-an*
n-i·tta· 'my brother-in-law' (man speaking)
n-i·tta·wiss 'my cousin'
w-i·wan 'his wife'
n-i·yaw 'my body'
nen-kašši 'my mother'

nen-kitik AN 'my knee'; pl. *-o·k*
  ne-kkakkwan 'my shin'; *ukkak-kuna·nk* 'on his shin'
ne-kka·t 'my leg'; pl. *-an; ekka·t* 'a leg'
ne-kkwan 'my liver'
nen-kwiss 'my son'
nen-kwisseˉ 'my little son'
  u-ma·nuwa·nk 'on his cheek'
ne-misseˉ 'my elder sister'
ne-miššo·miss 'my grandfather'; in address *nemiššo·*
ne-mo·te·ns 'my pocket'
ne-mo·wan pl. 'my droppings'
ne-našketi· AN 'my (bird's) tail'
ne-na·n AN 'the calf of my leg'
ne-nikk 'my arm'; pl. *-an;* *unikka·nk* 'on his arm'
ne-ninc 'my hand'; pl. *-i·n;* *eninc* 'a hand'
ne-ninci·kan, ne-ninci·ka·ns 'my fin'
ne-ninkuniss 'my sister's son' (man speaking)
ne-ninkwi·ʔekan AN 'my wing'
ne-ni·ca·niss 'my child'
  n-o·kkumiss 'my grandmother'; in address *no·kko·*
n-o·ss 'my father'
n-o·šeššeˉ 'my grandchild'
nem-pa·pa, nempa·pa·m 'my father'
nem-pi·ʔepi·sete·ʔ 'my lungs'
  ne-ppikkwan 'my back'; *uppik-kona·nk* 'on his back'
nem-pwa·m 'the back of my thigh'

ne-sikusiss 'my mother-in-law'
ne-sit 'my foot'; pl. *-an*
  u-so·wa·nak 'his (quadruped's) tail'
ne-ssayeˉ 'my elder brother'
  u-šikwan 'his (fish's) tail'
ne-šiniss 'my father-in-law'
ne-šiššeˉ 'my uncle'
ne-škanš AN 'my claw, hoof, nail'; pl. *-i·k*
ne-ški·nšik 'my eye'; pl. *-o·n;* *eški·nšik* 'an eye'
ne-ššimeˉ 'my younger brother or sister'
ne-štikwa·n 'my head'
nen-tassena·kke· 'my brisket'
nen-tatteka·wekan 'my backbone'
nen-tawe·ma· 'my sister' (man speaking), 'my brother' (woman speaking)
nen-tay 'my dog'
nen-tayeʔa·m 'my horse'
nen-ta·n, nen-ta·niss 'my daughter'
nen-ta·nkwe· 'my sister-in-law' (woman speaking)
nen-ta·ss 'my legging'; pl. *-an*
nen-te·ʔ 'my heart'; *ete·ʔ* 'a heart'
nen-te·neniw 'my tongue'
nen-te·nkway 'my face'
nen-te·škan AN 'my horn'
nen-to·n 'my mouth'
  u-to·nekkossuwan 'his kidneys'
nen-to·ntan 'my heel'
nen-to·skwan 'my elbow'
ne-tto·wak 'my ear'; pl. *-an*

a

a preverb with conjunct only: 'where; he who'

aw 'that' (an. sg.)

a·

a· 'come on!'
a·kim AN 'snowshoe'; pl. -*ak*
a·kkusi 'he is ill'
a·kkusiwin 'illness'
a·kkuškate· 'he has a stomach-ache'
a·kkuškate·ʔetiwak 'they have a stomach-ache'
a·kukwe·na·t 'he hugs him' (*n*)
a·kuwi·tta 'additional, extra'
a·mo· 'bee'
a·mpe·, *a·mpe·kišš* 'do, please; let it to be so'
a·muwa·t 'he drives him off' (*ʔw*)
a·nci preverb, 'changing place'
a·nci·we·nʔuwi 'he renews his effort'
a·nekkona̰ 'biscuit, cracker'
a·nekko·pecikan: nenta·nekko·-pecikan 'my great-grandchild'
a·nekkwat 'cloud'
a·nint 'some, a few'
a·ni· predicative, 'how (is it)?'
a·ni·ppi·šš predicative, 'where (is it)?'
a·ni·špi·cc predicative, 'when (is it)?'
a·ni·šš predicative, 'how (is it)?'
a·no 'to be sure, although'
a·nsekkank 'he changes it' (a garment) (doffs one and dons another)
a·nsekkoneye· 'he changes his clothes'
a·ntepi 'he changes his seat'
a·pa·pekkaʔekan 'key'
a·pecitto·t 'he uses it'
a·pena·pi 'he looks back'
a·pešiššin 'he revives'
a·petik 'necessarily; be sure to'
a·petta 'half, halfway, at the middle'
a·pettawena 'round the middle'
a·pettaweta·kke·ya·mekat 'it is halfway up the slope'
a·pettaweyaʔi· 'at the middle'
a·pettaweyaʔi·wan 'it is Thursday'
a·petta·tepikk 'at midnight'
a·pettoci·na·t 'he holds him round the middle '(*n*)
a·petto·škin 'half a filling'
a·pi·kenank 'he unwraps it'
a·ppeci 'very much, completely'
a·ppecipeso 'he tumbles down'
a·ppeciššin 'he falls to his death'
a·ppi· predicative, 'where (is it)?'
a·ppi·šš predicative, 'where (is it)?'
a·puwa· 'the weather turns warm'
a·puwa·t 'he unties him' (*ʔw*)
a·semakuma·pesowenak AN pl. 'suspenders'
a·sentipe·ppeso 'he carries his load with the pack strap tied round his forehead'
a·seya·n 'breech clout'

a·ssena· 'be careful! look out!'
a·sso·kka·n AN 'sacred story'
a·sso·kke· 'he tells a sacred story'
a·swa·kkussin 'it lies across a solid'
a·swa·kkussito·t 'he lays it across, leans it against, a solid'
a·swa·kkuššin 'he lies across a solid'
a·šekiteko·cin 'he falls backwards'
a·šepikk 'cliff, rock'
a·ši 'already, now'
a·šo· preverb, 'next' (of periods of time): eya·šo·-tepikkakk 'on the next night'
a·šo·nekkokenak AN pl. 'suspenders'
a·šukan 'bridge'
a·tte· 'it is extinguished'
a·tte·ʔank 'he extinguishes it by tool'
a·tte·škank 'he extinguishes it with his foot'
a·tuwa·ššin 'he lies face up'
a·w 'well, come on!'
a·wena·t 'he carries him off' (N)
a·ya 'oh!'
a·ya·nekko·peso 'he is tied in successive lengths'

c

ca·ca·mo 'he sneezes'
ca·keka·ʔank 'he chops it all'
ca·kesank 'he gets a burn in it'
ca·n 'John'
ca·nka·kkwe·ššin 'he lies with his head raised'
cekaceka·ne·šši̴ 'chickadee'
ce·ci·pa·n 'in various places, in different directions'
ci preverb: action in view; with initial change ci
ci·cci·kkeše·ʔank 'he pokes it (a fire)'
ci·cci·kkeše·ʔekan 'poker stick'
ci·kepi·k 'by the water'
ci·keta·ʔank 'he sweeps it with a broom'
ci·keta·ʔekan 'broom'
ci·keya·ʔi· 'close up, right next'
ci·ma·n 'canoe, boat'; pl. -an
ci·na·kwa 'yesterday'
ci·nti·ss, ci·nti·ssi̴ 'blue jay'
ci·pa·kkwe· 'he cooks'
ci·ss 'turnip'; pl. -an; esa·wi-ci·ss 'carrot'; mesko-ci·ss 'beet'
ci·ssekka·n 'conjuring tent'

e

eccika·te· 'it is placed'
ecice·ʔa·t 'he gets close to him'
eciceššin 'he lies upside down'
ecikke̴ 'tree stump'
ecina 'a short time'
ecitekki·sse· 'he falls face down'
ecitekki·ššin 'he lies face down'
ecitemo̴ 'red squirrel'
eʔa·w 'come on!'
ekacekki 'he is bashful'
ekate·ntam 'he is ashamed'
ekawa· 'he spears fish through the ice'
ekawa·nekamik 'shelter for ice fishing'
eka·cceno·n·ʔi 'it is tiny'

eka·ccete·ya· 'it is narrow'
eka·ccin 'it is small'
eka·cci·kat 'it is a small cloth or garment'
eka·cci·nˀi 'he is small'
eka·wa· 'with effort managing, just barely'
eka·wa·kkwa· 'it is shaded, sheltered'
eka·wa·na·t 'he longs for him' (N)
ekiceyaˀi·, *ekiceyaˀi·nk* 'on top of the thing'
ekici exocentric prenoun, 'on top': *ekici-eto·ppuwin* 'on the table'
ekintank 'he counts it, reads it, prices it'
ekiw 'those' (an. pl.); *ekiwe·ti* 'those over there'; *ekiwi* 'those'
ekkan 'bone'; *nentakkenim* 'my bone'
ekkawa·pema·t 'he watches him'
ekkawa·pi 'he watches'
ekkawe· preverb = *nekkawe·*
ekki 'earth, land'; *utakki·muwa·n* 'their pieces of land'
ekkikk AN 'kettle'; pl. *-o·k;* *nentakkikk* 'my kettle'
ekkikko·ns AN 'small kettle'
ekkita·kki 'on the land, hill'
ekkita·ttik 'on a stick, tree, branch'
ekkito 'he speaks thus, says so'
ekkituwin 'that way of speaking'
ekkiwe·nsĩ 'old man'; *utakkuwe·nsi·nˀeman* 'his old man; her husband'
ekkiwe·nsi·nˀuwi 'he is an old man'
ekko preverb 'so far, so long'
ekkokkuci·šš, *ekkokkuci·ššẽ* 'woodchuck'

ekkokkupina·kan 'basket'
ekkokkupina·kenikke· 'he makes baskets'
ekkona·šuwa·t 'he drives him away' (ˀw)
ekkossin 'it lies so high'
ekko·ci·šš 'louse'
ekko·sete· 'he is so long at the foot'
ekko·si 'he is so long, so tall'
ekkwa 'habitually, generally, on each occasion'
ekkwassema·n 'pumpkin, field squash'; pl. *-an*
ekkwa·ntuwa·kan 'ladder, stairway'
ekkwa·ntuwe· 'he climbs up on wood or solid'
ekkwa·pi·kat 'it is so long a string'
ekkwe· 'woman'; pl. *-wak*
ekkwe·sse·ns 'girl'
ekokkumita·ss 'sock'; *nentakukkometa·ssan* 'my socks'
ekomo 'he floats'
ekonta 'these' (an. pl.)
ekoski· 'he is anxious'
ekoteˀam (TI), *ekoteˀo* (AI) 'he canoes upstream'
ekotekkoni·si· 'he climbs up a slope'
ekotekkošuwe· 'he canoes (or swims) upstream'
eko·cin 'he hangs'
eko·n AN 'snow'
eko·na·kan 'tree house'
eko·na·t 'he hangs him up' (N)
eko·so 'he clings, hangs'
eko·tekkikkwa·n 'hook (or limb) on the kettle hanger'

eko·to·t 'he hangs it up'
ekwa emphatic postpositive
ekwaci·nk 'out of doors'
ekwaci·yeʔi·nk 'outside the place'
ekwaneʔank 'he covers it'
ekwaneʔoteso 'he covers himself up'
ekwa·peke·ssi 'mullet'; pl. *-wak*
ekwa·pi·kena·t 'he takes him out of the water' (*n*)
ekwa·ššema·t 'he takes him out of the water'
ekwa·wa·na·kk 'kettle hanger'
ekwa·wena·t 'he takes him out of the water' (*N*)
ekwa·we·peʔank 'he throws it out of a medium (water, fire) by tool'
ekwa·we·penank 'he throws it out of a medium by hand'
ekwa·we·pena·t 'he throws him out of a medium by hand' (*n*)
ekwiʔa·t 'he clothes him'
ekwit 'he wears it'
ekwiwin 'garment'; *nentakuwinan* 'my clothes'
ekwi·tepiwin 'chair'
ema· 'there'
ema·cwe·pena·t 'he wakes him up' (*N*)
emina 'everywhere' (?)
emino·nekkeˉ 'smoke hole'
empe· = *a·mpe·*
emwa·t 'he eats him'; independent, *utamwa·n*
ena postpositive, sign of yes-or-no question
enakente· 'it is priced so'
enake·kk 'bark'; *wi·kupi·mi·šši·--enake·kk* 'linden bark'

enake·kkukameko·ns 'bark hut'
enake·kkukamik 'bark house'
enakke·ya· 'in that direction'
enakkušiwe· 'he canoes (or swims) thither'
enama·t 'he bites him so'
enameʔe· preverb and prenoun, 'Christian worship'; *enameʔe·-ki·šekat* 'it is Sunday'
enamo 'the road goes thither'
enank AN 'star'; pl. *-o·k*
enanukki· 'he works thus'
enatenank 'he shapes it thus'
ena· postpositive, emphatic
ena·kkesank 'he burns it thus'
ena·kkunike· 'he enacts so, has a custom thus'
ena·kušši 'it is evening'
ena·pecitto·t 'he uses it thus'
ena·pentam 'he has such a vision'; *ena·pentank* 'he sees it so'
ena·pentamuwin 'such a vision'
ena·pete·ntam 'he derives such benefit'
ena·pi 'he looks thither'
ena·pi· 'he is strung thither or thus; it is strung thither or thus'
ena·t 'he says so to him' (*N*); *utiko·n* 'the other says so to him'
ena·wenkaʔank 'he moves, shapes it so, as or in sand or ashes'
ene·ntam 'he thinks so'; *nentine·-ntam* 'I think so'
ene·nti 'he stays out so long'
eni preverb, 'going on, on the way, in the course of time or action'

enika·suwin 'implement'; *nentaneka·suwinan* 'my implements'
enikke·kkemik 'on this side of the border'
enikwa 'until'
enim 'dog'; pl. -*o·k*
enimekki· 'Thunderer'
enimekki·kka· 'there is a thunderstorm'
enimekkoššin 'he lies face down'
enimošš 'dog'
enimo·ns 'little dog'
enimusse· 'he walks yon way'
enimussi·wekamik 'kennel'
enina·ttik 'hard maple'
enini 'man'
eninuwi·nš 'milkweed'
enišša· 'only, merely, in vain, in jest, in silly wise'
eniššena·pe· 'human being, Indian'
eniššena·pe·muttawa·t 'he speaks to him in an Indian language' (*aw*)
eniššena·pe·ns 'young Indian'
enill 'fish spear'; *nentanitt* 'my fish spear'
enittam = *nettam*
eniw 'that, those' (obv.) 'those' (inan. pl.); *eniwe·ti* 'those over there'; *eniwi* 'those'
eni·p 'elm'; pl. -*i·k*
eni·pi·šš 'leaf'; pl. -*an*
eni·pi·šša·po· 'tea'
enokki· 'he works'; *nentanukki·* 'I work'
enokki·ttuwa·t 'he works for him' (*aw*)
enokki·win 'work'
eno·c 'variously'

eno·ci prenoun 'various'; *eno·ci·-ke·ko·* 'all sorts of things'
eno·kki· 'he commissions people'
eno·na·t 'he orders, commissions, him' (*N*)
eno·suwin 'name'; *nentano·suwin* 'my name'
entaʔank 'he draws it (water) from there'
entaʔepa·n 'place from which one draws water'
entaʔepi· 'he draws water from there'
entasso preverb, 'so many times, so often'
enwa·we· 'he hiccoughs'
enwe· 'he speaks so'
enwe·pi 'he rests'
enwe·win 'such speech, such speech sound'
enwi 'bullet'; pl. *enwi·n*
epakkwa·n 'thatch'
epakkwe·yašk AN 'cattail reed'; pl. -*o·k*
epassekkawa·n 'shinny bag'
epassekkawe· 'she plays shinny' (the woman's double-ball game)
epateniss AN 'button'
epi 'he is there, he is at home'
epikkan 'pack strap, tumpline'
epino·cĩ 'child'
epino·ci·nʔuwi 'he is a child'
epino·ci·ns 'little child, baby'
eppaketank 'he throws it, pitches it'
eppane· 'always'
eppatto· 'he runs thither or thus'
eppiso 'he flies, speeds, thither'
eppiššemoni·k 'mat'; pl. -*in*

eppito·t 'he pulls it that way'
eppi· 'when'; *meno-eppi·* 'at the right time'; *iw eppi·* 'at that time'
eppi·tta·kunaka· 'the snow is so deep'
eppokwat 'it tastes so'
epwe·so 'he feels hot, he sweats'
epwi 'paddle'; pl. *epwi·n*; *nentapwi* 'my paddle'
epwi·ns 'small paddle'
esa·wa· 'it is yellow'
esa·wa·pikk 'brass'
esa·wesite· 'he has yellow feet'
esa·wi prenoun, 'yellow'
esipo·to·t 'he sharpens it'
eska?a·kan 'tent pole'
eskanesi 'he is lean'
essa postpositive, emphatic of novelty
essancekwan 'cache'
essaneko· squirrel; *esa·wi-essaneko·* 'fox squirrel'; *mekkate·-essaneko·* 'black squirrel'
essap AN 'net, seine'; pl. *-i·k*
essapa·p 'cord, rope'
essapa·pi·ns 'thread'
essassan, essassa͞ 'nest'; *utassessan utassessa·n?im* 'his nest'
essasswe·min 'cherry'
essa·nwe·se?a·t 'he keeps him amused'
essa·nwe·si 'he amuses himself'
essa·t 'he places him' (*SS*); independent *utassa·n*
essa·we· 'perch' (fish)
esse·ma· AN 'tobacco'; *nentasse·ma·* 'my tobacco'
essikena·kk 'blackbird'; pl. *-ok*

essin 'stone'; pl. *-i·n;* *kecci-essini·nk* 'at Chessening'
ešaški 'soil, earth'
eša· 'he goes thither'; *nentiša·* 'I go thither'
eša·mekat 'it goes thither'
eša·weškomenakat 'green head of a plant'; pl. *-o·n*
eša·weškwa· 'it is green, blue'
eša·weškwa·nte· 'it is a green house'
eša·wi prenoun 'yellow'
eši preverb, 'thither, thus'
ešicceka·na·t 'he works thus on him' (*N*)
ešicceka·tank 'he works thus on it'
ešicceka·te· 'it is done so, made so'
ešicceke· 'he makes things so, he does thus'
ešikan: nentašekan 'my sock, footcloth'
ešike·wenini 'carpenter'
ešikume·k 'dogfish'; pl. *-ok*
ešina·kwat 'it looks so'
ešina·šekkawa·t 'he chases (or sends) him thither' (*aw*)
ešina·šuwa·t 'he sends him thither' (*?w*)
ešinekka·netiso 'he names himself thus'
ešinekka·so 'he is named so'; *nentišenikka·s* 'that is my name'
ešinekka·tank 'he names it so, calls it so'
ešinekka·te· 'it is named so'
ešino·?emawa·t 'he shows it thus to him' (*aw*)
ešipeto·t 'he pulls it that way'
ešisseto·t 'he lays it so'

ešittekwe·ya· 'it flows as a stream in that direction'
ešittemawa·t 'he makes it for him' (*aw*); independent *utašettamuwa·n*
ešitto·t 'he makes it so, does it so; he arranges, makes it'; *nentašetto·n* 'I make it'
ešiwena·t 'he leads him thither' (*N*)
ešiweɪo·t 'he takes it thither'
ešiwe·pesi 'he behaves so, fares so'
ešiwe·puwa·t 'he knocks him that way' (*ʔw*)
ešiya· 'he is there; it is there'
eški preverbs 'at the beginning, for the first time'
eškonena·t 'he spares him from killing' (*N*)
eškote· 'fire'; *me·kwe·-eškote·nk* 'in the fire'
eškote·ns 'match'
eškote·ta·pa·n AN 'railway train'
eškote·wa·po· 'whiskey'
eškwa· preverb, 'having finished, after'
eškwa·c 'last, at the end'
eškwa·nte·m 'door'; *utaškwa·nte·muwa·* 'their door'
eškwa·ya·c 'last, at the end, late'
eškwe·ninc, eškwe·nenci·ns: nentaškwe·ninc nentaškwe·nenci·ns, 'my little finger'
eškwe·ta·kan 'youngest child'
eškwe·ya·nk 'in the rear, back'
ešpa·kunaka· 'there is deep snow'
ešpa·mekat 'it is high, tall'
ešpimessakonk 'upstairs'
ešpimink 'up aloft'
ešša postpositive, emphatic.

eššakuwe· 'he vomits'
eššakuwe·sekan 'water weed'
eššama·t 'he feeds him, gives him food'; independent *utaššema·n*
eššamo·cekan 'bait'
eššawe·kkwe·ššin 'he lies with his head turned to one side'
eššawe·ššin 'he lies on his side'
ešša·ke·šši͂· 'crawfish'
ešši prefixed to numbers, 'in excess of a decade'; *ešši-pe·šik* 'eleven'
eššikan 'black bass'
etamo·pi·l, etomo·pi·l 'automobile'
etašš postpositive, additive, 'and, then'
eta·kko·sete· 'he has feet of such size'
eta·wema·t 'he borrows from him'
eta·we· 'he gives credit, sells'; *utata·we·nan* 'he sells them'
eta·we·wekamik 'trading house, store'; pl. *-o·n*
eta·we·wenini 'trader, storekeeper'
etikkume·k 'whitefish'
etimene·wa·t 'he overtakes him' (*ʔw*)
etippesowin 'apron'
etissank 'he dyes it, paints it'
etomo·pi·l: see *etamo·pi·l*
eto·ppuwin 'table'
ettamuwa·t 'he places it for him' (*aw*)
ettawa·t 'he contends, bets, gambles, with him' (*aw*)
etta·tuwak 'they contend, bet, gamble, with each other'
ette·, ette·mekat 'it is there'

etto·t 'he places it there'; independent *utatto·n*
eya· 'he exists, is there'; *pi-eya·* 'he comes'
eya·, eya·mekat 'it exists, is there'
eya·muwa·t 'he gets it from him' (*aw*)
eya·nk 'he has it, gets it'
eya·wa·t 'he has him, gets him' (*aw*)
eye·kkusi 'he is tired'; *nentaye·kkos* 'I am tired'
eye·kkutiye·pi 'he is tired from sitting'; *nentaye·kkutiye·p* 'I am tired from sitting'
eye·kkwa· exocentric prenoun, 'at the end': *eye·kkwa·-ki·šik* 'End of the Sky' (Mr. Medler's Ojibwa name)
eye·yi·tuwaka·t 'on both legs'
eye·yi·tuwakkena 'at both sides of the road'
eye·yi·tuwayeˀi· 'at both sides, at both ends'
eye·yi·tuwinikk 'on both arms'
eyina·pi 'he looks around'

e·

e· changed form of preverb *a*
e· 'yes'
e·ka·c 'slowly'
e·mekkwa·n 'ladle'
e·mekkwa·ne·ns 'spoon'
e·nekokk 'with all one's might'
e·nekõ 'ant'
e·ntekwa 'it seems so'
e·ntekwe·n 'I wonder if it is so'
e·ntesso preparticle, 'every time'; *e·ntesso-kekiše·p* 'every morning'
e·ssa·wã 'muskmelon, cantaloupe'
e·sseka·k 'wood tick'; pl. -*ok*
e·ssepan 'raccoon'
e·ssepikkẽ 'spider'
e·ssĩ 'clam'
e·škam 'in the course of time, gradually, more and more'
e·šketamõ 'watermelon'
e·ššõ 'cabbage'
e·ššuwe·šk 'rifle'
e·tta 'only'

i

iw 'that, it' (inan. sg.)

i·

i·tik 'perhaps, I wonder'

k

ka 'no! wrong!'
ka preverb, future act: 'is to, shall'; used only with prefixes (*nenka-, ka-, uka-*) and under initial change (*ke·-*); cf. *ta*
ka· 'not, no', used with indepen-

dent verb or alone; *ka· ke·ko·* 'nothing'; *ka· wi·kka·* 'never'
ka·ci·nkwe·ni 'he makes a face'
ka·k 'porcupine'; pl. *-ok*
ka·ka·kešši⁓ 'crow'
ka·ka·škeci·ʔank 'he scrapes it'
ka·keke· 'all the time, forever'
ka·ki·keto 'he converses'
ka·ki·nekoya· 'it is pointed at both ends'
ka·ki·we·wak 'they severally go home'
ka·ncwe·penank 'he shoves it with his hand'
ka·ncwe·pena·t 'he shoves him with his hand' (*n*)
ka·nteʔikwa·ssuwin 'thimble'
ka·ntuwa·t 'he pushes him' (*ʔw*)
ka·skena·pa·kwe· 'he is thirsty'
ka·šeke·ns 'cat'
ka·škepa·cekan 'razor'
ka·tank 'he plants it'
ka·way AN 'quill of porcupine'; pl. *-ak*
ka·wetta·kemik 'all round the house'
ka·we· 'he is jealous'
kecci prenoun, 'big'; preverb, 'with force, much'
kecci-kwi·wesse·nsuwi 'he is a big boy'
kecci-mo·kkuma·nemo 'he speaks English' ("American")
kecci-mo·kkuma·ne·ns 'young white American'
kecci-mo·kkuma·nišš 'American fellow' (nickname of Mr. Medler among the Canadian Ojibwa of Walpole Island)

keccinekka·: ši-keccinekka·yan 'at thy right side'
keccipesowin 'belt'; *ukiccepisuwin* 'his belt'
kecci·na·kwa = *ci·na·kwa*
keka·nuka·te· 'he is long-legged'
keka·nwa·nekkwe· 'he has long hair'
kekiše·p 'in the morning'
kekiše·pa·wekat 'it is morning'
kekiššin 'he falls through the ice'
keki·kkema·t 'he exhorts him'
keki·pa·c 'foolishly'
keki·pa·ci preverb, 'foolishly, badly'
keki·pa·tesi 'he is bad, ill-behaved'; *nenkaki·pa·tis* 'I behave badly'
kekke·nema·t 'he knows him, knows about him'; independent *ukikke·nema·n*
kekke·ntank 'he knows it'; independent *ukikke·nta·n*
kekke·nta·kusi 'he is known'
kekke·ntemo·na·t 'he notifies him' (probably *N*)
kekkina 'all'
kekkino·ʔemawa·t 'he teaches him it' (*aw*)
kekkino·ʔema·kusi 'he is taught, gets schooling'
kekkino·ʔema·ti·wekamik 'school'; loc. *-onk*
kekkiše· 'charcoal'
kekkito·t 'he hides it'
kekwe· preverb, 'try to'
kekwe·ceci·nank 'he feels of it with his hand'
kekwe·cekkanetiwak 'they race'
kekwe·cekkanetiwin 'race'

kekwe·cema·t 'he asks him'; independent *ukakwe·cema·n*
kemiwan 'it rains'
kemo·tit 'he steals it'
kenaʔemawa·t 'he warns him against it' (*aw*)
kenake·: ka· kenake· 'by no means, not at all'
kenapac 'perhaps, probably'
kenawe·nema·t 'he takes care of him'; independent *ukanuwe·nema·n*
kena·cuwan 'it is beautiful'
kena·cuwi 'he is beautiful, handsome'
kencipeʔa·t 'he runs away from him'
kencipeʔiwe·wak 'they run away'
kencipettwa·tank 'he runs away with it'
kene·pik 'snake'; pl. -*o·k*
keno·na·t 'he addresses him' (*N*)
keno·si 'he is long, tall'
keno·še· 'pike' (fish)
keno·ya· 'it is long'
kenwa·kkusi 'he is a long timber, a tall tree'
kenwa·pi·kesi 'he (snake) is a long string'
kenwi·ntema·mekat 'it is deep water'
kepanekkaʔeke· 'he stops a hole in a tree'
kepatin 'it freezes over'
kepa·kkuʔank 'he closes it as or with a solid'
kepa·kkuʔika·te· 'it is closed up; it is canned'
kepa·kkuwa·t 'he locks him up' (*ʔw*)

kepe· preparticle, 'during, the length of': *kepe·-pepo·n* 'all winter'
kepe·yeʔi·, kepe·yeʔi·nk 'for a long while'
kepikka·na·t 'he passes him' (*N*)
kepikka·tank 'he passes it'
kepo·pecikan 'bag with a drawstring'
kepo·ssenẽ 'trousers'; *nenkipo·ssenẽ* 'my trousers'
keppaka·mekat 'it is thick'
kesi·ca·ne· 'he wipes his nose'
kesi·pi·kenank 'he washes it'; *nenkisi·pi·kena·n* 'I wash it'
kesi·pi·keninci· 'he washes his hands'
kesi·pi·kessakenike· 'he washes woodwork'
kesi·pi·keše· 'he takes a bath'
kesi·pi·ki·nkwe· 'he washes his face'
kesi·pwe·ška· 'he moves with scraping noise'
kesi·pwe·we·ška· 'he moves with repeated scraping noise'
kesi·sete·ššemowin 'door mat'
kessa·pi·ško·cekan 'sinker' (on a fishing line)
kessikke· 'he flies up'
kessina·mekat 'it is cold weather'
keša·pekkisank 'he heats it as metal'
keša·pekkite· 'it is heated as stone or metal'
keša·teke· 'he stays alone in the house'
keša·tte·, keša·tte·mekat 'it is hot weather'

keša·we·nceke·ški 'he is of envious disposition'
keša·we·ntam 'he is envious'
kešiso 'he is hot'; *nenkišis* 'I feel hot'
kešite·, *kešite·mekat* 'it is hot'
keši·kka· 'he goes fast'
keši·kka·petto· 'he runs fast'
keši·kkušiwe· 'he paddles or swims fast'
keši·peca·ne· 'his nose itches'; *nenkiši·peca·ne·* 'my nose itches'
keši·peka·te· 'his leg itches'
keši·pekoyuwe· 'his neck itches'
keši·peninci· 'his hand itches'
keši·pentipe· 'his head itches'
keši·pepikkwan 'his back itches'
keši·pepito·t 'he scratches it'
keši·pesite· 'his foot itches'
keši·peso 'he goes fast'
keši·peški·nšekwe· 'his eye itches'
keši·pešše· 'he itches'
keši·petto·ke· 'his ear itches'
keši·pi· 'he itches, he scratches himself'
keška·pekkaʔank 'he locks it'
keška·pekkaʔekan 'key'
keška·pekkaʔeka·te· 'it is locked'
keškiʔa·t 'he controls him'
keškiʔe·wesi 'he is able'
keškiʔe·wesiwin 'power'
keškikwa·sso 'he sews'
keškinekke·pesowin 'arm garter'
keškipena·t 'he manages to pull him' (*N*)
keškiso 'he endures'
keškita·sse·pesowin 'garter'
keškitto·t 'he controls it; he can do it'; *ka· ukašketto·ssi·n* 'he cannot do it'
kešsawa·t 'he hurts him' (*ʔw*)
ketaka·kko·ns 'fawn'
ketank 'he eats it all up'
ketima·kesi 'he is poor, in a plight'
keto·te· 'he crawls forth'
kettika·n 'field, farm'
kettika·ne·ns 'garden'; *nenkitteka·ne·nsink* 'in my garden'
kettika·tank 'he plants, raises it'
kettike· 'he farms'
kettimeški 'he is lazy'
kettisi: nenkittesi·mak 'my old folks, my parents'
keya·šk 'gull'; pl. -*ok*
keye· 'and, also'
ke· before pronouns, 'however, on the other hand, as for'
ke·ka· 'almost'
ke·keppi· 'after a while'
ke·ke·tt 'truly, surely'
ke·ko· 'something, anything'
ke·kwa with prohibitive verbs, 'do not'
ke·sepi·kenank 'he folds it up'
ke·ššuwa·kkussin 'it is loose on a solid'
ke·tin 'truly, really'
ki· preverb, completed action
ki·ceninci· 'he has a sore hand'
ki·ci·nkwe· 'he has a sore face'
ki··ʔa·t 'he escapes from him'
ki·kemanesite· 'his foot is asleep'
ki·keto 'he speaks'
ki·ke·tta· 'he furnishes food'
ki·ki·penkošši 'he is sleepy'
ki·kka·kkupina·t 'he pulls him free from a solid' (*N*)

ki·kki·škekkotank 'he cuts it repeatedly through'
ki·koʼ, *ki·ko·ns* 'fish'
ki·na·mekat 'it is sharp'
ki·nekokeʔank 'he chops it to a point'
ki·nepo·te· 'it is sharpened'
ki·nepo·to·t 'he sharpens it'
ki·nuwiški 'he tells a lie'
ki·siss AN 'sun, moon, month'; *mekko-ki·siss* 'February'; *si·sepa·kkutokke·-ki·siss* 'March'; *neme·peni-ki·siss* 'April; *wa·wa·ssekkone·-ki·siss* 'May'; *kettike·-ki·siss* 'June'
ki·ssa·te·nema·t 'he is sad about him'
ki·ssekkank 'he doffs it'
ki·ssekkoneye· 'he undresses'
ki·ssekkoneye·pena·t 'he pulls his clothes from him' (*N*)
ki·šekat 'it is day, it is a day'; *no·nko ki·šekakk* 'today'
ki·šekat 'day'; pl. *-o·n*
ki·šetto·t 'he finishes it'
ki·šik particle, 'day, by day': *kepe·-ki·šik* 'all day'; *eškwa·-enameʔe·-ki·šik* 'on Monday'; *nenko-enameʔe·-ki·šik* 'one week'
ki·ši·nkwe· 'he (Indian corn) is ripe'
ki·ši·tta· 'he finishes his work or action'
ki·ši·tta·mekat 'it finishes'
ki·ška·kkesank 'he burns it through'
ki·ška·kkuccito·t 'he tears it on a snag'
ki·ška·kkuʔank 'he chops it through as a solid'
ki·škeʔank 'he chops it through'
ki·škekaʔank 'he chops it through with an axe'
ki·škekkoceke· 'he cuts things through'
ki·škekkotank 'he cuts it through'
ki·škenakketoʼ 'tree stump'
ki·škentank 'he bites it through'
ki·škepo·cekan 'crosscut saw'
ki·škepo·to·t 'he saws it through'
ki·škešamuwa·t 'he cuts it through or off for him' (*aw*)
ki·škešank 'he cuts, slices it through'
ki·škešwa·t 'he cuts, slices him through'
ki·škuwa·t 'he chops him through' (*ʔw*)
ki·šo·ššin 'he lies warm'
ki·špenatemawa·t 'he buys it from him' (*aw*)
ki·špenato·t 'he buys it'
ki·špin 'if'
ki·šuwa·kkeci·ššin 'he lies curled up'
ki·wena·tesi 'he is crazy'
ki·weškwe·pi· 'he is drunk'
ki·wetta·wusse· 'he walks around in a circle'
ki·we· 'he goes home'
ki·weʼ 'so the story goes'
ki·we·petto· 'he runs home'
ki·we·tin 'the north; the north wind'; loc. *-onk*
ki·we·wena·t 'he takes him home' (*N*)
ki·we·weto·t 'he takes it home'

ki·wussa·na·t, ki·yussa·na·t 'he hunts him' (N)
ki·wusse·, ki·yusse· 'he hunts'
ko·ki· 'he dives'
ko·kko·kkuʔo· 'owl'
ko·kko·šš 'pig'
ko·kko·šše·ns 'little pig'
ko·kusseñ 'frog'
ko·ta·ššiñ 'rock bass'
kucicceke· 'he tries things, he tries'
kucici·nank 'he feels of it with his hand'
kucitto·t 'he tries it'
kukka·n 'go away'
kukko·mp, kukko·mpeñ 'cucumber'
kuma·ppi·, kuma·ppi·cc 'afterwards, finally'
kuma·t 'he swallows him'
kune·nkim (?) 'for a long time' (?)
kunima· 'perhaps, about, at a guess'
kunipeška· 'he falls out of the canoe'
kunsa·pi·, kunsa·pi·mekat 'it founders'
kuntamo·ceke· 'he fishes with hook and line'
kuntamo·na·t 'he catches him with hook and line' (N)
kuntank 'he swallows it'
kunta·kan 'throat'
kunta·ppene· 'he drowns'
kusa·pentam 'he tries to see a vision, he uses the conjuror's tent'

kusi 'he moves camp'
kusikwan 'it is heavy'
kussa·t 'he fears him'
kuškosi 'he wakes up'
kutacema·t 'he tests him by cold'
kuta·kumantank 'he tries to eat it, tastes of it'
kutta·mekosi 'he is terrible, formidable'
kutta·mekwat 'it is terrible, formidable'
kuttikusse·, kuttikuška· 'it tips over'
kuttikwe·penank 'he tips it over by hand'
kuwawa·t 'he chops him down' (ʔw)
kuwisse·mekat 'it falls over'
kuwiššemo 'he lies down'
kuyakk 'proper, good'
kwa·peʔank 'he scoops it up'
kwa·peʔikan 'dipper'
kwa·škuni 'he disembarks, descends from a wagon'
kwa·škwe·si 'he is clever'
kwe·cc 'just right'; *mi· kwe·cc* 'thanks!'
kwe·kkukkošuwe· 'he turns in a canoe or in swimming'
kwe·kkussito·t 'he turns it as it lies'
kwe·škuʔiwe·ssi 'Winged Startler'
kwi·škušši 'he whistles'
kwi·wesse·ns 'boy'
kwi·wesse·nsuwi 'he is a boy'

m

ma· enclitic: emphasizer, 'indeed'
ma·ca· 'he starts on his way, goes away'
ma·ca·mekat 'it starts off, goes away'
ma·ci· preverb, 'starting off, beginning'
ma·ci·ketto·t 'he makes it grow'
ma·ci·ki 'he starts to grow'
ma·ci·na·t 'he takes him away with him' (*N*)
ma·ci·pe ʔiwe·wak 'they run off'
ma·ci·peso 'he speeds away'
ma·ci·petto· 'he runs off'
ma·ci·ška· 'he gets along well'
ma·ci·temawa·t 'he makes it go away from him, takes it away for him' (*aw*)
ma·ci·to·t 'he takes it away with him'
ma·ci·tuwa·t 'he takes it away from him' (*aw*)
ma·ci·ya·ntuwe· 'he goes off climbing'
ma·ke· 'perhaps, or'
ma·mekka·te·ntam 'he is astonished'
ma·meppi· 'here'
ma·mi·cit 'he keeps eating it'
ma·muwi particle and preverb, 'all, all together, among them all'
ma·netta·nešši·ye ʔi· particle, 'woolen goods'
ma·no· 'nevertheless, let it be, anyway'
ma·nta 'this' (inan. sg.)
ma·pa 'this' (an. sg.)
ma·še ʔa·t 'he overpowers him'
ma·te ʔatto·t 'he starts to follow its trail, to follow it as a trail'
mecca·, mecca·mekat 'it is large'
mecca·tto·t 'he makes it large'
me ʔi·nkan 'wolf'
mekkakk 'box'; *nemakkakk* 'my box'
mekkakko·ns 'small box'
mekkakkussak 'barrel'; pl. *-o·n*
mekkama·t 'he takes something away from him, robs him'
mekkamuwa·t 'he finds it for him, on him' (*aw*)
mekkank 'he finds it'
mekkantwe· 'he robs people'
mekkate· 'gunpowder'
mekkate· prenoun, 'black'
mekkate·kke· 'he fasts'
mekkate·wa· 'it is black'
mekkate·wa·kemi·nkwe· 'he has black eyes'
mekkate·wa·nekkwe· 'he has black hair'
mekkate·wa·pekkisi 'he is black stone or metal'
mekkate·weški·nšekwa·n 'pupil of the eye'
mekkintepe· 'he has a big head'
mekkisin 'moccasin, shoe'; *nemakkesinan* 'my shoes'
mekkom AN 'ice'; loc. *-i·nk*
mekkomi·wa·po· 'ice water'
mekko·ns 'bear cub'
mekkwa 'bear'; pl. *-k*
mekkwaya·nẽ 'caterpillar'

mekkwe·nema·t 'he thinks of him, remembers him'
mekkwe·ntank 'he thinks of it, recalls it'
memašuwe· 'he copulates'
mema·cca·no·n 'they (inan.) are large'
mema·ccete·mekat 'it grows big'
mema·kuci·peto·t 'he squeezes it in his hand'
mema·kupito·t 'he squeezes it by hand'
mema·nka·ška· 'it runs in big waves, the waves run high'
mema·nkekkawe·wak 'they make big tracks'
mema·nkeninci· 'he has big hands'
mema·nkesite· 'he has big feet'
mema·nkešše· 'he has big ears'
mema·ntetowak 'they (an.) are large'
mema·sekka· 'it moves'
mena ᵖa·t 'he gives him drink'
menci prenoun and preverb, 'bad, badly'
mencikekkan 'fence'
mencikekkwe· 'bad woman'
mencikekkwe·wiss 'eldest sister'
mencikekkwe·wišš 'bad girl; the Silly Maiden'
menciko·te⁓ 'skirt'
mencinekka·wan AN 'mitten'
menci·kkuwiss 'eldest brother'
menci·min 'pease' (collective)
mene·ppwa· 'he is in need of smoking'
menikk 'so much, so many'; *a·ni·šš menikk* 'how much? how many?' *meno-menikk* 'just enough, quite enough'
menikkwe·t 'he drinks it'
menišše⁓ 'island'
menito· 'manitou, spirit'
menito·mene·ns 'wampum bead'
menito·ns 'beetle, insect'
menkate·ya· 'it is wide'
menka·we·pena·t 'he hinders, stops him' (probably *n*)
menki 'he barks'
menkiskan 'fishing hook'
menkiskene·ya·p 'fishing line'
menkoška·ce ᵖa·t 'he disturbs him'
menko·ss 'awl'
menkwakkemikessin 'it has mounds'
menkwakkemikeššin 'he lies in a mound'
menkwakkemikuwa·t 'he puts him in a mound'
meno pronoun, preverb, preparticle, 'good, well'
menoppukosi 'he tastes good'
menoppukwat 'it tastes good'
menosank 'he cooks it'
menose·kkwe· 'he cooks things, he cooks'
menoswa·t 'he cooks him'
menote· 'it is cooked'
meno·kkemi 'it is springtime'
meno·min 'rice'; *pekwaci-meno·min* 'wild rice'; *wa·pi-meno·min* 'cultivated rice'
menta·kukkwe· 'well-behaved woman; lady'
menta·kunini 'well-behaved or well-dressed man; gentleman'
menta·kwe·nema·t 'he likes him'

menta·kwe·ntank 'he likes it'
menta·min AN 'Indian corn'
menta·ssupi·ʔekan 'ten-spot'
menta·ssutapeʔikene·t 'it is ten o'clock'
menta·sswa·kk 'one thousand'
menta·sswi 'ten'
menta·še·nema·t 'he likes him'
mente·weka·n 'lodge for the Midewin Rite'
mente·wenini 'participant in the Midewin Rite'
mentimo·yẽ 'old woman'
mentito 'he is large'
mento·to· 'he takes a steam bath'
mento·to·ʔa·t 'he gives him a steam bath'
mento·to·wekamik 'hut for the steam bath'; loc. *-onk*
mentwe·ccekan 'flute'
mentwe·cceka·ns 'small flute'
mentwe·cceke· 'he plays music'
mentwe·nenkwi·ššin 'he moves with noise of wings'
mentwe·seke· 'he shoots'
mentwe·ška· 'he moves audibly'
menwa·kemi 'it is good liquid'
menwa·kemippetank 'he likes the taste of it as a liquid'
menwa·pecitto·t 'he has good use of it'
menwa·peme·weʔiwe·win 'blessing by a Higher Power'
menwa·peme·wesi 'he is blessed by a Higher Power, he has good luck'
menwa·peme·wesiwin 'good luck'
menwa·pentam 'he sees a good vision'

menwa·pentiso 'he likes his own looks'
mesineccikan 'picture'
mesineʔikan 'paper, piece of writing, book'; *nemasenaʔekan* 'my book'
mesineʔika·ns 'playing card'
mesisa·kk 'horsefly'; pl. *-ok*
mesisse· 'turkey'
mesko prenoun, 'red'
meskomin AN 'raspberry'
meskontepe· 'he is red at the head'
meskoti·ssemin AN 'bean'
meskwatessank 'he paints it red'
meskwa·nekkwat 'there are red clouds in the sky'
meskwa·pekkite· 'it is red hot'
meskwa·sse·ccekan 'red sash'
meskwa·te·ssĩ 'the common species of small turtle'
meskwi 'blood'
messan (pl.) 'firewood'
messat: *nemissat* 'my stomach'
messawe·nema·t 'he takes a liking to him, desires him'
messawe·ntank 'he takes a liking to it, desires it'
messimene·ns 'wheat'
mešakkwat 'the sky is clear'
meši·kkẽ 'hard-shell turtle'
meškawa·mekat 'it is hard, strong'
meškaweminekisi AN 'hard corn'
meškawesi, meškawesi· 'he is strong'
meškikki 'herb, medicine'
meškikki·wenini 'physician'
meškikki·wenini·wi 'he is a physician'
meškikkuwa·po· 'herb infusion'

meškimot 'bag'; *nemaškemot* 'my bag'
meški·kemin 'cranberry'
meškote· 'prairie'
meškote·ta·pa·n AN = *eškote·ta·-pa·n*
meškote·we·n ʔink 'at Flint' (Michigan)
mešši prenoun, 'big'
meššipeši· 'lion; Great Lynx'
mešši·mena·po· 'apple cider'
mešši·min AN 'apple'
mešwa·t 'he hits him with a missile'
mešwe· 'cottontail rabbit'
mettik 'piece of wood, stick', pl. *-o·n;* AN 'tree', pl. *-o·k;* *nemittekom* 'my tree'
mettiko·ns 'little stick'; AN 'small tree'
mettiko·nsekka· 'it is a place of small trees; there are many small trees'
mettikukamik 'log cabin'
mettikumi·šš 'oak tree'; pl. *-i·k*
mettikuna·kan 'wooden bowl'
mettikwa·kki·ns 'plot of wooded land'
mettikwa·p AN 'bow'; *umettikwa·-pi·n* 'his bow' (1.7)
mettikwa·pa·kk 'hickory tree'
mettikwa·pi·ns AN 'little bow'
meyaki prenoun, 'strange, foreign'
me·kkete·wekkoneye· 'priest'
me·kkete·wekkoneye·kkwe· 'nun'
me·kuya·k 'in the woods'
me·kuya·kekka· 'it is woodland'
me·kwa· 'at present, in the act, while'
me·kwa·c 'now'
me·kwe· exocentric prenoun, 'in, in the midst of'; *me·kwe·-meš-kote·* 'in the prairie'; *me·kwe·-eškote·nk* 'in the fire'
me·ma·twe· 'he sings'
me·mettikuninkwi·šše~ 'swallow'
me·mi·kwa~ 'butterfly'
me·mi·kwa·n ʔekka· 'there are many butterflies'
me·na·kuci~ 'bedbug'
me·nteke· 'especially'
me·yeki prenoun = *meyaki:* *me·yeki-pa·kke ʔa·kkwa·n* 'pheasant'
me·yo·ša predicative, 'it is long since'
mi· predicative, 'it is that, it was then'
mi·cena·t 'he defecates on him' (N)
mi·cit 'he eats it'
mi·ka·na·t 'he fights him' (N)
mi·ka·so 'he fights'
mi·ka·tuwak 'they fight each other'
mi·kkan 'road'; loc. *-a·nk*
mi·kka·ns 'path, trail'
mi·kkeno·t: nemi·kkeno·t 'my trousers'
mi·kkuwa·t 'he succeeds in hitting him' (probably *ʔw*)
mi·kwan AN 'feather'; *nemi·kunim* 'my feather'
mi·n 'blueberry'
mi·na·t 'he gives it to him' (N)
mi·nkwan AN = *mi·kwan*
mi·nuwa· 'again, also'
mi·si· 'he defecates'

mi·si·wa·kan 'privy'
mi·šeškokemik 'barn'
mi·šeškokka·: mi·šeškokka·k 'in the grass'
mi·šeškokuwa·m 'barn'
mi·šeško·ns 'blade of grass, weed'; *mi·šeško·nsan* pl. 'grass'
mi·šeško·nsekka·: mi·šeško·nsekka·k 'in the grass'
mi·šeško·nswa·nte· 'it is a green wooden thing'
mi·tenkwa·mi 'he defecates in his sleep'
mo·kkesse· 'he moves into view; he (sun) rises'
mo·kkuma·n 'knife'; *kecci-mo·kkuma·n* 'white American'
mo·kkuma·ne·ns 'small knife'
mo·kkuta·sso 'he whittles'
mo·nšwa·ka·ns 'scissors'
mo·nšwa·t 'he cuts his hair'
mo·nuwa·t 'he digs him up' (ʔw)
mo·škeʔan 'it is flooded; there is a flood'
mo·škemo 'he emerges'
mo·škene· 'he (kettle) is full'
mo·šwe·ka·ns 'handkerchief'
mo·šwe·n 'shawl'
muwi 'he weeps'
muwine·wa·t 'he attacks him' (ʔw)

n

na 'go on, do!'
na·kac 'later'
na·keʔana·t 'he tracks him' (N)
na·keʔatto·t 'he tracks it, follows it as a trail'
na·kusi 'he is visible'
na·mekkamekokka·te· 'it is built with a cellar'
na·mekkamik 'underground'
na·meyaʔi· 'underneath'
na·mi exocentric prenoun, 'under': *na·mi-nempa·kan* 'under the bed'
na·nan 'five'
na·na·ketawa·pentank 'he carefully looks it over'
na·na·š 'almost'
na·na·t 'he fetches him' (N)
na·neki·šekat 'it is Friday'
na·nemitena 'fifty'
na·nenkoso 'he lies repeatedly buried'
na·nenkotenonk 'sometimes'
na·nepa·yuwe· 'he yawns'
na·nepe·n 'only now when it is too late'
na·nkan 'it is light of weight'
na·no exocentric prenoun, 'five': *na·no-una·ka·ns* 'five cupfuls'
na·no·ceʔa·t 'he pursues him'
na·no·pi·ʔekan 'five-spot'
na·nwa·kk 'five hundred'
na·pekkank 'he wears it round his neck'
na·pekkawa·kan 'article of neckwear'
na·pekkwa·n 'ship'
na·pekwe·ppena·t 'he ropes him round the neck' (N)
na·pekwe·wa·t 'he catches him round the neck' (ʔw)

na·pešše·pesowin 'earring'
na·ppa·ni 'flour'
na·ssa·p 'in the same way, likewise, the same'
na·tekosi 'he acts boisterous'
na·temawa·t 'he helps him' (*aw*)
na·tema·ke· 'he helps'
na·tit 'he fetches it'
na·tuwe·ssi(?) 'Iroquois, Huron'
na·wekkwe· 'it is noon'; *ki·-eškwa·-na·wekkwe·k* 'this coming afternoon'
na·wekkwe·ya·kemi·nkwe· 'his eyes are in the noon state'
na·weyaʔi· 'in the middle, in the midst'
na·winc 'out on the open water'
necci·weʔa·t 'he scolds him'
necci·wette· 'it lies in disorder'
neʔa·nkenikkwe· 'daughter-in-law; *nenaʔa·nkenikkwe·m* 'my daughter-in-law'
neʔa·nkišš 'son-in-law'; *unaʔa·nkešši·man* 'his son-in-law'
neʔe·ntank 'he feels sure of it'
neʔiššin 'he adjusts himself in lying position'
nekka 'goose'; pl. *-k*
nekkawe· preverb, 'before another act, beforehand, first'
nekka·pa·weto·t 'he melts, liquefies it'
nekka·pa·we· 'he (snow) melts'
nekkwe·škuwa·t 'he goes to meet him' (*aw*)
nekkwe·ttekwe·ya·no·n 'they come together as streams, have a confluence'
nekkwe·ttuwa·t 'he answers him, consents to what he says' (*aw*)
nemanc 'however it be, whatever it be'
nemancenikka·: e·ši-nemancenikka·yan 'at thy left side'
nemanci preparticle, 'however it be, whatever it be': *nemanci-i·tik* 'however it may turn out to be'
nematepi 'he sits down, he sits'
neme· 'sturgeon'; *nento·neme·m* 'my sturgeon'
neme·pin, neme·peneˇ 'sucker' (fish)
neme·tto· 'he has left traces of his presence or activity'
nempakeca·ne· 'he is flat-nosed'
nempakena· AN 'corn-bread'
nempašša·ppeʔa·t 'he makes fun of him'
nempa· 'he sleeps'
nempa·kan 'bed'
nempa·ssuwi 'he instructs'
nempi 'water'; loc. *nempi·nk*
nempiss 'lake'
nempi·ška·kemi 'it is watery liquid'
nempi·šš 'water' (in portable quantity)
nempi·wa·kkusi 'he is drenched'; *kenimpi·wa·kkos* 'thou art drenched'
nempi·wekkameka· 'it is wet ground'
nempi·we·kat 'it is wet cloth'
nempo·kka·so 'he feigns dead'
nempo·p 'soup, broth'; loc. *-i·nk*

nempo·te·wi preverb, 'bashful, embarrassed': *nempo·te·wi-eya·'* he is bashful'

nempwa 'he dies'; *ne·mpot* 'when he died'

nempwa·cceʔa·t 'he visits him'

nempwa·kka· 'he is wise, learned'

nena·ʔeccika·te· 'it is put in order, repaired.'

nena·ʔessito·t 'he repairs it, puts it in place'

nena·ʔetta·ppenank 'he ties it in shape'

nena·ʔetto·t 'he puts it in shape, repairs it'

nena·metapi 'he sits a while or repeatedly'

nena·ntuwiʔa·t 'he doctors him'

nena·ntuwiʔekawa·t 'he does doctoring for him' (*aw*)

nena·ntuwiʔuwin 'doctoring'

neninkepinuweˉ 'screech owl'

nenkamo 'he sings'

nenkamuwin 'song'

nenkana·t 'he abandons him (*N*)

nenka·pa·weto·t 'he puts water on it, wets it'

nenkik 'otter'; pl. -*o·k* (or -*ok;* 6.2)

nenko exocentric prenoun, 'one': *nenko-pepo·n* 'one year'

nenkoci·ʔeke· 'he hoes'

nenkotwa·kk 'one hundred'

nenkotwa·ssemitena 'sixty'

nenkotwa·sso exocentric prenoun, 'six'

nenkotwa·sso·ška·wak 'they go as six'

nenkotwa·ssupi·ʔekan 'six-spot'

nenkotwa·sswa·kk 'six hundred'

nenkotwa·sswi 'six'

nenkotwe·wa·n 'one set, one pair'

nenkwaci 'somewhere, anywhere'

nenkwaci· 'off somewhere, away'

nenkwaʔank 'he buries it'

nenkwaʔeka·so 'he is buried'

nenkwana 'so thus it is, so it turns out'

nenkwatink 'at one time, once'

nenkwawa·t 'he buries him' (*ʔw*)

nenkwa·kan 'net of a spider'

nenkwa·na·t 'he snares him' (*N*)

nenkwa·nekkwat 'the sky clouds over'

nentawa· 'necessarily, needs, one had better'

nentawa·pema·t 'he seeks him'

nentawa·pentank 'he seeks it'

nentawe·nceke· 'he hunts'

nentawe·nema·t 'he desires him'

nentawe·ntank 'he desires it'

nentawe·nta·kwat 'it is desired'

nento preverb, 'seek to'

nentoma·t 'he calls him, asks for him'

nentopeni 'he goes on the war path'

nentošše· 'he listens'

nentotank 'he calls it, asks for it'

nentotemawa·t 'he asks him for it' (*aw*)

nessaškupo·ceke· 'he weeds, cultivates'

nessa·kkunank 'he opens it as a solid thing' (e.g., a door or window)

nessa·kkussin 'it stands open'

nessa·pa·weto·t 'he wets it'

nessa·t 'he kills him' (*SS*)

nessikkwe·ʔo 'he combs his hair'

nessimetana 'thirty'
nessink 'three times'
nessituttank 'he understands it'
nessituttawa·t 'he understands him' (*aw*)
nessituwak 'they kill each other'
nessituwinuwa·t 'he recognizes him' (*aw*)
nesso exocentric prenoun, 'three': *nesso-tepaʔeka·ns* 'three hours'
nessoki·šekat 'it is Wednesday'
nessokunakat 'it is three days'
nesso·pekat 'it has three leaves'; *ne·sso·pekakk* 'clover'
nesso·pi·ʔekan 'three-spot, trey'
nesswa·kk 'three hundred'
nesswa·pikk 'three dollars'
nesswi 'three'
neška·tesi 'he is angry'
neška·tesi·ttuwa·t 'he is angry at him' (*aw*)
neššikke· 'alone'
neššwa·ssemitena 'eighty'
neššwa·ssupi·ʔekan 'eight-spot'
neššwa·sswa·kk 'eight hundred'
neššwa·sswa·pikk 'eight dollars'
neššwa·sswi 'eight'
nettam 'first, at first'
nettama·ke· 'he kills something for someone, for people'
netta· preverb, 'skillfully, knowing how'
netta·weccike· 'he does things well'
netta·wekin 'it grows forth'
netta·wekitto·t 'he makes it grow'
ne·kaw 'sand'; loc. *ne·kuwi·nk*
ne·ko·te· 'he crawls under'
ne·kussito·t 'he puts it under something'

ne·kuwakkemika· 'it is a sandy place'
ne·kuwi·kka· sandy place'
ne·nepoš 'Nenabush' (the Culture Hero); obv. *-o·n*
ne·nepo·šo· = *ne·nepoš* (6. 4)
ne·no·kka·ssi, ne·no·kka·ssi·ns 'hummingbird'
ne·sse· 'he breathes'
ne·ya·p 'over again, back'
ne·yi·š 'both'
ni·ka·n 'in front, ahead, in the future'
ni·keʔa·t 'she gives birth to him'
ni·meʔiti·wekamik 'dance house'
ni·meʔituwak 'they dance together'
ni·mepa·kan 'water pail'
ni·meškaʔekan 'crest of the jay'
ni·metana 'forty'
ni·mi 'he dances'
ni·nemisi 'he is weak'
ni·nkuci 'somewhere'
ni·nte·ʔa·t 'he sends something to him'
ni·pena 'much, many'
ni·pete·ya·kkupiwak 'they sit in a row'
ni·pin 'in summer'
ni·puwa 'many'
ni·puwi 'he stands'
ni·sa·nat 'it is dangerous, there is danger'
ni·sa·ni preverb, 'dangerous'; *ni·sa·ni-eya·* 'it is a dangerous place'
ni·ssa·kkupina·t 'he pulls him down from a solid' (*N*)
ni·ssa·ntuwe· 'he climbs down, goes downstairs'

ni·ssekkošuwe· 'he canoes or swims downstream'
ni·sseyaʔi· 'below the place'
ni·š 'two'
ni·šena 'two loaves'
ni·šeno·n 'they (inan.) are two in number'
ni·šink 'twice'
ni·šo exocentric prenoun, 'two': *ni·šo-mekkakkussak* 'two barrels'
ni·šo·pi·ʔekan 'two-spot, deuce'
ni·šo·tto·ke· 'he has two ears'
ni·štena 'twenty'
ni·šuki·šekat 'it is Tuesday'
ni·šukonekat 'it is two days'
ni·šwa·kk 'two hundred'
ni·šwa·pikk 'two dollars'
ni·šwa·pi·k 'two strings'
ni·šwa·ssemitena 'seventy'
ni·šwa·ssupi·ʔekan 'seven-spot'
ni·šwa·sswa·kk 'seven hundred'
ni·šwa·sswa·pikk 'seven dollars'
ni·šwa·sswi 'seven'
ni·šwe·wa·n 'two sets, two pairs'
ni·šwe·wa·nekisuwak 'they are in two sets, they are two families'
ni·wa·kk 'four hundred'
ni·win 'four'
ni·wo exocentric prenoun, 'four'
ni·wo·pi·ʔekan 'four-spot'
ni·wukon, ni·yukon 'four days'
no·cemoʔa·t 'he cures him'
no·cemottemawa·t 'he cures it for him' (*aw*)
no·keka·puwi 'he comes to a halt'
no·kepiso 'he comes to a stop as he speeds'
no·kesse· 'he stops in his course'
no·kka·kunaka· 'there is soft snow'
no·kka·mekat 'it is soft'
no·na·kena·po· 'milk'
no·na·t 'she suckles him' (probably *N*)
no·na·wesso 'she suckles her child'
no·ni 'he sucks at the breast'
no·nkom, no·nkwa 'now, today'
no·ntank 'he hears it'; *no·ntam* 'he hears'
no·nta·kusi 'he is heard; he calls out'
no·nte· preverb, 'too soon, before the goal is reached'
no·ntuwa·t 'he hears him' (*aw*)
no·ppenana·t 'he follows, pursues him' (*N*)
no·tin 'wind'
nuwakekkwe·ššin 'he lies with lowered head'
nuwanc 'more'; *nuwanc penki·* 'less'
nuwatena·t 'he takes hold of him' (*n*)

o·

o·ci·, o·ci·ns 'housefly'
o·te·naw 'town'; loc. *o·te·na·nk* 'in town; at Detroit'
o·te·tto· 'he goes to town'
o·w (?) 'this thing'

p

pa·kentipe·ʔekan 'war club'
pa·kentipe·wa·t 'he smashes his head' (ʔw)
pa·kešše· 'he has a swelling'
pa·kkeʔa·kkwa·n 'hen, cock'; *me·yeki-pa·kkeʔa·kkwa·n* 'pheasant'
pa·kkwa·nemi·šš 'sumac'; pl. -*i·k*
pa·ma· 'later on, after a time'
pa·neššawa·n 'strip of jerked meat'
pa·pi· 'he waits'
pa·pi·ʔa·t 'he waits for him'
pa·pi·tto·t 'he waits for it'
pa·ppa·sse· 'red-headed woodpecker'
pa·ppeʔa·t 'he laughs at him'
pa·ppi 'he laughs'
pa·ssepito·t 'he crushes it with his hand' (e.g. a dish or an egg)
pa·škeci·ʔank 'he bursts it by tool as a small thing'
pa·škeci·ssin 'it falls and bursts'
pa·škeci·ška· 'he bursts open'
pa·škeʔank 'he bursts it by tool'
pa·škesank 'he shoots it with a gun'
pa·škesikan 'gun'
pa·škeswa·t 'he shoots him with a gun'
pa·šketiya·ma·t 'he bursts him at the rump by biting' (?)
pa·šketta·wenka· 'it is a dusty road; dust rises'
pa·tta·ma·t 'he accuses him'
pa·tta·šši·n 'he is trapped'
pa·tte· 'it is dry'
pa·tti·nat 'there is much of it'
pa·tti·neʔa·t 'he has much or many of him'
pa·tti·netto·t 'he has much or many of it'
pa·tti·no 'he is numerous'
pecci 'robin'
pecipeʔike·sse· 'he falls striking something'
pecipuwa·t 'he spears, transfixes him' (ʔw)
peci·nak 'just a little while ago, just now'
pekakkettank 'he hears it distinctly'
pekama·kan 'club, cudgel'
pekamepiso 'he arrives speeding'
pekamepite· 'it arrives speeding'
pekamusse· 'he comes in (under a spell)'
pekanta·nemat 'the wind strikes'
pekaškenat 'it rots to pieces'
pekaškešwa·t 'he cuts him up'
peka·n 'nut'; *wa·weye·-peka·n* 'walnut'
peka·na·kk 'walnut tree'
pekicwe·penank 'he throws it down'
pekiso 'he goes into the water, goes swimming, swims'
pekitank 'he throws it down'
pekitenamuwa·t 'he lets him have it' (aw)
pekitenank 'he sets it down'
pekitena·t 'he sets him down, lets him go, gives him permission' (n)

pekite·nema·t 'he holds funeral rites over him'
pekite·ntuwak 'they hold funeral rites one for another'
pekiw 'pitch'
pekkaʔank 'he breaks, severs it' (e.g. a cord)
pekkate· 'he is hungry'; *nempakkete·* 'I am hungry'
pekka·n 'differently, different'
pekka·nat 'it is different, it is another thing'
pekka·nesi 'he is different, he is another'
pekkiceciwan 'it flows as rapids'
pekkiketo·ne·wa·t 'he hits him on the mouth' (*ʔw*)
pekkina·ke· 'he wins from people, wins a contest'
pekkineˉ 'grasshopper'
pekkinuwa·t 'he wins from him' (*aw*)
pekkite·ʔutiso 'he strikes himself'
pekkitte·ʔutiwak 'they strike each other'
pekkitte·wa·t 'he strikes him' (*ʔw*)
pekkona·t 'he skins him' (*n*)
pekkopi·sse· 'he falls into the water'
pekkopi·ta·pa·na·t 'he pulls him into the water' (*N*)
pekkwakk 'arrow'; *upakkwakk* 'his arrow'
pekkwa·kkutwe· 'he plays ball'
pekkwa·kkwat 'ball'
pekkwe·ne·ncekan 'smudge bucket'
pekkwe·ne·ya· 'there is a fog'
pekkwe·pi·kemi 'it is muddied water'
pekkwe·šekan 'bread'
pekkwe·šeka·ns 'wheat'
pekokeʔike· 'he chops a hole'
pekone·te· 'it has a hole burned in it'
pekone·wa·t 'he makes a hole in him, pierces him' (*ʔw*)
pekone·ya· 'it has a hole in it'
pekone·ya·kkesank 'he burns a hole in it'
pekwaci prenoun, 'growing wild'
pekwaʔank 'he patches it'
pekwaʔemawa·i 'he patches it for him' (*aw*)
pekwanekkaʔeke· 'he chops a hole in a tree'
pekwatekkamik 'out in the wilds'
pekwawa·t 'he chops a hole in him' (*ʔw*)
pekwisse·ntam 'he hopes, wishes'; *nempakusse·ntam* 'I hope, I wish'
pema·kan 'cream'
pema·teka· 'he swims on, along, past'
pema·tesi 'he lives'; *nempima·tis* 'I live'
pemi preverb, 'on, along, past'
pemicuwan 'it flows on, along, past'
pemikkuwa·n 'track, footprint'
pemikkuwe· 'he leaves tracks'
pemineka·tank 'he carries it on his shoulder'
pemipeso 'he speeds or flies on, along, past'
pemipetto· 'he runs on, along, past'
pemipo·ceke· 'he plows'

pemisse· 'it goes by'; *uwe·ti ka·--pi-pemisse·k* 'last week'
pemiška· 'he goes by canoe, by boat'
pemita·pa·neko 'he goes by wagon'
pemosse· 'he walks on, along, past'
pemo·meko 'he goes on horseback'
pemo·ntank 'he carries it on his back'
pemwa·t 'he shoots him'
penakekkona·t 'he peels him'; independent *upanekikkuna·n* (N)
penakesikan AN 'hard-shell corn'
pena·kkusse· 'he falls off a log or a bridge'
pena·tesi 'he gets spoiled'
pena·tessin 'it gets spoiled lying or standing'
pene· 'partridge'
pene·ns, peneʼ 'young partridge'
pene·ssi 'bird' (of larger species)
pene·šši̴ 'bird' (of smaller species)
pene·šši·ns 'little bird'
penkissin 'it falls'
penkiššemo 'he (sun) sets'; *e·-penkiššemok* 'in the west'
penkiššin 'he falls'
penki· 'a little, few, small'
penki·šše̴ 'a little bit'
penkwi 'ashes'
pepaka·, pepaka·mekat 'it is thin'
pepakkekanteʔike· 'he threshes'
pepakuwiya·n 'shirt'; *nempapekiweya·n* 'my shirt'
pepakuwiya·ne̴ 'thin cloth'
pepankeššin 'he falls'
pepaššenše·ʔank 'he switches it'
pepa· preverb, 'about, around'
pepa·ma·ntuwe·petto· 'he runs about climbing'

pepa·ma·tesi 'he travels about'
pepa·mepiso 'he flies about'
pepa·meta·pa·neko 'he rides about in a wagon'
pepa·musse· 'he walks about, takes a walk'
pepa·tti·no 'he is numerous'
pepik 'flea'; pl. *-ok* (6. 2)
pepikwan 'musical instrument'
pepimusse· 'he walks on and on'
pepi·kumakkekki· 'toad'
pepi·wa·no·n 'they (inan.) are small'
pepi·wekkawe·wak 'they make small tracks'
pepo·n 'it is winter'
pepo·n 'winter'
pepo·nešši 'he winters'
peppaka·kkuʔikan 'black ashes'
pesa·n 'quiet, quietly'
pesa·ni preverb, 'quiet, quietly'
pesikwi· 'he gets up from sitting position'
pesintuwa·t 'he listens to him, obeys him' (*aw*)
peskane· 'it catches fire, kindles'
peska·pi· 'he comes back'
pessaka·kk AN 'board'; pl. *-ok*
pessaka·kko·ns AN 'slat'
pessakumin (AN?) 'sweet corn'
pessankwa·peššimo 'he dances with eyes shut'
pessankwa·pi 'he shuts his eyes'
peswa·pi·sseto·t 'he places it winding' (Cf. S 421-CFH)
pešikki 'cow'; *nempašekki·m* 'my cow'
pešikki·ns 'calf'
pešiššin 'he has a dangerous fall' (?)

pešiw 'lynx'
peškonuwa·t 'he misses him with a shot' (*aw*)
peškopena·t 'he plucks the feathers from him' (*N*)
peššakenake·kkuwa·t 'he peels the bark from him' (*ʔw*)
peššakenake·kkwe· 'he peels bark'
peššaki·kepina·t 'he skins him' (*N*)
peššanše·ʔank 'he hits it with a switch'
peššanše·ʔekan 'whip'
peššanše·ʔekana·ttik, peššanše·-ʔekane·ya·ttik 'whipstock'; pl. *-o·n*
peššiššik 'constantly, only, nothing but'
pešši·pena·t 'he skins him' (*N*)
petakkuwa·t 'he stings him (*ʔw*)
peta·sseke· 'Petoskey' (Michigan)
pe·cepatto· 'he runs slowly'
pe·cepiso 'he goes, flies slowly'
pe·ci·wi· 'he is weak'
pe·kka· 'unmoving, at rest'
pe·kkišš 'at the same time'
pe·nkuše·ʔo 'he dries himself'
pe·nkuše·ʔutiso 'he dries himself'
pe·nkuše·wa·t 'he dries him' (*ʔw*)
pe·pekka·n 'diverse, diversely'
pe·pešiššak 'empty-handed'
pe·ppe·šša·pi·kemo 'it goes in repeated streaks'
pe·šekon 'it is one'
pe·šeko·keši· 'horse'
pe·šeko·keši·wekamik 'stable'
pe·šeko·pi·ʔekan 'ace'
pe·šekwa·pikk 'one dollar'
pe·šekwa·pi·k 'one string or row'
pe·šik 'one'

pe·šša·pi·kemo 'it goes in a streak'
pe·ššo 'near, soon'
pi preverb, 'hither'
pi·ccin 'often'
pi·cema·kusi 'the smell of him comes hither'
pi·cema·kwat 'the smell of it comes hither'
pi·cema·ma·t 'he gets the smell of him'
pi·cema·ntank 'he gets the smell of it'
pi·cene·sseto·t 'he breathes it in'
pi·cene·ssin 'it is wafted hither'
pi·centipe·wa·t 'he smashes his skull' (*ʔw*)
pi·ku·ʔank 'he breaks it to pieces by tool'
pi·kussito·t 'he brings it down or drops it so as to break it to pieces'
pi·kuška· 'it breaks to pieces'
pi·kuššima·t 'he brings him down or drops him so as to break him to pieces'
pi·ma·ttetakunank 'he rolls it in his hand'
pi·ma·ttetakunike· 'he rolls things up in his hand'
pi·menakkwe· 'she rolls twine'
pi·meskotešši̇̄ 'snail'
pi·meskwa·pi·kenank 'he winds it round something'
pi·mettakenike· 'he rolls a cigarette'
pi·na·kemi 'it is clean liquid'
pi·na·t 'he brings him' (*N*)
pi·ncesse· 'he steps or falls in'
pi·nci·yeʔi·, pi·nci·yeʔi·nk 'inside'
pi·neccike· 'he cleans things'

pi·neʔa·t 'he cleans him'
pi·nekkameka·mekat 'it is a clean place'
pi·nette· 'it lies clean'
pi·nta·kan: nempi·nta·kan 'my pocket'
pi·nta·kkwa·na·t 'he smokes him' (tobacco) (*N*)
pi·nta·kkwe· 'he smokes'
pi·ntekana·t 'he brings him inside' (*N*)
pi·ntekato·t 'he brings it inside'
pi·nteke· 'he enters'
pi·nteke·yo·te· 'he crawls inside'
pi·ntekkoma·n 'knife sheath'
pi·ntenakkesse· 'he falls into a hollow tree'
pi·ntik 'inside'
pi·nto·mo 'he carries something in the fold of his garment'
pi·pa·ki 'he whoops, halloos'
pi·ssekkank 'he dons it'
pi·ssekkawa·kan 'jacket, coat'
pi·ssekkoneye· 'he gets dressed'
pi·ta·sepi· 'he belches'
pi·ti· call to chickens
pi·to·t 'he brings it'
pi·tte·wa·kemi 'it is foamy liquid'
pi·tte·wa·kemisse· 'it foams'; *pa·tte·wa·kemisse·k* 'beer'
pi·tuwa·t 'he brings it to him' (*aw*)
pi·wa·nak 'arrowhead'
pi·wa·nekõ· 'flint'; *pi·wa·nekõ·-nʔink* 'at the Saginaw Indian Reservation'; *pi·wa·nekõ·-si·pi* 'the Flint River'
pi·wa·no·n 'they (inan.) are small'
pi·wa·pekkona·kan 'iron dish'
pi·wa·pekko·ns 'wire'
pi·wa·pikk 'iron'; *pi·wa·pekko-a·šukan* 'iron bridge'
pi·wekkotema·kenan pl. 'shavings'
pi·wešši·nʔuwak 'they (an.) are small'
po·c 'surely'
po·ci·nkwe·ʔekan 'Indian bread baked in ashes'
po·kkete·ʔemin 'lemon'
po·kkete·ʔemina·po· 'lemonade'
po·kketo·nš AN 'pear'; pl. -*ak*
po·kkuka·te·peniteso 'he breaks his (own) leg'
po·kkupitemawa·t 'he breaks off a piece of it for him' (*aw*)
po·kkupito·t 'he breaks it in two'
po·kkuška· 'it breaks in two'
po·neʔa·t 'he ceases acting upon him'
po·nema·t 'he ceases talking to him'
po·netta· 'he ceases from his work or action'
po·ne·ntank 'he ceases thinking of it'
po·ni preverb, 'cease to'
po·ni· 'he alights from flight'
po·si 'he embarks, gets into a vehicle'
po·šo· 'good day!'
po·ta·kkwe·na·t 'he puts him in the kettle' (presumably *N*)
po·ta·tank 'he blows on it'
po·te·wa·temi· 'Potawatomi'
po·tta·kan 'mortar hole, mortar for pounding grain or meat'
po·tta·kena·ttik 'pestle'
po·tuwe· 'he makes a fire'
puwaʔank 'he knocks it off by

tool' (especially wild rice from the stalk)
puwaˀekan 'rice-gathering place'; loc. *-ink* a place near Saginaw.
puwa·na·t 'he dreams of him' (*N*)
puwa·tank 'he dreams of it'
pwa· preverb, especially with conjunct verbs, 'fail to, not'

s

sa·ka·sso 'he has the sun shining on him'
sa·ka·tte· 'there is bright sunlight'
sa·ka·tte·škuwa·t 'he (the sun) shines on him' (*aw*)
sa·kecina·šekkawa·t 'he chases him out' (*aw*)
sa·kecisse 'he runs out'
sa·keˀa·t 'he loves him'
sa·keˀituwak 'they 'ove each other'
sa·kekki· 'it grows forth'
sa·kekki· 'plant'; pl. *-no·n*
sa·keninci·ni 'he sticks out his hand'
sa·kesite·šši̇n 'he lies with his foot sticking out'
sa·keto·te· 'he crawls out'
sa·keto·te·petto· 'he crawls out running'
sa·ketto·t 'he is saving of it, he loves it'
sa·ki·na·nk 'at Saginaw'
sa·tte·wank 'on Saturday'
sekakkenank 'he stores it up'
sekakkenike· 'he stores things up'
seka·kkuˀikan 'nail'
sekika·te·ppena·t 'he ties him by the leg' (*N*)
sekimẽ 'mosquito'
sekipecikan 'buckle'
sekkaˀekan 'screw'

sekkaˀuwin 'cane'
sekkawa·t 'he lights him (a pipe)' (*ˀw*)
sekkwi 'he spits'
senakat 'it is difficult, costs much'
senakesi 'he is difficult, costs much'
senaketto· 'he has difficulty'
senakwe· 'he speaks in a difficult way'
senikuci·škank 'he rubs his feet on it'
senikupito·t 'he rubs it with his hand'
sesi·kkesi 'he is the oldest'
sessa·kesi 'he is stingy'
sesswe·kemiššin 'he leaps splashing'
sesswe·pi·keˀantuwa·t 'he sprinkles him with water' (probably *aw*)
se·ka·te·šši̇n 'he lies with a leg raised'
se·keˀa·t 'he frightens him'
se·kema·t 'he frightens him by speech'
se·kesi 'he is frightened'
se·kete·pwe· (AN?) 'burr'
si·kenamuwa·t 'he pours it out for him' (*aw*)
si·kenank 'he pours it out'
si·kwe·penank 'he spills it'

si·kwe·peškank 'he spills it with his foot or by body-movement'
si·nekki·keme· 'he blows his nose'
si·nena·t 'he milks her' (a cow) (n)
si·neškank 'he has a tight fit of it (a garment)'
si·pi 'river'
si·pi·we·ns, si·pi·we͂ 'brook, creek'

si·sepa·kkutokke· 'he makes sugar'
si·sepa·kkuto·ns 'piece of candy'
si·sepa·kkwat 'sugar'; nesi·sepa·kkutom 'my sugar'
si·wetta·kan 'salt'
so·kkupo 'it snows'
so·nka·kkuʔank 'he tightens it, makes it fast.'

š

ša·kena·šš 'Englishman, Canadian' also as family name
ša·kena·šši·mo 'he speaks English'
ša·ko·ceʔa·t 'he gets the better of him'
ša·nkessimetana 'ninety'
ša·nkesso·pi·ʔekan 'nine-spot'
ša·nkesswa·kk 'nine hundred'
ša·nkesswa·pikk 'nine dollars'
ša·nkesswi 'nine'
ša·nkwe·šši 'mink'
ša·pekkošuwe· 'he canoes or swims through'
ša·punika·ns 'needle'
ša·šeyi 'a long time ago'
ša·ši 'formerly, long ago'
ša·ššuwe·ya· 'it is square'
ša·wenonk 'in the south, to the south'
šekaška·ntuwe· 'flying squirrel'
šekaškwa·ceme͂ 'bloodsucker, leech'
šekate·nema·t 'he is impatient with him'
šeka·k 'skunk'; pl. -ok; loc. -onk 'at Chicago'
šeka·kuwi·nš AN 'onion'; pl. -i·k;

pekwaci-šeka·kuwi·nš 'wild onion'
šekina·wišš 'angleworm'
šekinkwa·m 'he wets his bed'
šekwa 'then, now'
šema·kan, šema·kenišš 'soldier'
šenin 'York shilling' (12½ cents)
šenkipe͂ 'diver-duck'
šenkišši̇n 'he lies extended, lies down, lies'
šenkwass 'weasel'
šepa·keninḳ loc., name of a place near Saginaw
šeya·w 'straight'
šeya·we·ca·ne· 'he has a straight nose'
šeya·we·mo 'it is a straight road, the road goes straight'
šeyi·kwa 'soon, in immediate prospect'
še·kwa·mekat 'it is dull'
še·ma·keni-uwe·ssi 'wasp'
ši·keme·wi·nš 'soft maple'
ši·kuna·t 'he empties him (a kettle)' (n)
ši·kwan AN 'grindstone'
ši·nke·nema·t 'he hates him'
ši·šši·ki 'he urinates'

ši·šši·p, ši·šši·pē 'duck'
šo·mena·po· 'wine'
šo·mi·nkwe·ni 'he smiles'
šo·neya· 'money'; *uša·wi-šo·neya·* 'gold'
šo·pi· 'he is slightly drunk'
šo·škucinuwe· 'he toboggans'
šo·škuššin 'he slips and falls'
šo·škwa·kkusi 'he is smooth wood'
šo·škwa·pekkat 'it is smooth stone or metal'
šo·škwa·pi·kesi 'he is a smooth string'
šo·škwa·tteˀe· 'he skates'
šo·šo·penakkonk 'in the treetop'
šo·šwa·pete· 'his teeth are on edge'
šuwe·nema·t 'he takes pity on him'
šwa·škusse· AN 'sleigh'
šwa·škusse·ns AN 'toboggan sled'

t

ta preverb, future, destiny or obligation rather than will; with prefixes *nenta·* or *nenka, keta·* or *ka;* with initial change *ke·* or *ta*
ta· 'he exists there, dwells there'; *e·nta·t* 'where he dwells, at his house'
ta·peško·keˀank 'he hews it square'
ta·ppene· 'he drowns'
ta·škekaˀekan 'wedge'
ta·škekawa·t 'he splits him (ˀw)
ta·ttekana·pi 'he looks up'
teccink 'so many times'
teka 'come! do!'
tekkaci 'he gets cold, catches a cold'
tekkacuwin 'a cold'; *utakkeciwin* 'the cold he has'
tekkama·puno 'he crosses'
tekkama·teka· 'he swims across'
tekkamekkomi· 'he crosses on the ice'
tekkamuˀa· 'he crosses'
tekkamuˀa·na·t 'he crosses over on him' (a log) (*N*)
tekka·kemi 'it is cold liquid, cold water'
tekke·ya·, tekke·ya·mekat 'the weather is cool'
tekkina·kan 'cradleboard'
tekkipi 'spring of water'
tekkokka·na·t 'he stamps on him' (*N*)
tekkokki· 'he stamps his foot'
tekkoma·t 'he bites him'
tekkona·t 'he holds him' (*n*)
tekkonekke·ško·so 'he is caught by the arm'
tekkonke· 'he bites people'
tekkopecike· 'he ties things fast'
tekkopena·t 'he ties him fast' (*N*)
tekkopeniteso 'he ties himself fast'
tekkopeto·t 'he ties it fast'
tekko·si 'he is short'
tekko·ya· 'it is short'
tekkwi·ntema·mekat 'it is shallow water'
tekonank 'he mixes it in'
tekoneke· 'he mixes things'
tekoswa·t 'he cooks him along' (with something else)

tekoššeno·mekat 'it arrives'
tekoššin 'he arrives'
teko· AN 'wave'
tekwa·ki 'it is autumn'
tenakkemikesi 'he is busy there, plays there'
tenakki· 'he dwells there'
tenakki·win 'residence'
tenawa 'that kind'
tena·nekito·n 'he talks there, he talks'
tenisank 'he cooks it there, he cooks it'
tenisi 'he dwells there'; *e·nteniseya·n* 'where I dwell'
teniso 'he is cooked there, he is cooked'
tenite· 'it is cooked there, it is cooked'
tenkiškuwa·t 'he kicks him' (*aw*)
tepaʔeka·ns 'hour'; *nenko-tepaʔeka·ns* 'one hour'
tepaʔeki·sesswa·n AN 'clock'
tepaʔemawa·t 'he pays him for it' (*aw*)
tepašši·šš 'small, low'
tepa·cemo 'he narrates, reports'
tepa·cetank 'he tells of it'
tepa·kkussin 'it lies fitting on wood'; *nenkwatink tepa·kkussink* 'one spool'
tepe·ntank 'he owns it'
tepe·w 'along the bank'
tepi 'there where, wherever'
tepikk 'at night'; *kepe·-tepikk* 'all night long'
tepikkat 'it is night'
tepikkonk 'last night'
tepinenci·pesowin 'ring' (for the finger); *nentipeninci·pesowin* 'my ring'
tepiško· 'in the same manner'
tepiško·sse· 'it reaches; the time has come'
tessakenwa·kemi 'it 'is stained liquid'
tesso exocentric prenoun, 'so many': *tesso-pepo·n* 'so many years'; preverb, 'so many times' *e·ntesso-tekoššink* 'every time he arrives'
tessokon 'so many days'
tessopepo·nekisi 'he is so many years old'
tessotepaʔekane·t 'it is so many o'clock'; *e·ntessotepaʔekane·k* 'what time it is'
tesso·na·kan 'trap'; *nentasso·na·kan* 'my trap'; *mekko-tesso·na·kan* 'bear trap'; *mettiko-tesso·na·kan* 'wooden trap'
tesso·so 'he is trapped'
teši preverb, 'there'; with initial change *e·nteši*
tešicceka·te· 'it is made there'; *e·ntešicceka·te·k* 'where it is made'
tešima·t 'he talks about him'
tešintank 'he talks about it'
tetakkukka·na·t 'he tramples on him' (*N*)
tetankeškawa·t 'he repeatedly kicks him' (*aw*)
teta·kkuka·te· 'he has short legs'
tetti·tepici·nank 'he rolls it'
te· preverb, 'reaching, enough'
te·penakkeno·so 'he has smoked enough'

te·penank 'he gets hold of it'
te·pena·pa·kwe· 'he quenches his thirst'
te·pena·t 'he gets hold of him' (*n*)
te·pene·ntank 'he has enough of it in his mouth'
te·pepina·t 'he seizes him' (*N*)
te·pettank 'he is reached by the sound of it'
te·petta·kusi 'he is within hearing, can be heard'
te·pwe· 'he speaks true'
te·pwe·ttank 'he believes it'
te·pwe·ttuwa·t 'he believes him' (*aw*)
te·te·pekkina·kk 'soft-shell turtle'
te·wa·kkukane· 'he has an ache in his bones'
te·wekkwe· 'he has a headache'
te·we·ˀekan AN 'drum'
to·kkeˀam 'he (fish) jumps from the water'
to·kkuntamuwa·t 'he (fish) bites at the bait for him' (*aw*)
to·tam 'he does so'
to·to·šša·po· 'milk'
to·tuwa·t 'he does so to him' (*aw*)
twa·ˀepa·n 'water hole in the ice'
twa·ššin 'he falls through the ice'

u

ucce·ppesi 'he is clever'
ucicca·k 'soul, spirit'; *meno-ucicca·k* 'good spirit'; *menci-ucicca·k* 'evil spirit'
ucipwe· 'Ojibwa'
ucipwe·mo 'he speaks Ojibwa'
ucipwe·muttawa·t 'he speaks Ojibwa to him' (*aw*)
ucipwe·ssin 'it is written in Ojibwa'
uci·ma·t 'he kisses him'
uci·pekke·ns 'small root'
uci·pikk 'root'; pl. *-an*
uka· 'pickerel'
ukima· 'chief; king-card'; *šema·keni-ukima·* 'jack-card'
ukima·kkwe· 'queen; queen-card'
ukima·wi 'he is chief'
ukkwe· 'maggot'
umi·mi· 'pigeon'
umpaˀuko 'he swells up'
umpa·pette· 'there is smoke or vapor rising'
umpi preverb, 'upward, rising'
umpinank 'he lifts it'
umpi·kwe·we·ššema·t 'he flaps him (wing) up with noise'
unakiš 'entrails'; pl. *-i·n*
unatenank 'he kneads it into shape'
una·c 'pleasantly, with pleasure'
una·kan 'bowl, dish'; *mettiko-una·kan* 'wooden bowl'; *pi·wa·pekko·-una·kan* 'iron dish'
una·ka·ns 'small dish, cup, drinking glass'; *na·no-una·ka·ns* 'five cupfuls'
unci particle and preverb, 'from there, since then, therefore'; *no·nkwa unci* 'from now on'
uncicuwan 'it flows from there'
uncika· 'he (kettle) leaks; it (vessel) leaks'
uncika·puwi 'he stands in that direction'

uncikka·mekat 'it comes from there'
uncinenituwak 'they kill each other for that reason'
uncipa· 'he comes from there'
uncipeso 'he speeds or falls from there'
uncipete· 'it speeds, sails, falls from there'
uncipeto·t 'he pulls it from there'
unci·ye̅ 'close by, next in order'
uniška· 'he gets up from lying position'
uniššeššin 'it is beautiful'
uni·ca·nessi 'he has a child'
uni·ca·ni 'he has a child'; *we·ni·ca·nit* 'the mother'
unsank 'he brings it to a boil'
unsa·m = *usa·m*
unsika·te· 'it is brought to a boil'
unso 'he (kettle) comes to a boil'
unswa·t 'he brings him (kettle) to a boil'
untako·cin 'he tumbles down from there, he tumbles down'
untama·kkume·šši̅ 'monkey'
untameʔa·t 'he keeps him occupied'
untameno 'he plays'
untamesi 'he is busy'
untametta· 'he is busy at something'
untami·kkank 'he busies or amuses himself with it'
unta·kkuwi· 'he shoots from there'
unta·nemat 'the wind blows from that direction'
unta·pette· 'there is smoke or vapor going up from there'
unta·tesi 'he is born there'

unte·, unte·mekat 'it comes to a boil'
untinank 'he takes it from there'
uppin AN 'potato'; pl. *-i·k;* *nento·ppeni·mak* 'my potatoes'; *pekwaci-uppini·k* 'wild potatoes'
uppwa·kan AN 'pipe' (for smoking)
usa·m 'excessively, too much'
usa·mena·ntam 'he fasts too long'
usa·menkwa·m 'he oversleeps'
ussassetam 'he coughs'
ussa·ššekop 'slippery elm'
ušicceka·te· 'it is arranged, made'
ušikuni 'he has a fishtail'; *we·šekonit* 'he who has a fishtail', as a man's name
ušipi·ʔank 'he pictures, draws, writes it'
ušipi·ʔeka·ns 'pencil'
ušitto·t 'he arranges, makes it'
uši·tta· 'he gets ready'
uškini·kekkwe· 'young woman'
uškini·ki 'he is young'
uškinuwe· 'young man'
uškinuwe·wi 'he is a young man'
uški·nšekokka·cekanan pl. 'eye-glasses'
ušo·ma·nekkiwa·pikk 'copper'
ušo·neya·mi 'he has money'
uššašk 'muskrat'; pl. *-ok*
uššaško̅ 'muskrat'
uššaškukamik 'muskrat house'
utapeʔaki·sesswa·ni 'he has (something as) a clock'
utatteka·kumin AN (also inan.?) 'blackberry, timberberry'
utayi 'he has a dog'
uta·pa·n AN 'wagon'
uta·pa·ne·ns AN 'hand sled'

uta·ppenank 'he picks it up'
uta·ppena·t 'he picks him up, takes him up' (*n*)
uta·ppepiso 'he has a fit'
uta·ppeškate·peniko 'he has cramps'
uta·wa· 'Ottawa Indian'
ute·ʔemin 'strawberry'
uttama·t 'he draws at him' (a pipe)
uttikkwan 'branch'
uwa preverb, 'go off and'; with prefix *nentawa*
uwašševe· 'more'
uwaššetta 'beyond, farther'
uwaya 'someone'
uwe·kwe·n 'whoever it be'
uwe·nepi 'he seats himself'
uwe·ne·, *uwe·ne·šš* 'who is it?'
uwe·ssi: *še·ma·keni-uwe·ssi* 'wasp'
uwe·ssĩ 'animal, creature'
uwe·šeʔa·t 'he dresses him up, decks him out, paints his face'
uwe·šeʔo 'he dresses up, decks himself out, paints himself'
uwe·šeššin 'he lies in place'
uwe·ti 'that over there'
uwiti 'that, there, then'
uwi· preverb = *uwa*
uwi·cekkiwe·nʔetiwak 'they are friends together'
uwi·nke· 'with all one's might'
uwo·ssi 'he has (someone as) a father'; *we·yo·ssecik* 'the man's children'

w

wa·ʔo·nẽ 'whippoorwill' (I. 13)
wa·ka·kkuta·ttekokke· 'he makes axe handles'
wa·ka·kkuta·ttik 'axe handle'; pl. *-o·n*
wa·ka·kkuto·ns 'hatchet'
wa·ka·kkwat 'axe'
wa·keca·ne· 'he has a curved nose'
wa·kepinuwẽ 'screech owl'
wa·kk AN 'fish egg'; pl. *-ok* 'roe'; *uwa·kkuman* 'her (female fish's) roe'
wa·kkwa·kemi·nkwe· 'he has gray eyes'
wa·kuššẽ 'fox'
wa·nekka·n 'pit'
wa·pank 'tomorrow'
wa·pa·kemi·nkwe· 'he has gray eyes'
wa·pa·nekkwat 'white cloud'
wa·pekan 'clay'
wa·peka·k 'white porcupine'
wa·pema·t 'he sees him'
wa·pentaʔetiwak 'they show things to each other'
wa·pentaʔuwe· 'he shows things, exhibits'
wa·pentamuwa·t 'he sees it for him' (*aw*)
wa·pentank 'he sees it'
wa·pentiso 'he sees himself'
wa·pentiwak 'they see each other'
wa·peso 'he is ripe'
wa·peška· 'it is white'
wa·peška·pekkat 'it is white metal'; *eya·peška·pekkakk* 'silver'
wa·peškintepe· 'he is white-headed'
wa·peškisi 'he is white'

wa·peškitessank 'he paints it white'
wa·peški·we· 'he has white flesh'; *eya·peški·we·cik* 'the white people'
wa·peškokki· 'marsh'
wa·pete· 'it is ripe'
wa·pi prenoun, 'white'
wa·pow 'Walpole' (in 'Walpole Island')
wa·po·so·, wa·po·so͞ 'rabbit'
wa·po·weya·n 'blanket'
wa·po·weya·ne·ns 'small blanket'
wa·ssa 'far'
wa·ssekkoci·ʔank 'he polishes it'
wa·ssekkone·ncekan 'lamp'
wa·ssekkone·ncekana·po· 'kerosene'
wa·ssemo 'he (Thunderer) flashes'; *wa·ssemowak* 'there is lightning'
wa·sse·ccekan 'window'
wa·sse·ccekana·pikk 'window glass'
wa·ssi͞ 'bullhead' (fish)
wa·šše·ya·kemi 'it is clear water'
wa·wan 'egg'; pl. -*o·n*
wa·wa·pekono·ci͞ 'mouse'
wa·wa·pema·t 'he looks at him'
wa·wa·pemowin 'mirror'
wa·wa·ssekkone͞ 'flower'
wa·wa·ssekkone·: wa·wa·ssekkone·--ki·siss 'the flower month, May'
wa·wa·ške·šši 'deer'
wa·wa·te·ssi 'firefly'
wa·weno·ns 'egg'; *uwa·weno·nseman* 'her (bird's) eggs'
wa·weye· prenoun, 'round'
wa·weye·keʔank 'he hews it round'
wa·weye·mo·we 'he has round droppings'
wa·weye·ya· 'it is round'

wa·wi·ntemawa·t 'he promises it to him' (*aw*)
wena·cenkošši 'he has a nightmare'
wene·nema·t 'he forgets him'
wene·ntank 'he forgets it'
weniʔa·t 'he loses him'
wenina 'everywhere'
weniššin 'he gets lost'
wenitto·t 'he loses it'
weškipeto·t 'he pulls it zigzag'
we·ci·ka·we·ssi 'cricket'
we·kune·šš 'what is it?'
we·kutakwe·n 'whatever it be'
we·nepikk 'for a little while'
we·neppanat 'it is easy, costs little'
we·pekkamekat 'the goings-on begin'
we·pena·t 'he casts him off' (probably *n*)
we·petta· 'he begins his work or activity'
we·petta·teso 'he hits himself'
we·pi preverb, 'begin to'
we·ppecika·ns 'hammer'
we·ppetawa·t 'he hits him' (*aw*)
we·šše·šk 'rifle'
we·we·ncekano͞ 'horned owl'
we·we·ni 'properly, correctly; thanks!'
we·we·no·k 'with ample space'
we·wi·nepa͞ 'squash'
we·wi·p 'quickly, right away'
we·wi·peška· 'he goes hurrying'
we·wi·petta· 'he hastens his work or action'
we·wi·pe·nta·kwat 'it is urgent'
wi· preverb, future, intent; with prefixes *ni·* or *nuwi·, kuwi·, uwi·*

wi·ceka·ma·t 'he dances with him'
wi·cenokki·ma·t 'he works with him'
wi·cesse·ma·t 'he goes with him'
wi·ci·wa·t 'he accompanies him' (*i·w*)
wi·kka· 'after an interval of time, with delay, late'; *ka· wi·kka·* 'never'
wi·kkuma·t 'he invites him to a meal'
wi·kkupina·t 'he pulls him in' (*N*)
wi·kkupito·t 'he pulls it in'
wi·kkuppina·t 'he ties him up' (*N*)
wi·kkwe·kema· 'there is a bay'
wi·kkwe·pecikan 'love medicine'
wi·kkwe·pena·t 'he puts him under a love spell' (*N*)
wi·kkwe·tonk 'at the bay' (a place name)
wi·kupi·mi·šš 'linden'; *wi·kupi·mi·šši·-enake·kk* 'linden bark'
wi·kuwa·m 'house'
wi·kuwa·me·ns 'little house'
wi·mpenakkesi AN 'hollow tree'
wi·mpenakketo⁻ 'hollow stump or log'
wi·na·kemi 'it is dirty liquid'
wi·na·nke· 'turkey buzzard'
wi·nekkamekisi 'he makes a mess'
wi·nena·kusi 'he looks dirty'
wi·neninci· 'he has dirty hands'
wi·neninci·ššin 'he gets his hands dirty'
wi·neno 'he is fat'
wi·nentipe· 'he has a dirty head'
wi·nesite·ššin 'he gets his feet dirty'
wi·ntemawa·t 'he tells it to him' (*aw*)
wi·ntema·tuwak 'they tell it one to another'
wi·pa 'early, soon'
wi·sseni 'he eats'
wi·sseniwin 'food'
wi·teke· 'he lives with someone, he (or she) is married'
wi·teke·ma·kan 'wife'; *ni·teke·ma·kan* 'my wife'
wi·teke·ma·t 'he lives with him; he (she) is married to her (him)'
wi·teke·ntuwak 'they live together, they are married to each other'
wi·to·kkuwa·t 'he goes with him, helps him in an undertaking' (*aw*)
wi·to·ppuma·t 'he eats with him'
wi·weci·na·t 'he wraps him up' (*n*)
wi·wekkwa·n 'hat'
wi·wekkwa·ne·ns 'little hat'
wi·wekkwe·ci·nank 'he wraps it up'
wi·wekkwe·ci·na·t 'he wraps him up' (*n*)
wi·wekkwe·nank 'he wraps it up'
wi·we·keci·na·t 'he wraps him in cloth' (*n*)
wi·yak 'some sort'
wi·ya·ss 'meat, flesh'
wuwa·pema·t 'he repeatedly sees him'

INDEX

This index covers items of grammatical importance and matters of potential ethnographic interest. References are as described on page xi.

A

abbreviations   page xi
accretions of suffixes 2. 6-7; 18
actor 5. 7
address 6. 7
alphabetical order   page xi
anaphora 20. 48-9
animate 5. 2
animate intransitive verbs 5.7; 7.2-8; 8.2-8; 9.1, 4-6; 12
antecedent 20.5
assibilation (irregular mutation) 3.21-4

B

base forms 3.1
bibliography   Preface
Bluejay (totem character?) T23
bread, making T25-6
burial rites T24

C

Carlisle Indian School   Preface; T8-9
categories of inflection 5
changed tense of conjunct 5.18, 20
citation-forms   Preface
composition 1.1; 2.2; 10
compounding form; of nouns 6.12; of verbs 9.9
concord 20.3
conjunct dubitative 5.24.
conjunct indicative 5.18
conjunct order 5.13; 8; 20.6, 39-40
conjunct preterit 5.23
conjunct preterit dubitative 5.25
connective -*yi*- 3.18-20
co-ordination 20.46-7
cross references, style of   page xi
cross reference (grammatical) 20.2, 35

D

delayed imperative mode 5.27; 9.4
demonstrative pronoun expressions 20.12

demonstrative pronouns 6.23-4, 27
dependent nouns 6.19-21
dependent root 4.14; 19.2
deverbal finals 2.6
deverbal medials 2.7
dialects and dialect variation   Preface; T1
direct forms (TA) 7.13, 14-8; 8.13-20
double-object verbs 5.11; 20.27
dubitative modes 5.13; 7.6-8, 11-2; 7.17-8, 21; 8.6-8, 12, 19-21, 28-9, 35-6
dubitative pronoun expressions 20.15
dubitative pronouns 6.25; 20.45

E

enclitics 20.7-9
endings, inflectional 2.1; 4.10
English Words in Ojibwa 1.1
ethnological texts T19-29, 31(?)
exclusive first person plural 5.4; 20.26
exocentric prenouns 10.7

F

fasting and visions T22-3, 31
finals 2.3, 6; 4.12; 11-17; animate intransitive 12; inanimate intransitive 13; noun 11; particle 16; pseudo-transitive 15; transitive animate 14; transitive inanimate 15.
first person 5.4
fish-spearing T14
formal object 5.12
forms 2-20

G

gender 5.2
goal of movement 20.28
Great Lynx T23
Great Serpent T23

H

Hurons T32

I

I—thee forms (TA) 7.13, 24-5
imperative 5.13, 27; 9.1-8
impersonal verbs 5.10
inanimate 5.2
inanimate intransitive verbs 5.7; 7.9-12; 8.9-12; 13
inclusion of words or phrases between members of compound 10.12
inclusive first person plural 5.4
indefinite pronoun expressions 20.13
indefinite pronouns 6.26
independent dubitative 5.16
independent dubitative preterit 5.17
independent indicative 5.14
independent order 5.13; 7
independent preterit 5.15
indicative modes 5.13; 7.2, 9, 14, 19, 22, 24, 26; 8.2, 9, 14, 21, 23, 30, 32
inflection 5-9
inflection, categories of 5
inflectional endings 2.4; 4.10
informant Preface
initial change 2.1; 4.2-5
instrument 20.28
internal combination or sandhi 3
interrogative pronoun expressions 20.14
interrogative pronouns 6.25
intransitive 5.7
inverse forms (TA) 7.13, 19-21; 8.13, 21-2
iterative tense 5.18, 21; 8.3, 10, 15, 22

L

local forms of nouns 6.8-11
local-noun expressions 20.13, 28, 32
love medicine T28-30

M

me-forms (TA) 8.13, 23-9
medial suffixes 2.5; 4.12-3; 17
medicine T19-20, 28-30
Medler, Andrew (informant) Preface
Mirror Being T31
mode 5.13
morphologic processes 4
morphology 2-19
morphophonemes 3.2
morphophonemics 3
mutation 3.21-4

N

negation, negative modes 5.13, 26; 7.4, 7, 10, 15, 18, 20, 23, 25, 28; 8.4, 7, 16, 25, 27; 20.6, 30, 33
Nenabush T35-8
noun expressions 20.16-20
nouns 5.1-3, 5-6; 6.1-21; 11
noun, local, expressions 20.13, 28, 32
noun, local form of 6.8-11
number 5.3, 8, 10, 12; 6.1-6; specialization of verb stems for 5.8

O

object 5.7
obviation 5.11; 6.1-6; 20.4
order 5.13
Ottawa Preface

P

participles 5.18, 22-4; 8.3, 10, 15, 18, 22, 24, 33; 20.6, 21, 38
particle expressions 20.10
particles 16; 20.10, 42-4
particles, predicative 20. 42-4
parts of speech 5.1
passive Foreword; 5.7; 7.2, 14, 19; 8.2, 14, 21, 32
person 5.4
personal pronoun expressions 20.11
personal pronouns 6.22
phonemes Foreword; Preface; 1
plural 5.3
possessed themes of nouns 6.13-18
possession 5.6
postmedial elements 2.7; 18.2
postradical elements 2.8; 19.12-16
predicative particles 20.42-4
prefinal elements 2.6; 18.3-4
prefixes 4.6-9
premedial elements 2.7; 18.4
prenouns 10.4-7
prenouns, exocentric 10.7
preparticles 10.13
preterit modes 5.13; 7.5, 8, 12, 16; 8.5, 8, 11, 17-18, 20, 26-7, 29, 31, 34, 36
preverb 10.8-12
primary word formation 2.5; 11-19
prohibitive mode 5.27; 9.5-8; 20.6
pronouns 6.22-7
pronunciation 1

proximate 5.5
pseudo-intransitive 5.12; 7.27, 29
pseudo-object 5.9
pseudo-transitive 5.9; 7.3

R

Rabbit (myth character) T33-4
reduplication 2.8; 4.17; 19.4-10
relative reference 20.5
relative roots 5.20; 10.11, 14; 20.5, 31, 35
reminiscences T1-10, 24, 28, 29
roots 2.8; 19

S

sacred stories T33-8
secondary derivation 2.3, 4; 11-19
second person 5.4
sentence-types 20.50-1
simple tense of conjunct 5.18-9
singular 5.3
sounds 1
subordinate clauses 20.38-45
substantive expressions 20.11-22
sweat lodge T19-20
syntax 20

T

tense 5.13, 18
thee-forms (TA) 8.13, 30-1
themes 2.1
third person 5.4
thou-me forms (TA) 7.13, 22-3
Thunderers T10, 23
time, telling T27
transitive 5.7
transitive animate verbs 5.7; 7.13-25; 8.13-31; 9.2, 4-5, 7; 14
transitive inanimate verbs 5.7; 7.26-9; 8.32-6; 9.3, 8; 15

V

verb expressions 20.24-37
verbs 5.7-27; 7-9; 12-15
visions and fasting T22-3, 31
vocative 6.7

W

Walpole Island, life on T15-18
weather, predicting T10
wild rice, harvesting T4-6
word formation 4.11-17; 11-19
word order 20.7, 29; 20 *passim*

www.ingramcontent.com/pod-product-compliance
Lightning Source LLC
Chambersburg PA
CBHW021138230426
43667CB00005B/162